> 新闻出版重大科技工程项目管理及相关成果丛书

数字版权保护技术研发工程论文选辑

Selected Edition of Theses on the National DRM R&D Project

魏玉山 主编 张凤杰 张从龙 副主编

中国书籍出版社
China Book Press

编 委 会

主 任：孙寿山

副主任：张毅君　谢俊旗　魏玉山

成 员：冯宏声　刘成勇　张　立　武远明　张树武

《数字版权保护技术研发工程论文选辑》

主　编：魏玉山
副主编：张凤杰　张从龙
统　稿：张凤杰　李　欣

序 言

版权保护，是新闻出版业得以繁荣发展的前提，新闻出版业是版权产业的重要组成部分。信息技术的飞速发展，在给人们带来内容消费便捷的同时，也使侵权盗版变得更加容易。如果任由侵权盗版恣意横行，版权产业链将难以正常运转，内容企业的创新积极性将会下降，经济效益将无法保障，社会效益也将无从实现。

党中央、国务院高度重视版权产业的发展，做出一系列重大部署。政府主管部门不断加强顶层设计，完善相关政策、法律，加大执法力度，并通过实施"项目带动战略"，加强相关技术研发与应用，全面应对信息技术给版权产业带来的冲击。

早在十年前，原新闻出版总署就提出四项新闻出版重大科技工程的建设目标，由国家数字复合出版系统工程提供数字化生产系统，由数字版权保护技术研发工程（简称"版权工程"）提供版权保护与运营的技术保障，由中华字库工程提供用字保障，由国家知识资源数据库工程提供出版业向知识服务转型升级的全面支撑。四大工程先后列入国家"十一五"与"十二五"时期文化发展规划纲要，在国家财政的支持下陆续启动。

版权工程2007年6月启动可行性论证，2010年1月获准立项，2011年7月正式启动，共18个分包、26项课题，建设内容涵盖标准研制、技术研究、系统开发、平台搭建、总体集成、应用示范等多个方面，参与工程研发、集成、管理任务的单位24家。工程总目标是：探索数字环境下的版权保护机制，为出版单位数字化转型提供政府主导的第三方公共服务平台，为数字出版产业发展提供一整套数字版权保护技术解决方案。

在总局新闻出版重大科技工程项目领导小组的直接领导下，重大科技工程项目领导小组办公室积极推进，总体组、工程管控、总集、标准、监理以及各技术研发单位、应用示范单位共同努力，圆满完成了版权工程预定任务，取得了多方面的成果。

一是完成了工程的总体目标，实现了多项技术突破。按照总体设计方案，版权工程研究制定了四类25项工程标准与接口规范，形成了一套数字版权保护技术标准体系，在此基础上，突破传统版权保护技术手段，研发并形成了内容分段控制技术、多硬件绑定技术、富媒体保护技术、数字水印嵌入技术、媒体指纹提取技术、可信交易计数技术等版权保护核心支撑技术；针对移动出版、互联网出版、出版单位自主发行等业务模式，开发了五类版权保护应用系统，完成了五类数字版权保护技术集成应用示范；搭建了数字内容注册与管理、版权保护可信交易数据管理、网络侵权追踪三个公共服务子平台；经过整理与集成，最终形成了综合性的数字版权保护技术管理与服务平台。

二是获得多项知识产权，形成一系列相关成果。在技术研发过程中，版权工程共申请发明专利41项（其中5项已授权），登记软件著作权62件，在国内外媒体上发表论文42

篇。同时，为了解全球范围内相关领域最新的科技创新成果、发展方向和发展趋势，版权工程管控包委托第三方知识产权机构开展了专利检索分析、知识产权规避设计、专利池建设建议方案编制等工作，形成了一系列知识产权相关成果。

三是积累了重大科技工程项目管理的经验。版权工程是原新闻出版总署组织开展的第一个国家重大工程。在此之前，我们对重大科技工程项目管理缺乏经验，在工程的实施过程中，我们一边探索工程的管理体制与管理机制，一边组织工程的研发。通过工程的实施，我们形成了一套比较可行的工程管理体系，形成了包括财务管理、进度管理、质量管理等一批工程管理制度，积累了重大科技工程项目管理的经验。

在版权工程全面完工之际，及时总结工程项目管理经验，认真梳理工程创新成果，并加以展现和传播，具有重要意义。为此，版权工程总体组在总局重大科技工程项目领导小组指导和支持下，对工程标准、已发表论文、专利检索分析成果物进行梳理，对工程过程管理内容与质量控制举措等进行总结，形成系列丛书并予以出版。

版权工程时间跨度较长，参与单位较多，人员变动较大，相关成果物本身专业性、技术性非常强，整理、汇编起来非常不易；再加上丛书编写人员时间、精力有限，该套丛书在材料选取、内容校正、综合分析等方面肯定会存在不足。但瑕不掩瑜，本套丛书的出版，无疑可以为新闻出版行业类似项目的开展以及数字版权保护技术领域相关研究提供重要的经验借鉴和资料参考。

期望新闻出版行业以及社会各界以本套丛书的出版为契机，更加关注数字版权保护技术的研发与应用，共同推动版权工程成果的落地转化，利用高新技术手段，破解版权保护难题，为创新发展保驾护航，促进社会主义先进文化的大发展、大繁荣！

2016 年 12 月 12 日

出版说明

数字版权保护技术研发工程（简称版权工程）是列入国家"十一五"与"十二五"时期文化发展规划纲要的重大科技专项，是国家新闻出版广电总局新闻出版重大科技项目之一，是推进新闻出版业转型升级、实现持续发展、构建新兴业态的重要保障。在总局重大科技工程项目领导小组的直接领导下，总局重大科技工程项目领导小组办公室积极推进，总体组、工程管控、总集、标准、监理以及各分包研发单位、应用示范单位通力协作，攻坚克难，共同完成各项既定任务，取得了丰硕成果。

2016年12月2日，版权工程召开整体验收会并顺利通过专家验收，验收专家对工程成果及工程管理和工程研发各方给予高度评价，一致认为版权工程立项定位明确，管理思路清晰，工作过程扎实、成果效果显著。

作为总局率先完成的新闻出版重大科技项目，数字版权保护技术研发工程除向行业及社会提供一套技术成果外，还将研发过程中产生的研究论文、专利检索分析报告、工程标准以及过程管理文档等汇编成书，供业界参考。这本身也是工程取得的另一形式的成果。

本套丛书共四部、七册，基本情况如下：

1. 《数字版权保护技术研发工程过程管理与质量控制》：在介绍工程基本情况基础上，重点介绍了工程过程管理、质量控制的主要内容与方法，以及知识产权管理、软件测评管理等专项管理的"软技能"。此外，还有工程项目管理各阶段文档编写的要求（附模板）以及工程研发成果简要情况；

2. 《数字版权保护技术研发工程论文选辑》：在工程研发过程中，各分包在中外媒体上公开发表的相关论文42篇。综合考虑论文质量及作者意愿，总体组分为"安全技术研究"、"相关算法研究"、"其他相关研究"三辑，选编了28篇论文成果结集出版；

3. 《数字版权保护技术研发工程专利检索与分析》：以第三方知识产权公司专利检索分析成果为基础，从工程72个技术检索主题中选取了55个技术检索主题进行重点介绍。这些技术主题涉及"多硬件环境相关技术"、"加密认证相关技术"、"数字水印相关技术"、"内容比对相关技术"、"内容访问控制相关技术"、"其他相关技术"等六大方面。由于篇幅较大，分为上、下两册出版；

4. 《数字版权保护技术研发工程标准汇编》：以工程研究制定的标准成果为基础，系统介绍了工程管理类标准、基础类标准、数据类标准以及工程接口协议类标准等四类26项标准。由于篇幅较大，分为上、中、下三册出版。

丛书出版是工程成果转化的形式之一。版权工程既定的研究建设任务虽已基本结束，但后续推广应用工作才刚刚开始。只有工程成果得到广泛应用，众多工程参与者的付出才得到切实回报，工程成果的价值才能得以真正显现。此刻我们所要吹响的绝非船到码头车到站的"熄灯号"，而是动员各有关方面不忘初心、继续前进的"集结号"。

让我们继续努力，共同推动版权工程成果的落地转化，为新闻出版业数字化转型升级提供有力支撑，为传统出版与新兴出版融合发展提供有力支撑！

张毅君
2016 年 12 月 9 日

前　言

为应对信息技术飞速进步带来的挑战，促进新闻出版业态转型融合发展，国家新闻出版广电总局（原新闻出版总署）从产业需求出发，集众智力顶层设计，提出了数字复合出版系统工程、数字版权保护技术研发工程（简称版权工程）、中华字库工程、知识资源数据库工程等四项重大科技工程的建设目标并被先后列入国家"十一五"与"十二五"时期文化发展规划纲要。根据国家规划的分工部署于2007年开始可行性研究论证和相关立项工作；2011年，在国家财政的大力支持下，版权工程、中华字库工程率先启动研发。

版权工程是首个完成研发的新闻出版重大科技工程。在总局重大科技工程项目领导小组的直接领导、重大科技工程项目领导小组办公室的积极推进下，版权工程总体组、管控、总集、标准、监理与其他各研发参与方协同努力，圆满完成了版权工程预定的建设任务，取得了多方面的重要技术成果。其中，已发表论文体现了相关技术领域研发的重点和难点，是该工程创新性的重要标志。

按照项目合同书的约定，版权工程共有9个分包、10家项目承担单位涉及论文发表任务，拟发表论文数量为38篇。截至2016年6月，经过工程总体组审核与确认，已公开发表的相关论文总计42篇，版权工程论文发表任务超额完成。

在工程全面完工之际，版权工程总体组在总局新闻出版重大科技工程项目领导小组的指导和支持下，通过征询论文作者意见，将已发表的工程论文成果进行梳理并结集汇编成册，作为"新闻出版重大科技工程项目管理及相关成果丛书"之一予以出版，旨在展现版权工程技术创新成果，加强与业界分享及交流，同时为数字版权保护技术领域相关研究提供参照和借鉴。

本书共收录版权工程论文28篇，其中11篇以英文形式在国外媒体上发表。根据这些论文研究主题的相关性，版权工程总体组将其归结为三个大类，每个大类一辑，编作三辑出版。其中：

第一辑"安全技术研究"共收录相关论文12篇；

第二辑"相关算法研究"共收录相关论文8篇；

第三辑"其他相关研究"共收录相关论文8篇。

由于论文数量较多，涉及的作者较多，本书不再集中列示各位作者姓名，而是按照各分包提交的论文成果署名情况，分署于相应的论文之中。

借此机会，谨对版权工程的顺利完工表示祝贺，对版权工程各参与单位、全体参与人员包括本书所收录及未收录的所有论文的作者一并表示敬意！

谢俊旗

2016年11月28日

目 录

第一辑　安全技术研究 / 1

云计算环境中支持隐私保护的数字版权保护方案 / 3

A Study on Parameters of Image Encryption Based on Moire Pattern（基于莫尔条纹的图像加密技术参量研究）/ 16

基于行为的访问控制应用于多级安全信息系统 / 25

基于代理重加密的多媒体数字版权授权协议 / 33

面向多级安全的结构化文档描述模型 / 41

A DRM Interoperability Architecture Based on Local Conversion Bridge with Proxy Re-Cryptography（一种基于代理重加密的本地转换桥的 DRM 互操作架构）/ 49

Image Tamper Detection Based on the DCT Coefficients Model（基于 DCT 系数模型的图像篡改检测）/ 57

Homomorphic Encryption Based Data Storage and Query Algorithm（基于数据存储和查询算法的同态加密）/ 67

高效的选择密文安全的单向代理重加密方案 / 77

新型通用格式多媒体数字版权管理系统设计与实现 / 93

基于 UCON 模型的移动数字出版版权保护系统研究与设计 / 108

基于数字水印的 PDF 完整性认证研究 / 116

第二辑　相关算法研究 / 125

一种基于 H.264/AVC 的视频可逆脆弱水印算法 / 127

A Video Watermarking Algorithm of H.264/AVC for Content Authentication（一种 H.264/AVC 格式的视频内容认证水印算法）/ 138

An Audio Zero-watermarking Algorithm Based on Wavelet and Cepstrum Coefficients Mean Comparison（一种基于小波和倒谱系数平均值比较的音频零水印算法）/ 147

An Algorithm to Control Watermarking Capacity Using PSNR（一种基于峰值信噪比的水印容量控制算法）/ 154

A New Echo Hiding Algorithm with High Robustness（一种新型的高鲁棒回声消除算法）/ 160

A Visual Hiding Algorithm Based on Human Visual System（基于人类视觉系统的视觉隐匿算法）／167

Reversible Data Hiding based on Histogram Technique（基于直方图技术的可逆数据隐藏算法）／174

Ciphertext Query Algorithm for Character Data Based on DAS Model（基于DAS模型的密文查询字符数据的算法）／201

第三辑　其他相关研究／213

数字版权保护技术带来的变化／215

访问控制模型研究进展及发展趋势／219

细粒度超媒体描述模型及其使用机制／232

基于AOP的数据库应用安全控制的设计与实现／240

面向动态框架的数据交互规范研究／251

基于iOS系统阅读的数字版权保护技术初探／259

基于移动客户端的电子阅读器客户端设计与开发／262

数字版权保护技术在百科类工具书中的应用探索／266

第一辑
安全技术研究

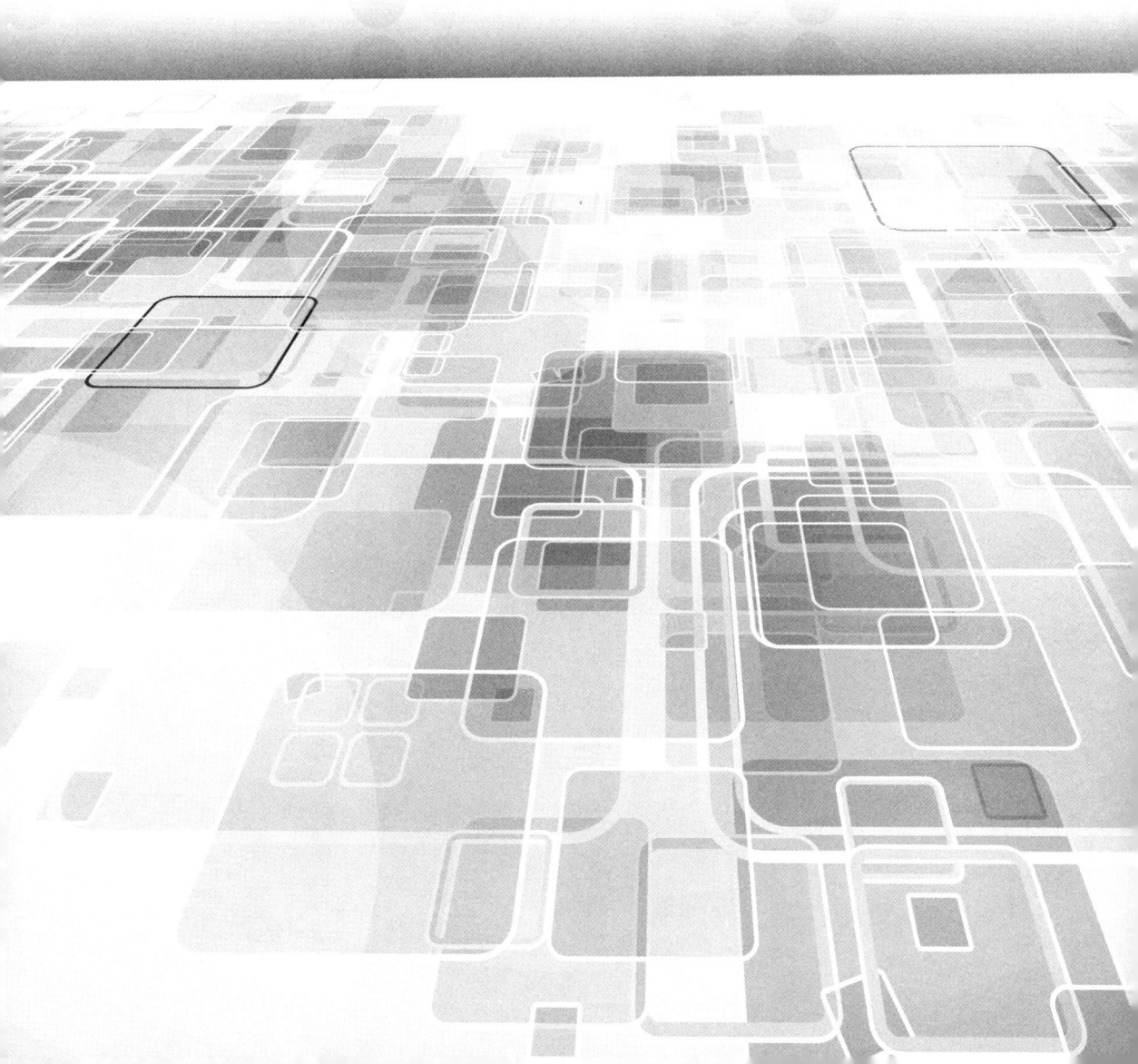

云计算环境中支持隐私保护的数字版权保护方案

黄勤龙　马兆丰　傅镜艺　杨义先　钮心忻

1　引言

随着互联网和云计算技术的快速发展和不断普及，云计算在提高使用效率的同时，为数字内容安全与用户隐私保护带来极大的冲击与挑战[1]。数字版权管理（digital rights management，DBM）通过数字内容的加密和安全许可等一系列手段防止数字内容的非法误用，确保数字内容在公平、合理、安全许可框架下的条件使用和消费[2-5]。

云计算以动态的服务计算为主要技术特征，有着较大的灵活性和成本优势。企业能够将内容存储和运营外包给云服务提供商，而不需自己购买设备和维护系统，还能在存储需求变化时灵活地增减云资源的租用。同时，用户也能够方便地通过不同终端接入云服务，使用海量的数字内容。然而，如何保护云环境下数字内容的安全性和合理使用，同时防止云服务提供商挖掘或者泄露用户隐私信息是云计算环境中数字版权保护无法回避的核心问题。

针对云计算环境中数字版权保护的需求，本文提出一种云计算环境中支持隐私保护的数字版权保护方案，实现数字内容版权全生命周期的保护和用户隐私的保护。本文的贡献主要有3个方面。

（1）提出云计算环境中数字内容版权全生命周期保护和用户隐私保护的框架，包括系统初始化、内容加密、许可授权和内容解密4个主要协议，支持云计算环境中细粒度的用户授权和灵活的应用模式。

（2）采用基于属性基加密和加法同态加密算法的内容加密密钥保护和分发机制，保证内容加密密钥的安全性。内容加密密钥由主密钥、授权密钥和辅助密钥3部分组成，其中主密钥使用内容提供商设置的访问策略加密，授权密钥和辅助密钥分别由授权服务器和密钥服务器加密分发给用户，用户只有在其属性满足密文的访问策略并且拥有有效许可证的情况下才能基于加法同态加密算法解密出内容加密密钥。

（3）允许用户匿名向云服务提供商订购内容和申请授权，有效保护用户的隐私，同时防止云服务提供商、授权服务器和密钥服务器等收集用户使用习惯等敏感信息。

---

* 本文选自《通信学报》，第35卷第2期，2014年2月，第95–103页

2 相关工作

云计算技术带来的大规模在线存储和按需使用的模式，使越来越多的用户选择云计算作为内容的存储平台。然而，数字内容的全生命周期保护包括内容的安全性、内容的合理使用等，是云计算发展和应用中面临的关键问题。在云计算快速发展的推动下，国内外学者在云环境下版权保护方面的研究也在不断深入，并取得不少研究成果，主要集中在内容安全、访问控制和隐私保护等方面[6~15]。

（1）数字内容安全。内容加密是保护云环境中内容安全的基本手段，JAFARI 等人在 2011 年的 ACMDRM 会议上提出支持云存储环境的数据版权保护方案[6]，通过加密用户上传的数字内容，并限制访问者对内容的使用权利，保护内容的安全性。该方案不依赖于可信的云服务提供商，但是不支持细粒度的用户授权。另外，在 JAFARI 等人的方案中，数据拥有者在为用户授权时，使用用户的公钥加密内容加密密钥，导致用户解密的计算复杂度较高。针对内容加密密钥的保护，WANG 等人提出云计算中基于 SIM 卡的移动版权保护方案 CS-DRM[7]，使用对称加密技术加密内容加密密钥。但是，该方案需要通过 SIM 卡提前协商对称密钥，实用性不高，同时会泄露用户使用内容的习惯。

PETRLIC 也提出云计算环境中支持细粒度授权的版权保护方案[8]，允许内容提供商将加密的内容上传到云服务提供商，并设置使用权限。用户在使用内容时，云服务提供商利用代理重加密技术将内容重加密为用户公钥加密的内容，确保只有该用户才能解密，并且在重加密过程中，云服务提供商也无法知道内容的明文。该方案虽然可以保证内容在云环境中的安全性，但是用户每次使用内容时都需要重加密内容，当用户数量达到一定规模时会带来很大的额外开销。

另外，同态加密也广泛应用于数字内容的安全保护，SAMANTHULA 等人提出了云计算环境中基于代理重加密和同态加密技术的内容安全共享方案[9]。CORENA 等人也提出了基于云计算的财务数据安全整合和存储的方案[10]，该方案基于加法同态加密和秘密共享技术实现数据在密文状态下的运算。

（2）内容访问控制。密文的访问控制是云计算环境下加密内容安全使用的关键问题，WU 等人提出了一种云计算环境下基于属性基加密的内容保护方案[11]，以实现灵活的访问控制。洪澄等人在属性基加密的基础上提出一种内容保护和访问控制方案[12]，设计出一种基于秘密共享方案的云端重加密方法，在不损失安全性的前提下将一部分重加密代价转移到云端，降低权限管理的复杂度，实现密文访问控制。MULLER 等人首次提出基于属性基加密的数字版权保护方案[13]，通过静态规则和动态规则实现版权内容的合理使用。其中，静态规则是通过设置密文的访问策略，实现用户的访问控制，动态规则是将用户允许使用的权限通过许可证分发给用户，实现内容的使用控制。

（3）用户隐私保护。针对云计算环境下用户使用内容时隐私保护的问题，CONRADO 等人最早提出支持隐私保护的版权保护方案[14]，允许用户匿名购买内容和申请授权。但是，该方案基于智能卡实现，缺乏实用性。PERLMAN 等人提出基于匿名现金和盲签名技术的用户隐私保护方案[15]，允许用户匿名使用内容，同时防止云服务提供商跟踪用户的使用行为，但是不支持细粒度的用户授权。在 PERLMAN 等人方案的基础上，PETRLIC 等人提出一种云计算环境中支持灵活用户授权的内容版权保护方案[16]，该方案基于同态加密和秘密共享技术实现云服务器上加密内容的授权管理，结合重加密机制防止云服务器收集用户的敏感数据。然而，该方案同样在用户每次使用内容时都需重加密内容，效率较低。

本文在上述工作成果的基础上，提出适用于云计算环境的数字内容版权全生命周期保护方案，允许内容提供商上传加密内容到云存储环境，采用属性基加密和加法同态加密算法分发内容加密密钥，不仅保护内容的安全性，支持灵活的访问控制，而且允许用户匿名获取内容和授权，同时防止云服务提供商获得用户使用内容的记录。

3 预备知识

3.1 CP-ABE

属性基加密（ABE）最初由 SAHAI 和 WATERS 提出[17]，它以属性为公钥，将密文和用户私钥与属性关联，能够灵活地表示访问策略，当用户的私钥与密文的访问策略相互匹配时，该用户才能解密密文。ABE 包括密钥策略（KP-ABE）以及密文策略（CP-ABE）2类。其中，CP-ABE 的密文与访问策略关联，更加适合于云计算环境下的访问控制。

CP-ABE 算法包括以下 4 个组成部分。

（1）$ABE\ Setup\ O$。生成系统公钥 PK 和系统主密钥 MK。

（2）$ASK = ABE\ KeyGen\ (AS, MK)$。使用用户属性 AS 和 MK 生成用户的属性私钥 ASK。

（3）$CT = ABE\ Encrypt\ (AP, M, PK)$。使用访问策略 AP 和 PK 将数据明文 M 加密为密文 CT。

（4）$M = ABE\ Decrypt\ (ASK, CT)$。如果用户的属性 AS 满足访问策略 AP，使用属性私钥 ASK 解密密文 CT 得到明文 M。

3.2 加法同态加密

同态加密技术允许用户对加密数据进行直接运算或处理，是实现云计算安全中密文处理和隐私保护的重要基础。同态加密[18]是在 1978 年由 RIVEST 等人提出的，是基于数学难题的计算复杂性理论的密码学技术。2009 年，GENTRY 提出了基于多项式环上理想格的全同态加密算法[19]。2010 年，DIJK 等人提出针对整数加密的全同态加密算法[20]。

基于同态加密算法，可以对加密数据进行运算或处理，而不再需要先进行解密。CASTELLUCCIA 等人提出一种加法同态加密算法[21]，满足如表 1 所示的属性，包括加密算法、解密算法和密文加法，该方案是可证明安全的。

表 1 加法同态加密算法

加密算法	解密算法	密文加法
$c = Enc(m,k,M) = m + k(\mod M)$，其中，$M$ 是一个大整数，$m \in [0, M-1]$，$k \in [0, M-1]$。	$Dec(c,k,M) = c - k(\mod M)$。	如果 $c1 = Enc(m1,k1,M)$，$c2 = Enc(m2,k2,M)$，其中，$m1 + m2 \in [0, M-1]$，则有 $Dec(c1 + c2, k1 + k2, M) = m1 + m2$。

4 云计算环境中版权保护需求

（1）灵活性

云计算由于可扩展性和灵活性等特性，能够满足用户对数字内容不断增长的需求，并且支持按需使用的业务模式。因此，云计算环境中的版权保护方案在保证数字内容安全性的前提下应满足灵活的业务需求和细粒度的用户授权，并且支持内容提供商设置灵活的访问控制。同时，云计算为用户提供使用便利，用户可以随时随地使用不同终端访问云服务提供商，购买和租用数字内容。因此，云计算环境中的版权保护方案应支持灵活的应用模式。

（2）安全性

云计算允许内容提供商将内容发布到云存储平台，并快速分发给用户，因此版权保护方案应保证内容的安全性，防止由于云服务系统内部人员失职、外部黑客攻击等引起的数字内容泄露，保护内容提供商的合法权利。同时，为了保证数字内容的合理使用，版权保护方案应确保数字内容只能被授权用户访问，防止假冒攻击和重放攻击等非授权访问，并且支持许可证的撤销。

（3）隐私保护

用户通过云服务提供商订购内容时，版权保护方案应防止内容提供商和云服务提供商等获取用户身份信息，保证用户的匿名性。另外，云服务提供商在为用户提供内容服务的同时，往往通过网页等技术收集并分析用户的使用记录，为用户精准地推荐相关内容。因此，版权保护方案应防止云服务提供商收集用户的使用记录等敏感信息，保护用户的隐私。

5 方案设计思想

基于 CP-ABE 和加法同态加密算法，本文提出一种半可信云计算环境中支持隐私保护的数字版权全生命周期保护方案，保护版权内容在上传、存储、传输和使用等环节的安全性和合理使用。如图 1 所示，数字版权保护方案涵盖属性机构、内容提供商、密钥服务器、授权服务器、云服务提供商和用户等组成部分。

（1）属性机构：属性机构是可信的服务器，为用户分配属性，并生成用户的属性私钥通过安全信道分发给用户。

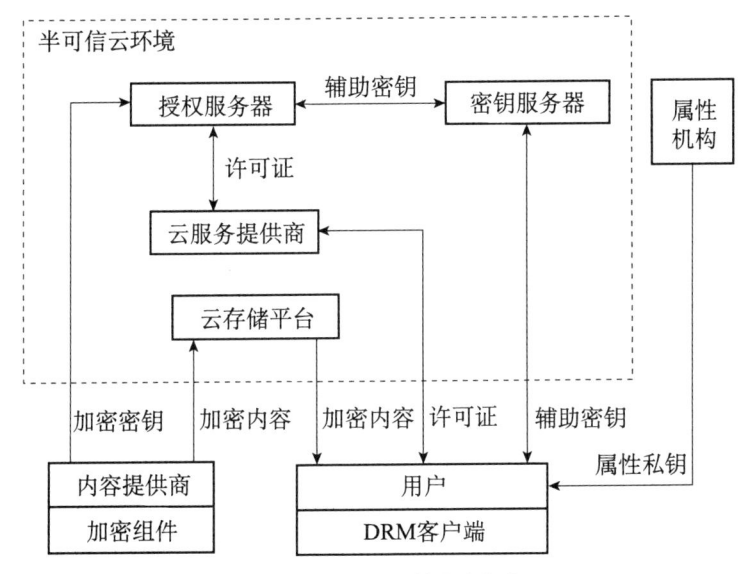

图 1　数字版权保护方案框架

（2）内容提供商：内容提供商通过加密组件使用随机的主密钥、授权密钥、辅助密钥相加得到内容加密密钥，使用内容加密密钥加密准备上传的数字内容，并将加密后的数字内容发布到云存储平台。同时，内容提供商通过访问策略加密主密钥以实现用户的访问控制。

（3）密钥服务器：密钥服务器接收内容提供商加密的辅助密钥，在申请内容解密时为已授权用户提供辅助密钥。另外，在授权服务器撤销许可证后，密钥服务器拒绝已撤销许可证的内容解密请求。

（4）授权服务器：授权服务器根据云服务提供商的内容订购请求，为用户生成许可证，并通过云服务提供商分发给用户。许可证中包含加密的授权密钥以及时间限制、次数限制等细粒度授权，并使用授权服务器的私钥签名。

（5）云服务提供商：云服务提供商向用户提供内容服务，用户通过云服务提供商购买内容提供商的内容并获取许可证，在此过程中云服务提供商不能获取明文内容、用户隐私和敏感信息。

（6）用户：用户获取加密的内容后，通过云服务提供商向授权服务器申请许可证，在使用内容时向密钥服务器申请辅助密钥。用户设备上的可信 DRM 客户端首先利用属性私钥解密出主密钥，然后基于加法同态加密算法解密出授权密钥与辅助密钥的和，再与主密钥相加得到内容加密密钥并解密明文内容。DRM 客户端在执行内容使用权利约束的同时，保护内容加密密钥和明文内容不被窃取或者转存。

下面介绍数字版权全生命周期保护中系统初始化、内容加密、许可授权和内容解密 4 个主要的协议。文中用到的符号定义如表 2 所示。

表 2 相关符号定义

符号	含义
SP, U	云服务提供商,用户
S, K	授权服务器,密钥服务器
PK, MK	系统公钥/主密钥
AS	用户属性
AP	访问策略
ASK	属性私钥
CID	内容标识
PCD, ECD	明文内容,加密内容
CMK, LK, AK	主密钥,授权密钥,辅助密钥
CEK	内容加密密钥
UK	用户的随机密钥
HK	同态密钥
LIC	用户许可证
T	时间戳
Enc O, Dec O	加密/解密运算
Sig O	私钥签名运算

5.1 系统初始化协议

系统初始化时,属性机构定义系统属性为 $A = \{a_1, a_2, a_3, \cdots, a_n\}$,公开发布系统公钥 PK,并秘密保存系统主密钥 MK。

用户注册时,根据用户的属性 AS 为用户生成属性私钥 ASK,并通过安全信道发送给用户秘密保存。

$$ASK = ABE.KeyGen(AS, MK)$$

5.2 内容加密协议

在内容加密阶段,内容提供商的加密组件生成随机的 CEK,再使用 CEK 基于对称加密算法加密内容提供商上传的内容。

Step 1 内容提供商的加密组件随机生成长度为 l 的 CMK、LK 和 AK,并相加得到 CEK。

$$CEK = CMK + LK + AK \in [0, M-1],\text{其中} M \geq 2^{l+1}$$

Step 2 加密组件使用 CEK 加密 PCD,并把加密结果 ECD 发布到云存储平台。

$$ECD = Enc(CEK, PCD)$$

Step 3 内容提供商设置该内容的访问策略 AP,加密组件基于 CP-ABE 算法使用 AP 加密 CMK,使用授权服务器的公钥 PK_S 加密 LK,并将结果一并发送给授权服务器,同时使用密钥服务器的公钥 PK_K 加密 AK 发送给密钥服务器。

$$CP \to S: ABE.Enc(AP, CMK, PK) \parallel Enc(PK_S, LK) \quad CP \to K: Enc(PK_K, AK)$$

5.3 许可授权协议

用户通过云服务提供商订购内容后，云服务提供商向授权服务器申请 LIC，授权服务器根据用户的订购权限生成 LIC，并通过云服务提供商分发给用户。许可授权协议时序如图 2 所示。

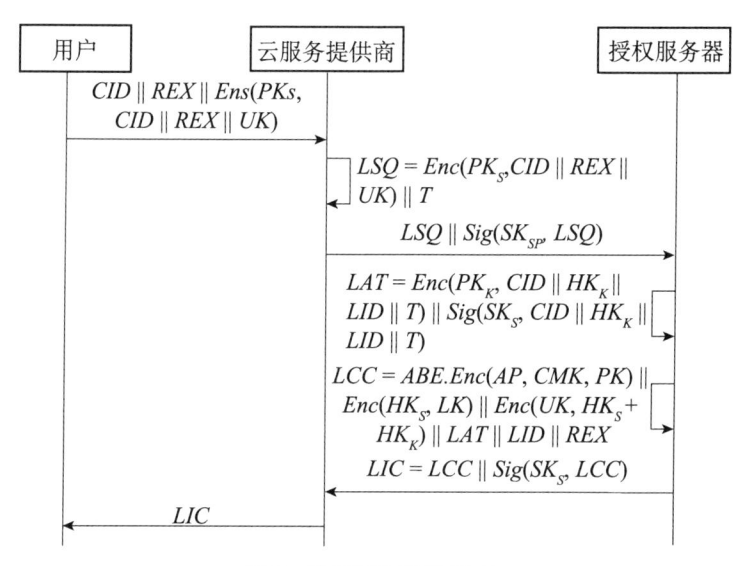

```
用户                          云服务提供商                        授权服务器
 │   CID ‖ REX ‖ Ens(PKs,         │                                  │
 │   CID ‖ REX ‖ UK)              │                                  │
 │ ──────────────────────────────>│                                  │
 │                                │ LSQ = Enc(PKs, CID ‖ REX ‖       │
 │                                │ UK) ‖ T                          │
 │                                │                                  │
 │                                │   LSQ ‖ Sig(SKSP, LSQ)           │
 │                                │ ────────────────────────────────>│
 │                                │                                  │ LAT = Enc(PKK, CID ‖ HKK ‖
 │                                │                                  │ LID ‖ T) ‖ Sig(SKS, CID ‖ HKK ‖
 │                                │                                  │ LID ‖ T)
 │                                │                                  │ LCC = ABE.Enc(AP, CMK, PK) ‖
 │                                │                                  │ Enc(HKS, LK) ‖ Enc(UK, HKS +
 │                                │                                  │ HKK) ‖ LAT ‖ LID ‖ REX
 │                                │   LIC = LCC ‖ Sig(SKS, LCC)      │
 │                                │<──────────────────────────────── │
 │            LIC                 │                                  │
 │<───────────────────────────────│                                  │
```

图 2　许可授权协议时序

Step 1　用户随机生成密钥 UK，向云服务提供商提交内容订购请求，包括 CID、用户使用权限 REX 和许可授权请求 LAQ。其中，LAQ 包括 CID、REX 和 UK，并使用 PK_S 加密。

$$LAQ = Enc(PK_S, CID \| REX \| UK)$$
$$U \to SP: CID \| REX \| LAQ$$

Step 2　云服务提供商处理用户的内容订购请求后，向授权服务器提交许可生成请求 LSQ 和签名。其中，LSQ 包括 LAQ 和 T 等。

$$LSQ = LAQ \| T$$
$$SP \to S: LSQ \| Sig(SK_{SP}, LSQ)$$

Step 3　授权服务器收到许可生成请求 LSQ 和签名后，验证 LSQ 的签名是否正确，并验证 T 是否有效。验证通过后，授权服务器首先使用 SK_S 解密出 CID、REX 和 UK。其次，授权服务器根据 CID 随机生成长度为 l 的 HK_S 和 HK_K（满足 $HK_S + HK_K \in [0, M-1]$，其中每个内容的 HK_K 均相同）。根据许可证权利描述为用户生成 LIC 并返回给云服务提供商。LIC 中包括 AP 加密的 CMK、HK_S 加密的 LK、许可授权凭证 LAT 和许可证标识 LID 等，并使用 SK_S 签名。

$$LAT = Enc(PK_K, CID \| HK_K \| LID \| T) \| Sig(SK_S, CID \| HK_K \| LID \| T)$$
$$LCC = ABE.Enc(AP, CMK, PK) \| Enc(HK_S, LK) \|$$
$$Enc(UK, HK_S + HK_K) \| LAT \| LID \| REX$$
$$S \to SP: LIC = LCC \| Sig(SK_S, LCC)$$

Step 4　云服务提供商将 LIC 发送给用户，用户使用 PK_S 验证 LIC 的完整性，并保存 LIC。

5.4 内容解密协议

用户使用内容时，将已申请的 LIC 中的 LAT 发送给密钥服务器请求 AK。用户获取 AK 后，基于加法同态加密算法解密出 LK 与 AK 的和。内容解密协议时序如图 3 所示。

```
用户                                                                密钥服务器
 |  Enc(PK_K, CID || HK_K || LID || T) || Sig(SK_S, CID || HK_K || LID || T)  |
 |------------------------------------------------------------------------->|
 |                         Enc(HK_K, AK)                                    |
 |<-------------------------------------------------------------------------|
 | CMK = ABE.Dec(ASK, ABE.Enc(AP, CMK, PK))                                  |
 | HK_S + HK_K = Dec(UK, Enc(UK, HK_S + HK_K))                               |
 | LK + AK = Dec(HK_S + HK_K, Enc(HKS, LK) + Enc(HK_K, AK))                  |
 | PCD = Dec(CMK + LK + AK, ECD)                                             |
```

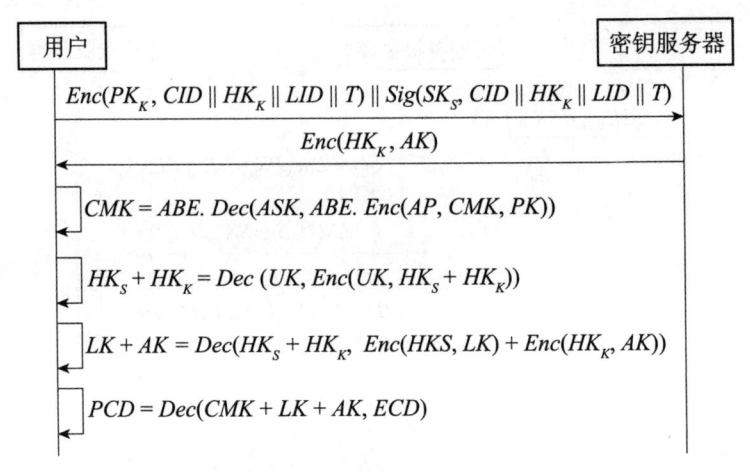

图 3　内容解密协议时序

Step 1　用户使用内容时首先判断 LIC 是否存在，若 LIC 存在并且有效时，用户从 LIC 提取出 LAT 发给密钥服务器申请 AK。

$$U \rightarrow K: Enc(PK_K, CID \| HK_K \| LID \| T) \| Sig(SK_S, CID \| HK_K \| LID \| T)$$

Step 2　密钥服务器收到 LAT 后，使用 PK_S 验证 LAT 的完整性，并使用 SK_K 解密出 CID 和 HK_K。然后，密钥服务器使用 SK_K 解密出该内容的 AK，并使用 HK_K 加密 AK 后，将 $Enc(HK_K, AK)$ 返回给用户。

$$K \rightarrow U: Enc(HK_K, AK)$$

Step 3　用户使用 ASK 从 LIC 中解密出 CMK。

$$CMK = ABE.Dec(ASK, ABE.Enc(AP, CMK, PK))$$

Step 4　用户使用 UK 从 LIC 中解密出 $HK_S + HK_K$。

$$HK_S + HK_K = Dec(UK, Enc(UK, HK_S + HK_K))$$

Step 5　基于加法同态加密算法，用户使用 $(HK_S + HK_K)$ 解密出 $(LK + AK)$。

$$LK + AK = Dec(HK_S + HK_K, Enc(HK_S, LK) + Enc(HK_K, AK))$$

Step 6　用户使用 CEK 解密 ECD，并按照 LIC 中的 REX 执行权利约束。

$$PCD = Dec(CMK + LK + AK, ECD)$$

6　方案应用模式

（1）云在线应用模式

云计算将大量计算资源、存储资源与内容资源通过网络连接在一起，推动了在线应用和在线内容服务的快速发展。本文方案支持云环境下数字内容在线使用场景下灵活的版权控制，例如在线播放多媒体内容、在线阅读电子书等。用户通过安装在终端的 DRM 客户端向授权服务器在线申请许可证,获取许可证后实时解密在线传输的加密内容流,并按照许可证中规定的权利进行使用控制。通过方案中的隐私保护方法,用户不仅可以享受云计算带来的在线数字内容服务,而且无需担心隐私和敏感记录的泄露。

(2)云超级分发应用模式

云计算通过 CDN 等技术消除网络运营商之间的互通瓶颈,将数字内容分发到离用户最近的网络节点,为用户提供更快的内容超级分发服务。本文方案支持许可证与内容独立分发的模式,加密的数字内容可以在用户之间或者用户的不同终端设备之间进行超级分发。用户使用加密内容时,需要通过云服务提供商向授权服务器申请许可证。本文方案不但满足云环境中数字内容分发和共享的需求,而且保护用户使用内容过程中的隐私。

7 方案分析

7.1 正确性分析

已知 $HK_S + HK_K \in [0, M\text{-}1]$,$LK + AK \in [0, M\text{-}1]$,$M$ 是一个大整数。

基于 CASTELLUCCIA 等人提出的加法同态加密算法[21]可以得出

$$Enc(HK_S, LK) + Enc(HK_K, AK)$$
$$= Enc(HK_S + HK_K, LK + AK)$$

则由上述等式,可得

$$(LK + AK) = Dec(HK_S + HK_K, Enc(HK_S, LK) + Enc(HK_K, AK))$$

由 $CEK = CMK + LK + AK$,用户可以正确解密内容。

7.2 安全性分析

定理 1 用户只有满足访问策略并获取有效的许可证后才能解密内容。

加密服务器使用 CEK 加密数字内容,用户只有获取 CEK 才能解密内容。用户通过云服务提供商向授权服务器申请 LIC,LIC 中包含 AP 加密的 CMK、HK_S 加密的 LK、$Enc(UK, HK_S + HK_K)$ 和 LAT 等。在使用加密内容时,用户将 LIC 中的 LAT 发送给密钥服务器,密钥服务器验证有效后,返回 $Enc(HK_K, AK)$ 给用户,用户然后使用属性私钥 ASK 解密出 CMK,再基于加法同态加密算法解密出 CEK。因此,用户只有满足属性结构并获取有效的许可证后才能解密内容。另外,撤销的用户由于无法通过密钥服务器获取加密的 AK,因此也无法解密内容。

定理 2 云服务提供商、授权服务器和密钥服务器均无法获得内容加密密钥。

在许可授权阶段,由于 CMK 使用 AP 加密,因此云服务提供商和授权服务器均无法获得 CEK。在内容解密阶段,密钥服务器可以根据 $Enc(PK_K, AK)$ 解密出 AK,但是无法获得 CMK 和 LK,因此也无法获得 CEK。另外,如果攻击者试图伪造 LAT,随机生成 HK_K' 并发送 $Enc(PK_K, CID \| HK_K' \| T) \| Sig(SK_S', CID \| HK_K' \| T)$ 给密钥服务器。密钥服务器使用 PK_S 验证签名 $Sig(SK_S', CID \| HK_K' \| T)$ 不通过,攻击者无法获取 AK。因此,云服务提供商也不能联合攻击者获得 CEK。

定理 3 攻击者不能重放云服务提供商的许可生成请求。

在许可授权阶段,云服务器提供商向授权服务器提交许可生成请求。攻击者试图重放许可生成请求，发送 $LSQ' \parallel Sig(SK_{SP}, LSQ')$ 给授权服务器。授权服务器验证 LSQ' 的签名正确，然后使用 SK_S 解密 $LAQ \parallel T'$ 得到 LAQ 和时间戳 T' 等，但是验证时间戳 T' 与授权服务器时间不符。因此，攻击者无法通过重放攻击获取授权服务器颁发的许可证。

7.3 隐私保护分析

（1）匿名性

用户在内容订购时，生成随机的 UK 向授权服务器申请授权，云服务提供商和授权服务器无法获取用户的身份信息。用户在使用内容时向密钥服务器提交的 LAT 也不包含用户的身份信息。因此，本文方案能够保证用户的匿名性，防止泄露用户的身份信息。

（2）敏感记录保护

用户向云服务提供商订购内容时，随机生成密钥 UK 封装在许可授权请求中发送给云服务提供商。由于每次订购时 UK 都不相同，因此云服务提供商无法将该内容订购请求与特定的匿名用户联系起来，也无法收集匿名用户的内容订购记录。同时，许可授权申请中每次的时间戳 T 都不相同，因此授权服务器也无法统计特定匿名用户的授权记录。

用户在使用内容时，向密钥服务器提交 LAT，由于 HK_K 是随机生成的，并且每个内容的 HK_K 均相同，因此密钥服务器也无法分析用户的内容使用习惯。

通过以上分析，本文方案能够有效防止用户敏感记录的泄露和分析。

7.4 实验分析

（1）实验环境

下面将设计实验对本文方案的性能进行分析。实验环境是 Ubuntu 12.10 虚拟机（Intel Core i5 2.53 GHz，分配 2 GB 内存）。实验的编码实现基于 cpabe 库[22]，对称加密算法使用 128bit AES 算法。

（2）实验结果

针对不同内容大小和属性个数的情况进行加密和解密实验，图 4 展示了访问策略中属性个数为 8 的情况下加密和解密时间开销与内容大小的对比关系，图 5 展示了解密时间开

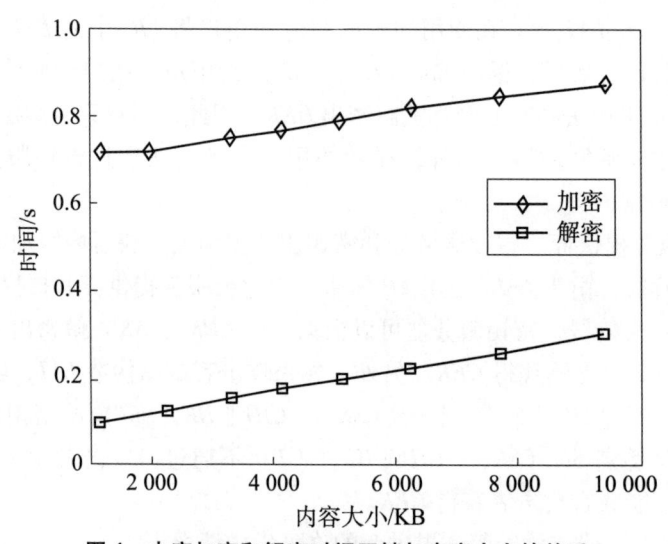

图 4 内容加密和解密时间开销与内容大小的关系

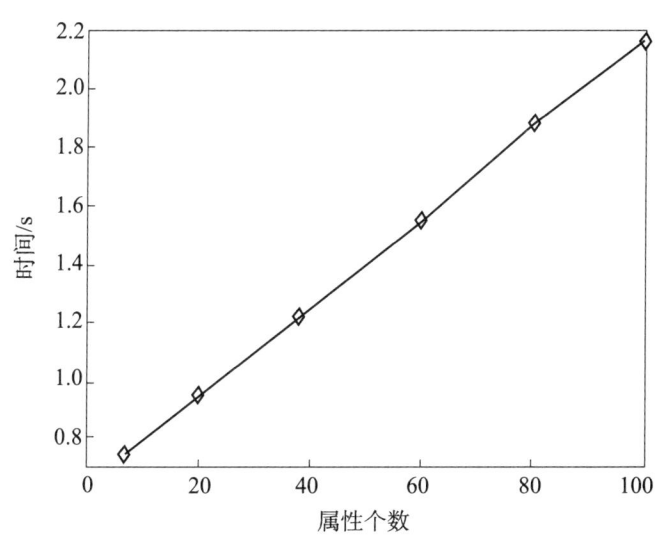

图 5 内容解密时间开销与属性个数的关系

销与访问策略中属性个数的对比关系。实验结果可以看出，加密和解密的时间开销与内容大小和访问策略中属性个数成线性关系，加密 10 M 大小的内容所需的时间小于 1 s，解密时间也远小于加密时间，因此，本文所提方案在内容加密和解密操作的时间开销方面具有优势。

7.5 与其他方案的比较

本文方案使用对称加密算法加密内容，保护内容的安全性，支持许可证的细粒度用户授权，如是否允许播放、时间限制和次数限制等，同时支持在线和超级分发应用模式。通过引入 CP-ABE 和加法同态加密机制分发内容加密密钥，保证内容加密密钥的安全性。另外，本文在保证用户匿名性的同时，能够防止用户敏感记录的泄露和分析。本文方案与现有的云计算环境中内容保护方案对比分析的结果如表 3 所示。

表 3 云计算环境中内容保护方案功能对比分析

方案	内容加密	内容加密密钥保护	内容重加密	细粒度授权	许可证分发	用户匿名	敏感记录保护	在线模式	超级分发模式
文献［6］	对称加密	公钥加密	不需要	不支持	独立分发	不支持	不支持	不支持	支持
文献［7］	对称加密	对称加密	不需要	不支持	独立分发	不支持	不支持	不支持	支持
文献［12］	对称加密	属性基加密	不需要	支持	独立分发	支持	不支持	支持	不支持
文献［13］	对称加密	属性基加密	不需要	支持	独立分发	支持	不支持	支持	支持
文献［16］	加法加密	加法同态加密	需要	支持	独立分发	支持	支持	支持	不支持
本文	对称加密	属性基加密和加法同态加密	不需要	支持	独立分发	支持	支持	支持	支持

与文献［6，7］相比，本文方案支持细粒度的用户授权，同时允许用户匿名使用云计算环境中的版权保护服务，保护用户敏感记录。与文献［16］相比，本文方案使用对称加密算

法加密内容，安全性更高，并且在使用内容时不需要重新加密内容，效率更高，同时也支持超级分发模式。与文献［12，13］相比，本文方案支持对用户敏感记录等隐私的保护。

8　结束语

针对云计算环境中数字版权保护的需求，本文提出一种云计算环境中支持隐私保护的数字版权保护方案。首先，提出云计算环境中数字内容版权全生命周期保护和用户隐私保护的框架，描述了数字内容版权全生命周期中系统初始化、内容加密、许可授权和内容解密4个主要的协议。其次，本文提出基于属性基加密和加法同态加密算法的内容加密密钥保护和分发机制，保证内容加密密钥的安全性。内容加密密钥由主密钥、授权密钥和辅助密钥组成，分别独立加密分发到用户。用户在其属性满足密文的访问策略并且拥有有效许可证的情况下，可以首先解密出主密钥，然后基于加法同态加密算法解密出授权密钥与辅助密钥的和，最后得到内容加密密钥。同时，本文允许用户匿名向云服务提供商订购内容和申请授权，有效保护用户的隐私，防止云服务提供商、授权服务器和密钥服务器等收集匿名用户使用习惯等敏感信息。此外，本文支持云计算环境中灵活的业务模式和许可证的细粒度授权，支持在线和超级分发应用模式。

安全性、隐私保护和实验分析表明，与现有的云计算环境中数字版权保护方案相比，本文方案灵活性及安全性较高，能够有效保护用户的隐私，支持灵活的访问控制，在云计算环境中具有较好的实用性。

参考文献

［1］冯登国，张敏，张妍，等. 云计算安全研究［J］. 软件学报，2011，22（1）：71-83.
FENG D G, ZHANG M, ZHANG Y, et al. Study on cloud computing security［J］. Journal of Software, 2011, 22（1）: 71-83.

［2］俞银燕，汤帜. 数字版权保护技术研究综述［J］. 计算机学报，2005，28（12）：957-968.
YU Y Y, TANG Z. A survey of the research on digital rights manage-ment［J］. Chinese Journal of Computers, 2005, 28（12）: 957-968.

［3］马兆丰，范科峰，陈铭等. 支持时空约束的可信数字版权管理安全许可协议［J］. 通信学报，2008，29（10）：153-164.
MA Z F, FAN K F, CHEN M, et al. Trusted digital rights management protocol supporting for time and space constraint［J］. Journal on Com-munications, 2008, 29（10）: 153-164.

［4］ZHANG Z Y, PEI Q Q, YANG L, et al. Establishing multi-party trust architecture for DRM by using game-theoretic analysis of security policies［J］. Chinese Journal of Electronics, 2009, 18（3）: 519-524.

［5］QIU Q, TANG Z, LI F, et al. A personal DRM scheme based on social trust［J］. Chinese Journal of Electronics, 2012, 21（4）: 719-724.

［6］JAFARI M, SAFAVI-NAINI R, SHEPPARD N P. A rights management approach to protection of privacy in a cloud of electronic health records［A］. Proceedings of the 11th Annual ACM Workshop on Digital Rights Management [C]. Chicago, USA, 2011. 23-29.

[7] WANG C K, ZOU P, LIU Z, et al. CS-DRM: a cloud-based SIM DRM scheme for mobile internet [J]. Eurasip Journal on Wireless Communi- cations and Networking, 2011, 2011: 1-30.

[8] PETRLIC R. Proxy re-encryption in a privacy-preserving cloud com-puting DRM scheme [A]. Proceedings of the 4th International Sympo-sium on Cyberspace Safety and Security, CSS 2012 [C]. Melbourne, Australia, 2012. 194-211.

[9] SAMANTHULA B K, HOWSER G., ELMEHDWI Y, et al. An effi-cient and secure data sharing framework using homomorphic encryption in the cloud [A]. Proceedings of the 1st International Workshop on Cloud Intelligence [C]. Istanbul, Turkey, 2012. 1-8.

[10] CORENA J C, OHTSUKI T. Secure and fast aggregation of financial data in cloud-based expense tracking applications [J]. Journal of Net-work and Systems Management, 2012, 20 (4): 534-560.

[11] WU Y D, WEI Z, DENG R H. Attribute-based access to scalable media in cloud-assisted content sharing networks [J]. IEEE Transactions on Multimedia, 2013, 15 (4): 778-788.

[12] 洪澄, 张敏, 冯登国. 面向云存储的高效动态密文访问控制方法 [J]. 通信学报, 2011, 32 (7): 125-132.
HONG C, ZHANG M, FENG D G. Achieving efficient dynamic cryp-tographic access control in cloud storage [J]. Journal on Communications, 2011, 32 (7): 125-132.

[13] MULLER S, KATZENBEISSER S. A new DRM architecture with strong enforcement [A]. Proceedings of the 5th International Conference on Availability, Reliability, and Security, ARES 2010 [C]. Krakow, Poland, 2010. 397-403.

[14] CONRADO C, PETKOVIC M, JONKER W. Privacy-preserving digital rights management [A]. Proceedings of the Secure Data Man-agement 2004 [C]. Toronto, Canada, 2004. 83-99.

[15] PERLMAN R, KAUFMAN C, PERLNER R. Privacy-preserving DRM [A]. Proceedings of the 9th Symposium on Identity and Trust on the Internet, IDtrust 2010 [C]. New York, USA, 2010. 69-83.

[16] PETRLICR, SORGE C. Privacy-preserving DRM for cloud computing [A]. Proceedings of 26th IEEE International Conference on Advanced Information Networking and Applications Workshops, WAINA 2012 [C]. Fukuoka, Japan, 2012. 1286-1291.

[17] SAHAI A, WATERS B. Fuzzy identity-based encryption [A]. Proceedings of EUROCRYPT 2005 [C]. Aarhus, Denmark, 2005. 457-473.

[18] RIVEST R, SHARMIR A, DERTOUZONS M. On Data Banks and Privacy Homomorphisms [M]. Orlando: Academic Press, 1978.

[19] GENTRY C. Fully homomorphic encryption using ideal lattices [A]. Proceedings of the 41st Annual ACM Symposium on Theory of Computing [C]. New York, USA, 2009. 169-178.

[20] DIJK M, GENTRY C, HALEVI S, et al. Fully homomorphic encryption over the integers [A]. Proceedings of Advances in Cryptology-Eurocrypt 2010 [C]. Riviera, France, 2010. 24-43.

[21] CASTELLUCCIA C, MYKLETUN E, TSUDIK G. Efficient aggregation of encrypted data in wireless sensor networks [A]. Proceedings of the Second Annual International Conference on Mobile and Ubiquitous Systems: Networking and Services [C]. San Diego, USA, 2005. 109-117.

[22] BETHENCOURT J, SAHAI A, WATERS B. Advanced crypto software collection[EB/OL]. http://acsc.cs.utexas.edu/cpabe/.

A Study on Parameters of Image Encryption Based on Moire Pattern[*]

Zhe-Ming Weng　Dao-Shun Wang　Shun-Dong Li　Xiang-Yang Luo

Ⅰ　Introduction

When two images are superimposed, a new different pattern appears. This kind of pattern is called 'moiré pattern'. Based on this phenomenon, Muñoz-Rodríguez and Rodríguez-Vera [1] proposed a novel image encryption based on moiré pattern performed by computational algorithms. A certain reference fringe pattern is used to encrypt a secret image. The secret image can be reconstructed by simple computation with the same parameters. Ragulskis and Aleksa [2, 3] improved this algorithm and proposed an image hiding algorithm based on time-averaging moiré. The secret image can be reconstructed by naked eye when a time-averaging moiré pattern is harmonically oscillated in a predefined direction. Based on their algorithm, Ragulskis and Aleksa [4] proposed an image hiding algorithm based on time-averaged fringes produced by non-harmonic oscillations. Ragulskis et al. [5] proposed an image hiding algorithm based on circular moire fringes. Sakyte et al. [6] proposed an image hiding algorithm based on near-optimal moiré gratings. Palivonaite et al. [7] proposed an image hiding algorithm in time-averaged deformable moiré gratings. Petrauskiene et al. [8] proposed a dynamic visual cryptography based on chaotic oscillations. In these improved algorithms [2 - 8], the basic generating equations and parameters are almost the same as those in [1]. Experimental results of [1 - 8] did not give related parameters, nevertheless, we know that the reconstruction quality may be different when we use the same algorithm with different parameters (about this point, see Fig. 1 of section 2). So, it is worthwhile to study the relationship among reconstruction quality and parameters of generating equations.

This paper is organized as follows. Section 2 reviews the algorithm proposed by Muñoz-Rodríguez and Rodríguez-Vera and discusses two superimposition models for grey-scale image. In Section 3, we propose a method to calculate the reconstruction quality and give its relationship with parameters of generating equations. Then in Section 4, we use the proposed method to compare and discuss the reconstruction quality in another image hiding algorithm based on moiré pat-

---

[*] 本文选自 2014 IEEE Workshop on Electronics, Computer and Applications, 第 914 - 917 页

tern. Section 5 concludes the paper.

II Previous Works

Muñoz-Rodríguez and Rodriguez-Vera [1] proposed an image encryption based on moiré pattern performed by computational algorithms. It is one of the most typical image hiding algorithms based on moire pattern. A certain reference fringe pattern is used to encrypt a secret image. The secret image can be reconstructed by simple computation with the same parameters.

This algorithm is reviewed as follows.

TABLE 1   ALGORITHM PROPOSED BY MUÑOZ-RODRíGUEZ AND RODRíGUEZ-VERA

Input: a, b, f_0, and the secret image $f(x, y)$
Output: encrypted image $I_D(x, y)$
Construction: for every pixel in $f(x, y)$
　　　　　compute $I_D(x, y)$ according to (2)
Revealing: for every pixel in $I_D(x, y)$
　　　　compute $I_R(x, y)$ according to (1)
　　　　compute $M_p(x, y)$ according to (3)

In this algorithm, $I_R(x, y)$ denotes the reference fringe pattern and it can be obtained as

$$I_R(x,y) = a + b\cos(2\pi f_0 x), \qquad (1)$$

where a and b are the background intensity and contrast of the fringe pattern, respectively, and f_0 is the fundamental frequency.

$I_D(x, y)$ denotes the encrypted image and it is described as

$$I_D(x,y) = a + b\cos[2\pi f_0 x + f(x,y)], \qquad (2)$$

where the intensity function $f(x, y)$ stands for the secret image.

$M_p(x,y)$ denotes the moiré pattern and it is described by

$$M_p(x,y) = I_R(x,y) + I_D(x,y) \qquad (3)$$

According to (1) and (2), the value of the pixel is between $a - b$ and $a + b$. So we can let a, $b > 0$. In image processing, a white pixel is represented as a 0, and a black pixel is represented as a 1. In general, we can let $a = 0.5$ and $b = 0.5$, and then the value of the pixel is between 0 and 1. We can let $M_p(x,y) = 1$ when $M_p(x,y) = I_R(x,y) + I_D(x,y) > 1$.

In printing and image processing, Multiply mode [10] is commonly used to obtain moiré pattern when superimposing two grey-scale images. If a white pixel is represented as a 0 and a black pixel is represented as a 1, the moire pattern is described by

$$M_p(x,y) = 1 - [1 - I_R(x,y)] \cdot [1 - I_D(x,y)]$$
$$M_p(x,y) = I_R(x,y) + I_D(x,y) - I_R(x,y) \cdot I_D(x,y) \qquad (4)$$

We use the secret image in [1] as experimental image. Using the above algorithms with different f_0, partial experimental results are shown in Fig 1.

Figure 1. Reconstructed images with different f_0: (a) $f_0 = 0.5$; (b) $f_0 = 0.4$

From the experimental results above we can see that encrypted images with different parameters can reconstruct the secret image correctly, but we cannot tell the difference between two similar reconstructed images like Fig. 1 (a) and Fig. 1 (b).

III The Discussion on Parameter Values and Reconstruction Quality

In section 2, we note the fact that when difference between two parameters is very small, it is difficult to distinguish one reconstructed image from another by human vision, such as Fig. 1 (a) and Fig. 1 (b). Traditionally, image quality has been evaluated by human subjects. This method, though reliable, is expensive and too slow for real-world applications. So computational models that can automatically predict perceptual image quality are needed [9]. Refer to the definition of Wang et al. [11, 12]'s average contrast, next we give a definition of 'average contrast' in image hiding algorithms based on moiré pattern.

Definition 1. *For a secret image with a grey-levels*, $M_p^{(i)}$ *denotes the moiré pattern of the ith grey-level area in it. The average grey-level of* $M_p^{(i)}$ *is*

$$\overline{\beta}^{(i)} = \frac{1}{T} \cdot \sum_{x=0}^{T-1} M_p^{(i)}(x,y), \tag{5}$$

where T is the minimum period of the generating equations. When T is big enough, then

$$\overline{\beta}^{(i)} = \frac{1}{T} \cdot \int_0^T M_p^{(i)}(x,y) dx, \tag{6}$$

Average contrast betwenn the ith and the $(i+1)$ the average grey-levels is

$$\alpha^{(i+1,i)} = \overline{\beta}^{(i+1)} - \overline{\beta}^{(i)}, i = 0, \cdots, g-2 \tag{7}$$

Using **Definition 1**, we give the analysis about parameter f_0 and reconstruction quality below.

Lemma 1. Let $f_0 \in R$, then there are integers p and q, with $q \neq 0$, such that $f_0 = \frac{p}{q}$. Then the minimum period of the generating equations is $T = q$.

Proof: We prove this lemma by two steps.

(i) According to (2), $I_D(x+q,y) = a + b\cos\left[2\pi \cdot \dfrac{p}{q} \cdot (x+q) + f(x,y)\right] = a + b\cos\left[2\pi p + 2\pi \cdot \dfrac{p}{q} \cdot x + f(x,y)\right] = a + b\cos\left[2\pi \cdot \dfrac{p}{q} \cdot x + f(x,y)\right] = I_D(x,y)$.

Let $f(x,y) = 0$, then $I_R(x,y) = I_R(x+q,y)$. So q is a period of the generating equations.

(ii) Proof by contradiction: If there exists $q' < q$ and $I_D(x,y) = I_D(x+q',y)$ for any given x, then $I_D(x+q',y) = a + b\cos\left[2\pi \cdot \dfrac{p}{q} \cdot (x+q') + f(x,y)\right] = a + b\cos\left[2\pi \cdot \dfrac{pq'}{q} + 2\pi \cdot \dfrac{p}{q} \cdot x + f(x,y)\right] = a + b\cos\left[2\pi \cdot \dfrac{p}{q} \cdot x + f(x,y)\right]$.

So $\dfrac{pq'}{q}$ is an integer, namely $\dfrac{p}{q}$ is not a simplest fraction. It is contradict with our precondition. So q is the minimum period of the generating equations.

Theorem 1. Let $f_0 = \dfrac{p}{q}$, then $\bar{\beta}^{(i)} = \dfrac{1}{q} \cdot \sum_{x=0}^{q-1} M_p^{(i)}(x,y) = \dfrac{1}{q} \cdot \sum_{x=0}^{q-1} M'^{r(i)}_p(x,y)$, where $f'_0 = \dfrac{1}{q}$ in $M'^{(i)}_p(x,y)$.

Proof: We need to prove that $\sum_{x=0}^{q-1}\left(a + b\cos\left[2\pi \cdot \dfrac{p \cdot x}{q} + f(x,y)\right]\right) = \sum_{x=0}^{q-1}\left(a + b\cos\left[2\pi \cdot \dfrac{x}{q} + f(x,y)\right]\right)$. As p, q, x and y are all integers, if $p \cdot x \leq q-1$, there exists $k = p \cdot x$ in the right formula than $M_p^{(i)}(k,y)$. If $p \cdot x > q-1$, namely $p \cdot x \geq q$, then $a + b\cos\left[2\pi \cdot \dfrac{p \cdot x}{q} + f(x,y)\right] = a + b\cos\left[2\pi \cdot \dfrac{p \cdot x}{q} - 2\pi \cdot n + f(x,y)\right] = a + b\cos\left[2\pi \cdot \dfrac{p \cdot x - q \cdot n}{q} + f(x,y)\right]$. There exists an integer n and $(p \cdot x - q \cdot n) \in [0, q-1]$. So there also exists $k' = (p \cdot x - q \cdot n)$ in the right formula that $M_p^{(i)}(x,y) = M'^{(i)}_p(k',y)$. According to Lemma 1, the minimum period of the generating equations is $T = q$, so items in the left formula will be one-one mapping to items in the right formula, thus the theorem is proven.

Ragulskis and Aleksa [2] analyzed the algorithm in [1]. The generating equations can be expressed as

$$I_1(x) = \cos^2\left(\dfrac{\pi}{\lambda}x\right) = \dfrac{1}{2} + \dfrac{1}{2}\cos\left(\dfrac{2\pi}{\lambda}x\right) \tag{8}$$

$$I_2(x) = \cos^2\left(\dfrac{\pi}{\lambda}(x - f(x))\right) = \dfrac{1}{2} + \dfrac{1}{2}\cos\left(\dfrac{2\pi}{\lambda}x - \dfrac{2\pi}{\lambda} \cdot f(x)\right) \tag{9}$$

They proved the following conclusion and we use it as a lemma.

Lemma 2[2]. $f(x,y)$ should be mapped into 0 and π.

Proof: Let $a = 0.5$ and $b = 0.5$, then (1) is same as (8) and (2) is same as (9). We learn from [2] that $0 \leq f(x) \leq \dfrac{\lambda}{2}$, so $f(x,y) = \dfrac{2\pi}{\lambda} \cdot f(x) \in [0, \pi]$.

Theorem 2. Let $f_0 = \dfrac{p}{q}$, when T is big enough, then the expected value of $\bar{\beta}^{(i)}$ is

(i) $\bar{\beta}^{(i)} = 1 - \dfrac{1}{\pi} \cdot \sin\left(\dfrac{\pi}{2} - \dfrac{\pi \cdot i}{2 \cdot (g-1)}\right)$ by Sum mode,

(ii) $\bar{\beta}^{(i)} = \dfrac{3}{4} - \dfrac{1}{8}\cos\left(\dfrac{\pi \cdot i}{g-1}\right)$ by Multiply mode.

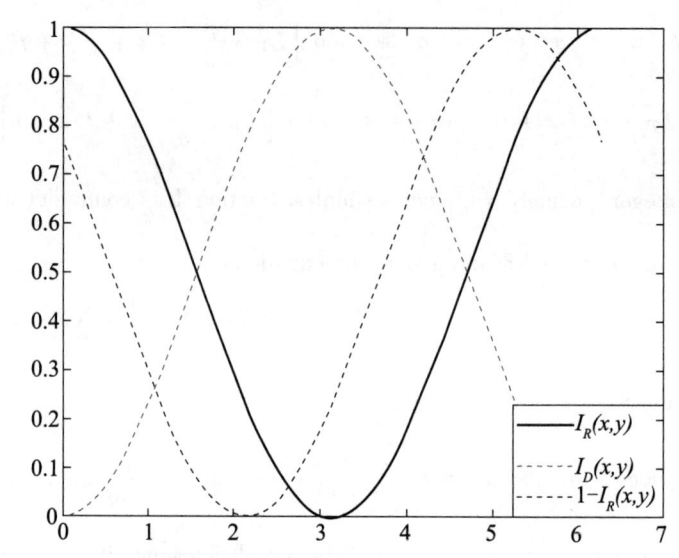

Figure 2 Equation image of I_R, I_D and $1 - I_R$

Proof: According to Theorem 1, if $f_0 = \dfrac{p}{q}$, we can use $f'_0 = \dfrac{1}{q}$ to calculate the average grey-level. The value of the ith grey-level $f^{(i)}(x,y)$ can be mapped into $\dfrac{\pi \cdot i}{g-1}$.

To prove (i), when we superimpose two grey-scale images by Sum mode, the moiré pattern is described by

$$M_p(x,y) = \begin{cases} I_R(x,y) + I_D(x,y), & if(I_R(x,y) + I_D(x,y)) < 1 \\ 1, & else \end{cases} \quad (10)$$

According to (10), $M_p(x,y) = I_R(x,y) + I_D(x,y)$ when $I_D(x,y) < 1 - I_R(x,y)$. It is easy to figure out that $I_D(x,y) < 1 - I_R(x,y)$ when $x \in \left(\dfrac{1}{4f'_0} - \dfrac{\pi \cdot i}{4\pi f'_0 \cdot (g-1)}, \dfrac{3}{4f'_0} - \dfrac{\pi \cdot i}{4\pi f'_0 \cdot (g-1)}\right)$. According to Definition 1, the average grey-level is

$$\bar{\beta}^{(i)} = f'_0 \cdot \left(\dfrac{1}{2f'_0} + \int_{\frac{1}{4f'_0} - \frac{\pi \cdot i}{4\pi f'_0(g-1)}}^{\frac{3}{4f'_0} - \frac{\pi \cdot i}{4\pi f'_0(g-1)}} (I_R(x,y) + I_D(x,y))dx\right)$$

$$\bar{\beta}^{(i)} = 1 - \dfrac{1}{\pi} \cdot \sin\left(\dfrac{\pi}{2} - \dfrac{\pi \cdot i}{2 \cdot (g-1)}\right), i = 0,\cdots,g-1 \quad (11)$$

To prove (ii), when we superimpose two grey-scale images by Multiply mode, the moiré pattern is described by (4). According to Definition 1, the average grey-level is

$$\overline{\beta}^{(i)} = f'_0 \cdot \int_0^{\frac{1}{f'_0}} (I_R(x,y) + I_D(x,y) - I_R(x,y) \cdot I_D(x,y)) dx$$

$$\overline{\beta}^{(i)} = \frac{3}{4} - \frac{1}{8}\cos\left(\frac{\pi \cdot i}{g-1}\right), i = 0, \cdots, g-1 \quad (12)$$

Corollary 1. $\overline{\beta} \in \left[1 - \frac{1}{\pi}, 1\right]$ and average contrast between black and white is $\overline{\alpha} = \frac{1}{\pi}$ by Sum mode.

Proof: According to Theorem 2, $\overline{\beta}^{(i)} = 1 - \frac{1}{\pi} \cdot \sin\left(\frac{\pi}{2} - \frac{\pi \cdot i}{2 \cdot (g-1)}\right)$ is a monotonic function. So the average grey-level of the 0th grey-level area (white) is $1 - \frac{1}{\pi}$, the average grey-level of the $(g-1)$th grey-level area (black) is 1. So $\overline{\beta} \in \left[1 - \frac{1}{\pi}, 1\right]$ and average contrast between black and white is $\overline{\alpha} = \frac{1}{\pi}$.

Corollary 2. $\overline{\beta} \in \left[\frac{5}{8}, \frac{7}{8}\right]$ and average contrast between black and white is $\overline{\alpha} = \frac{1}{4}$ by Multiply mode.

Proof: According to Theorem 2, $\overline{\beta}^{(i)} = \frac{3}{4} - \frac{1}{8}\cos\left(\frac{\pi \cdot i}{g-1}\right)$ is a monotonic function. So the average grey-level of the 0th grey-level area (white) is $\frac{5}{8}$, the average grey-level of the $(g-1)$th grey-level area (black) is $\frac{7}{8}$. So $\overline{\beta} \in \left[\frac{5}{8}, \frac{7}{8}\right]$ and average contrast between black and white is $\overline{\alpha} = \frac{1}{4}$.

Theorem 2 shows the expected value of the average grey-level when T is big enough. When T is not so big, the following table shows the comparisons of reconstruction qualities with different T and f_0 by Definition 1.

TABLE II. RELATIONSHIP BETWEEN T, f_0 AND RECONSTRUCTION QUALITY BY SUM MODE.

minimum period T	fundamental frequency f_0	Average contrast	
		Sum mode	Multiply mode
2 *	1/2	0.5	0.5
3	1/3	0.333	0.25
4	1/4	0.25	0.25
5	1/5 (or 2/5)	0.324	0.25
6	1/6	0.333	0.25
7	1/7 (or 2/7, 3/7)	0.321	0.25
8	1/8 (or 3/8)	0.302	0.25
9	1/9 (or 2/9, 4/*)	0.320	0.25
10	1/10 (or 3/10)	0.324	0.25

From the result, we observe that the reconstruction qualit is best when $f_0 = 0.5$ regardless of which superimposition model we use. It is because in this marked condition, $T = 2$ is too small. When T becomes bigger, average contrast by Sum mode approaches $\frac{1}{\pi} = 0.318$, which is same as Corollary 1. Average contrast approaches $\frac{1}{4} = 0.25$, which is same as Corollary 2. Also, when $f_0 = \frac{p}{q}$, average contrast is same as when $f_0' = \frac{1}{q}$, which is stated in Theorem 1.

In the above analysis, we propose some methods to calculate the reconstruction quality of the algorithm in [1]. So these methods can give an objective evaluation of the reconstruction quality.

Ⅳ Experimental Results and Discussions

The basic generating equations and parameters are almost the same in [2 – 8], in this section we will show reconstruction qualities with different λ.

Using (8) and (9) to be our generating equations, the moiré pattern is described by

$$I_d(x) = \frac{1}{2}(I_1(x) + \bar{I}_2(x)),$$

$$\text{where } \bar{I}_2(x) = 1 - \bar{I}_2(x). \tag{13}$$

Next we can figure out the reconstruction quality by using *Average contrast*.

According to (8), the period of the pattern image is λ. The value of the ith grey-level $f^{(i)}(x)$ cab be mapped into $\frac{\lambda \cdot i}{2 \cdot (g-1)}$. According to Definition 1, the average grey-level is

$$\bar{\beta}^{(i)} = \frac{1}{\lambda} \cdot \int_0^\lambda \left(\frac{1}{2} \cdot \left(\cos^2\left(\frac{\pi}{\lambda}x\right) + 1 \right) - \cos^2\left(\frac{\pi}{\lambda} \cdot \left(x - \frac{\lambda \cdot i}{2 \cdot (g-1)}\right)\right) \right) dx$$

$$\bar{\beta}^{(i)} = \frac{1}{2}, i = 0, \cdots, g-1 \tag{14}$$

When $i = 0$, namely $f(x) = 0, I_d(x) = \frac{1}{2}$ for any given x, However, when $i \neq 0, \bar{\beta}^{(i)} = \frac{1}{2}$ for any given i. So the reconstructed image can only be regarded as a binary image.

As $I_d(x) = \frac{1}{2}$ for any given x when $i = 0$, average contrast between black and white can be redefine as

$$\alpha^{(g-1,0)} = \bar{\beta}^{(g-1)} - \bar{\beta}^{(0)} = \frac{1}{T} \cdot \int_0^T \left| M_p^{(g-1)}(x,y) - \bar{\beta}^{(0)} \right| dx \tag{15}$$

The following table shows the comparisons of reconstruction qualities whith different λ.

TABLE III RELATIONSHIP BETWEEN A AND RECONSTRICION QUALITY IN [2-8]

Pitch of the grating λ	Average contrast
2	0.5
3	0.333
4	0.25
5	0.324
10	0.324

From the result, we can see that the reconstructed image can only be regarded as a binary image in [2-8]. The reconstruction quality is best when $\lambda = 2$.

V Conclusion

In this paper, we find the difference among reconstructed images with different parameters by image hiding algorithm based on moiré. We use average contrast to calculate the reconstruction quality and give its relationship with parameters of generating equations. Experimental results show that high reconstruction quality can be obtained by comparing different parameters.

Acknowledgment

This research was supported in part by the National Natural Science Foundation of China (Grant Nos. 61170032, 61272435, 61373020, and 61379151), and in part by the Project of General Administration of press and publication of China (GAPP-ZDKJ-BQ/15-2).

References

[1] J. A. Muñoz-Rodríguez, R. Rodriguez-Vera. Image encryption based on moiré pattern performed by computational algorithms. Optics Communications, 2004, 236 (4) 295-301.

[2] M. Ragulskis, A. Aleksa, L. Saunoriene. Improved algorithm for image encryption based on stochastic geometric moiré and its application. Optics Communications, 2007, 273 (2): 370-378.

[3] M. Ragulskis, A. Aleksa. Image hiding based on time-averaging moiré. Optics Communications, 2009, 282 (14) 2752-2759.

[4] M. Ragulskis, A. Aleksa, Z. Navickas. Image hiding based on timeaveraged fringes produced by non-hannonic oscillations. Journal of Optics A: Pure and Applied Optics, 2009, 11 (12): 125411.

[5] M. Ragulskis, A. Aleksa, J. Ragulskiene. Image hiding based on circular moiré fringes. WSEAS Transactions on Mathematics, 2010, 9 (2) 90-99.

[6] E. Sakyte, R Palivonaite, A. Aleksa, et al. Image hiding based on near-optimal moire gratings. Optics Communications, 2011, 284 (16): 3954-3964.

[7] R. Palivonaite, A. Aleksa, A. Paunksnis, et al. Image hiding in timeaveraged deformable moire gratings. Journal of Optics, 2014, 16 (2): 025401.

[8] V Petrauskiene, R. Palivonaite, A. Aleksa, et al. Dynamic visual cryptography based on chaotic oscil-

lations. Communications in Nonlinear Science and Numerical Simulation, 2014, 19 (1): 112-120.
[9] Z. Wang, A. C. Bovik. Modern image quality assessment, Morgan &Claypool Publishers.
[10] S. Cimato, R. De Prisco, A. De Santis. Colored visual cryptography without color darkening. Theoretical Computer Science, 2007, 374 (1): 261-276.
[11] D. S. Wang, F. Yi, X. Li. Probabilistic visual secret sharing schemes for gray-scale images and color images. Information Sciences, 2011, 181 (11) 2189-2208.
[12] D. S. Wang, L. Dong, X. Li. Towards shift tolerant visual secret sharing schemes. IEEE Transactions on Information Forensics and Security, 2011, 6 (2) 323-337.

基于行为的访问控制应用于多级安全信息系统

李凤华　史国振　张晶辉　李　莉

引言

针对网络应用的安全需求，先后出现了多种访问控制模型，如基于角色的访问控制模型 RBAC（role-based access control）[1-3]、基于任务的访问控制模型 TBAC（traskbased access control）[4-5]、与时空相关的访问控制模型[6-7]、面向分布式的访问控制模型[8-9]等。虽然部分已有模型涉及了与访问控制相关的时态因素和位置因素，但缺乏了对多级安全信息系统中位置、软硬件平台、时态等环境因素的综合考虑。文献[10]针对角色、环境和时态对权限分配的影响给出了环境状态、时态状态以及行为的概念，提出了基于行为的访问控制模型 ABAC（action-based access control）。文献[11]在此基础上，通过引入受限的时态状态和环境状态，给出了管理行为的定义和 ABAC 管理模型的结构。文献[12]给出了 Web 环境下基于行为的访问控制安全体系结构，在此体系结构中，行为服务器管理行为信息，域服务器决定请求资源的安全序列，以及资源服务器响应用户的请求，其中资源服务器存储的资源使用了不同的安全序列。文献[13]基于 ABAC 模型，给出了协作信息系统访问控制的流程；提出了包含用户请求、用户身份、口令、角色、时态状态、环境状态、生命期等安全属性的安全关联及其产生方法；给出了一种安全认证协议，用来实现用户与行为服务器、资源管理服务器之间交换与 ABAC 模型相关的安全属性，并使用 UC 模型证明该协议的安全性。

多级安全信息系统是指允许存储具有不同敏感等级信息的系统，允许具有不同安全标识和授权的用户按照"知其所需"的原则处理系统信息的系统，阻止没有安全标识、没有授权或者没有获取信息需求的用户访问信息的系统[14]。然而，环境状态则是影响多级安全信息系统中访问控制策略的重要因素，虽然文献[13]给出了协作信息系统访问控制流程，但没有具体描述环境服务器的实现方法。针对环境状态 E 在多级安全信息系统中的重要性，本文在协作信息系统访问控制流程基础上提出了 ABAC 的多级安全信息系统访问控制机制，通过环境服务器中的网络位置探测器获得网络位置信息，通过时间戳服务器获取时态状态。本文具体介绍网络位置探测器。

---

* 本文选自《计算机工程与设计》，第33卷第1期，2012年1月，第106-110页

1 网络位置探测原理

环境状态 E 可以表示为 [EN | EL | EH | ES][10-11]，其中 EN 表示事件发生的网络逻辑位置信息，包括 MAC 地址和 IP 地址；EL 表示事件发生的网络物理位置信息；EH 表示事件发生时用户使用的硬件信息；ES 表示事件发生时用户的软件信息。本文对用户的网络逻辑位置与网络物理位置进行了探测，通过网络位置探测器来获得网络位置。

网络位置探测器的作用是为环境服务器提供登录到多级安全信息系统的主机的网络物理位置信息和网络逻辑位置信息，包含了网络物理位置探测器和网络逻辑位置探测器两个部分，网络物理位置探测器是用来获取目的主机的网络物理位置，即主机所在的具体地点，网络逻辑位置探测器是用来获取目的主机的网络逻辑位置，即主机的 MAC 地址与 IP 地址。网络位置探测器的部署如图 1 所示，下面具体介绍两个模块的实现框架。

1.1 网络逻辑位置探测

网络逻辑位置探测器是基于动态主机配置协议 DHCP（dynamic host configuration protocol）和 WinPcap（windows packet capture）[15]实现的。

在多级安全信息系统中，DHCP 服务器用来为内部网络主机分配动态的 IP 地址。为了便于管理，本文在信息系统中只设计了一个提供 DHCP 服务的服务器，也就是环境服务器。当主机登录后，向服务器发送请求，该主机只会收到来自环境服务器的响应，每当环境服务器向主机发送一个 DHCPACK 报文，就表示一台主机登录到多级安全信息系统中。同时，需要获取的网络逻辑位置信息也记录在 DHCPACK 报文的 yiaddr 字段和 chaddr 字段中。yiaddr 字段表示服务器分配给客户端的 IP 地址，当 DHCP 服务器响主机的 DHCP 请求时，将分配给该主机的 IP 地址填入此字段；chaddr 字段记录主机的 MAC 地址，当主机发出 DHCP 请求报文时，将 MAC 地址填入此字段，DHCP 服务器使用此字段来唯一标识一台主机。DHCP 消息类型则记录于 option 字段中，当 code = 53，length = 1，value = 5 时，此字段表示 DHCP 报文类型为 DHCPACK。

网络逻辑位置探测器获取网络逻辑位置的过程包括内核部分和用户数据分析部分，其中内核部分负责从网络中捕获和过滤数据；用户分析部分负责协议分析、数据处理、抽取网络信息，2.1 节中介绍网络逻辑位置探测器的实现方法。

1.2 网络物理位置探测

网络逻辑位置探测器检测到有主机登录到多级安全信息系统后，获取到该主机的网络逻辑位置信息，并将网络逻辑位置信息发送给网络物理位置探测器，作为网络物理位置探测器抽取该主机网络物理位置信息的依据。

在环境服务器上的 DHCP 服务为主机提供 IP 地址的过程中，DHCP 包经由的交换机学习了该主机的 MAC 地址，将其记录到地址转发表中（端口号-MAC 地址）。本文使用地址转发表中交换机端口号与 MAC 地址的对应关系来探测主机与环境服务器之间的链路关系，根据位置信息表来确定主机的物理位置，此方法的核心在于获取交换机地址转发表的方法。

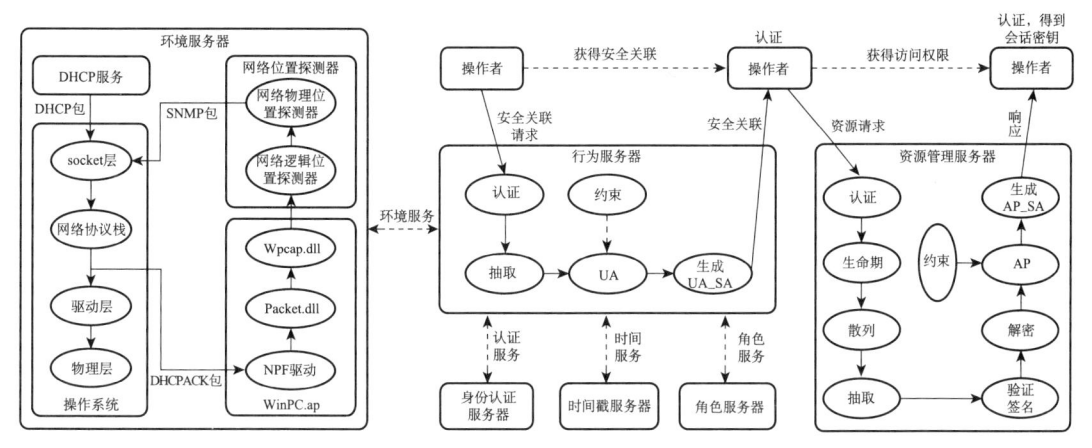

图 1　基于 ABAC 的多级安全信息系统访问控制机制

在日常生活中，网管人员通常使用远程登录交换机，使用交换机控制台命令查询的方法来获取交换机的地址转发表。这种方法相对简单，只需几条命令即可获得所需信息，但不同品牌的交换机的命令是不同的，同一品牌的不同型号的交换机的命令也是不同的，没有统一的标准，所以这种方法只限于特定的网络，既不具备可扩展性，也不具备通用性。网络物理位置探测器则采用了基于简单网络管理协议 SNMP（simple network management protocol）的网络管理方法来获取交换机的地址转发表。其中，管理信息库 MIB（management information base）包含所有可被查询和修改的参数。本文中涉及的 MIB 对象包括 RFC1493 Bridge MIB 描述的地址转发表 dot1dTpFdbTable、RFC2674 QBridge MIB 描述的地址转发表 dot1qTpFdbTable，以及 RFC 1213 MIB-2IP 功能组描述的路由表 IpRouteTable。2.2 节中详细介绍网络逻辑位置探测器的实现方法。

2　网络位置探测器的实现

2.1　网络逻辑位置探测器的实现

网络逻辑位置探测器用于获取多级安全信息系统中主机的网络逻辑位置信息，是基于环境服务器的 DHCP 服务实现的。当一台主机登录到多级安全信息系统中，DHCP 服务为该主机动态分配 IP 地址，在确认阶段，DHCP 服务向该主机发送 DHCPACK 数据包，该数据包中包含所提供的 IP 地址以及该主机的 MAC 地址，也就是我们所需要的网络逻辑位置信息。网络逻辑位置探测器使用 WinPcap 捕获 DHCPACK 数据包，分析数据，读取 yiaddr 字段和 chaddr 字段，即网络逻辑位置信息。网络逻辑位置探测器依据主机 IP 地址查询数据库中的 Vlan 信息表获取该主机的 Vlan 信息。网络位置探测器使用 MySQL 数据库管理 Vlan 信息表，表的结构如表 1 所示，该表记录了多级安全信息系统的 Vlan 信息，Vlan 的 IP 地址的范围与 DHCP 服务的 IP 作用域对应。实现网络逻辑位置探测器的具体流程如图 2 所示。

2.2　网络物理位置探测器的实现

网络物理位置探测器用于获取多级安全信息系统中主机的网络物理位置信息，是基于

SNMP 协议实现的。网络物理位置探测器收到网络逻辑位置探测器发送的网络逻辑位置信息后，根据网络逻辑位置信息中的 MAC 地址探测主机的网络物理位置。网络物理位置探测器向交换机发送 SNMP 报文，依据地址转发表和路由表获取与目的主机连接的交换机的端口号，查找数据库中的位置信息表便得到目的主机的物理地址。网络位置探测器使用 MySQL 数据库管理位置信息表，表的结构如表 2 所示，该表记录了多级安全信息系统中设备的位置信息。实现网络物理位置探测器的具体流程如图 3 所示。

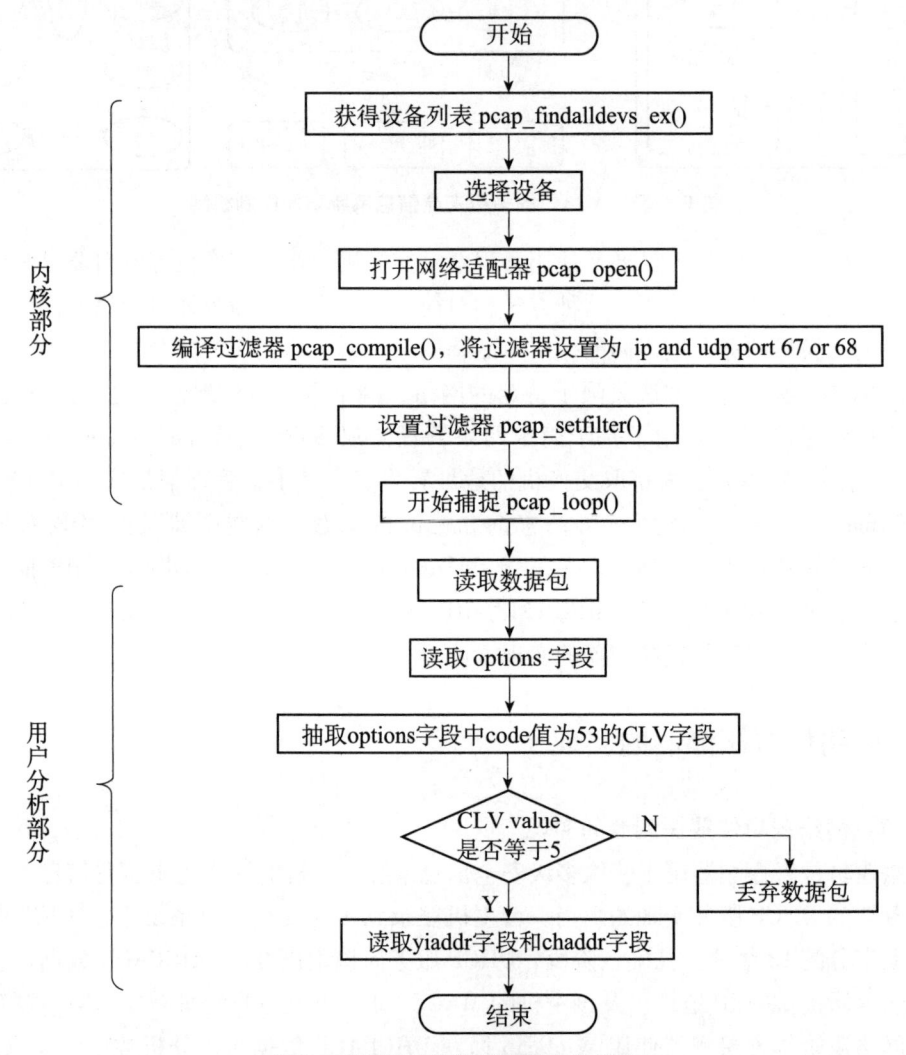

图 2　网络逻辑位置探测器实现流程

表 1　Vlan 信息表

字段名	数据类型	说明
VlanID	INTEGER	主键，唯一标识 Vlan
StartIP	VARCHAR（45）	记录该 Vlan 的起始 IP 地址，对应 DHCP 的 IP 作用域的起始 IP 地址
EndIP	VARCHAR（45）	记录该 Vlan 的终止 IP 地址，对应 DHCP 的 IP 作用域的终止 IP 地址
VlanInfo	VARCHAR（45）	记录该 Vlan 的信息

2.3 网络位置探测器的示例

本文在环境服务器上设计并实现了网络位置探测器，示例测试的网络拓扑结构如图 4 所示，其中，交换机 Switch1 型号为 H3C S5500 EI，交换机 Switch2 型号为华为 Quidway S2000 系列。环境服务器的操作系统为 Windows Server 2003，配置 DHCP 服务，创建了 3 个 IP 作用域，分别为 3 个 Vlan 分配 IP 地址，IP 地址范围为"172.16.66.226～172.16.66.236"，"172.16.66.100～172.16.66.116"，"172.16.66.131～172.16.66.140"，子网掩码为 255.255.255.224，并将多级安全信息系统中的客户端电脑设置为自动获取 IP 地址的方式。

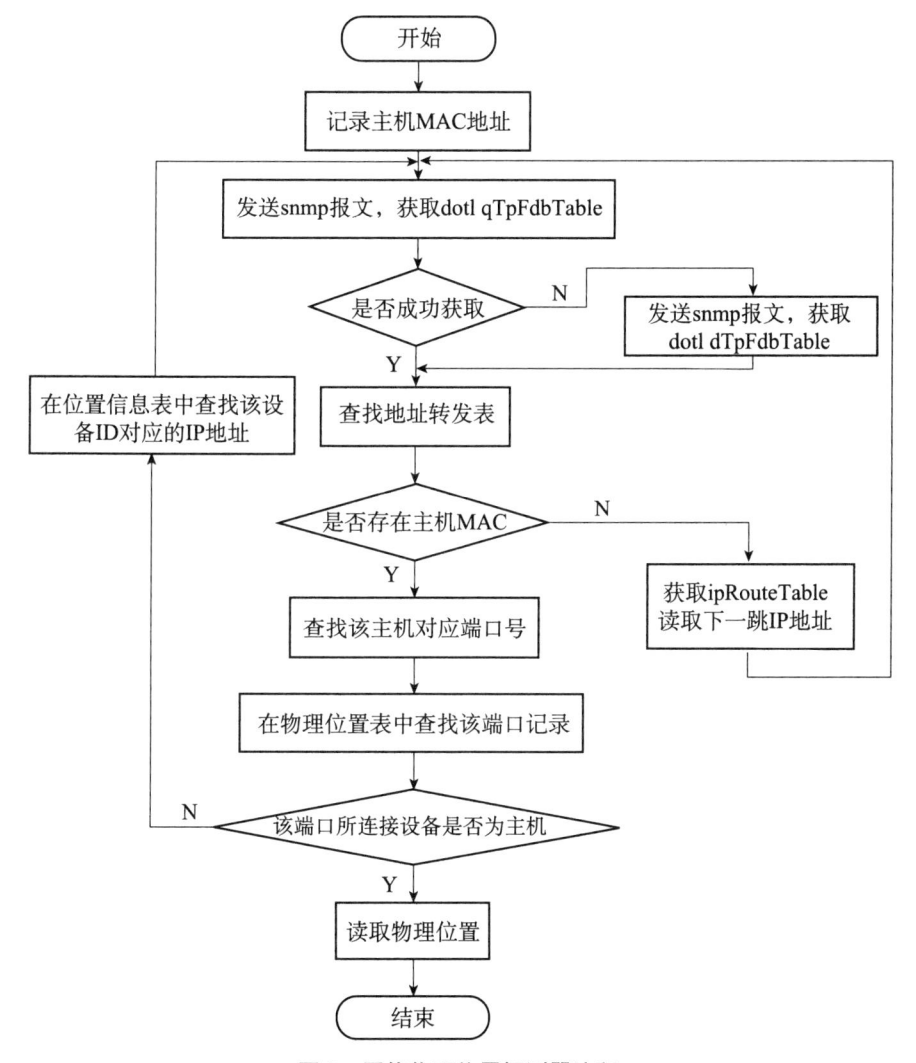

图 3　网络物理位置探测器流程

表 2　位置信息

字段名	数据类型	说明
ID	INTEGER	主键，该设备的 ID，唯一标识表中的设备
DeviceName	VARCHAR（45）	记录该设备的名称
DeviceIP	VARCHAR（45）	记录该设备的 IP 地址

(续表)

字段名	数据类型	说明
SwitchPort	INTEGER	记录该交换机的某一端口号
DeviceID	INTEGER	记录与该端口连接的设备的 ID
DeviceFlag	INTEGER	记录与该端口连接的设备的类型,1 表示交换机,0 表示主机
DeviceLocation	VARCHAR(45)	记录该设备的物理位置,主机的物理位置用于探测器查询,交换机的用于维修

由于在 IP 地址动态获取过程中采用广播方式发送报文,因此 DHCP 只适用于 DHCP 客户端和服务器处于同一个子网内的情况。对于图 4 的网络环境下,需要 Switch1 上配置 DHCP 中继服务,并配置 Vlan 接口 1 对应 DHCP 服务器 IP 作用域 1,Vlan 接口 2 对应 IP 作用域 2,Vlan 接口 3 对应 IP 作用域 3。由于网络物理位置探测器是基于 SNMP 协议实现的,Switch1 和 Switch2 均开启了 SNMP 服务。

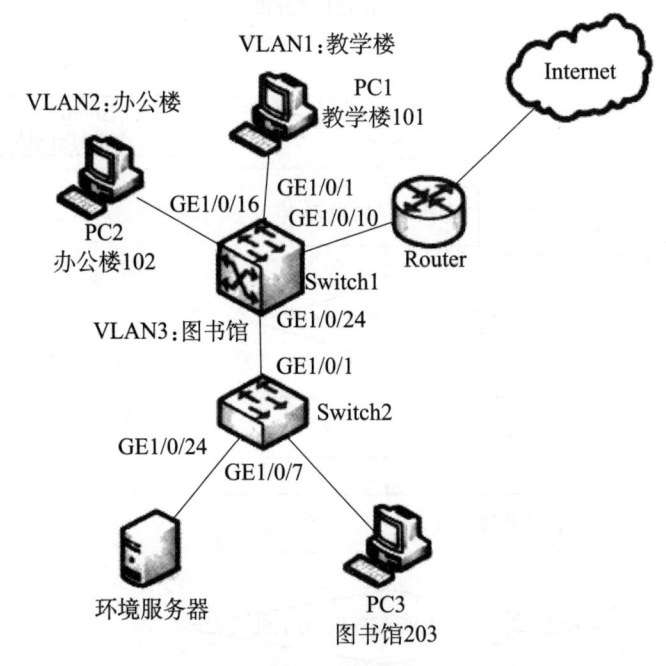

图 4 网络拓扑

当有主机接入时,如 PC1 接入网络,网络逻辑位置探测器获得网络逻辑位置信息后,将其发送给网络物理位置探测器,网络物理探测器读取 Switch2 的地址转发表,此地址转发表中没有目的主机 PC1 的 MAC 地址,网络物理位置探测器则读取 Switch2 的路由表,得到下一个目的交换机的 IP 为 172.16.66.98,即 Switch1。网络物理位置探测器读取 Switch1 的地址转发表,PC1 的 MAC 地址对应的端口为 1,根据 Switch1 的 IP 地址与端口号查找物理位置表,得到 PC1 的物理位置为"教学楼 101"。同样,当 PC2 登录网络时,也可得到 PC2 的网络位置信息。

当 PC3 登录网络时,网络位置探测器的网络逻辑位置探测器捕获 DHCPACK 包,分析数据包,记录 PC3 的网络信息,显示 PC3 的 IP 地址、MAC 地址和 Vlan 信息,并将 PC3

的网络逻辑位置信息发送给网络物理位置探测器，网络物理位置探测器读取 Switch2 的地址转发表，PC3 的 MAC 地址对应的端口为 7，根据 Switch2 的 IP 地址与端口号查找物理位置表，得到 PC3 的物理位置为"图书馆 203"。图 5 为 PC1、PC2 和 PC3 接入到多级安全信息系统后的，网络位置探测器获得的 PC1、PC2 和 PC3 的网络位置信息。

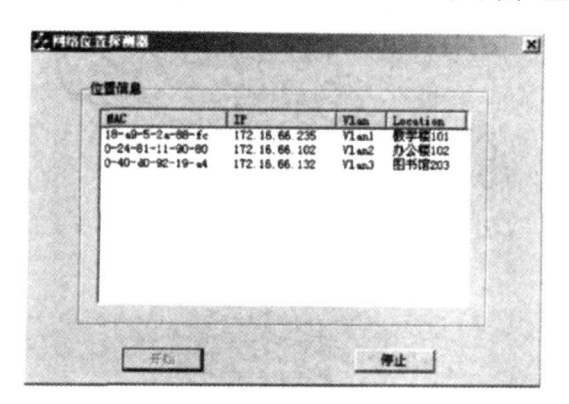

图 5　演示界面

3　结束语

基于行为的访问控制模型 ABAC 的行为包含了角色、环境状态和时态状态，行为的状态随着角色、环境状态和时态状态的不同而动态变化。环境状态的获取是基于行为图 5 演示界面的访问控制模型应用的前提，为了实现 ABAC 模型，本文给出了在多级安全信息系统中 ABAC 的位置探测器的设计框架，提出了依赖 DHCP 协议提取网络逻辑位置的方法，以及基于 SNMP、MIB 提取网络物理地址的方法，最后以示例的形式描述了位置探测器的实现方法。

参考文献

［1］ Ferraiolo D F，Sandhu R，Gavria S，et al. Proposed NIST standard for role-based access control ［J］. ACM Transactions on Information and System Security，2001，4 (3)：224-274.

［2］ Bammigatti P H. Generic WA-RBAC：role based access control model for web applications ［C］. Proceedings of the 9th International Conference on Information Technology. Bhubaneswar，India：IEEE Computer Society，2006：237-240.

［3］ Takabi H，Amini M，Jalili R. Enhacing role-based access control model through fuzzy recations ［C］. Proceedings of the Third International Symposium on Information Assurance and Security. Manchester，UK：IEEE Computer Society，2007：131-136.

［4］ DENG Ji-Bo，HONG Fan. Task-based access control model ［J］. Journal of Software，2003，14 (1)：76-82 (in Chinese).［邓集波，洪帆. 基于任务的访问控制模型 ［J］. 软件学报，2003，14 (1)：76-82.］

［5］ ZHANG Dong-wen，PEI Xing，QIU Ji-Qing，et al. A delegation model for time constraints-based TRBAC ［C］. Proceedings of the Eighth International Conference on Machine Learning and Cybernetics.

Baoding, China: IEEE Press, 2009: 2027-2032.

[6] Ardagna C, Cremonini M, Damiani E, et al. Supporting Location based conditions in access control policies [C]. Proceedings of the ACM Symposium on Information, Computer and Communications Security. Taipei, Taiwan: ACM Press, 2006: 212-222.

[7] Damiani M, Bertino E, Catania B. GEO-RBAC: a spatially aware RBAC [J]. ACM Transactions on Information and System Security, 2007, 10 (1): 1-42.

[8] LIU Song-yun, HUANG He-jiao. Role-based access control for distributed cooperation environment [C]. Proceedings of Interna-tional Conference on Computationlai Intelligence and Securiity. Beijing, China: IEEE Computer Society, 2009: 455-459.

[9] WU Xian, QIAN Pei-de. Research on policy domain access control model in distributed systems [C]. Proceedings of Nine International Conference on E-Business and Information System Security. Wuhan, China: IEEE Press, 2009: 1-6.

[10] LI Fenghua, WANG Wei, MA Jianfengm, et al. Action-based access control model [J]. Chinese Journal of Electronics, 2008, 17 (3): 396-401.

[11] LI Feng-hua, WANG Wei, MA Jian-feng, et al. Aion-based access control model and administration of action [J]. Acta Electronia Sinica, 2008, 36 (10): 1881-1890 (in Chinese). [李凤华, 王巍, 马建峰, 等. 基于行为的访问控制模型及其行为管理 [J]. 电子学报, 2008, 36 (10): 1881-1890.]

[12] LI Fenghua, WANG Wei MA Jianfcng, et al. Action-based access control for web services [J]. Journal of Information Assurance and Security, 2010, 5 (3): 162-170.

[13] LI Feng-hua, WANG Wei, MA Jian-feng, et al. Access control model and its application for collaborative information systems [J]. Journal on Communications, 2008, 29 (9): 116-123 (in Chinese). [李凤华, 王巍, 马建峰, 等. 协作信息系统的访问控制模型及其应用 [J]. 通信学报, 2008, 29 (9): 116-123.]

[14] Tan Z Y, Liu D, Lin J. Availability analysis method of multilevel security models with credibility characteristics [C]. Proceeding of International Conference on Networks Security, Wireless Communications and Trusted Computing, 2009: 175-178.

[15] WinPcap Documentation [DB/OL]. http://www.winpcap.org/docs/dois_412/html/main html, 2010.

基于代理重加密的多媒体数字版权授权协议*

黄勤龙,马兆丰,傅镜艺,钮心忻

互联网技术的飞速发展在使数字内容传播日益便捷的同时,也带来许多版权纠纷。数字版权管理(digital rights management,DRM)通过数字内容的制作、发行、安全许可和计费等一系列手段防止数字内容的非法误用,确保数字内容在公平、合理、安全许可框架下使用和消费。目前的 DRM 方案包括开放移动联盟 DRM 和 microsoft media DRM 等[1]。

现有的多媒体数字版权保护方法分为两大类:一类是基于数字水印的方法,将版权等水印信息隐藏在数字媒体中;另一类是基于加密技术的方法,采用数字加密和身份认证的方法,限制非授权用户的使用,并保证授权用户的正常使用。相比之下,基于加密技术的方法更具有普遍性,学术界提出了很多基于加密技术的版权保护方案[2]。

现有的 DRM 方案中,用户通常将数字内容传送至 DRM 服务器进行加密,再通过 DRM 服务器授权给其他用户使用。一旦服务器遭受攻击,就会有用户数字内容泄露的风险。因此,在用户对 DRM 服务器并不完全信任的情况下,如何保护数字内容的安全性,实现数字内容的合理使用,这是目前数字版权保护面临的关键问题。

针对这一问题,提出了代理重加密方案[3]。在代理重加密方案中,一个半可信的代理者可以把用授权人的公钥加密的密文转化为被授权人的公钥加密的密文。在这个过程中,代理者不能获取明文的任何消息。代理重加密在分布式文件系统的安全管理以及云计算等场景中已得到广泛应用。

1 相关工作

代理重加密方案在 1998 年欧洲密码学年会上首次被提出[3],并由 Ateniese 等[4]在网络和分布式系统安全研讨会议和 2007 年美国计算机学会计算机与通信安全会议上相继给出其规范的形式化定义。

目前,在代理重加密方面已有大量研究,包括单向或双向代理重加密方案和基于代理重加密的数字版权管理机制等。Taban 等[5]提出一种安全并满足互操作性的数字版权管理机制。该机制中增加了跨域操作管理者,实现域 A 中的许可证转换为域 B 中的许可证,而

---

* 本文选自《北京邮电大学学报》,第 36 卷第 6 期,2013 年 12 月,第 7 – 12 页

管理者不能对许可证进行解密或者单独生成域 A 或域 B 中的许可证。Lee 等[6]提出一种安全和共同盈利的 DRM 互操作机制，通过指定代理重加密者，允许内容提供商重加密内容以实现不同格式的数字内容共享，避免泄露数字内容明文，但是该机制在内容共享过程中需要重加密内容。Ma 等[7]提出了一种基于代理重加密的版权内容共享模型，通过代理重加密内容实现不同用户和设备之间按需共享内容，同时支持限制内容共享次数。Petrlic 等[8]提出了一种基于云平台的内容统一发布和保护方案，允许用户通过云平台订购和使用不同内容提供商发布的内容，但是该方案在用户每次使用内容时都需要重加密内容。

针对多媒体内容，笔者提出一种基于代理重加密的多媒体数字版权授权协议。该协议引入密钥代理服务器，允许内容提供商在客户端加密多媒体内容，内容使用者获取加密的多媒体内容后向许可证服务器申请许可证，内容使用者下载许可证后向密钥代理服务器提交内容加密密钥重加密申请，密钥代理服务器重加密内容加密密钥后返回给内容使用者，而许可证服务器无法获取内容加密密钥明文。该协议在内容使用和共享过程中不需要重新加密内容。在该协议的基础上，实现了云计算环境下的数字电视节目内容共享平台。

2 协议设计模型

笔者提出的基于代理重加密的多媒体数字版权授权协议主要包括内容平台、许可证服务器、密钥代理服务器、内容提供商和内容使用者等。该协议引入代理重加密机制，允许内容提供商加密多媒体内容，内容使用者获取内容和许可证服务器分发的许可证后，通过密钥代理服务器获取代理重加密后的内容加密密钥再解密多媒体内容，保证了多媒体内容在存储、传输和使用过程中的安全性。

如图 1 所示，基于代理重加密的多媒体数字版权授权协议的主要过程如下。

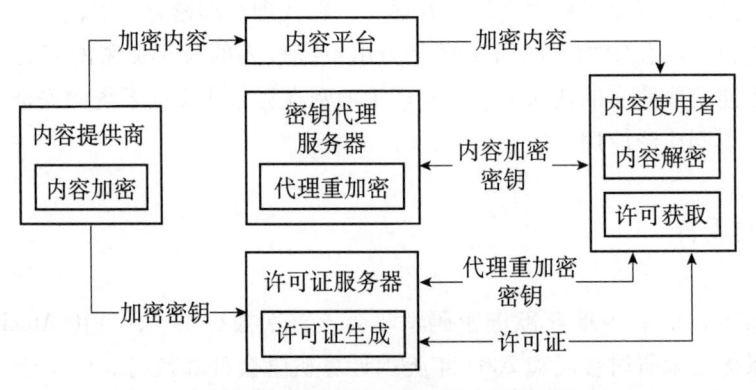

图 1 基于代理重加密的多媒体数字版权授权协议

（1）内容使用者向许可证服务器注册，许可证服务器为内容使用者生成代理重加密密钥。

（2）内容提供商随机生成内容加密主密钥和内容加密辅助密钥，两者加密生成内容加密密钥。内容提供商使用内容加密密钥加密多媒体内容，并使用密钥代理服务器公钥加密内容加密辅助密钥保存在内容头中，与加密内容一起通过内容平台分发给内容使用者，而内容加密主密钥则加密发送给许可证服务器保存。

（3）内容使用者下载加密的多媒体内容后，向许可证服务器申请许可证，许可证服务器根据内容使用者的权利申请为内容使用者生成并分发许可证，许可证中包含许可证服务器公钥加密的内容加密主密钥和用户的使用权利（包括时间、次数等）等。

（4）内容使用者获取许可证后，向密钥代理服务器申请代理重加密内容加密主密钥。密钥代理服务器将许可证中许可证服务器公钥加密的内容加密主密钥代理重加密为内容使用者公钥加密的内容加密主密钥，同时使用私钥解密出文件头中密钥代理服务器公钥加密的内容加密辅助密钥，并使用内容使用者公钥加密内容加密辅助密钥，加密的结果与代理重加密的内容加密主密钥一并发送给内容使用者。

（5）内容使用者使用私钥解密出内容加密主密钥和内容加密辅助密钥，两者加密生成内容加密密钥，内容使用者再使用内容加密密钥解密多媒体内容，并按照许可证中的权利描述使用多媒体内容。

该协议的参数如表 1 所示。

表 1 基于代理重加密的多媒体数字版权授权协议参数

名称	含义
I_u	用户标识
I_c	内容标识
$K_{a,u}$	代理重加密密钥
K_m	内容加密主密钥
K_a	内容加密辅助密钥
K_e	内容加密密钥
M	明文多媒体内容
K_r	代理重加密后的内容加密主密钥
C	版权保护内容格式
V	允许使用的权利
T	权利描述信息
P	公钥
S	私钥
Q	版权信息
W	许可证申请
N	许可证正文
F	内容加密密钥重加密申请

2.1 内容使用者注册

内容使用者向许可证服务器注册，许可证服务器为内容使用者生成代理重加密密钥，如图 2 所示。

步骤 1 内容使用者向许可证服务器提交注册请求，请求包括内容使用者公钥 P_u。

$$U \to S : I_U \parallel P_u$$

步骤 2 许可证服务器验证内容使用者的身份，如果验证通过则生成内容使用者的代理重加密密钥。

$$K_{a,u} = G(S_a, P_u)$$

步骤 3 许可证服务器使用内容使用者公钥 P_u 加密代理重加密密钥并返回给内容使用者。

$$A \rightarrow U: E(P_u, K_{a,u})$$

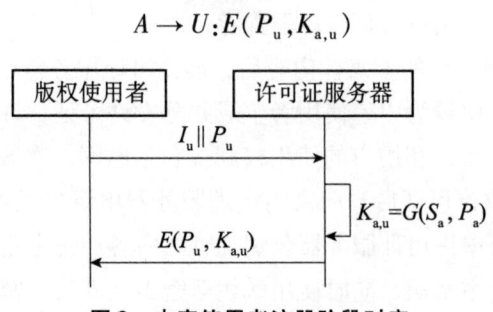

图2 内容使用者注册阶段时序

2.2 内容加密

内容提供商随机生成内容加密密钥，使用内容加密密钥加密并打包多媒体内容，如图3所示。

步骤1 内容提供商随机生成内容加密主密钥 K_m 和内容加密辅助密钥 K_a，使用 K_m 加密 K_a 得到内容加密密钥。

$$K_e = E(K_m, K_a)$$

步骤2 内容提供商使用 K_e 加密多媒体内容 M，按照格式打包加密后的内容并上传至内容平台。内容头包括内容标识 I_c 和密钥代理服务器公钥 P_k 加密的 K_a 等信息。

$$C = \{I_c \parallel E(P_k, K_a) \parallel E(K_e, M)\}$$

步骤3 内容提供商将内容标识 I_c、内容加密主密钥 K_m 以及允许内容使用者使用的权利 V（时间和次数等）等版权信息加密发送给许可证服务器。

$$Q = \{I_c \parallel E(P_a, K_m) \parallel E(P_a, V)\}$$

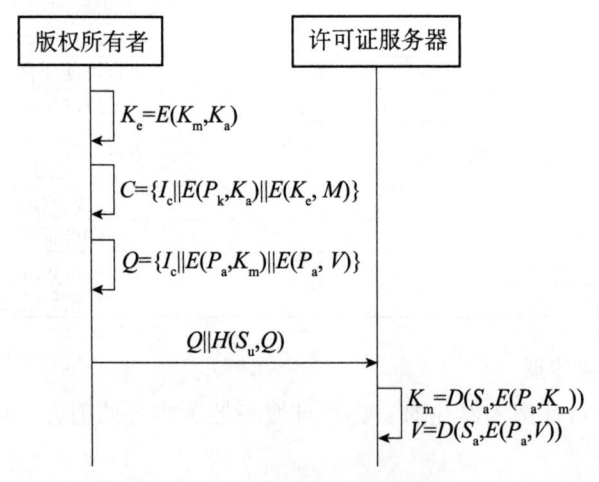

图3 内容加密阶段时序

步骤4 内容提供商使用私钥 S_u 签名 Q，签名结果与 Q 一并发送给许可证服务器。

$$U \rightarrow A: Q \parallel H(S_u, Q)$$

步骤5 许可证服务器验证版权信息的签名，验证通过后，使用私钥 S_a 解密出 K_m 和 V 并保存。

$$K_m : D(S_a, E(P_a, K_m))$$
$$V = D(S_a, E(P_a, V))$$

步骤6 内容提供商将加密打包后的内容上传到内容平台，供内容使用者下载。

2.3 许可授权

内容使用者下载加密的多媒体内容后，向许可证服务器申请许可证，许可证服务器根据权利申请为内容使用者生成许可证，如图4所示。

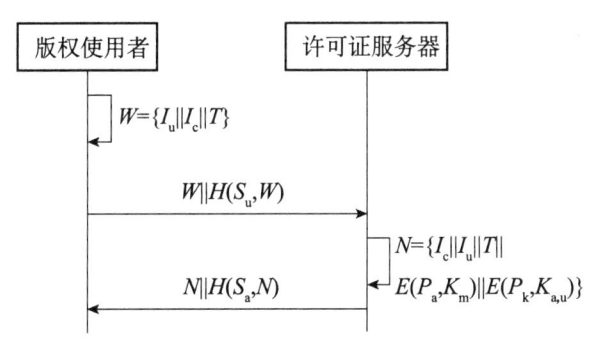

图4 许可授权阶段时序

步骤1 内容使用者从内容平台下载加密后的内容后，在无有效许可证的情况下，DRM客户端提示内容使用者申请许可证再使用内容。

步骤2 内容使用者向许可证服务器提交许可证申请，包括用户标识 I_u、内容标识 I_c 和权利描述信息 T 等。

$$W = \{I_u \| I_c \| T\}$$

步骤3 内容使用者使用私钥 S_u 签名许可证申请，并发送许可证申请给许可证服务器。

$$U \to A : W \| H(S_u, W)$$

步骤4 许可证服务器验证许可证申请的签名。验证通过后，检查内容使用者申请的权利信息是否在内容提供商规定的权利 V 范围内，同时查询该内容使用者的代理重加密密钥 $K_{a,u}$，并为该内容使用者生成许可证。许可证中包含内容标识 I_c、用户标识 I_u、权利描述信息 T、许可证服务器公钥 P_a 加密的 K_m 和密钥代理服务器公钥 P_k 加密的 $K_{a,u}$ 等。

$$N = \{I_c \| I_u \| T \| E(P_a, K_m) \| E(P_k, K_{a,u})\}$$

步骤5 许可证服务器使用私钥 S_a 签名许可证，并将签名后的许可证发送给内容使用者。

$$A \to U : N \| H(S_a, N)$$

2.4 代理重加密

内容使用者获取许可证后，向密钥代理服务器申请代理重加密内容加密密钥，如图5所示。

步骤1 内容使用者获取许可证后，验证许可证签名。验证通过后，向密钥代理服务器提交内容加密密钥重加密申请。申请包括内容头中使用密钥代理服务器公钥 P_k 加密的 K_a、许可证中许可证服务器公钥 P_a 加密的 K_m 和密钥代理服务器公钥 P_k 加密的 $K_{a,u}$。

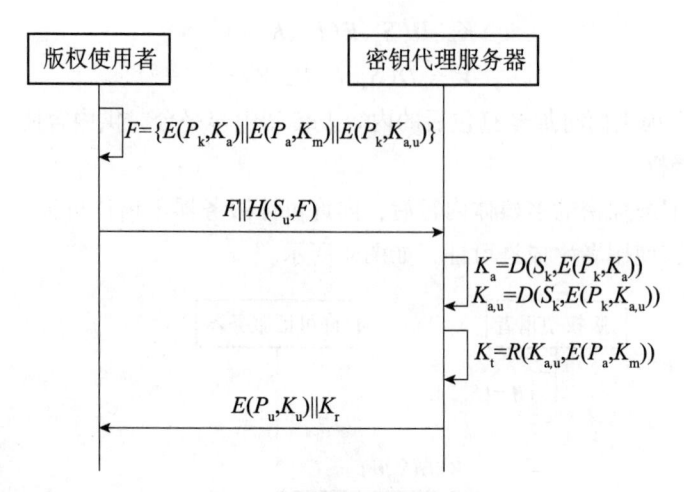

```
          版权使用者                    密钥代理服务器
              │                             │
              │◄── F={E(P_k,K_a)‖E(P_a,K_m)‖E(P_k,K_{a,u})} ──│
              │                             │
              │── F‖H(S_u,F) ──►            │
              │                             │┐ K_a=D(S_k,E(P_k,K_a))
              │                             ││ K_{a,u}=D(S_k,E(P_k,K_{a,u}))
              │                             │┘
              │                             │┐ K_t=R(K_{a,u},E(P_a,K_m))
              │                             │┘
              │◄── E(P_u,K_u)‖K_r ──        │
```

图 5 代理重加密阶段时序

$$F = \{E(P_k, K_a) \| E(P_a, K_m) \| E(P_k, K_{a,u})\}$$

步骤 2 内容使用者使用私钥 S_u 签名内容加密密钥申请,并将申请发送给密钥代理服务器。

$$U \rightarrow K: F \| H(S_u, F)$$

步骤 3 密钥代理服务器验证内容使用者提交的内容加密密钥代理重加密申请的签名。验证通过后,使用私钥 S_k 解密出 K_a 和 $K_{a,u}$。

$$K_a = D(S_k, E(P_k, K_a))$$
$$K_{a,u} = D(S_k, E(P_k, K_{a,u}))$$

步骤 4 密钥代理服务器使用代理重加密密钥 $K_{a,u}$ 对许可证服务器公钥 P_a 加密的 K_m 进行代理重加密,结果为

$$K_r = R(K_{a,u}, E(P_a, K_m))$$

步骤 5 密钥代理服务器使用内容使用者公钥 P_u 加密 K_a,连同代理重加密后的 K_m 发送给内容使用者。

$$K \rightarrow U: E(P_u, K_a) \| K_r$$

2.5 内容解密

步骤 1 内容使用者使用私钥 S_u 解密出 K_a。

$$K_a = D(S_u, E(P_u, K_a))$$

步骤 2 内容使用者使用私钥 S_u 解密代理重加密后的 K_m。

$$K_m = D(S_u, K_r)$$

步骤 3 内容使用者使用 K_m 加密 K_a,生成内容加密密钥 K_e。

$$K_e = E(K_m, K_a)$$

步骤 4 内容使用者使用 K_e 解密出多媒体内容,并按照许可证描述的权利进行使用。

3 协议实现方案

在提出协议的基础上,实现了云计算环境下的数字电视节目内容共享平台,完成数字

电视节目的安全共享,主要过程如下。

(1) 用户注册。用户(网络视频提供商)通过 DRM 客户端在内容共享平台注册,平台为用户生成代理重加密密钥。

(2) 电视节目加密。内容提供商(电视台)使用 DRM 客户端加密数字电视节目,加密完成后 DRM 客户端将版权信息发送给内容共享平台,并将加密的数字电视节目上传到内容共享平台的云存储中。

(3) 电视节目授权。用户从内容共享平台选择合适的数字电视节目后,提交订购申请(订购的有效时间等),内容共享平台为该用户生成并分发授权许可证。

(4) 电视节目解密。用户获取数字电视节目的许可证后,在使用数字电视节目时,DRM 客户端向内容共享平台申请代理重加密后的内容加密密钥,DRM 客户端再解密出内容加密密钥,并按照许可证中的权利进行播放。

内容共享平台不仅保护内容提供商的合法权利,而且保证数字电视节目在存储、传输和使用过程中的安全性。

4 协议安全性分析

(1) 内容使用者只有获取合法许可证后才能解密内容

内容提供商使用 K_e 加密多媒体内容,内容使用者必须向许可证服务器申请才能获取许可证,许可证中包含许可证服务器公钥加密的 K_m。内容使用者向密钥代理服务器申请代理重加密 K_m,密钥代理服务器返回内容使用者公钥加密的 K_m 和 K_a,只有内容使用者可以用自己的私钥解密出 K_m 和 K_a。因此,内容使用者只有获取合法许可证后才能解密内容。

(2) 抵抗攻击者与许可证服务器的合谋攻击

许可证服务器保存着 P_a 加密的 K_m,只有许可证服务器可以用自己的私钥 S_a 解密出 K_m。攻击者获取加密后的多媒体内容后,可以联合许可证服务器获取 K_m,但 K_a 是由 P_k 加密保存在内容头中,只有密钥代理服务器可以用自己的私钥 S_k 解密出 K_a。因此,攻击者与许可证服务器无法解密出 K_a,也就无法获得 K_e。

(3) 抵抗攻击者与密钥代理服务器的合谋攻击

攻击者获取加密的多媒体内容后,在代理重加密阶段,由于 K_a 是由 P_k 加密保存在内容头中,密钥代理服务器可以用自己的私钥 S_k 解密出 K_a,并且可以使用 $K_{a,u}$ 将许可证服务器公钥加密的 K_m 代理重加密成内容使用者公钥加密的 K_m,而密钥代理服务器无法获取 K_m 明文。因此,攻击者可以联合密钥代理服务器获取 K_a,但无法获取 K_m。

5 协议比较分析

笔者所提出的协议与文献[2,8]提出的协议均支持内容提供商使用统一的内容发布平台,对比结果如表 2 所示。从对比结果看出,笔者所提出的协议支持半可信的 DRM 服务器,采用对称加密算法加密多媒体内容,通过代理重加密许可证实现内容的共享,不需要重新加密内容,效率和安全性更高。

表 2 数字版权授权协议对比

协议	DRM 服务器	内容加密方	内容加密算法	内容共享方式
文献［2］	可信	内容平台	对称加密算法	许可证
文献［8］	半可信	内容提供商	模加算法	重加密内容
本文	半可信	内容提供商	对称加密算法	重加密许可证

6 结束语

提出一种基于代理重加密的多媒体数字版权授权协议。

（1）该协议引入密钥代理服务器，允许内容提供商在客户端加密多媒体内容，加密后的多媒体内容发送给半可信的内容平台和许可证服务器。

（2）内容使用者从内容平台下载加密的多媒体内容后，向许可证服务器申请许可证。

（3）内容使用者下载许可证后，向密钥代理服务器提交内容加密密钥重加密申请，密钥代理服务器重加密内容加密密钥后再发送给内容使用者.

该协议采用加密方式存储多媒体内容，保证多媒体内容的安全性，同时密钥代理服务器完成内容加密密钥的转换，保证内容加密密钥的安全性，能够有效抵抗合谋攻击，效率及安全性较高。

参考文献

［1］马兆丰，范科峰，陈铭，等. 支持时空约束的可信数字版权管理安全许可协议［J］. 通信学报，2008，29（10）：153-164.
  Ma Zhaofeng, Fan Kefeng, Chen Ming, et al. Trusted digital rights management protocol supporting for time and space constraint［J］. Journal on Communications，2008，29（10）：153-164.

［2］Wang Chaokun, Zou Peng, Liu Zhang, et al. CS-DRM：a cloud-based SIM DRM scheme for mobile internet［J］. Eurasip Journal on Wireless Communications and Networking, 2011（1）：1-30.

［3］Blaze M, Bleumer G, Strauss M. Divertible protocols and atomic proxy cryptography［C］//Advances in Cryptology-EUROCRYPT1998，International Conference on the Theory and Application of Cryptographic Techniques. Espoo：LNCS 1403，1998：127-444.

［4］Ateniese G, Fu K, Green M, et al. Improved proxy re-encryption schemes with applications to secure distributed storage［J］. ACM Transactions on Information and System Security，2006，9（1）：1-30.

［5］Taban G, Cardenas A A, Gligor V D. Towards a secure and interoperable DRM architecture［C］//Proceedings of the 6th ACM Workshop on Digital Rights Management. New York：ACM Press，2006：69-78.

［6］Lee S, Park H, Kim J. A secure and mutual-profitable DRM interoperability scheme［C］// ISCC 2010. New York：IEEE Inc，2010：75-80.

［7］Ma Guojun, Pei Qingqi, Wang Yuchen. A general sharing model based on proxy re-encryption［C］// IIHMSP 2011. Piscataway：IEEE Computer Society，2011：248-251.

［8］Petrlic R, Sorge C. Privacy-preserving DRM for cloud computing［C］// WAINA 2012. Piscataway：IEEE Computer Society，2012：1286-1291.

面向多级安全的结构化文档描述模型

苏铿　李凤华　史国振　李莉

1　引言

随着网络、数字出版等技术的进步，阅读终端的飞速发展，使文档阅读的需求发生了巨大的变化，要求文档能够面向多样化、普及化的终端，既有版式的清晰性和条理性，也要具备流式的内容可变性，并能够自适应终端屏幕大小。结构化文档融合了流式和版式描述信息，面向多样化的阅读、显示需求，已经逐步成为互联网信息传播的重要载体。针对结构化文档格式的研究一直是文档描述的重点。一个文档可以采用层次化组织的物理和逻辑结构进行描述，物理结构反映文档的布局，逻辑结构反映文档的组织。文档的物理结构和逻辑结构的整体构成了文档模型[1]。

访问控制最初面向大型机资源共享的需求，传统的访问控制研究经历了自主访问控制、强制访问控制、基于角色的访问控制等模型。为了适应分布式网络环境的特点，出现了基于任务的访问控制、面向分布式和跨域的访问控制、与时空相关的访问控制等模型。云计算、移动计算等的出现，使得访问控制的研究向细粒度、多要素的方向发展，基于属性的访问控制、基于行为的访问控制等模型相继出现。目前，如何针对网络环境下信息的传输进行对象化、细粒度的访问控制，满足用户个性化需求的同时，保证信息资源合理、合法使用成为了访问控制研究面临的新挑战。

多级安全[2]主要关注信息的分级管理和访问授权，保证不同安全级别的信息只能被享有相应权限的用户访问，BLP[3]、Biba[4]等模型通过实施严格的强制访问控制策略，在一定程度上保护了信息的机密性和完整性。

目前，泛在网络环境下的信息多以结构化文档的方式进行交互和传播，而且随着在线交互设备的多样化，结构化文档的访问控制及安全属性描述已经逐渐走向对象级、细粒度，即文档包含子文档，子文档包含对象，客体的访问控制以对象为单位。现有的结构化文档描述模型中缺少针对访问控制和多级安全的支持，导致在多级安全环境下，结构化文档的机密性、完整性受到威胁，基于结构化文档的访问控制不能迎合多级安全的需求。因此本文提出一种面向多级安全的结构化文档描述模型，能够保证文档流式和版式信息完备，并解决结构化文档在日趋复杂的网络环境下机密性、完整性、访问控制等问题。

---

* 本文选自《通信学报》，第33卷第Z1期，2012年9月，第222-227页

2 结构化文档

结构化文档同时描述了文档的版式信息和流式信息，能够更好地适用于自适应显示。在众多的结构化文档描述模型中，PDF、XPS 和 CEBX 较为成熟。其中，Adobe 推出的 PDF 1.3 规范引入了 logical structure，PDF 1.4 规范引入了 tagged PDF 来完善流式信息的表达；其后又将 XML 引入，用于对 MARS 文档格式中信息进行结构化的描述。李宁等人针对"标文通"与 Tagged PDF 的信息交换进行了实验，为减少办公文档的跑版问题提供了积极的借鉴意义[5]。微软公司也在其固定版式文件 XPS（XML paper specification）中采用类似的方式对逻辑结构信息进行了兼容[6]，但是以上研究并没有完全解决信息数据的结构化问题。Bloechle 等人基于 Dori 模型开展了一系列的研究工作，于 2006 年提出了 XCDF[7] 格式，XCDF 文档与 Tagged PDF 相比，版式信息与流式信息的结合更为紧密合理，并且采用了 XML 来描述相关信息，使得其构造、使用更为方便，基于上述研究，文献［8］提出了一种从已有固定版式文档中重新构造文档逻辑结构的方法——Dolores。为了缩小文档体积、便于使用，Bloechle 对 XCDF 格式进行了优化[9]。

北大方正公司 2005 年在原来 CEB 版式结构文档的基础上启动了 CEBX 计划，并吸收 Tagged-PDF、MARS 流式特征，推出了 CEBX 1.1 版本，能够较好地解决版式和流式文档的融合问题，并分别针对移动设备和文档存储，提出了 CEBX 1.2-M 和 CEBX 1.2-A 版本。CEBX 采用了打包的形式，将文档整体描述、安全描述、版式信息、流式信息以及资源和物理层信息进行整合。CEBX 添加了文档整体安全描述[10]，能够实现整个文档及其包含文件的加密、签名以及整体使用权限的定义，并且支持 DRM 解决方案，初步解决了结构化文档在网络传输和使用过程中的机密性、完整性等问题。

但是，随着分布式计算、移动计算、云计算以及泛在计算的出现，网络环境日趋复杂，如何对结构化文档进行多级安全管理，并满足用户随时、随地访问结构化文档的控制需求，成为结构化文档描述的未来的研究方向。

3 面向多级安全的结构化文档的描述模型

3.1 面向多级安全的结构化文档描述

针对上述结构化文档在泛在网络环境中面临的访问控制和多级安全管理问题，本文将基于 CEBX 等结构化文档描述方法，提出一种如图 1 所示的新型结构化文档描述模型。该模型分为 2 个层次，第 1 层包含了文档入口、文档安全属性描述、文档根节点、页面信息、文档逻辑结构描述、文档样式结构描述。其中，文档入口描述了文档的安全属性、基础信息、文档根节点等内容及其相互关联关系；文档安全属性描述了对文档信息进行加密和签名所使用的算法、密钥以及初始向量等信息；文档根节点的定义主要用于实现文档的嵌套和包含，描述了文档及其子文档之间的逻辑关系，子文档同样包含了文档入口、安全属性描述等信息；文档逻辑结构描述与文档样式结构描述对文档的元素组织形式、显示方式进行了描述，包含了文档章、节等的组织结构和样式表等信息；页面信息描述了页面的逻辑组成、关联关系、数量等信息。为了进一步描述结构化文档所包含资源及其物理数据，定义了模型的第 2 个层次，包含页面，每个页面由资源目录、资源描述和物理数据组成。资源是对一组图元或其他数据描述的集合。在页面中出现的图元、使用的数据或者结构都保存在资源中，在需要使用时从相应的资源中读取。一个文档可以包含一个或多个资源。

在图 1 所示的结构化文档模型中，文档逻辑结构描述、文档样式结构描述需要在网络传输和使用中保证其完整性，从而保证文件格式和版式的正常显示。并且需要保证文档所包含资源的合法使用，因此需要结合目前网络环境的多样性和用户访问个性化的需求，为资源描述添加安全属性描述，包含该资源的域安全属性、时态属性、环境属性，为了能够满足多级安全管理的需求，为安全属性描述添加了安全级别和访问范畴的定义。

文档逻辑结构和样式结构描述的完整性标识保证了结构化文档在网络传输过程中文档格式、显示形式等描述的完整、不可篡改；资源安全属性描述的添加能够为用户提供在任意时间、任意地点对任意资源合法访问的控制以及满足资源多级管理的需求。

3.2 安全属性描述

安全属性描述包含了文档整体的安全属性描述、针对逻辑结构描述和样式结构描述的完整性标识以及针对资源访问控制和多级安全管理的环境、时态、安全等级、访问范畴和域安全属性的描述。综合各类不同安全属性描述的特点，为图 1 中的描述模型添加安全属性描述定义，说明如图 2 和表 1 所示。

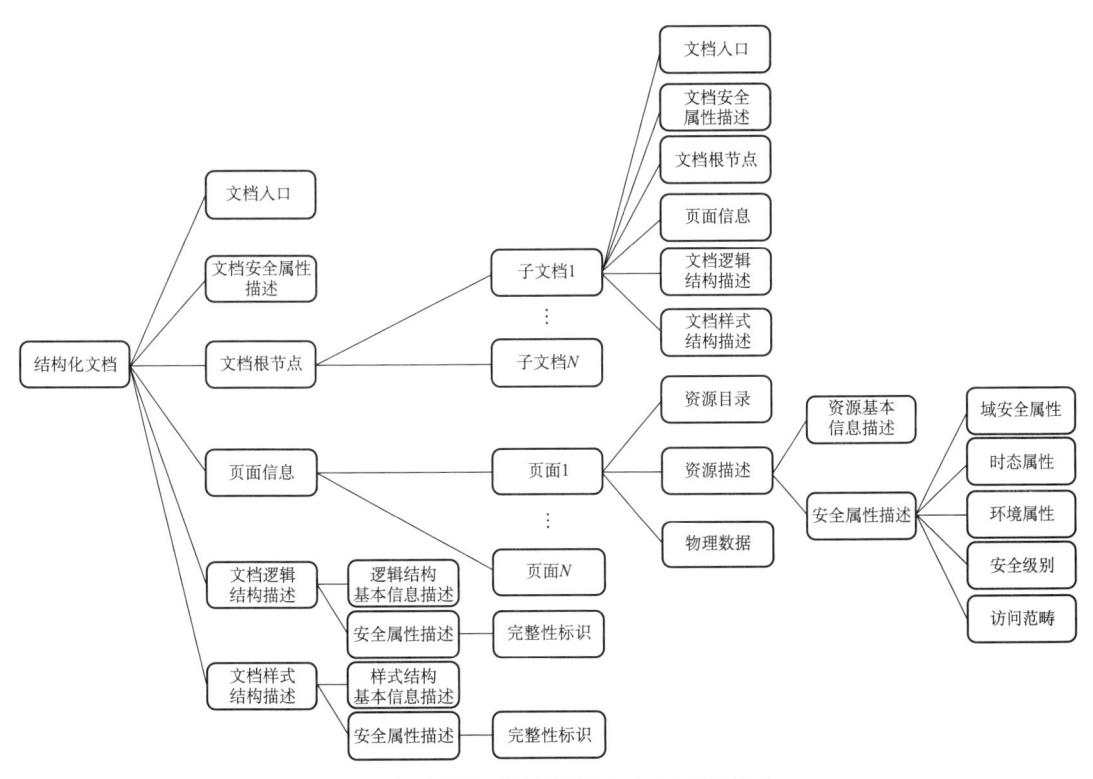

图 1　泛在网络环境下结构化文档描述模型

访问控制标签（access control label）主要包含了权限描述、权限对象、用户信息、管理员信息、域安全属性、时态属性、环境属性、安全级别和访问范畴。其中，权限定义了

Read、Write、Create、Modify 4 类，并且可以依据需要将其具体化，例如：针对多媒体文件，可以定义为 View（查看）、Play（播放）等。为了保证权限信息的完整性，为该项内容定义了签名标签。为了支持对结构化文档跨域流通时的控制，定义了域安全属性，主要描述在传播过程中所经由域的约束信息。时态、环境属性的定义用于对用户访问进行控制，结合基于行为的访问控制模型[11]，时态和环境属性分别标识了可以对文档及其对象进行访问的时间区段和环境要求。安全等级和访问范畴的定义为多级安全管理提供支持，安全级别标识了能够访问该文档或者资源对象主体的最低安全级别，访问范畴则标识了访问主体所处的组信息，例如：部门、系部等。

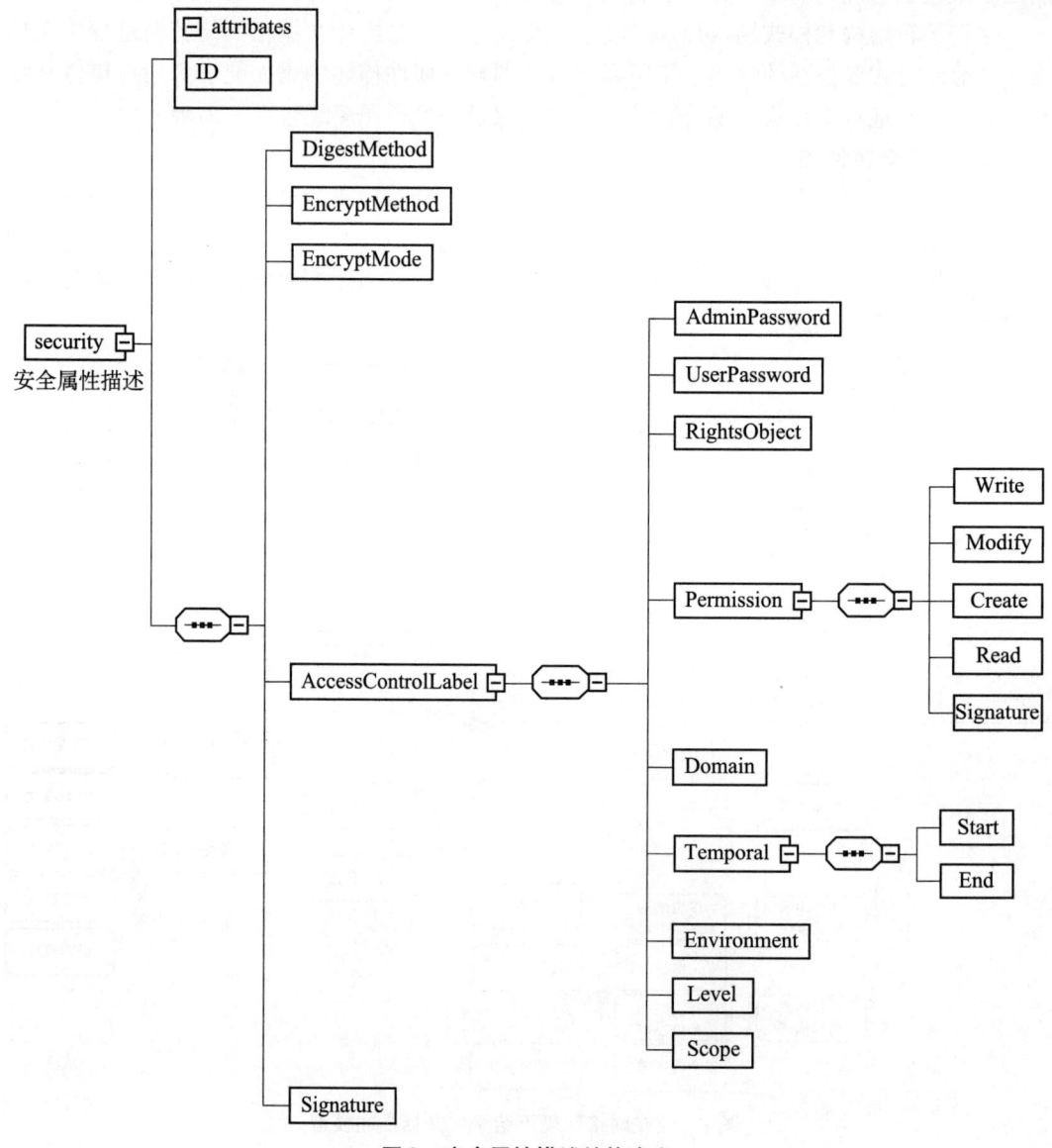

图 2　安全属性描述结构定义

签名标签的定义主要用于保证文档及其相关信息的完整性，该标签中定义了签名所使用的算法、签名的有效期以及签名生成的数据即完整性标识信息，如图 3 所示。其中，ID 为数字签名的唯一标识，TimeStamp 为时间戳，用于记录签名时间和数字签名的有效期。由于结构化文档描述文件包含信息较多，在进行数字签名前，需要生成摘要数据。Digest Method 和 Digest Value 分别表示了摘要算法和摘要数据。SignatureMethod 和 SignatureValue 分别对应签名算法和签名数据。CertificationType 和 CertificationData 分别描述用于验证签名的证书类型和证书数据。在网络数据的传输过程中，接收方将依据接收到文档的 Signature 中摘要算法、签名算法、证书数据中的公钥信息生成验签数据，并与摘要数据对比以确认结构化文档该部分信息的完整性。

用户可以根据需求的不同而选取不同的字段，针对文档逻辑结构描述和样式结构描述需要选取 Signature 标签；针对资源的安全属性描述则需要选取访问控制标签，Signature 标签可以按照需要取舍。

表 1 安全属性描述标签说明

名称	说明
ID	该安全性描述的唯一标识
DigestMethod	为支持文档及其对象的签名需求，为文档定义使用的摘要算法
EncryptMethod	为了支持文档及其对象的加解密，为其定义加解密算法
EncryptMode	加密模式
AccessControlLabel	定义了该结构化文档访问控制相关的信息，包含了管理员、用户的密码、权利描述对象、权限描述、时态、环境、安全级别以及范畴等
Signature	数字签名，用于文档及其对象完整性描述

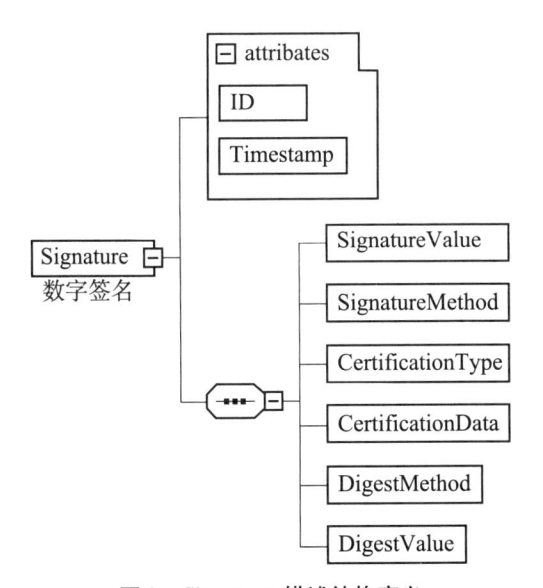

图 3 Signature 描述结构定义

3.3 安全属性描述实例

为了进一步说明图 1 所示模型以及图 2、图 3 所描述结构的使用方法，本节将给出一个针对性的实例。定义结构化文档的逻辑结构和样式结构描述的完整性标签，采用 MD5 算法计算消息摘要，RSA 算法生成签名，证书采用 X.509 格式，签名生成时间为当前系统时间。对应的安全属性描述文件 Security_ 1.xml 如下。

```
< ?xml version = "1.0" encoding = "UTF-8"? >
< Security ID = "001" >
…
< Signature ID = "01" TimeStamp = "2010 - 05 - 08 08:08:08" >
< DigestMethod > MD5 < /DigestMethod >
< DigestValue >…< /DigestValue >
< SignatureMethod > RSA < /SignatureMethod >
< SignatureValue >…< /SignatureValue >
< CertificationType > X.509 < /CertificationType >
< CertificationData >…< /CertificationData >
< /Signature >
< /Security >
```

针对该结构化文档的访问控制需求，例如，该文档的访问时间是上午 8 点到下午 5 点，地点为公司内部，可以被安全级别 3 及以上级别部门 A 的人员进行修改操作。Domain 标签将记录该文档在跨域传递过程中经由安全域的信息，如 ID、网络位置等内容。具体描述文件 Security_ 2.xml 如下。

```
< ?xml version = "1.0" encoding = "UTF-8"? >
< Security ID = "001" >
…
< AccessControlLabel >
< AdminPassword >…< /AdminPassword >
< UserPassword >…< /UserPassword >
< RightsObject >
    < Permission >
        Modify
    < /Permission >
< /RightsObject >
< Domain >
…
< /Domain >
< Temporal >
    < Start >08:00:00< /Start >
    < End >17:00:00< /End >
```

```
</Temporal>
<Environment>In Company</Environment>
<Level>3</Level>
<Scope>Department A</Scope>
</AccessControlLabel>
…
</Security>
```

4　安全性分析

4.1　完整性

结构化文档安全属性描述模型为结构化文档、子文档及其对象定义了安全属性标签，包含了完整性标记，能够保证逻辑结构描述、样式结构描述以及资源和数据在网络传输过程中的完整性和不可篡改性。

4.2　机密性

该模型支持为文档及其描述文件和资源的加密，可以定义对应的加解密算法、工作模式、密钥以及初始化向量。能够保证在文档传输和使用过程中，数据信息的机密性。

4.3　访问控制

安全属性描述中包含域属性、时态、环境属性，为用户描述访问时所处的物理环境、软硬件平台、时间状态等信息，并对结构化文档进行对象级的环境、时态约束。文档管理系统通过定义用户与结构化文档，添加主客体环境、时态标签，实现结构化文档的多要素访问控制，进一步适用于分布式计算、云计算、泛在计算等复杂网络环境。

4.4　多级安全管理

安全属性描述中包含的安全级别和访问范畴能够约束主客体的安全级别及所属范围，针对不同的安全级别设置不同的访问规则及其操作类型，从而对结构化文档实现多级安全管理。

5　结束语

分布式计算、移动计算、云计算以及泛在计算的出现推动了信息化社会的发展，结构化文档作为一种融合了版式和流式信息的表现形式，在网络信息的传播中扮演了重要的角色。但是，网络环境的复杂特性为结构化文档的访问控制带来了新的挑战，不同的网络环境、物理位置、用户角色、时间状态等使得传统的访问控制方式不能够适用于多样化环境下的结构化文档管理。而且，多级安全的出现使得结构化文档的描述日趋复杂。因此，需要一种结合多种访问要素、具有多级安全特征的结构化文档描述方法。本文通过对传统结构化文档描述模型的研究，结合访问控制和多级安全需求，提出了一种面向多级安全的结构化文档描述模型定义和描述方法，定义了安全属性的描述结构，并给出了相应的 XML

描述实例。该模型能够解决结构化文档在网络跨域流转过程中逻辑结构描述、样式结构描述以及资源数据的完整性和机密性问题，保证结构化文档的合理、合法使用。

参考文献

［1］ KLINK S, DENGEL A, KIENINGER T. Document structure analysis based on layout and textual features［A］. Proceedings of the 4th IAPR International Workshop on Document Analysis Systems［C］. Rio de Ja-neiro, Brazil. 2000. 99 – 111.

［2］ The future of multi-level secure (MLS) information systems［EB/OL］. http：//csrc. nist. gov/nissc/1998/ proceedings /panelF3. pdf, 1998.

［3］ BELL D E. Looking Back at the Bell-LaPadula model［A］. Proceedings of the 21st Conference On Annual Computer Security Applications［C］. Washington, DC, USA, 200. 337 – 351.

［4］ BIBA K J. Integrity Considerations for Secure Computer Systems［R］. MTR-3153, The Mitre Corporation, 1977, 04.

［5］ 李宁, 田英爱, 侯霞, 等. 办公文档与固定版式文档格式关系探讨［J］. 电子学报, 2008, 36 (B12)：128 – 132.
LI N, TIAN A Y, HOU X, et al. A discussion on relationship between revisable and non-revisable document formats［J］. Acta Electronica Sinica, 2008, 36 (B12): 128 – 132.

［6］ Microsoft Corporation. XPS Specification and Reference Guide［S］. 2010, 06, 30.

［7］ BLOECHLE J L, RIGAMONTI M, HADJAR K, et al. Xcdf：a canonical and structured document format［A］. Proceedings of the 7th International Workshop on Document Analysis Systems［C］. Nelson, New Zealand, 2006. 141 – 152.

［8］ BLOECHLE J L, PUGIN C, INGOLD R. Dolores：an interactive and class-free approach for document logical restructuring［A］. Proceedings of the 8th International Workshop on Document Analysis Systems［C］. Nara, Japan, 2008. 644 – 652.

［9］ BLOECHLE J L, LALANNE D, INGOLD R. OCD：an optimized and canonical document format［A］. Proceedings of the 10th International Conference on Document Analysis and Recognition［C］. Barcelona, USA, 2009. 236 – 240.

［10］ CEBX/Mv1. 2 Standard Manual［S］. 2011. 8.

［11］ 李凤华, 王巍, 马建峰, 等. 基于行为的访问控制模型及其行为管理［J］. 电子学报, 2008, 10, 36 (10)：1881 – 1890.
LI F H, WANG W, MA J F, et al. Access control model and admini-stration of action［J］. Acta Electronica Sinica, 2008, 10, 36 (10): 1881 – 1890.

A DRM Interoperability Architecture Based on Local Conversion Bridge with Proxy Re-Cryptography*

Lihao Su   Weiwei Zhang   Ru Zhang   Jianyi Liu

Introduction

In digital contents age, conflicts always exist between copyrights protection and making most of the Internet to share information. Various Digital Rights Management (DMR) Standards are introduced and applied to all kinds of devices, which however gives rise to new problems such as content consumers cannot share contents between devices by just copying them from one device to another conveniently and freely.

Different DRM standards have their respective implementation details of encryption algorithm and packaging format to wrap content. Also semantic rules for rights expression language in license are diverse between different DRM standards. Without compromising these security properties, DRM Interoperability system distributes content and license in required DRM format to devices or transfers content and license from one DRM format to another between devices while keep rights consistent in the process.

Related Work and Our Design Principle

Generally, there are two types of interoperable schemes that approach device's DRM-specific requirements, one is based on distribution in which each device receives content from domain managers in desired format such as in [1, 2], another is based on sharing between devices to transform the content of one device's format to another's through DRM translation such as in [3, 4].

Early interoperability scheme [5] approaches Digital contents transformation with neutral format. Devices translate the source's DRM-specific contents into the neutral format when exporting it and then convert the received neutral format to destination's required contents format when importing it. Underlying requirements in this proposal include that all devices have to agree with neutral format generation algorithm, which is weakly feasible.

Earlier proposal by [6], downloads heterogeneous DRM components as software to extend DRM agents functionality, provides various API to meet DRM agent's knowledge requirements for transformation between different DRMs. But license translation may spin out of control at devices' end.

Similarly, [3] transfers interoperable process to DRM agent in terminal devices, and DRM service providers only support these devices in different domains with necessary information such as compatible Rights Object (RO) and profile.

[1] uses an DRM Interoperability agent, which employs proxy re-encryption scheme for content protection, but it only takes effect in content distribution channel from providers to end devices, so it requires content acquisition from Internet source when a new device wants to share an owned content.

[2] tries to install Trusted Platform Module (TPM) in Local Domain Manager (LDM), so content scrambling key SCK_m can be securely encrypted inside TPM without software based encryption algorithm. However tamper-resistance through hardware is not economically feasible for existing PCs according to [7].

[4] provides bases and preliminaries of DRM backgrounds for our proposal, it presents a basic application of proxy re-encryption. In its content sharing scenario between end devices, proxy re-encryption diverts the workload of encrypting K_m to semi-trusted proxy. Source device sends K_m under its own public key to proxy to be re-encrypted into a message under destination devices' public key. But this scenario impractically assumes that exporting and importing terminal devices uses identical encryption algorithm. And their scheme mentions nothing about using license to constrain action of translation and re-encryption by third party. Our proposal resolves these problems by separating encryption into 2 layers, with first inside layer universally adopted by all providers, the second layer could be customized by different DRM schemes.

Above all, our main consideration for a secure and efficient DRM conversion scheme follows the principles as below:

(1) Guarantee secure communication between participants through encryption.

(2) Minimize the number of participants and the amount of communication data for key exchange and re-encryption key generation.

(3) Minimize calculation requirements for end devices.

Proxy Re-encryption Algorithm Preliminary

We employ the Proxy Re-encryption scheme raised by Improved proxy re-encryption schemes [8].

Definitions:

ABilinear Map is a map e: $G_1 \times \hat{G}_1 \to G_2$ in which the following properties are satisfied:

(1) G_1 and G_2 are groups of the same prime order q;

(2) for all $a, b \in Z_q, g \in G_1, h \in \hat{G}$, then $e(g^a, h^b) = e(g, h)^{ab}$ is efficiently computable;

(3) the map is non-degenerate, i.e. if g generates G_1 and h generates $\hat{G}_1$, then $e(g, h)$ generates G_2;

There are two levels of encryption in proxy re-cryptography.

The level 1 encryption algorithm encrypts messages under A's public key so that the encrypted message can only be decrypted under A's private key.

The level 2 encryption algorithm encrypts messages under A's public key while the encrypted message can be re-encrypted with $rk_{A \to B}$ so that it can be decrypted under B's private key.

For global system parameters which all entities share, there are random generators $g \in G_1$ and $Z = e(g, g) \in G_2$, in which G_1 and G_2 are two groups of the same prime order with a bilinear map $G_1^2 \to G_2$. So Re-cryptography can be divided in the following setting and functions:

(1) Alice has private key (a_1, a_2, g^{a_2}) and public key (Z^{a_1}, Z^{a_2}); Bob has private key (b_1, b_2, g^{b_2}), public key (Z^{b_1}, Z^{b_2}) and delegatee key (g^{b_1}).

(2) Re-Encryption Key (Alice to Bob) Generation: $g^{b_1 a_2} = (g^{b_1})a_2$ is generated by Alice, who finds out Bob's public key g^{b_1} as delegatee key and invokes her own private key a_2 as a delegator key.

(3) First Level Encryption with Alice's public key: Message M is encrypted to get $(Z^{a_1 k}, M \cdot Z^k)$, In which $Z_{a_1 k} = (Z^{a_1})^k$ and K is randomly generated by Sender.

(4) First level Decryption with Alice's private key: $M \Rightarrow \dfrac{M \cdot Z^k}{Z^k} = \dfrac{M \cdot Z^k}{(Z^{a_1 k})^{\frac{1}{a_1}}}$

(5) Second level Encryption with Alice's public key: $(g^k, M \cdot Z^{a_2 k})$ In which $M \cdot Z^{a_2 k} = M \cdot (Z^{a_2})^k$ and K is randomly generated by Sender

(6) Re-Encryption with Re-key: $(Z^{b_1 a_2 k}, M \cdot Z^{a_2 k})$ In which $Z^{b_1 a_2 k} = e(g^k, g^{b_1 a_2})$

(7) Re-Encryption Decryption with Bob's private key: $M = \dfrac{M \cdot Z^{a_2 k}}{Z^{a_2 k}} = \dfrac{M \cdot Z^{a_2 k}}{(Z^{b_1 a_2 k \frac{1}{b_1}})}$

System Architecture

In the following section, an elaborate introduction of our proposed system will be presented and functions of each component in the architecture will be explained. For content flow to be published and purchased freely in the digital content market and consumed conveniently among devices, the complete DRM system involves two processes, as is illustrated in Fig. 1: 1. Content purchase and distribution process; 2. Content sharing process.

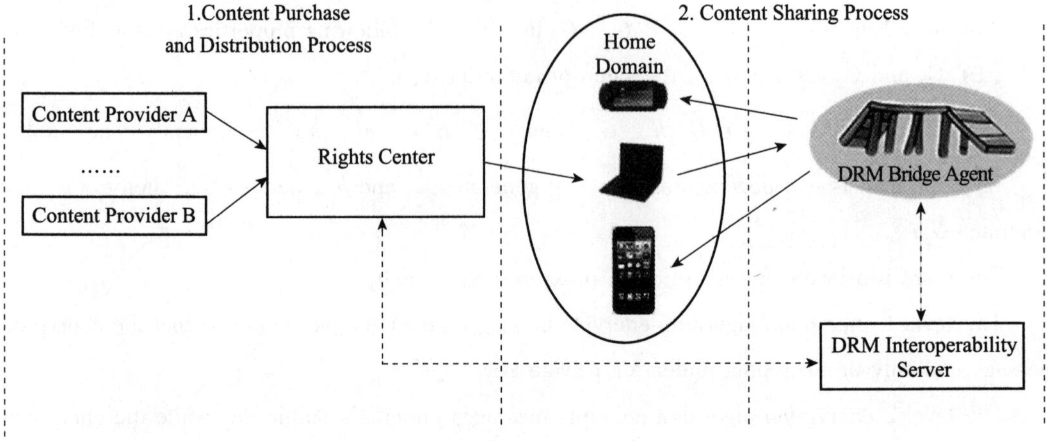

Fig. 1: Complete architecture of the proposed interoperability system

Content encryption key re-encryption steps. Our paper presumes that some contents have been purchased from providers. Hence we will focus mainly on content sharing process.

Here is a step layout to explain how our protocol works. The following descriptive steps only illustrates protection for content encryption key K_m.

Note that $AE_{1,2}$ (M, K) means level 1 and level 2 asymmetric encryption respectively and SE (M, K) means symmetric encryption of message M with key K. PAC (M) means packaged message M in certain digital content file format.

Step 1: After obtaining his devices such as Device A PC and Device B mobile phone, user needs to register them in the conversion domain which belongs to a Domain Bridge Agent (DBA). In this case, there are Devices A and B, so domain manager DBA ask for ID of A, B and notifies the Trusted DRM Interoperability Server (DIS) to look for Device A's pair of public key (g^{a_0}, g^{a_r}) and private key (a_0, a_r) and B's public key (Z^{b_0}) from their manufacturers.

Step 2: For the first time Device A sends a request to DBA asking for content m's conversion, DBA connects with DRM server and receives re-encryption key (rk) list for A from DRM server. Since DRM Server knows all devices public/private key pairs, it takes charge of generating rk pairs securely. A's list for N sessions of rk pairs comes as:

$$(AE_1(t_1,PK_X),g^{a,t_1/a_0};AE_1(t_2,PK_X),g^{a,t_2/a_0};AE_1(t_3,PK_X),g^{a,t_3/a_0};\cdots;$$
$$AE_1(t_N,PK_X),g^{a,t_N/a_0})$$

In which for every AE_1 (t_i, PK_x) (i = 1, 2, $\cdots$, N), ti means temporary private key for destination device in every conversion session. And for each pair of session key, x in AE_1 (t_i, PK_x) stands for all devices except A, therefore $g^{a,t_i/a_0}$ in ith session can be $rk_{A \to X}$ for all destination devices.

Step 3: After uploading its content m and license to Bridge, a conversion session starts. DRM bridge agent firstly extract Rights Object for m and get RO_m. Contained in RO_m, K_{mis} encrypted by A's public key in second-level: $AE_2(K_m, PK_a) = (g^{a_0 k}, K_m \cdot Z^{a,k})$, in which $g^{a_0 k} =$

$(g^{a_0})^k$ and $K_m \cdot Z^{a,k} = K_m \cdot (Z^{a_r})^k$ and K is randomly generated by Sender. For ith conversion from A to B, DBA picks up $(AE_1(t_i, PK_b), g^{a_r t_i/a_0})$ and re-encrypt $AE_2(K_m, PK_a)$ with the calculation of $e(g^{a_0 k}, g^{a_r t_i/a_0})$ to get $(Z^{a_r t_i k}, K_m \cdot Z^{a,k})$.

When conversion finished, DRM agent in A downloads a new License in which RO_m was removed and Virtual Monotonic Counter (VMC) is decremented by one by DBA. And along with the download process, DBA sends license update notification to DRM agent to decrement its VMC to make it consistent with new license. So A can no longer render m. This license update mechanism guarantees that at anytime only one device in the conversion domain can render m within its validation period. Then DBA generates RO_m for B's License. When B logged in the conversion domain, it downloads the converted Content m. Only B can decrypt $AE_1(SK_t, PK_b)$ with its private key $PK_b = b_0$ and get $SK_t = t_i$, so it can further decrypt $(Z^{a_r t_i k}, K_m \cdot Z^{a,k})$ and get Km. Complete conversion steps for content and license are illustrated in Figure 2:

Device A   DRMBridgeAgent   DBridgeServer   Device B

$CReq(ID_M, ID_A, PK_A) \rightarrow$

        $CReq(ID_M, ID_A, PK_A) \rightarrow$ Session Key List Acquisition

AE_1 (rk—list, PK_A), $\leftarrow$ in which rk—list = $(AE_1(t_i, PK_x))$, $g^{a,t/a_0}$

(x stands for devices other than A in the domain),

Content: $PAC_{DRM_A}(SE_{DMR_A}(SE_0(m, K_m), K_A))$;

RO: $AE_1(K_A, PK_{Br})$, $AE_2(K_m, PK_A)$

DRM Bridge Agent's Conversion:

$AE_1(K_A, PK_{Br}) \rightarrow K_A$ decrypted with DBA's secret key SK_{Br}

$PAC_{DRMA}(SE_{DRMA}(SE_0(m, K_m), K_A)) \rightarrow SE_0(m, K_m) \rightarrow$

Generate $K_B \rightarrow PAC_{DRMB}(SE_{DMRB}(SE_0(m, K_m), K_B))$

Encrypt K_B with B's public key $\rightarrow AE_1(K_B, PK_B)$,

Pick $(AE_1(t_i, Z^{b_0}))$, $g^{a,t/a_0}$, from rk-list to re-encrypt $AE_2(K_m, PK_A)$

$= (g^{a_0 k}, K_m \cdot Z^{a,k})$ as $e(g^{a_0 k}, g^{a,t/a_0}) \rightarrow Z^{a,t,k}$

Insert $(Z^{a,t,k}, Km \cdot Z^{a,k}) = AE_1(K_m, PK_t)$ and $AE_1(t_1, Z^{b_0})$

$= AE_1(SK_t, PK_B)$ to RO_m for B's Liense

(PK_{Br} and SK_{Br} stands for DBM Bridge Agent's public key and private key).

($PK_t = Z^{t_1}$) and $SK_t = t_i$ represent temporary public and private key for ith session

---

             Content and License (RO) Conversion

Content: $PAC_{DRM_B}(SE_{DMRB}(SE_0(m, K_m), K_B))$;

RO: $AE_1(K_B, PK_B)$, $AE_1(K_m, PK_t)$, $AE_1(SK_t, PK_B)$

$\longrightarrow$

Fig. 2 Procedure of content and license conversion

User operation steps. Source device user: Register (First time) → Log in → Upload (Content, License) → Convert → Download (License)

Destination device user: Register (First time) → Log in → Upload (License) → Download (License, Content)

Security Analysis and Comparison

What distinguishes our proposal to [1, 2, 3] is that we build our interoperability framework based on local third party, leaving content provider out of interoperability service so that distribution channel would be simplified without installing various DRM interfaces. This feature is our proposal's biggest advantage over [1] which incorporates multiple entities to accomplish re-encryption key issuing through 9 rounds of negotiations. Besides, [1] only applies one layer of encryption over raw content which undermines system's flexibility.

The proposed rk list update mechanism embodies our earlier design principle 2 of minimizing the amount of communication data for key exchange and re-encryption key generation and principle 3 of transferring the translation and re-encryption burden to DIS and DBA from end device. These feature highlights our proposal in comparison with [3, 4] which relies on end devices to accomplish DRM adaptation.

Time consumption for one conversion is reduced both in communication and at terminal agent side. Similar to [1], we implement a prototype using the Proxy re-cryptography Library (PRL) [9] in Linux system. A complete re-encryption process is executed and evaluated in functions and in overall session. We compare our scheme to designated proxy re-encryption (DPRE) proposed by [1], which multiplies an addition proxy private key π on exponent of second level encrypted cipher text $(g^k, M \cdot Z^{a_2\pi k})$ and re-encrypt as e $(g^k, g^{a_2 b_1})$ $\pi = Z^{b_1 a_2 \pi k}$ to implement proxy designation. Functions that comprise the whole re-encryption process in [3] are respectively denoted below:

gen params (): generate domain parameters; *keygen* (): generate a public/private key pair; *level*1 *encrypt* (): perform first-level encryption; *level*2 *encrypt* (): perform second-level encryption; *delegate* (): generate a re-encryption key; *re-encrypt* (): re-encrypt a second-level encrypted message; *decrypt* (): decrypt an encrypted message

Our advantage in time consumption is demonstrated in table 1:

We use gettimeofday () to get time difference before and after a function and measure this function's duration. We deploy this testing program on Intel Core (TM) 3.10 GHZ CPU and 1.98G RAM, linux Cent OS.

In the above, N represents the number of re-encryption keys in list. A complete conversion in DPRE comprises of key generation, level2 encryption, delegation, re-encryption and decryption, except that gen params () happens once and for all. A usual complete conversion in our proposal constitutes of key generation, level 2 encryption, delegation, re-encryption and decryption, in which level 2 encryption and delegation usually takes no time due to acquisition form static rk list storage.

Table 1 Time consumption for each function in PRL

Functions	DPREDuration (us)	Our proposal Duration (us)	
gen params ( )	28 775.7	28 925.9	
keygen ( )	12 762.7	11 868.7	
level 1 encrypt ( )	1 489.8	1 517.4	
level 2 encrypt ( )	12 725.8	First-time conversion	3 067.7
		Usual conversion	0
delegate ( )	3 215.8	rk-list update	2 768.4 * N
		Usual conversion	0
re-encrypt ( )	7 550.9	6 699.7	
decrypt ( )	1 412.6	1 376.4	
complete conversion	67 933.3	50 388.1	

We notice that in the bold statistic there's a notable time consumption drop in level 2 encrypt ( ) and re-encrypt ( ) in our proposal because exponential calculation with π for proxy designation is left out. And in usual conversion sessions, level 2 encrypt ( ) takes no time because source content is ready in form of level 2 encrypted cipher text under source device's public key, and re-encryption key acquisition costs no time because the keys are available in rk list.

Summary and Further Considerations

Defects of our proposal lie in DRM property disclosure to Conversion Bridge, for DRM bridge agent has to know the specifications of each DRM rules and policies in order to convert RO and wrapped content. And similar to [2] our proposal assumes all content providers and DRM agents at terminal devices use a universal standard content encryption algorithm for raw content protection, this is a high demanding preliminary.

And as to the domain concept in consistence with foundation proposal in [3], we have to consider that as new devices join a conversion domain, the complications concerning rk list update, storage and management would get severe in geometric multiple growth, involving every end device in the domain.

And with regarding to Principle 1, actually key refreshment only takes effects in the second half of transmission from bridge to destination device. So other security measures to protect the confidentiality of K_m and raw content has to be further implemented to our proposal.

Acknowledgments

This work was collaboratively supported in part with funds from
（1） Beijing Natural Science Foundation's project（90604022）（4122053）.
（2） National Natural Science Foundation's project（61003284）.
（3） Fundamental Research Funds for the Central Universities（2013RC0310）.
（4） Press Publication Major Science and Technology Engineering Project（GXTC-CZ-1015004/09）（GXTC-CZ-1015004/15-1）.
（5） National Key Technology Research and Development Program（2012BAH08B02）.
（6） National 863 Program（2012AA012606）.

References

[1] A secure and mutual-profitable DRM interoperability scheme; Lee Sangho, Park Heejin; Kim, Jong; IEEE Symposium on Computers and Communications, ISCC 2010

[2] Secure interoperable digital content distribution mechanisms in a multi-domain architecture; Win, Lei Lei; Thomas, Tony; Emmanuel, Sabu; MULTIMEDIA TOOLS AND APPLICATIONS, SEP 2012

[3] Interoperable DRM Framework for Multiple Devices Environment; Hwang, Seong Oun; Yoon, Ki Song; ETRI JOURNAL, AUG 2008.

[4] Towards a secure and interoperable DRM architecture; Taban, Gelareh; Cárdenas, Alvaro A.; Gligor, Virgil D; Proceedings of the ACM Workshop On Digital Rights Management, DRM'06. Co-located with the 13th ACM Conference on Computer and Communications Security, 2006

[5] D.-W. Nam, J.-S. Lee, and J.-H. Kim, "Interlock system for DRM interoperability of streaming contents," in Proceedings of IEEE International Symposium on Consumer Electronics 2007, ISCE 2007

[6] ISO/IEC 14496-13, "Information technology: Generic coding of moving pictures and associated audio information, part 2: IPMP on MPEG-2 systems," 2002.

[7] Barhoush, Malek; Atwood, J. William; Requirements for enforcing digital rights management in multicast content distribution; TELECOMMUNICATION SYSTEMS, SEP 2010

[8] Improved proxy re-encryption schemes with applications to secure distributed storage Ateniese, Giuseppe; Fu, Kevin; Green, Matthew; Hohenberger, Susan; ACM Transactions on Information and System Security, 2006.

[9] The JHU-MIT Proxy Re-cryptography Library, http://spar.isi.jhu.edu/prl/.

Image Tamper Detection Based on the DCT Coefficients Model*

JIANG Wenfeng ZHANG Ru LIU Jianyi

I Introduction

Now, in the digital age of the rapid development of technology, the means of digital image tampering has become increasingly diverse. With the emerging image processing software and image processing software features escalating, tampered images becomes more and more simple, which makes the image appear a great deal of worry as the traditional forensic methods, therefore, how to identify whether an image has been tampered has become one of the important research topics in recent years, while the ability to roughly determine the type of image tampering has put forward higher requirements on this subject. In recent years, many scholars introduced stable distribution into the fitting dct coefficient model for the image steganography detection, although mentioned for image tamper detection but did not in-depth study, this article use the stable distribution fitting the dct coefficient model to research the image tamper detection, found that for the same model camera photo, image tamper detection can achieve good results.

II Statistical Characteristics of DCT Coefficients

Jpeg image coder process, as Figure 1 shown:

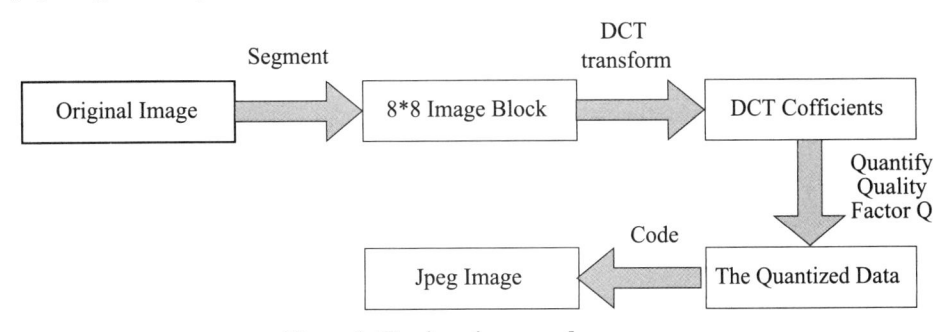

Figure 1. The jpeg image codec process

---

* 本文选自2nd International Conference on Computer Science and Network Technology (ICCSNT 2012), 第798-802页

It can be seen that JPEG images are stored quantized DCT coefficients, among them, the low-frequency components of the image will be concentrated in the upper left corner, where the F (0, 0), referred to as direct current (DC) coefficients, and the remaining 63 values known as the exchange (AC) coefficients. Usually the values of the DC coefficients are relatively large, and they do not exist significant statistical regularity, so this article discusses only the statistical model of the AC coefficients. Up to now, there are already a large number of scholars do in-depth research on the statistical model of the AC coefficients, in which the literature i ii iii suggests AC coefficients meet laplace distribution. Literatureivv mentioned DCT coefficients can not fully obey Gaussian model, because the high-frequency portion of the DCT coefficients tend to exhibit a heavier tail than the Gaussian distribution. Generalized Gaussian distribution (GGD) is more suitable for image DCT coefficients model, because its tail fading slower than the Gaussian distribution. However, GGD is not always suitable for low-IF section of the DCT coefficients. According to the Literature vi, the tail of the DCT coefficients of high magnitude sequence and GGD index fading is not attached, which led to a degradation in detection performance. Literature vii that the the SαS model is applicable to non-Gaussian heavy tail data, the model is more flexible, more fully describe the low-frequency coefficients of DCT. The literatureviii suggests that the stable distribution can better fit the AC coefficients.

III The Calculation of the Probability Density and the Parameters Estimated of the Symmetric a Stable Distribution Model

Stable distribution does not have an explicit probability density function, but the function can be characterized by inverse Fourier transform, i. e.

$$f(x;\alpha,\beta,\sigma,\mu) = \frac{1}{2\pi}\int_{-\infty}^{\infty} \varphi(t) e^{-ixt} dt \tag{1}$$

in which

$$\varphi(t) = \exp[it\mu - |ct|^{\alpha}(1 - i\beta\mathrm{sgn}(t)\varphi)] \tag{2}$$

Four parameters respectively determined the a stable distribution characteristics of tailing ($0 < \alpha \leq 2$), symmetry properties ($-1 \leq \beta \leq 1$), dispersion ($0 < c < \infty$) and location ($-\infty < \mu < \infty$), For symmetric α stable distribution ($S\alpha S$), the symmetry parameters $\beta = 0$, therefore, the characteristic function of the $S\alpha S$ model can be written as the following formula:

$$\varphi(t) = \exp(it\mu - |ct|^{\alpha}) \tag{3}$$

When using $S\alpha S$ model to fitting the JPEG image AC coefficient distribution model, using the mean μ of the sample data to estimate the location parameters μ, using the variance σ of the sample data to estimate the dispersion parameters c, to estimate the tailing features, mainly has the maximum likelihood estimation method, sample quantile law, sample characteristic function method, the fractional lower order moment method, extreme order statistics law, and dynamic estimation method ix. Taking into account the Computation of the common method is relatively large, this paper adopts the posterior method x to detemine the parameter of a, that is assume

JPEG image AC coefficients distribution meet SαS model, and then select α parameters in a certain step length traversing a number between 0 - 2, calculate the fitting degree of the model probability density function and the sample data distribution function, select the smallest fitting degree model corresponding parameters as the estimated actual parameters.

The calculation of the probability density has been the main obstacle to the application of the α stable distributions, the numerical methods based on fast inverse Fourier transform (IFFT). used in this article mentioned in the literaturexi. If calculate the probability density values of N interval of T points, need to use the N eigenvalues samples involved in computing, the N points can be expressed as $x_k = (k - 1 - (N/2))T, k = 1, \cdots, N$, at the same time N-uniform sampling in the integration interval of the t ($-\infty, \infty$), these sample points can be expressed as: $t_n = 2\pi(n - 1 - N/2)/NT, n = 1, \cdots, N$, then the above fornula (1) may be converted into

$$f(x_n) = \frac{1}{NT} \sum_{i=1}^{N} \varphi(t_n) e^{-it_n \cdot x_n}, n = 1, \cdots, N \qquad (4)$$

Use the MATLAB emulator IFFT method can approximately calculated the probability density of each point of the SαS model.

Ⅳ Fitting of Several Distribution and Jpeg Image AC Coefficient

This article take the goodness-of-fit test of the probability distribution of is the Kolmogorov-Smirnov (KS) test. KS test statistic t is defined as follows:

$$t = \max_{i=1,2,\cdots,M} |F_X(x_i) - F(x_i)|$$

Sample distribution function is defined as:

$$F_x(z) \begin{cases} 0, z < x_{(1)} \\ \frac{n}{M}, x(n) \leq z < x_{n+1}, n = 1,2,\cdots,M | -1, X(n), n = 1,\cdots,M \\ 1, z \geq x_{(M)} \end{cases}$$

We selected 2000 pieces of the original photo from 11 kinds of camera, using KS test to measure the fitting degree between the AC coefficients distribution curve and a typical statistical distribution curve. The experiment results show that the fitting degree of the AC coefficients between with laplace distribution and stable distribution differ not quite, while differ less between the AC coefficients and GGD. Table 1 lists the KS fitting degree of the AC coefficients between with laplace distribtuion, stable distribution and GGD of the 3 original photos shown in Figure 2. But previous literature, however, considered the stable distribution is more suitable for medium and low frequency AC coefficients. In order to achieve the low frequency AC coefficients and the statistical distribution curve fitting, We remove the AC coefficients value of 0, 1, - 1, and then use the KS test to measure the fitting degree between the AC coefficients distribution curve and a typical statistical distribution curve. The experiment informed that the stable distribution has the minimum fit with the low-frequency AC coefficients. Table 2 lists the KS fitting degree of the low frequency AC coefficients between with laplace distribution, stable distribution and GGD of the 3 original photos shown in Figure 2.

(a)

(b)

(c)

Figure 2. Three original pictures

TABLE I. KS GOODNESS FIT OF AC COEFFICIENTS OF THE PICTURES OF FIGURE 2

Classic statistic model	(a)	(b)	(c)
Laplace	0.433341	0.567229	0.324662
GGD	0.030686	0.005451	0.034217
$S\alpha S$	0.485935	0.70937	0.378011

TABLE II. KS GOODN ESS FIT OF THE LOW FREQ UENCY AC COEFFICIENTS OF THE PICTURES OF FIGURE2

Classic statistic model	(a)	(b)	(c)
Laplace	0.047112	0.071934	0.044283
GGD	0.020781	0.00268	0.022596
$S\alpha S$	0.019069	0.001845	0.021064

Ⅴ The Impact of the Common Tampering Operations on the Statistical Characteristics of the AC Coefficients

A. Re-compression of JPEG images

During compression, the JPEG image usually choose a quality factor Q for compression, greater Q, the smaller compression ratio, the more image details of reservations, on the contrary, smaller Q, greater compression ratio, the smaller image detail information retained.

As shown in Figure 3, the first step of general JPEG image tampering operations is jpeg image decompression, and then modify the image on the pixel level, and then compressed into a new jpeg image, at this time, if the gap between jpeg image compression quality factor Q^2 and the camera compression quality factor Q^1 which used when the image initially generated is relatively large, it will affect the statistical characteristics of the AC coefficients, and if with little difference, then the statistical characterustics of the AC coefficients in jpeg images will not change significantly.

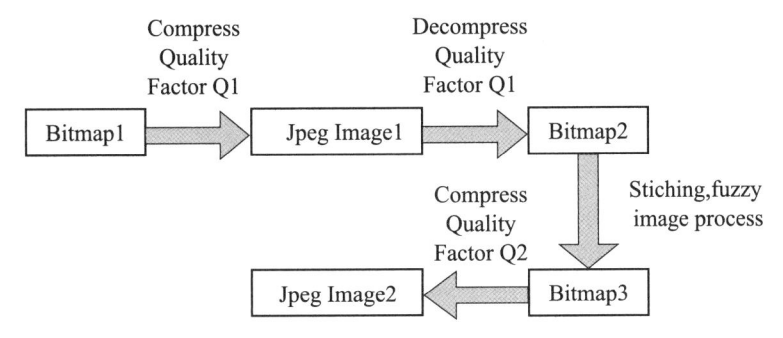

Figure 3. General jpeg image tampering process

Experiment found that the α parameter of the best fit between the AC coefficients in the original image of the Canon IXUS 950 IS camera and the stable distribution stabilized in a range of values, and the α parameter of the image which is re-compression by quality factor 95 is closest to the α parameter of the original image, while the others are deviated from the α parameter of the original image, and the trend is that the quality factor and 95 differ bigger, the α parameter deviated from farther, as shown in Figure 4. We can use the opencv tools to read the Canon IXUS 950 IS model camera raw image quality factor of about 98, which also verified before saying. We respectively select 100 images of 20 different models of cameras from the image library to do the above experiment, found still meet the above-mentioned law, but the α parameters for each model camera raw images will vary.

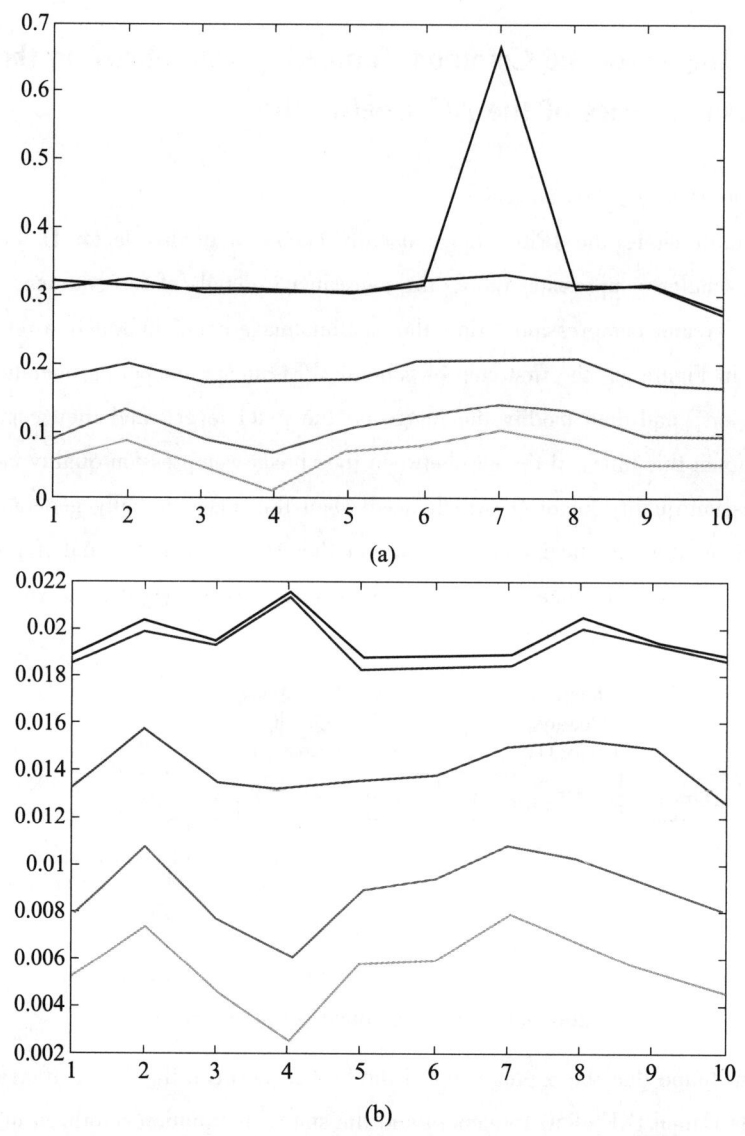

Figure 4. The α parameter and the ks degree of the best fit between the AC coefficients and the stable distribution of the images which are 10 original images of Canon IXUS 950 IS camera models re – compressed by different compression factor Q ((a) represents the α parameter, (b) represents the ks degree; The red represents 10 Original α parameter curve, the green represents the quality factor of 95, the blue represents the quality factor of 90, the yellow represents the quality factor of 80, black represents the quality factor of 70. In this paper, we used the ACDSee6.0 Software to re – compressed.)

B. Image blur

In image processing, in order to remove noise or smooth details, usually need the image obfuscation. Because the image noise and detail information is usually stored in the high – frequency component of the image, so the image blur operation will cause the high – frequency component attenuation, AC coefficient closer to 0, the probability density curve becomes sharp, and the corresponding parameter α becomes smaller, as shown in Figure 5.

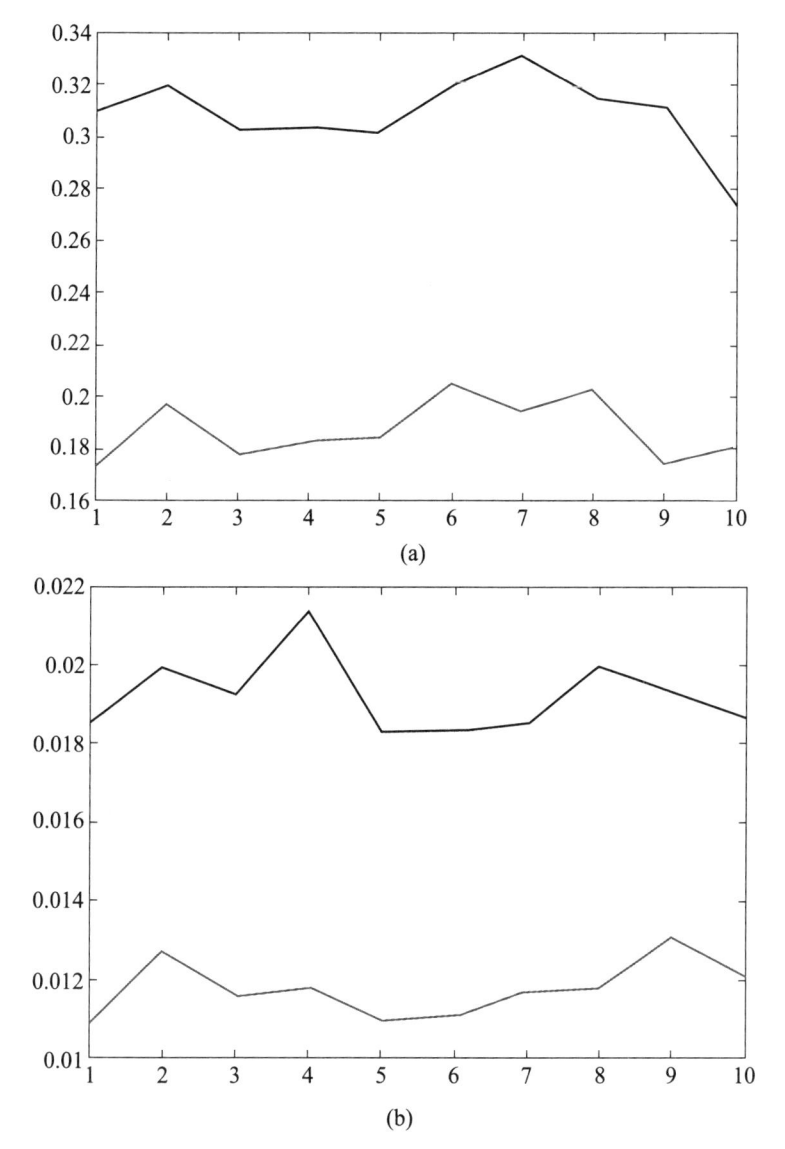

Figure 5. The contrast of the α parameter and the ks degree of 10 original images of Canon IXUS 950 IS and of the images which are 10 original images after the global fuzzy operation and recompressed by the quality factor of 95. ((a) represents the α parameter, (b) represents the ks degree; the red represents the original images, the green represents the images have been tampered. In this paper, we used the ACDSee6.0 Software to image blur).

C. Image sharpening

The purpose of the image sharpening process is to make the edges of the image, the contour lines as well as the details of the image becomes clear, the fundamental reason for the images become fuzzy after the smoothed is that the images are average or integral calculation, and therefore its inverse operation (differential operation) can make the image becomes clear. From the frequency domain to consider, the substance of the image blur is that its high frequency component is attenuated, thus the image sharpening operation substantially enhances the high-frequency component of the original image. And after sharpening processing of the image reflected in spatial domain is the AC coefficient probability density curve becomes smooth and the parameter α corresponding become large, as shown in Figure 6.

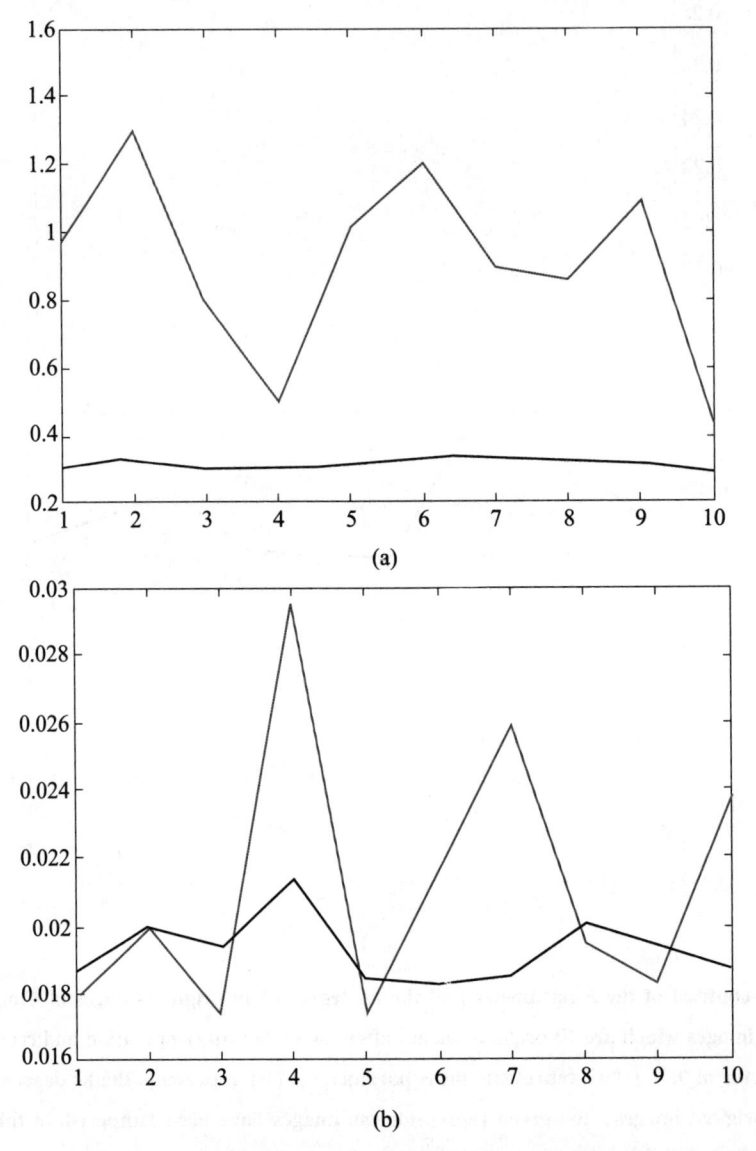

Figure 6. The contrast of the α parameter and the ks degree of 10 original images of Canon IXUS 950 IS and of the images which are 10 original images after the global sharpening operation and recompressed by the quality factor of 95. ((a) represents the α parameter, (b) represents the ks degree; the red represents the original images, the green represents the images have been tampered. In this paper, we used the ACDSee6.0 Software to image sharpening).

Ⅵ Image Tamper Detection Method Based on DCT Coefficients Model and Detection Result

We can see from the last chapter, the global fuzzy operation will cause the α parameter of images smaller, global sharpening will cause the α parameter larger, while the secondary compressing operation will also cause the α parameter of the image becomes larger or smaller, thus, the discrimination of the image tampering based on the image α parameters become the next step.

In the image tampering type detection, because the last process of image tampering operation usually have the re-compression process, the image tampering type detection must first identify detected whether the image after re-compression process, if the α parameter deviate from the normal range, then recompress the image to be detected by the camera image quality factor, if the re-compression of the image after coefficient still deviates from the normal range, then the image to be seized is after the recompression operation. If the image to be detected is not through the re-compression operation, and its α parameter is smaller than the normal, then determine it after the global fuzzy or other cause DCT coefficients model become lanky tampering types of operations; Conversely, if its α parameter is bigger than the normal, then determine it after the global sharpening or other cause DCT coefficients model become flat tampering types of operations.

In this paper, using the α parameter and the ks degree of the image as characteristic parameters, using the SVM vector machine as classifier, select the Canon IXUS 950 IS model camera raw image, global blur and sharpen global each 30 images as training samples, detecting the same camera model but different photographs of the original image, the images after global fuzzy and global sharpening each 50 samples, the test results for the global blur: the false alarm rate of 6%, undetected rate of 8%; global sharpening: the false alarm rate is 4%, the the undetected rate was 10%.

Ⅶ Conclusion

In sum, compared to the other common distribution, the stable distribution fit better with the low frequency AC coefficients, and can better reflect the true situation of the low frequency AC coefficients distribution in the image. At the same time, when use and the fitting degree to reflect the image tampering of the same model camera image, it show good regularity. Therefore, in discussing the JPEG detection of common types, the α parameter of the best fit between the AC coefficients and the stable distribution can be used as the discriminant features. In the actual operation, it is possible to build a database, storing the characteristic value ranges of the different tamper operations of the different camera's images, for the image to be detected, computing the eigenvalues and then comparing with the values in the database, the output corresponding type of tampering is the estimated type of image tampering.

Acknowledgements

This work is supported by

National Natural Science Foundation of China (61003284), Beijing Natural Science Foundation (4122053) and Digital copyright protection technology research and development projects (GXTC-CZ-1015004/09, GXTC-CZ-1015004/15-1)

References

[1] Reininger R, Gibson J. Distribution of the two-dimensional DCT coefficients for images, IEEE Trans. Commun, vol. COM-31, June 1983, pp. 835-839.

[2] Muller F. Distribution shape of two-dimensional DCT coefficients of natural images, Electron. Letter., vol. 29, no. 22, Oct. 1993, pp. 1935-1936.

[3] Jos hi RL, Fischer T R. Comparison of generalized Gaussian and Laplacian modeling in DCT image coding, IEEE Signal Processing Letters, vol. 2, no. 5, 1995, pp. 81-82.

[4] Hernandez J. R., Amado M., and Perez-Gonzalez F., DCT-domain water-marking techniquesfor still images: Detector performance analysis and a new structure [J], IEEE Trans cation on Image Process., 2000, 9: 55-68

[5] Birney K. A. and Fischer T. R., On the modeling of DCT and subband image data for compression [J], IEEE Trans. Image Process., 1995, 4 (2): 186-193

[6] Hernandez J. R., Amado M., and Perez-Gonzalez F., DCT-domain water-marking techniquesfor still images: Detector performance analysis and a new structure [J], IEEE Trans cation on Image Process., 2000, 9: 55-68

[7] Adler R., Feldman R., and Taqqu M. S., A Guide to Heavy Tails: Statistical Techniques and Applications [M]. Boston, MA: Birkhauser, 1998

[8] Alexia Briassouli, Panagiotis Tsakalides, Athanasios Stouraitis. Hidden Messages in Heavy-Tails: DCT-Domain Watermark Detection Using Alpha-stable Models. IEEE Transactions on Multimedia. VOL. 7. NO. 4. August 2005. pp700-714.

[9] Cao Jian Wen, Qiu Tian Shuang. The Study on the Dynamic Parameter Estimation of Stable Distribution., Dalian University of Technology, 2005

[10] Mao Jia Fa, Lin Jia Jun. Research of Universal Hidden Information Detecting Based on the Cover Image Describing. Huazhong University of Science & Technology, 2008

[11] Lv Xiao Rui, Huang Rui Guang. Model Simulation and Parameter Estimation of Alpha Stable Distribution., Huazhong University of Science & Technology, 2008

Homomorphic Encryption Based Data Storage and Query Algorithm*

Chunyun Di   Chenlei Cao   Ru Zhang   Jianyi Liu

Introduction

With the rapid development of the Internet as well as the arrival of data intensive society, cloud computing and related technologies attract more and more attention. Cloud computing combines the resources on the Internet as a unified entity, providing users with powerful computing resources and adequate storage space. While users enjoy the services provided by the cloud, they don't need to care the process about data computing, storage and management on the cloud. Large-scale data is migrated from the user client to the cloud storage server, which greatly reducing the user's burden about data management.

However, once the data stored on the cloud server, the user won't restrict the unauthorized operation from the cloud system. To protect data security, users store the data in encrypted form on the cloud. Although ciphertext storage improves security, it complicates the process of data query quickly.

To solve the above problems, this paper proposes a ciphertext query algorithm according to the multiplication homomorphic encryption characteristic of RSA. On this basis, this paper sorts and displays the ciphertext query result efficiently by using the calculation method of the ciphertext similarity, which is the combination of inclined angle's cosine of vector, vector's mapping length and words' weight.

Related Work

In the ciphertext retrieving field, the main solutions are as follows: linear search algorithm, secure index method, public key encryption with keyword search and homomorphic encryption technology.

In terms of linear search, Song et al. [1] proposed the linear retrieving algorithm, encrypt-

---

* 本文选自 Advanced Materials Research Vols. 846 – 847 (2014), 第 1582 – 1589 页

ing every word in the file. This algorithm has the features as follows: simple, quick, flexible, extensible and better resistance to statistic analysis.

Goh et al. [2] proposed a method called secure index. Secure index is a data structure, which only needs O (1) time complexity to search a word by "threshold" and is a more secure ciphertext retrieval method. Curtmola et al. [3] proposed an encryption retrieval method of adaptive security definition, which resolved the problem of attackers referred to the search results to generate retrieving operation in [2].

In the field of public key encryption with keyword search, Boneh et al. proposed a public key encryption with keyword search algorithm (PEKS) in [4], which enables the email server to return all the information that contains the query keywords to user without knowing any secret information. This method uses public key encryption algorithm to encrypt data, and enhances the security. It also solves the problem of key distribution. However, PEKS has some problems like low encryption and decryption efficiency, low retrieval efficiency, complex computation, high consuming of CPU and client memory, and not applicable to search for multiple keywords. Qin Liuy et al. proposed an efficient privacy preserving keyword search scheme (EPPKS) and a secure and privacy preserving keyword searching method (SPKS) in [5] and [6], and further addressed the problems of PEKS.

The homomorphic encryption algorithm gets great concern in recent years. It was proposed by Rivest et al. in [7] in 1978. The homomorphic characteristic of the algorithm ensures the computing on encrypted data without leaking data information. Later on, Sander and Tschudin proposed an addition and multiplication homomorphic encryption schemes over the integer ring in [8]. Then Gentry first announced the fully homomorphic encryption [9] using ideal lattice in 2009, and studied in detail in [10]. Among the existing encryption algorithm, RSA and ElGamal encryption algorithm possess the characteristic of multiplication homomorphic, and Paillier encryption algorithm has the characteristic of addition homomorphic [11].

This paper proposes a ciphertext query algorithm according to the multiplication homomorphic encryption characteristic of RSA. On receiving the ciphertext query item and the number of matching elements, the algorithm queries the ciphertext data and returns query result. To efficiently sort the query result, this paper proposes a similarity calculation method after fully considering the importance of inclined angle's cosine of vector, vector's mapping length and words' weight on data sorting.

System Architecture and Algorithm Designing

A. Data storage and query architecture

The architecture for ciphertext data storage and query in this paper is shown in Figure 1, the architecture consists of three components: a data owner, a data user and cloud storage server.

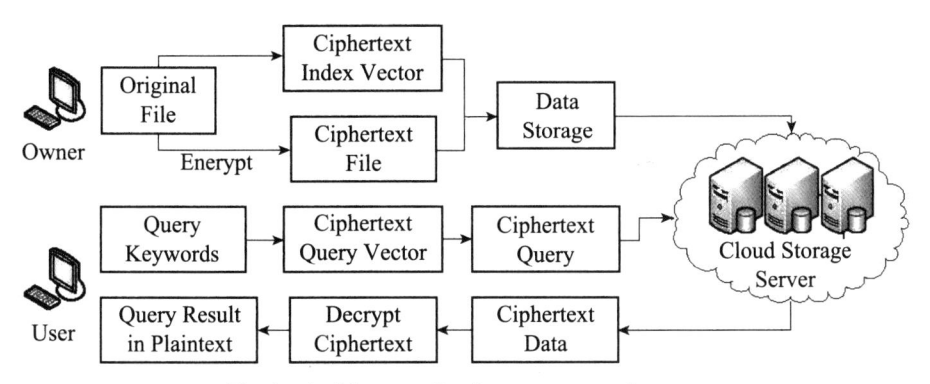

Fig. 1. Architecture for data storage and query

The data owner is responsible for the encryption of original data and the generation of the ciphertext index vector. When user performs data query operation, the user generates the ciphertext query vector, and sends the query vector and other relevant information to the cloud server for ciphertext query. The cloud server calculates and processes the ciphertext in accordance with the query conditions, and returns ciphertext query result to the user. On receiving the ciphertext query result, the user decrypts the ciphertext data and displays the plaintext data query result to user.

B. Ciphertext storage method

In order to describe the proposed algorithm in detail, this paper first gives the following definitions:

Definition 1. Index vector I_i. I_i represents the ciphertext index vector of plaintext file D_i: $I_i = ((i_{i1}, w_{i1})(i_{i2}, w_{i2}), (i_{in}, w_{in}))$, i_{ik} is the Kth ciphertext index element, and w_{ik} represents the weight of the Kth element in ciphertext index.

Definition 2. Index element frequency $tf_{ik} = f_{ik} / \sum_{j=1}^{n} f_{ij}$. tf_{ik} represents the frequency [12] of the element in I_i. f_{ik} is the number of occurrences of the index element in the file.

Definition 3. Inverted index frequency idf. idf reflects the importance of index elements in the file dataset. The typical form is as follows [12]: $idf_k = \log(N/n_k)$. N is the number of the file in the dataset, n_k is the number of file in which the index element appeared.

Definition 4. Weight. According to the typical weight of file [12], the weight of index elements can be designed as follows: $w_{ik} = \dfrac{(\log(f_{ik}) + 1) \cdot \log(N/n_k)}{\sqrt{\sum_{k=1}^{n}[(\log(f_{ik}) + 1) \cdot \log(N/n_k)]^2}}$

Definition 5. Query vector Q. $Q = (q_1, q_2, \cdots, q_t)$, q_k is the Kth query element. Every query element has the same importance in query vector.

Method 1. Ciphertext data storage.

Step 1. Generate ciphertext index vector:

Firstly, data owner generates plaintext keywords, and calculates the weight w_{ij} of the keywords in the current file. Secondly, data owner encrypts each plaintext keywords by RSA encryption algorithm with key $PK = (e, n)$, and then generates the ciphertext index vector: $I_i = ((i_{i1}, w_{i1}) (i_{i2}, w_{i2}) \cdots, (i_{in}, w_{in}))$.

Step 2. Encrypt original data by symmetric encryption algorithm.

Step 3. Associate the ciphertext query vector with ciphertext for data query.

Step 4. Send ciphertext index vector and ciphertext data to the cloud storage server for storage.

C. Ciphertext query method

The method of ciphertext query uses the multiplication homomorphic characteristic of RSA public key encryption algorithm.

Encrypt two plaintext data m_1 and m_2 with the public key (e, n). $E(\cdot)$ means the encryption.

$c_1 = E(m_1) \equiv m_1^e \bmod n$; $c_2 = E(m_2) \equiv m_2^e \bmod n$.

Ciphertext c_1 and c_2 meet the following operations:

$c_1 \otimes c_2 = (m_1^e \bmod n) \otimes (m_2^e \bmod n) = (m_1^e \cdot m_2^e) \bmod n = (m_1 m_2)^e \bmod n = E(m_1 m_2)$

$E(m_1) \otimes E(m_2) = E(m_1 m_2)$. We can come to the conclusion that RSA public key encryption algorithm has the homomorphic multiplication characteristic.

Algorithm 1. Ciphertext query algorithm. Data user queries ciphertext data that is stored in the cloud server. The specific steps are as follows:

Step 1. Data user extracts query keywords, and generates the query vector Q. Q includes three query elements q_1, q_2, q_3, and $Q = (q_1, q_2, q_3)$.

Step 2. Data user uses the owner's public key (e, n) to process query elements, and obtains ciphertext query item Cq_i. Ciphertext query item contains three elements: $Cq_3 = (\prod_{i=1}^{3} q_i)^e \bmod n$, two elements: $Cq_2 = (q_i \cdot q_j)^e \bmod n$, $1 \leq i, j \leq 3$, $i \neq j$, and one element: $Cq_1 = (q_i)^e \bmod n$, $1 \leq i \leq 3$. Send the ciphertext query item and the number of elements to cloud server for query.

Step 3. Cloud server queries and matches data according to the information sent by the user. The specific steps are as follows: (a) According to the number of elements, cloud server randomly takes k elements from ciphertext index vector I_i for multiplication, and obtains Im_k, $Im_k = i_{ix} \otimes i_{iy} \otimes \cdots \otimes i_{iz}$. i_{ix}, i_{iy}, i_{iz} denote the Xth, Yth and Zth element of ciphertext index vector. Take k = 3 as an example, $Im_3 = i_{ix} \otimes i_{iy} \otimes i_{iz}$, x, y, z are different from each other.

(b) Compare the ciphertext query item Cq_3 with Im_3 and get flag.

(c) If $Cq_3 = Im_3$, flag = 1, cloud server returns the ciphertext index element's weight and other relevant information to compute similarity. Otherwise, flag = 0, Cq_3 does not match with Im_3 cloud server does not return data.

Similarly, this paper can query the ciphertext data which is matched with any k elements of the query vector, and get the weight of matched index elements.

D. Query result sorting method

This paper sorts the query result effectively by calculating the similarity between ciphertext index vector and query vector.

Similarity, refers to the level of relevance between two files. The common method is to calculate the inclined angle's cosine of vectors. The smaller inclined angle is, the higher the similarity is.

This paper proposes a similarity calculation method after fully considering the importance of inclined angle's cosine of vector, vector's mapping length and words' weight on data sorting, and achieves the efficient sort of query result. For a detailed description of the implementation process of the similarity algorithm, this paper gives the following definitions.

Definition 6. The inclined angle's cosine of vectors, refers to the inclined angle's cosine of query vector and index vector. Query vector $Q = (q_1, q_2, \cdots, q_t)$ includes t query elements. The space coordinates value of Q is $(1/\sqrt{t}, 1/\sqrt{t}, \cdots, 1/\sqrt{t})$ after the normalization processing. Index vector I_i includes n index elements. For vector I_i, first, sets the position of index element which matches with the query element of Q is 1, otherwise 0. If the query vector Q has k elements matching with the index elements of I_i, we can obtain the following space coordinates value of I_i after normalization processing: $(\underbrace{1/\sqrt{n}, 1/\sqrt{n}, \cdots, 1/\sqrt{n}}_{k}, \underbrace{0, 0, \cdots, 0}_{n-k})$. The cosine value of vector I_i and Q is:

$$\cos\theta_i = \cos(I_i, Q) = \frac{\sum_{j=1}^{k}(1/\sqrt{t}) \cdot (1/\sqrt{n})}{\sqrt{\sum_{j=1}^{k}(1/\sqrt{n})^2} \cdot \sqrt{\sum_{j=1}^{k}(1/\sqrt{t})^2}} = \frac{\frac{k}{t \cdot n}}{\sqrt{\frac{k}{n} \cdot 1}} = \sqrt{\frac{k}{t}} \quad (1)$$

The greater the inclined angle's cosine is, the closer query vector is to index vector.

Definition 7. Total query weight TW_i. If the query vector Q has k query elements matching with the index elements of I_i, TW_i is set to be the sum of the weight of elements in I_i, which match with query elements in Q. The representation is as follows:

$$TW_i = \sum_{j=1}^{k} w_{ij} \quad (2)$$

Under the same conditions, the greater the total query weight is, the higher the degree of matching between the query vector and index vector is.

Definition 8. Matching length, is the mapping length of the index vector on the query vector, as shown in figure 2.

Matching length can be expressed as follows: $L_i = |I_i| \cdot \cos\theta_i$. $\cos\theta_i$ is the inclined angle θ_i's cosine of vectors. $|\cdot|$ refers the size of a set. $|I_i|$ is the size of the index vector I_i. $|Q|$ is the size of the query vector Q.

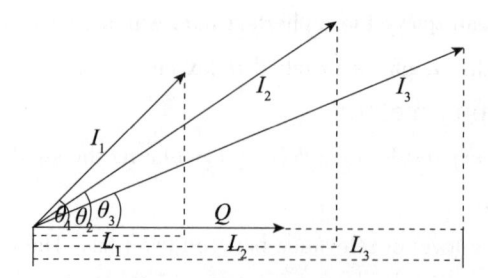

Fig. 2 Matching length

Definition 9. Matching distance $dist_i$. The representation of matching distance is as follows:

$$dist_i = \begin{cases} L_i - |Q|, & L_i \geq |Q| \\ |Q| - L_i + |I_{max}|, & L_i < |Q| \end{cases} \quad (3)$$

The reason of adding $|I_{max}|$ while $L_i \leq |Q|$ is that it is easier to find the matching index elements under the condition of $L_i > |Q|$.

The smaller the matching distance is, the closer query vector is to index vector, and the higher the degree of matching between the query vector and index vector is.

Algorithm 2. The method of calculating similarity between query vector and index vector I_i can be expressed as follows:

$$Sim_i = \cos^2\theta_i \cdot \left(1 + \frac{1}{dist_i + 1}\right) \cdot TW_i \quad (4)$$

The reasons that this paper uses $\cos^2\theta_i$ in the method of calculating similarity are: (1) to enlarge the importance of inclined angle of vectors in similarity calculation; (2) to increase the difference value of similarity between different index vectors; The larger the difference value between Sim_i is, the easier to sort query result.

The smaller $dist_i$ is, the closer the index vector is to query vector. $dist_i$ is counterproductive to Sim_i, so this paper uses the reciprocal of $dist_i$ in calculating Sim_i. Why this paper uses the reciprocal of $(dist_i + 1)$ in similarity calculation method is because: (1) to ensure that the calculation is still meaningful while $dist_i = 0$; (2) to avoid the reciprocal of $dist_i$ tending to infinity while $dist_i \xrightarrow{\infty} 0$. Additionally, using $\left(1 + \frac{1}{dist_i + 1}\right)$ is because "1" is the original coefficient of algorithm, and it indicates the effect of $dist_i$ based on the original data. It reflects the counterproductive of $dist_i$ to Sim_i.

Now, take an example to illustrate the similarity calculation.

Example 1. Suppose the index vectors of three file D_1, D_2 and D_3, which are queried by query vector $Q = (q_1, q_2, q_3)$, are in the form of: $I_1 = ((i_{11}, 0.5), (i_{12}, 0.8), (i_{13}, 0.3), (i_{14}, 0.1))$, $I_2 = ((i_{21}, 0.9), (i_{22}, 0.4), (i_{23}, 0.2), (i_{24}, 0.6), (i_{25}, 0.3))$ and $I_3 = ((i_{31}, 0.9), (i_{32}, 0.5), (i_{33}, 0.1))$. q_1 and q_2 match with i_{11} and i_{12} of I_1, q_1, q_2 and q_3 match with i_{21}, i_{22} and i_{23} of I_2, q_2 and q_3 match with i_{31} and i_{32} of

I_3. According to the given data and formulas (1) to (4) we can obtain the data as shown in Table 1. The first column indicates the subscript of the index vector I_i which matches the query vector. The second to the fifth column are the inclined angle's cosine, matching distance, total query weight and similarity value respectively.

Table 1 Similarity calculation table

i	cosine	matching distance	total weight	similarity
1	0.816	0.266	1.3	1.551
2	1	2	1.5	2
3	0.816	5.551	1.4	1.076

The above table shows that the similarity between query vector Q and index vector I_2 is the highest, so it should be ranked first when returned by query result; The similarity between Q and I_3 is the smallest, so it should be ranked last while returning query result;

With Method 1, Algorithm 1 and Algorithm 2 proposed above, this paper describes how to create ciphertext index vector, how to query ciphertext by using the multiplication homomorphic encryption characteristic of RSA, and how to calculate the similarity method to sort data results.

System Implementation and Statistics Analysis

A. System implementation

This paper designs and implements a test system for ciphertext data storage, query and sort according to system architecture in Figure 1, Method 1, Algorithm 1 and Algorithm 2.

In the test system, the server hardware runtime environment is as follows: Intel (R) Core (TM) i7-3770 CPU@ 3.40GHz, 8.00GB memory. The server software operating environment is: Windows 7 and Web-logic 12C. The development languages are Java and SQL. The development environment includes Spring 3.1, Java JDK 1.7 and some third party open source architecture.

This system implements the encryption of sensitive data, extraction and generation of the ciphertext index vector on the data owner client. In the implementation process, this paper uses AES-128 as the original file encryption algorithm and RSA -1024 as the keywords encryption algorithm. After receiving the ciphertext query information from data user, the cloud server queries ciphertext according to the query condition and returns the corresponding data. Thus the system simulates the cloud-oriented ciphertext data storage and query services.

B. Statistics analysis

In order to test feasibility and rationality of the proposed ciphertext query algorithm, this paper compares the ciphertext query item with ciphertext index vector according to the multiplication homomorphic encryption characteristic of RSA, using the ciphertext data query time. This paper uses RSA-1024 bits public key as the encryption key, taking both Chinese phrases and English phrases as query elements and plaintext index elements for testing. To illustrate the algorithm performance, this paper gives the following definition:

Definition 10. Ciphertext query time T_q. From the moment that the server receives query condition to the time the server finds the matching data.

In order to test the indicator in Definition 10, This paper takes Q = {"Lincoln", "president", "declaration"} as query vector, CI10, CI20, CI30, CI50 CI60, CI70, CI80, CI90 and CI100, which contain 10, 20, 30, 50, 60, 70, 80, 90 and 100 index elements, as ciphertext index vector. The specific steps are as shown in Algorithm 1. We can obtain the statistics results as shown in Table 2. The first row in Table 2 is the number of matching elements, the first column is the number of index elements, the unit of query time is milliseconds (ms).

Table 2 Ciphertext query time

(ms)	0	1	2	3
10	0	6	16	15
20	0	4	32	21
30	0	4	40	39
50	3	3	62	56
60	3	3	81	68
70	3	3	102	86
80	3	3	116	102
90	3	3	132	128
100	3	3	160	156

The graphical representation of the test result is as shown in Figure 3. The abscissa in Figure 3 represents the number of ciphertext index elements, and the ordinate is the ciphertext query time T_q. T3 is the query time which matches three elements of query vector; T2 is the query time which matches two elements; T1 is the query time which matches one element; T0 represents the query time which does not match with query vector. In addition, T4 is the plaintext query time.

From Table 2 and Figure 3, we know that the more index elements are, the larger the T_q is, while the matching element is greater than 1. Moreover, T2 > T3 is because the more the combinations of elements are, the larger the T_q is. For three query elements and 100 index elements, the maximum query time. $T_{max} \leqslant 160ms$. The ciphertext query time basically meets the needs of user.

T4 is larger than T0 and T1 when the number of matching elements are 0 and 1. This is because the ciphertext query directly calculates the numerical value, and the plaintext query should deal with string. T2 and T3 is larger than T4 when the number of matching elements are 2 and 3. This is because the ciphertext query have to multiply each of the two or three elements of ciphertext index vector first, and this process is time-consuming.

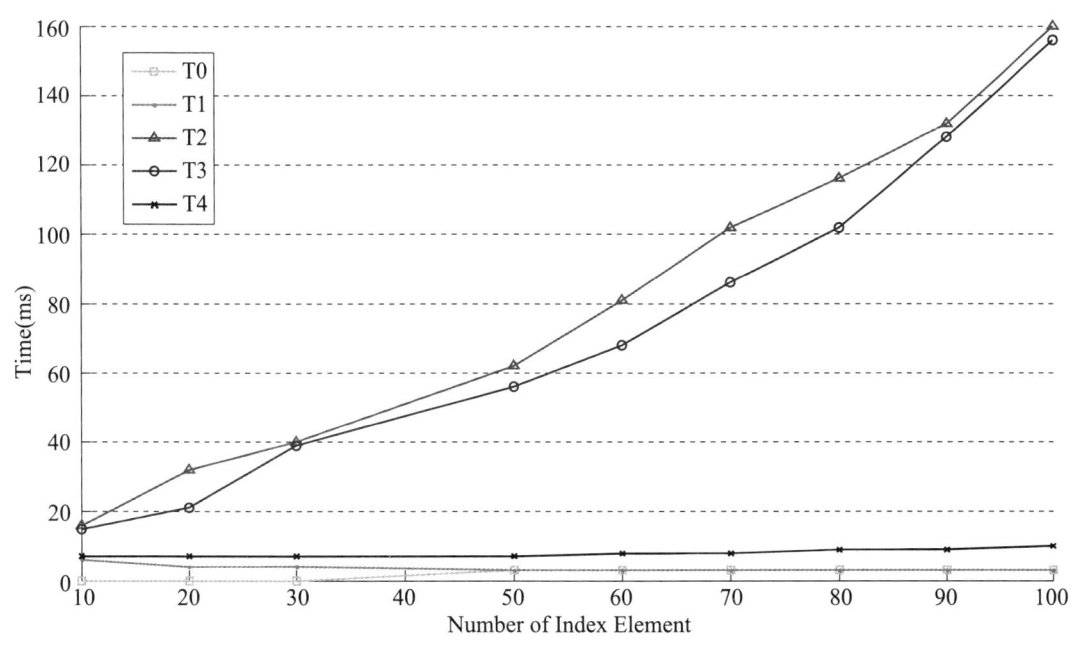

Fig. 3 Ciphertext query time

Conclusion

In this paper, the ciphertext data storage and query algorithm consists of three parts: the generation and storage of ciphertext data, the query of ciphertext, and the sort of query result. Data owner generates ciphertext index vector by the RSA public key encryption algorithm and stores the corresponding data. After receiving the ciphertext data query conditions from data user, the cloud server queries ciphertext data according to the multiplication homomorphic encryption characteristic of RSA. This method queries ciphertext data without decrypting data. So it reduces the decryption overhead and improves the computing performance. Besides, it strengthens the anti-attack capability of the algorithm. This paper gets the similarity value by calculating the inclined angle's cosine of vector, vector's mapping length and words' weight, and sorts the query result according to the similarity value. Finally, the ciphertext query time is evaluated in a lab environment. The more index elements and combinations of index elements are, the more query time is consumed. The test result shows that the algorithm is highly secured and the query time is acceptable to users.

To gradually increase the availability and security of the system, We will make improvements from the following two aspects in the future. Firstly, improve the execution efficiency and query accuracy of the query algorithm; secondly, develop more secure and efficient access control policy during the data storage process, and implement real-name ciphertext data storage in combination with the method given in literature [13].

Acknowledgement

This work was collaboratively supported in part with funds from: 1. Beijing Natural Science Foundation's project (90604022) (4122053). 2. National Natural Science Foundation's project (61003284). 3. Fundamental Research Funds for the Central Universities (2013RC0310). 4. Press Publication Major Science and Technology Engineering Project (GXTC-CZ-1015004/09) (GXTC-CZ-1015004/15-1). 5. National Key Technology Research and Development Program (2012BAH08B02). 6. National 863 Program (2012AA012606).

References

[1] D. Song, D. Wagner, and A. Perrig. Practical techniques for searches on encrypted data. in Proc. of the IEEE Symposium on Security and Privacy' 00. 2000. pp. 44 – 55.

[2] E. Goh. Secure indexes. in Cryptology ePrint Archive. Report 2003/216. 2003.

[3] R. Curtmola, J. Garay, S. Kamara, and R. Ostrovsky. Searchable symmetric encryption: Improved definitions and efficient constructions. in Cryptology ePrint Archive. Report 2006/210. 2006.

[4] Boneh D, Crescenzo G, Ostrovsky R, Persiano G. Public key encryption with keyword search. In: Cachin C, Camenisch J, eds. LNCS 3027. Heidelberg: Springer-Verlag. 2004. 506 – 522.

[5] Qin Liuy, Guojun Wang, and Jie Wuz. An Efficient Privacy Preserving Keyword Search Scheme in Cloud Computing. In: Computational Science and Engineering, 2009. CSE '09. International Conference on (Volume: 2). Aug. 2009. 715 – 720.

[6] Qin Liuy, Guojun Wang, and Jie Wuz. Secure and privacy preserving keyword searching for cloud storage services. appear in Journal of Network and Computer Applications. 9 March 2011.

[7] Rivest R L, Adleman L M, and Dertouzos M L. On Data Banks and Privacy Homomorphisms. in: Foundations of Secure Computation. 1978, pp. 169 – 178.

[8] T. Sander and C. Tschudin. Towards mobile cryptography. In Proceedings of the IEEE Symposium on Security and Privacy. Oakland, CA, 1998. IEEE Computer Society Press.

[9] Gentry C. Fully homomorphic encryption using ideal lattices [C]. // Proceedings of 41st ACM Symposium on Theory of Computing (STOC 09), ACM press, New York, 2009: 169 – 178.

[10] Gentry C. A fully homomorphic encryption scheme [D/OL]. Stanford University, 2009. http://crypto.stanford.edu/craig.

[11] Shidou Yan, Nian Liu, Zichen Li. The homomorphism analysis of public key cryptosystem. Journal of Beijing Elrctronin Science and Technology Institute. June 2012.

[12] Written by W. Bruce Croft, Donald Metzler, Trevor Strohman, translated by Ting liu, Bing Qin. Search engines information retrieval in practice. China Machine Press.

[13] Chenlei Cao, Ru Zhang, Mengyi Zhang, Yixian Yang. IBC-based entity authentication protocols for federated cloud systems. (identity-based cryptography) (Report). KSII Transactions on Internet and Information Systems, May 1, 2013.

高效的选择密文安全的单向代理重加密方案*

张维纬　张茹　刘建毅　钮心忻　杨义先

1　引言

在1998年的欧洲密码学年会上，Blaze等[1]首次提出了代理重加密（PRE，proxy re-encryption）的概念，在一个代理重加密方案中，一个拥有转换密钥的半可信代理者可以把用Alice公钥加密的消息m所得的密文转换为用Bob公钥加密的消息m所得到的密文，但这个过程中半可信代理者不能获得关于消息m的任何信息。近年来，PRE在很多场合得到了应用，如加密电子邮件的转发[1]。此外，代理重加密还可以应用于分布式文件系统[2,3]、DRM互操作系统中内容加密密钥或多媒体内容的转换[4,5]、云环境中用户文件的加密和传感器网络中用户敏感数据的分类加密[6,7]等。

以分布式文件系统为例，Alice在不完全可信的服务器上存储了以其公钥加密的文件，允许它在指定的用户访问，但Alice可能无法在每次用户进行数据访问时都在线进行密文转换。采用代理重加密方案，Alice可以使用自己的私钥及指定用户的公钥计算一个重加密密钥，存储于代理服务器上，当用户访问文件时，服务器用相应的重加密密钥将密文重加密成可由用户私钥解密的密文。代理重加密方案的性质保证了代理服务器无法获得明文，也无法得知Alice与用户的私钥。

Blaze等[1]首次提出了双向PRE方案。Ateniese等[2]利用双线性配对构造了3种单向PRE方案，他们的PRE方案都只是在DBDH假设的标准模型下满足选择明文安全（CPA，chosen-plaintext attack）的。但实际的应用场合通常都要求密文满足选择密文安全（CCA，chosen-ciphertext attack）。Canetti等[8]首次利用CHK（canetti-halevi-katz methodology）[9]技术构造了一种在标准模型下满足CCA安全的双向多跳PRE方案，但是与Ateniese等[2]提出的双向PRE方案的缺点一样，该方案也不能抵抗共谋攻击。他们留下了一个公开的问题，即如何构造一个在标准模型下单向CCA安全的PRE方案。值得注意的是，构造一个单向PRE方案比双向PRE方案困难，因为任何双向的PRE方案都可以通过单向的PRE方案实现。Libert等[10]首次提出了一种在标准模型下能抵抗共谋攻击的单向PRE方案，该方案只满足重放选择密文安全（RCCA，replayable chosen ciphertext attack），RCCA安全级别

---

* 本文选自《通信学报》，第34卷第7期，2013年7月，第87−97页

比 CCA 低，因为 RCCA 安全模型中不允许敌手询问挑战明文的任何形式的密文解密预言机。Weng 等[11]利用 Hohenberger 等[12]所提出的签名方案中的一个技巧及借助伪随机函数族构造了一个标准模型下 CCA 安全的单向单跳的 PRE 方案。

上述文献［2，8，10，11］所提出的 PRE 方案都需要双线性配对运算，而运行一次双线性对运算的时间至少是椭圆曲线上点乘运算的 20 倍以上[13]。针对这个问题，有学者提出无需双线性配对运算构造的 PRE 方案[14,15]，但这些方案都是在随机预言模型下 CCA 安全的。正如 Canetti 等[16]指出的那样，存在这样的实际签名和加密方案，在随机预言模型中是安全的，但任何具体实现都是不安全的。

近年来，也有学者提出了基于身份的 PRE 方案[17,18]、基于关键词搜索的 PRE 方案[6,7]等。但如何在标准模型下构造一个高效的单向、单跳的 PRE 方案仍然是一个有待解决的重要问题。

本文使用 CHK 技术和随机填充技术构造了一种新的高效的单向、单跳 PRE 方案，并且在无需随机预言机的模型下证明了方案的 CCA 安全性。该方案只需要一次强签名函数以及单向、抗碰撞的散列函数。所提方案在安全性和运算效率方面都优于 LV 方案[10]，而在同等安全性条件下，运算效率优于 WJ 方案[11]。

2 预备知识

2.1 双线性配对

令群 $\mathbb{G}_1$ 和群 $\mathbb{G}_2$ 是 2 个乘法有限循环群，它们的阶为素数 p，双线性配对 $e: \mathbb{G}_1 \times \mathbb{G}_1 \to \mathbb{G}_2$ 满足如下条件。

（1）双线性：$\forall g, h \in \mathbb{G}_1, \forall a, b \in \mathbb{G}_p$，均有 $e(g^a, h^b) = e(g, h)^{ab}$ 成立。

（2）非退化性：存在 $g, h \in \mathbb{G}_1$，使 $e(g^a, h^b) \neq 1_{\mathbb{G}_2}$ 成立，其中，$1_{\mathbb{G}_2}$ 表示群 $\mathbb{G}_2$ 的单位元。

（3）可计算性：存在一个有效的算法使得对于 $\forall g, h \in \mathbb{G}_1$ 均可计算 $e(g, h)$。

2.2 复杂性假设

本方案的复杂性假设与文献［10，11］相同，即基于 3-弱判定型双线性迪菲-赫尔曼求逆（3-wDBDHI，3-weak decision bilinear Diffie-Hellman inversion）假设。即给定 $(g, g^a, g^{a^2}, g^{a^3}, g^b, Q) \in \mathbb{G}_1^5 \times \mathbb{G}_2$，其中，$a, b \in \mathbb{Z}_p^*$ 未知，判断 $Q = e(g, g)^{b/a}$ 是否成立。文献［10］已经证明，该问题也等价于给定 $(g, g^{1/a}, g^a, g^{a^2}, g^b, Q) \in \mathbb{G}_1^5 \times \mathbb{G}_2$，判断 $Q = e(g, g)^{b/a^2}$ 是否成立。

一个概率性多项式时间（PPT，probabilistic polynomial-time）算法 $\mathcal{B}$ 如果满足：

$$| \Pr[\mathcal{B}(g, g^{1/a}, g^a, g^{a^2}, g^b, Q = e(g, g)^{b/a^2}) = 1]$$
$$- \Pr[\mathcal{B}(g, g^{1/a}, g^a, g^{a^2}, g^b, Q = e(g, g)^c) = 1] | \geq \varepsilon$$

其中，$a, b, c \in \mathbb{Z}_p^*$，则称算法 $\mathcal{B}$ 能够以优势 ε 求解群 $(\mathbb{G}_1, \mathbb{G}_2)$ 中的 3-wDBDHI 问题。

若对于任意 t-时间的算法 $\mathcal{B}$，均无法以优势 ε 求解群 $(\mathbb{G}_1, \mathbb{G}_2)$ 中的 3-wDBDHI 问

题，则称群 ($\mathcal{G}_1$, $\mathcal{G}_2$) 中的 (t, ε) – 3 – wDBDHI 假设成立。

2.3 一次性强签名函数[10]

一次强签名函数 $Sig = (\mathcal{G}, \mathcal{S}, \mathcal{V})$ 包括 3 个算法，即密钥产生算法 $\mathcal{G}$、签名算法 $\mathcal{S}$ 和验证算法 $\mathcal{V}$。输入安全参数 k，密钥产生算法 $\mathcal{G}$ 输出密钥对 (svk, ssk)，对于消息 m，如果签名值为 $\sigma = \mathcal{S}(ssk, m)$，则验证函数 $\mathcal{V}(\sigma, svk, m)$ 输出 1，否则输出 0。

与文献 [8, 10] 一样，提出的方案也需要强的不可伪造的一次签名函数，即要求不存在 PPT 的敌手能够为签名的消息产生一个有效的新签名。

定义 1 $Sig = (\mathcal{G}, \mathcal{S}, \mathcal{V})$ 是一个强的一次签名函数，如果对于任何的 PPT 函数 $\mathcal{F}$，伪造签名值成功的概率 Adv^{SIG} 是可忽略的。此处 Adv^{SIG} 的定义为

$$Adv^{SIG} = \Pr[(ssk, svk) \leftarrow \mathcal{G}(1^k); (m, St) \leftarrow \mathcal{F}(svk);$$
$$\sigma \leftarrow \mathcal{S}(ssk, m); (m', \sigma') \leftarrow F(m, \sigma, svk, St):$$
$$\mathcal{V}(\sigma', svk, m') = 1 \wedge (m', \sigma') \neq (m, \sigma)]$$

其中，St 表示 $\mathcal{F}$ 的状态信息。

3 单向 PRE 的模型定义

3.1 单向 PRE 的定义

定义 2 一个单向单跳代理重加密方案包括如下算法。

Setup (1^k)：输入安全参数 1^k，系统参数产生函数输出一个全局公开参数 par。

KeyGen (par) → (pk, sk)：输入全局公开参数 par，密钥产生算法 KeyGen 输出公钥 pk 和私钥 sk。

Enc_2 (par, pk, m) → C：输入公钥 pk、明文 m 和全局公开参数 par，加密算法 Enc_2 输出第 2 层密文 C。

Enc_1 (par, pk, m) → C：输入公钥 pk、明文 m 和全局公开参数 par，加密算法 Enc_1 输出第 1 层密文 C。

ReKeyGen (par, sk_i, pk_j) → $rk_{i \to j}$：输入私钥 sk_i、公钥 pk_j 和全局公开参数 par，重加密密钥产生算法 ReKeyGen 输出重加密密钥 $rk_{i \to j}$。

ReEnc (par, $rk_{i \to j}$, C_i) → C_j：输入重加密密钥 $rk_{i \to j}$、密文 C_i 和全局公开参数 par，重加密算法 ReEnc 输出重加密密文 C_j 或者错误符号 ⊥。

Dec_2 (par, sk, C) → m：输入私钥 sk、第 2 层密文 C 和全局公开参数 par，解密算法 Dec_2 输出所对应的明文 m 或者错误符号 ⊥。

Dec_1 (par, sk, C) → m：输入私钥 sk 和第 1 层密文 C 和全局公开参数 par，解密算法 Dec_1 输出所对应的明文 m 或者错误符号 ⊥。

正确性：对于明文空间中的明文 m 和任意的两对公私钥对 (pk_i, sk_i), (pk_j, sk_j) ← KeyGen (1^k)，必须满足以下的条件：

$$Dec_1 (sk_i, Enc_1 (par, pk_i, m)) = m$$
$$Dec_2 (sk_i, Enc_2 (par, pk_i, m)) = m$$

$$\mathrm{Dec}_1\ (sk_j,\ \mathrm{ReEnc}\ (\mathrm{ReKeyGen}\ (par,\ sk_i,\ pk_j),$$
$$\mathrm{Enc}_2\ (par,\ pk_i,\ m)))\ =m$$

代理重加密算法应该允许多种类型的加密形式[2]，如第 1 层加密（Enc_1）和第 2 层加密（Enc_2）。第 1 层密文不能被重加密，而第 2 层密文可以被加密成第 1 层密文的形式。这样定义的目的是给发送者选择的余地。发送者可以根据不同的应用场景选择加密算法，即可以加密一个消息只给 Alice 或 Alice 及其下一级的访问用户。

3.2 单向 PRE 的安全性定义

通过 2 个游戏分别定义第 1 层密文和第 2 层密文的安全性。

Game1 Uni-PRE2-CCA：单向代理重加密方案第 2 层密文的 CCA 安全性定义。

阶段 1 敌手 $\mathcal{A}$ 以任何次序询问以下预言机。

公钥产生预言机 $\mathcal{O}_{pk}\ (i)$：挑战者 $\mathcal{B}$ 输入全局参数 par，运行算法 KeyGen（par）得到公私钥对（$pk_i,\ sk_i$），把 pk_i 返回给敌手 $\mathcal{A}$。

注：以下预言机输入均包括全局参数 par。

私钥产生预言机 $\mathcal{O}_{sk}\ (pk_j)$：敌手 $\mathcal{A}$ 输入公钥 pk_j，挑战者 $\mathcal{B}$ 返回 pk_j 对应的 sk_j 给敌手 $\mathcal{A}$。

重加密密钥产生预言机 $\mathcal{O}_{\mathrm{ReKeyGen}}\ (pk_i,\ pk_j)$：敌手 $\mathcal{A}$ 输入（$pk_i,\ pk_j$），挑战者 $\mathcal{B}$ 返回重加密密钥 $\mathrm{rk}_{i\to j} = ReKeyGen\ (\mathrm{sk}_i,\ \mathrm{pk}_j)$。

重加密预言机 $\mathcal{O}_{\mathrm{ReEnc}}\ (pk_i,\ pk_j,\ C_i)$：敌手 $\mathcal{A}$ 输入（$pk_i,\ pk_j,\ C_i$），挑战者 $\mathcal{B}$ 返回重加密密文 $C_j = \mathrm{ReEnc}\ (\mathrm{ReKeyGen}\ (sk_i,\ pk_j),\ C_i)$。

解密预言机 $\mathcal{O}_{\mathrm{Dec}_1}\ (pk,\ C)$：敌手 $\mathcal{A}$ 输入（$pk,\ C$），C 为第 1 层密文。挑战者 $\mathcal{B}$ 运行 $\mathrm{Dec}_1\ (sk,\ C)$，并将结果返回给敌手 $\mathcal{A}$。

注释 1 为敌手 $\mathcal{A}$ 提供第 2 层密文的解密预言机是没有必要的，因为 $\mathcal{A}$ 总是可以用获得的重加密密钥加密第 2 层密文从而获得第 1 层密文，再询问第 1 层密文解密预言机得到第 2 层密文对应的明文。

挑战阶段：一旦敌手 $\mathcal{A}$ 决定阶段 1 可以结束了，就会输出 2 个等长的明文 m_0 和 m_1 及一个要挑战的公钥 pk_i^*，这里 pk_i^* 必须满足：pk_i^* 由预言机 $\mathcal{O}_{pk}$ 获得且敌手 $\mathcal{A}$ 在阶段 1 没有进行私钥预言机 $\mathcal{O}_{sk}\ (pk_i^*)$ 查询。$\mathcal{B}$ 随机选择 $b \in \{0,\ 1\}$，把 $C_{i^*} = \mathrm{Enc}_2\ (pk_i^*,\ m_b)$ 发送给敌手 $\mathcal{A}$。

阶段 2 $\mathcal{A}$ 可以任何次序继续询问以下预言机。

公钥产生预言机 $\mathcal{O}_{pk}\ (i)$：挑战者 $\mathcal{B}$ 的回答与阶段 1 一样。

私钥产生预言机 $\mathcal{O}_{sk}\ (pk_j)$：敌手 $\mathcal{A}$ 输入公钥 pk_j，如果 $pk_j = pk_i^*$ 或者（$pk_i^*,\ pk_j$）是预言机 $\mathcal{O}_{\mathrm{ReKeyGen}}$ 的输入或者（$pk_i^*,\ pk_j,\ C_i^*$）是预言机 $\mathcal{O}_{\mathrm{ReEnc}}$ 的输入，则挑战者 $\mathcal{B}$ 输出 $\bot$，否则挑战者和阶段 1 一样回答。

重加密密钥产生预言机 $\mathcal{B}_{\mathrm{ReKeyGen}}\ (pk_i,\ pk_j)$：敌手 $\mathcal{A}$ 输入（$pk_i,\ pk_j$），如果 $pk_i = pk_i^*$ 并且 pk_j 是 $\mathcal{O}_{sk}$ 的一个输入，那么挑战者 $\mathcal{B}$ 输出 $\bot$，否则挑战者和阶段 1 的回答一样。

重加密预言机 $\mathcal{O}_{\mathrm{ReEnc}}\ (pk_i,\ pk_j,\ C_i)$：敌手 $\mathcal{A}$ 输入（$pk_i,\ pk_j,\ C_i$），如果（pk_i,

C_i）=（pk_i^*，C_i^*）并且 pk_j 是预言机 $\mathcal{O}_{sk}$ 的一个输入，那么挑战者 $\mathcal{B}$ 输出 ⊥，否则挑战者和阶段 1 的回答一样。

解密预言机 $\mathcal{O}\text{Dec}_1$（pk_j，C_j）：$\mathcal{B}$ 输入（pk_j，C_j），若（pk_j，C_j）=（pk_i^*，C_i^*）或 C_j = ReEnc（$rk_{i\to j}^*$，C_i^*），则挑战者 $\mathcal{B}$ 输出 ⊥，否则挑战者和阶段 1 的回答一样。

以上输入的公钥 pk_i 和 pk_j 都必须由预言机 $\mathcal{O}_{pk}$ 产生。

猜测阶段：敌手 $\mathcal{A}$ 输出一个猜测 $b' \in \{0, 1\}$。如果 $b = b'$，则敌手 $\mathcal{A}$ 赢得了这个游戏。

定义 3 敌手 $\mathcal{A}$ 针对方案 Uni-PRE2-CCA 安全性的优势为

$$Adv_{\mathcal{A}}^{\text{Uni-PRE2-CCA}}(1^k) = |\Pr[b=b'] - \frac{1}{2}|$$

若对于所有多项式 t 时间的敌手 $\mathcal{A}$，分别进行最多 q_{pk}、q_{sk}、q_{ReKeyGen}、q_{ReEnc}、q_{Dec_1} 次查询后，均有 $Adv_{\mathcal{A}}^{\text{Uni-PRE2-CCA}}(1^k) \leq \varepsilon$，则称该单向 PRE 方案是（$t$，$q_{pk}$，$q_{sk}$，$q_{\text{ReKeyGen}}$，$q_{\text{ReEnc}}$，$q_{\text{Dec}_1}$，$\varepsilon$）- Uni-PRE2-CCA 安全的。

Game2 Uni-PRE1-CCA：单向代理重加密方案第 1 层密文的 CCA 安全性。

注释 2 在单向单跳的 PRE 中，是无法对第 1 层密文进行再次转换的。所以允许敌手 $\mathcal{A}$ 获得任意的重加密密钥（包括从目标公钥到其他他已经被敌手获得其私钥对应公钥的重加密密钥），因此在这个游戏中就没有必要为敌手提供重加密预言机查询，因为 $\mathcal{A}$ 可以用获得的重加密密钥进行重加密操作。由注释 1 可知，也没有必要为敌手提供第 2 层密文的解密预言机查询。游戏如下。

阶段 1 除了不询问重加密预言机 $\mathcal{O}_{\text{ReEnc}}$，其他的与 Game1 的阶段 1 相同。

挑战阶段：一旦敌手 $\mathcal{A}$ 决定阶段 1 可以结束，就会输出 2 个等长的明文 m_0 和 m_1 及一个要挑战的公钥 pk_i^*，这里 pk_i^* 必须满足：pk_i^* 由预言机 $\mathcal{O}_{pk}$ 获得并且 $\mathcal{A}$ 在阶段 1 没有进行私钥预言机 $\mathcal{O}_{sk}$（pk_i^*）查询。$\mathcal{B}$ 随机选择比特 $b \in \{0, 1\}$，把 C_i^* = Enc$_1$（pk_i^*，m_b）发送给敌手 $\mathcal{A}$。

阶段 2 敌手 $\mathcal{A}$ 可以任何次序继续询问以下的随机预言机。

公钥产生预言机 $\mathcal{O}_{pk}$（i）：与阶段 1 相同。

私钥产生预言机 $\mathcal{O}_{sk}$（pk_j）：敌手 $\mathcal{A}$ 输入公钥 pk_j，如果 $pk_j = pk_i^*$，则挑战者 $\mathcal{B}$ 输出 ⊥，否则挑战者和阶段 1 一样回答。

重加密密钥产生预言机 $\mathcal{O}_{\text{ReKeyGen}}$（$pk_i$，$pk_j$）：敌手 $\mathcal{A}$ 输入（pk_i，pk_j），挑战者 $\mathcal{B}$ 返回重加密密钥 $rk_{i\to j}$ = ReKeyGen（sk_i，pk_j）。

解密预言机 $\mathcal{O}\text{Dec}_1$（pk，C）：若（pk，C）=（pk_i^*，C_i^*），则挑战者 $\mathcal{B}$ 输出 ⊥，否则挑战者和阶段 1 的回答一样。

猜测阶段：敌手 $\mathcal{A}$ 输出一个猜测 $b' \in \{0, 1\}$。如果 $b = b'$，则敌手 $\mathcal{A}$ 赢得了这个游戏。

定义 4 敌手 $\mathcal{A}$ 针对方案 Uni-PRE1-CCA 安全性的优势为

$$Adv_{\mathcal{A}}^{\text{Uni-PRE1-CCA}}(1^k) = |\Pr[b=b'] - \frac{1}{2}|$$

若对于所有多项式 t 时间的敌手 $\mathcal{A}$，分别进行最多 q_{pk}、q_{sk}、$q_{ReKeyGen}$、q_{Dec_1} 次查询后，均有 $Adv_{\mathcal{A}}^{\text{Uni-PRE1-CCA}}(1^k) \leq \varepsilon$，则称该单向 PRE 方案是 $(t, q_{pk}, q_{sk}, q_{ReKeyGen}, q_{Dec_1}, \varepsilon)$ – Uni-PRE1-CCA 安全的。

4 本文提出的 PRE 方案

LV 方案[10]利用 CHK 技术实现了对第 2 层密文有效性的公开验证，但他们第 1 层密文的部分密文 $(C'_2, C''_2 C'''_2)$ 可以是 $(C'^s_2, C''^{1/s}_2 C'''^s_2)$（$s$ 是随机数）的任意形式，在第 1 层密文解密时，无法对第 1 层密文的唯一性进行有效验证，因此它们的第 1 层密文只是 RCCA 安全的。构造一个 CCA 安全、单跳、单向的 PRE 方案的关键是对原始密文（第 2 层密文）和重加密后的密文（第 1 层密文）进行有效性的验证。原始密文有效证的验证保证了该密文是由授权者产生的，而重加密后的密文的有效性验证则保证了该密文是由代理产生的。本文构造的方案基于双线性变换、CHK 变换及密钥填充方案。CHK 技术保证密文转换前后不变密文元素的完整性，并通过随机填充技术及散列函数的单向性和抗碰撞性验证了改变密文的唯一性。本文方案中的第 1 层和第 2 层密文的完整性都可以得到有效验证，实现 CCA 安全。

4.1 方案的构造

填充技术以往用于设计密码方案，例如 RAS-OAEP[19,20]、PSS[21]等。Wang 等[18]首次利用随机填充技术构造基于身份信息的单向代理重加密方案。本文利用 CHK 技术和随机填充技术构造一个单向、单跳的 PRE 方案，包括如下算法。

Setup (1^k)：令明文的空间为 $\mathcal{M} = \{0, 1\}^{k_0}$，其中，$k_0 < k$ 并且 $\frac{2}{2^{k_0}}$ 与 $\frac{1}{2^{k-k_0}}$ 的值小到可以忽略。令群 G_1 和群 G_2 是 2 个乘法有限循环群，它们的阶为素数 p，设 g_1、g、u、v 为 $\mathbb{G}_1$ 的生成元，并且映射 $e: \mathbb{G}_1 \times \mathbb{G}_1 \to \mathbb{G}_2$ 是一个双线性配对映射。选取一个目标防碰撞的散列函数 $\mathcal{H}: \{0, 1\}^* \to \mathbb{G}_1$。选取一个强的不可伪造的一次签名函数 $\text{Sig} = (\mathcal{G}, \mathcal{S}, \mathcal{V})$。最后输出系统的参数：$par = (\mathcal{M}, k, k_0, \mathbb{G}_1, \mathbb{G}_2, g, g_1, p, u, v, e, \text{Sig}, \mathcal{H})$。

KeyGen (par)：用户 i 随机选取 $x_i \in Z_p^*$，输出公钥 $pk_i = g^{x_i}$ 和私钥 $sk_i = x_i$。

ReKeyGen (par, sk_i, pk_j)：输入 par 及用户 i 的私钥 $sk_i = x_i$ 和用户 j 的公钥 $pk_j = g^{x_j}$，该算法输出重加密密钥 $rk_{i \to j} = pk_j^{1/sk_i} = g^{x_j/x_i}$。

Enc_1 (par, pk_j, m)：输入 par 及公钥 pk_j 和明文 $m \in \mathcal{M}$，该算法按如下步骤产生第 1 层密文。

(1) 随机选择一次签名密钥对 $(svk, ssk) \leftarrow G(1^k)$，并且设置 $C_1 = svk$。

(2) 随机选择 $r \in \mathbb{Z}_p^*$ 及 $r_1 \in \{0, 1\}^{k-k_0}$，然后计算

$C_2 = g_1^r$；

$C_3 = e(pk_j, g)^r$；

$C_4 = (m \parallel r_1) \cdot e(g, g)^r$；

$C_5 = (u^{svk} \cdot v)^r$；

$C_6 = H(m \| r_1 \| C_5) \cdot C_5^{r_1}$。

(3) 对 (C_2, C_4, C_5, C_6) 进行一次签名，得到签名值 $\sigma = S(ssk, (C_2, C_4, C_5, C_6))$，输出的第 1 层密文 $C_j = (C_1, C_2, C'_3, C_4, C_5, C_6, \sigma)$。

$\text{Enc}_2(par, pk_i, m)$：输入 par 及公钥 pk_i 和明文 $m \in \mathcal{M}$，该算法按如下步骤产生第 2 层密文。

(1) 随机选择一次签名密钥对 $(svk, ssk) \leftarrow \mathcal{G}(1^k)$ 并且设置 $C_1 = svk$。

(2) 随机选择 $r \in \mathbb{Z}_p^*$ 及 $r_1 \in \{0, 1\}^{k-k_0}$，然后计算

$C_2 = g_1^r$；

$C_3 = pk_i^r$；

$C_4 = (m \| r_1) \cdot e(g, g)^r$；

$C_5 = (u^{svk} \cdot v)^r$；

$C_6 = H(m \| r_1 \| C_5) \cdot C_5^{r_1}$。

3) 对 (C_2, C_4, C_5, C_6) 进行一次签名，得到签名值 $\sigma = S(ssk, (C_2, C_4, C_5, C_6))$，输出的第 2 层密文 $C_i = (C_1, C_2, C_3, C_4, C_5, C_6, \sigma)$。

$\text{ReEnc}(par, rk_{i \to j}, C_i)$：输入 par、重加密密钥 $rk_{i \to j}$ 及针对公钥 pk_i 的第 2 层密文 $C_i = (C_1, C_2, C_3, C_4, C_5, C_6, \sigma)$，并根据如下的条件判断 C_i 的有效性

$$\mathcal{V}(C_1, \sigma, (C_2, C_4, C_5, C_6)) = 1 \tag{1}$$

$$e(C_3, u^{C_1} \cdot v) = e(pk_i, C_5) \tag{2}$$

若式（1）或式（2）不成立，输出 $\perp$。否则计算 $C'_3 = e(C_3, rk_{i \to j}) = e(pk_j, g)^r$，并输出针对公钥 pk_j 的第 1 层密文：$C_j = (C_1, C_2, C'_3, C_4, C_5, C_6, \sigma)$。

$\text{Dec}_1(par, sk_j, C_j)$：用户 j 用私钥 sk_j 按照如下步骤对第 1 层密文 $C_j = (C_1, C_2, C'_3, C_4, C_5, C_6, \sigma)$ 进行解密。

(1) 验证式（1）是否成立，如果不成立，输出 $\perp$，否则继续以下的步骤。

(2) 计算 $m' = \dfrac{C_4}{C'_3{}^{(1/sk_j)}}$。

(3) 解析 m' 为 $(m \| r_1)$，m 为 $k_0 \text{bit}$，r_1 为 $(k - k_0)$ bit。

(4) 验证 $C_6 = H(m' \| C_5) \cdot C_5^{r_1}$ 是否成立，如果不成立，输出 $\perp$，否则，输出 m。

$\text{Dec}_2(par, sk_i, C_i)$：用户 i 用私钥 sk_i 按如下步骤对第 2 层密文 $C_i = (C_1, C_2, C_3, C_4, C_5, C_6, \sigma)$ 进行解密。

(1) 如果式（1）或式（2）不成立，则输出 $\perp$，否则 继续以下的步骤。

(2) 计算 $m' = \dfrac{C_4}{e(C_3, g)^{(1/sk_i)}}$。

(3) 解析 m' 为 $(m \| r_1)$，m 为 $k_0 \text{bit}$，r_1 为 $(k - k_0)$ bit，并输出 m。

注释 3 本文利用 CHK 技术保证密文转换前后不变密文元素的完整性，第 2 层密文元素 $C_3 = pk_i^r$ 的完整性通过双线性配对运算验证，第 1 层密文元素 C'_3 的完整性通过随机填充

技术及散列函数的单向性和抗碰撞性验证。因此本文方案中的第 1 层和第 2 层密文的完整性都可以得到有效验证，实现 CCA 安全，下面将证明方案的 CCA 安全性。

4.2 安全性证明

本文通过定理 1 和定理 2 分别证明所提方案的 CCA 安全性。

定理 1 假设 Sig 是一个不可伪造的一次强签名函数，并且群（G_1，G_2）的 3-wDBDHI 假设成立，那么，本方案是 Uni-PRE2-CCA 安全的。

证明 假设 Sig 是一个不可伪造的一次强签名函数，如果存在一个敌手 $\mathcal{A}$ 可以攻破本文所提方案的（t，q_{pk}，q_{sk}，$q_{ReKeyGen}$，q_{ReEnc}，q_{Dec_1}，ε）-Uni-PRE2-CCA 安全性，则存在一个挑战者 $\mathcal{B}$ 可以攻破群（G_1，G_2）的（t'，ε'）-3-wDBDHI 假设，其中 ε'，t' 满足

$$\varepsilon' \geq \left| \pm \varepsilon \cdot \left(\frac{1}{\mathrm{e}\,(1+q_{sk}+q_{rk})} \left(\frac{1-q_{ReEnc}+q_{Dec_1}}{p} \right) \right) - Adv^{SIG} \right|$$

$$t' \leq t + q_{ReEnc} \cdot (3t_p + 3t_e) + q_{Dec_1} \cdot (1 \cdot t_p + 3t_e)$$

其中，e 表示自然对数的底。t_p 表示一个双线性配对运算时间，t_e 表示一个模指数运算时间。根据假设，Adv^{SIG} 是可忽略的。

给定 3 - wDBDHI 输入实例（g，$A_{-1} = g^{1/a}$，$A_1 = g^a$，$A_2 = g^{a^2}$，$B = g^b$，Q），其中，a，$b \in \mathbb{Z}_p^*$ 且未知。挑战者 $\mathcal{B}$ 的目标是判断 $Q = e(g, g)^{b/a^2}$ 是否成立。挑战者 $\mathcal{B}$ 为敌手 $\mathcal{A}$ 建立如下的公开参数：$\mathcal{B}$ 执行 $\mathcal{G}(1^k) \to (svk^*, ssk^*)$，然后随机选择 α_0，α_1 和 α_2，其中，α_1、$\alpha_2 \in \mathbb{Z}_p^*$，设置 $g_1 = A_2^{\alpha_0}$，$u = A_1^{\alpha_1}$，$v = A_1^{-\alpha_1 \cdot svk^*} \cdot A_2^{\alpha_2}$。挑战者 $\mathcal{B}$ 和敌手 $\mathcal{A}$ 按照如下的方式进行交互。

阶段 1 $\mathcal{B}$ 构造如下预言机。

公钥预言机 $\mathcal{O}_{pk}(i)$：挑战者 $\mathcal{B}$ 随机选取 $x_i \in \mathbb{Z}_p^*$，然后选择随机数 $c_i \in \{0, 1\}$，其中，$\Pr[c_i = 1] = \theta$，$\Pr[c_i = 0] = 1 - \theta$。如果 $c_i = 1$，设定 $pk_i = g^{x_i}$，否则设定 $pk_i = A_2^{x_i}$。最后，挑战者 $\mathcal{B}$ 将元组（pk_i，x_i，c_i）加入列表 T_{PK}，并将 pk_i 返回给敌手 $\mathcal{A}$。

私钥产生预言机 $\mathcal{O}_{sk}(pk_i)$：挑战者 $\mathcal{B}$ 从列表 T_{PK} 中找出元组（pk_i，x_i，c_i）。如果 $c_i = 1$，将 $sk_i = x_i$ 返回给敌手 $\mathcal{A}$，并把 pk_i 记录在列表 T_{SK} 中；否则 $\mathcal{B}$ 输出 Abort 并终止游戏。

重加密密钥产生预言机 $\mathcal{O}_{ReKeyGen}(pk_i, pk_j)$：挑战者 $\mathcal{B}$ 从列表 T_{PK} 中找出元组（pk_i，x_i，c_i）和（pk_j，x_j，c_j），根据如下情况为敌手 $\mathcal{A}$ 产生重加密密钥 $rk_{i \to j}$。

（1）若 $c_i = 1$：挑战者 $\mathcal{B}$ 设定 $rk_{i \to j} = pk_j^{1/x_i}$ 并将结果返回给敌手 $\mathcal{A}$，再把（pk_i，pk_j）记录在列表 T_{RK} 中。

（2）若 $c_i = c_j = 0$：挑战者 $\mathcal{B}$ 设定 $rk_{i \to j} = g^{x_j/x_i}$ 并将结果返回给敌手 $\mathcal{A}$，再把（pk_i，pk_j）记录在列表 T_{RK} 中。

（3）若 $c_i = 0 \wedge c_j = 1$：挑战者 $\mathcal{B}$ 输出 Abort 并中止游戏。

重加密预言机 $\mathcal{O}_{ReEnc}(pk_i, pk_j, C_i)$：挑战者 $\mathcal{B}$ 首先检查 pk_i 和 pk_j 是否都在列表 T_{PK} 中，如果不存在，则 $\mathcal{B}$ 输出 $\perp$ 并退出游戏。否则解析 C_i 为（C_1，C_2，C_3，C_4，C_5，C_6，σ），按照式（1）和式（2）检查密文的有效性，若式（1）或式（2）不成立，则输出 $\perp$

并退出模拟游戏，否则 $\mathcal{B}$ 进行如下操作。

①若 $c_i = 0 \wedge c_j = 1$：挑战者 $\mathcal{B}$ 在没有产生转换密钥 $rk_{i \to j}$ 的情况下为敌手 $\mathcal{A}$ 进行重加密操作。如果 $C_1 = svk^*$，则 $\mathcal{B}$ 输出 Abort 并终止游戏，否则，$\mathcal{B}$ 计算

$$\left(\frac{C_5}{C_2^{a_2/a_0}}\right)^{\frac{1}{a_1 \cdot (svk-svk^*)}} = \left(\frac{(u^{svk} \cdot v)^r}{(g^{a^2 \cdot a_0 \cdot r})^{a_2/a_0}}\right)^{\frac{1}{a_1 \cdot (svk-svk^*)}} = \left(\frac{A_1^{a_1 \cdot svk \cdot r} \cdot A_1^{-a_1 \cdot svk^* \cdot r} \cdot A_2^{a_2 \cdot r}}{g^{a^2 \cdot a_2 \cdot r}}\right)^{\frac{1}{a_1 \cdot (svk-svk^*)}}$$

$$= \left(\frac{g^{a \cdot a_1 svk \cdot r} \cdot g^{-a \cdot a_1 svk^* \cdot r} \cdot g^{a^2 \cdot a_2 r}}{g^{(a^2 \cdot a_2 \cdot r)}}\right)^{\frac{1}{a_1 \cdot (svk-svk^*)}} = (g^{ara_1(svk-svk^*)})^{\frac{1}{a_1 \cdot (svk-svk^*)}}$$

$$= g^{ar} = A_1^r \tag{4}$$

计算 $e(A_1^r, A_{-1})^{x_j} = e(g^{ar}, g^{1/a})^{x_j} = e(pk_j, g)^r = C_3'$。最后将 $\boldsymbol{C}_j = (C_1, C_2, C_3', C_4, C_5, C_6, \sigma)$ 返回给敌手 $\mathcal{A}$，并把 $(pk_i, pk_j, \boldsymbol{C}_i)$ 记录在列表 T_{RE} 中。

②若 $c_i = 0 \wedge c_j = 1$ 不成立，则按照重加密密钥预言机 $\mathcal{O}_{\text{ReKeyGen}}$ 的方法产生重加密密钥 $rk_{i \to j}$，然后运行 ReEnc($rk_{i \to j}, \boldsymbol{C}_i$) 并将结果返回给敌手 $\mathcal{A}$，并把 $(pk_i, pk_j, \boldsymbol{C}_i)$ 记录在列表 T_{RE} 中。

第 1 层解密预言机 $\mathcal{O}_{\text{Dec}_1}(pk_j, \boldsymbol{C}_j)$：挑战者 $\mathcal{B}$ 首先检查 pk_j 是否都在列表 T_{PK} 中，如果不存在，$\mathcal{B}$ 输出 ⊥ 并终止游戏。否则 $\mathcal{B}$ 解析 $\boldsymbol{C}_j = (C_1, C_2, C_3', C_4, C_5, C_6, \sigma)$，如果 $C_1 = svk^*$，$\mathcal{B}$ 输出 Abort 并中止游戏，否则进行如下操作。

①若 $c_j = 1$，则 $sk_j = x_j$，则 $\mathcal{B}$ 运行 Dec1($\boldsymbol{C}_j, sk_j$) 并将结果返回给敌手 A。

②若 $c_j = 0$，验证式（1）是否成立，如果不成立，输出 ⊥ 并退出游戏，否则，由式（4）得到 A_1^r，再计算 $e(A_1^r, A_{-1}) = e(g^{ar}, g^{1/a}) = e(g, g)^r$，则 $m' = \frac{C_4}{e(A_1^r, A_{-1})}$，解析 m' 为 $(m \| r_1)$，验证 $C_6 = H(m' \| C_5) \cdot C_5^{r_1}$ 是否成立，如果不成立，输出 ⊥ 并退出游戏，否则，输出 m。

挑战阶段：一旦敌手 $\mathcal{A}$ 决定阶段 1 可以结束，就会输出 2 个等长的明文 m_0 和 m_1 及要挑战的公钥 pk_i^*。如果 pk_i^* 所对应的 $c_i^* = 1$，$\mathcal{B}$ 输出 Abort 并中止游戏。否则，$\mathcal{B}$ 选择随机数 $b \in \{0,1\}$ 并计算：

$$C_1^* = svk^*$$

$$C_2^* = B^{\alpha_0} = (g^{a^2})^{\alpha_0 \cdot \frac{b}{a^2}} = (A_2^{\alpha_0})^{r^*} = g_1^{r^*}$$

$$C_3^* = B^{x_i^*} = B^{b \cdot x_i^*} = (g^{a^2 \cdot x_i^*})^{\frac{b}{a^2}} = (pk_{i^*})^{r^*}$$

$$C_4^* = (m_b \| r_1^*) \cdot \mathcal{Q}$$

$$C_5^* = B^{\alpha_2} = (g^b)^{\alpha_2} = (g^{a^2 \cdot \alpha_2})^{\frac{b}{a^2}}$$

$$= (g^{a \cdot \alpha_1 (svk^* - svk^*)} \cdot g^{a^2 \cdot \alpha_2})^{\frac{b}{a^2}}$$

$$= (g^{a \cdot \alpha_1 svk^*} \cdot g^{-a \cdot \alpha_1 svk^*} \cdot g^{a^2 \cdot \alpha_2})^{\frac{b}{a^2}}$$

$$= (A_1^{\alpha_1 svk^*} \cdot A_1^{-\alpha_1 svk^*} A_2^{\alpha_2})^{\frac{b}{a^2}}$$

$$= (u^{svk^*} \cdot v)^{\frac{b}{a^2}} = (u^{svk^*} \cdot v)^{r^*}$$

$$C_6^* = H(m_b \| r_1^* \| B^{\alpha_2}) \cdot (B^{\alpha_2}) r_1^*$$

$$= H(m_b \parallel r_1^* \parallel C_5^*) \cdot (C_5^*)^{r_1^*}$$
$$\sigma^* = \mathcal{S}(ssk^*, (C_2^*, C_4^*, C_5^*, C_6^*))$$

将挑战密文 $C_{i^*} = (C_1^*, C_2^*, C_3^*, C_4^*, C_5^*, C_6^*, \sigma^*)$ 返回给 $\mathcal{A}$。显然，若 $r^* = \frac{b}{a^2}$，当 $\mathcal{Q} = e(g,g)^{\frac{b}{a^2}}$ 成立时，C_i^* 必是一个针对 pk_i^* 的有效密文。

阶段 2 $\mathcal{B}$ 构造如下的预言机。

公钥预言机 $\mathcal{O}_{pk}(i)$：和阶段 1 的回答一样。

私钥产生预言机 $\mathcal{O}_{sk}(pk_j)$：如果 $pk_j = pk_i^*$ 或者 (pk_i^*, pk_j) 在列表 T_{RK} 中或者 (pk_i^*, pk_j, C_i^*) 在列表 T_{RE} 中，则挑战者 $\mathcal{B}$ 输出 $\perp$ 并退出游戏。否则和阶段 1 回答一样。

重加密密钥产生预言机 $\mathcal{O}_{ReKeyGen}(pk_i, pk_j)$：如果 $pk_i = pk_i^*$ 并且 pk_j 在列表 T_{SK} 中，则挑战者 $\mathcal{B}$ 输出 $\perp$ 并退出游戏。否则和阶段 1 回答一样。

重加密预言机 $\mathcal{O}_{ReEnc}(pk_i, pk_j, C_i)$：如果 $(pk_i, C_i) = (pk_i^*, C_i^*)$ 且 pk_j 在列表 T_{SK} 中，则挑战者 $\mathcal{B}$ 输出 $\perp$ 并退出游戏。否则和阶段 1 回答一样。

第 1 层解密预言机 $\mathcal{O}_{Dec_1}(pk_j, C_j)$：如 (pk_i^*, pk_j, C_i^*) 在列表 T_{RE} 中，挑战者 $\mathcal{B}$ 输出 $\perp$，否则挑战者和阶段 1 的回答一样。

猜测阶段：最后，敌手 $\mathcal{A}$ 输出猜测 $b' \in \{0, 1\}$。如果 $b = b'$，那么挑战者 $\mathcal{B}$ 输出 1 作为其针对 3-wDBDHI 实例的回答；否则，挑战者 $\mathcal{B}$ 输出 0。

概率分析：定义 Abort 为敌手 $\mathcal{A}$ 在与挑战者 $\mathcal{B}$ 交互时发生的中断事件。

假设敌手 $\mathcal{A}$ 最多进行了 q_{sk}、$q_{ReKeyGen}$、q_{ReEnc}、q_{Dec_1} 次预言机 $\mathcal{O}_{sk}$、$\mathcal{O}_{ReKeyGen}$、$\mathcal{O}_{ReEnc}$、$\mathcal{O}_{Dec_1}$ 查询。在阶段 1 和阶段 2 对预言机 $\mathcal{O}_{sk}$、$\mathcal{O}_{ReKeyGen}$ 查询中关于 c_i 的 Abort 不会发生的概率分别为 $\theta^{q_{sk}}$ 及 $(\theta + (1-\theta)^2)^{q_{rk}}$。由于在进行 $\mathcal{O}_{ReEnc}$、$\mathcal{O}_{Dec_1}$ 查询中，出现 $C_1 = svk^*$ 最大的概率为 $1/p$，因此查询 $\mathcal{O}_{ReEnc}$、$\mathcal{O}_{Dec_1}$ 中 Abort 不会发生的概率为 $\left(1 - \frac{q_{ReEnc} + q_{Dec_1}}{p}\right)$。在挑战阶段关于 c_i 的 Abort 不会发生的概率为 $(1-\theta)$。因此，在模拟中，关于 coin 的 Abort 不会发生的概率为

$$\Pr[\neg \text{Abort}] = \theta^{q_{sk}}(\theta + (1-\theta)^2)^{q_{rk}}(1-\theta) \cdot \left(1 - \frac{q_{ReEnc} + q_{Dec_1}}{p}\right) \geq \theta^{q_{sk} + q_{rk}}(1-\theta)\left(1 - \frac{q_{ReEnc} + q_{Dec_1}}{p}\right)$$

当 $\theta = \frac{q_{sk} + q_{rk}}{1 + q_{sk} + q_{rk}}$ 时，$\theta^{q_{sk} + q_{rk}}(1-\theta)$ 取得最大值，最大值为 $\frac{1}{e(1 + q_{sk} + q_{rk})}$。从而得出

$$\Pr[\neg \text{Abort}] \geq \frac{1}{e(1 + q_{sk} + q_{rk})}\left(1 - \frac{q_{ReEnc} + q_{Dec_1}}{p}\right)$$

其中，e 表示自然对数的底。

当 Abort 不会发生并且 $T = e(g,g)^{b/a^2}$ 时，由于挑战密文恰好是对 m_b 的有效加密密文。此时，

$$\Pr[\mathcal{B}(g, g^{1/a}, g^a, g^{a^2}, g^b, \mathcal{Q} = e(g,g)^{b/a^2}) = 1]$$
$$= \Pr[\mathcal{B}(g, g^{1/a}, g^a, g^{a^2}, g^b, \mathcal{Q} = e(g,g)^{b/a^2}) = 1 \mid \text{Abort}].$$

$$\Pr[\text{Abort}] + \Pr[\mathcal{B}(g, g^{1/a}, g^a, g^{a^2}, g^b, \mathcal{Q} = \mathrm{e}(g,g)^{b/a^2}) = 1 | \neg \text{Abort}] \cdot \Pr[\neg \text{Abort}]$$
$$= (1/2) \cdot \Pr[\text{Abort}] + \Pr[b = b' | \neg \text{Abort}] \cdot \Pr[\neg \text{Abort}]$$

当 Abort 不会发生且 $\mathcal{Q}$ 是 $\mathbb{G}_2$ 的一个随机元素时，挑战密文是对 $\mathbb{G}_2$ 上一个随机元素的加密密文。

此时敌手 $\mathcal{A}$ 的优势是伪造一次签名。此时
$$\Pr[\mathcal{B}(g, g^{1/a}, g^a, g^{a^2}, g^b, \mathcal{Q} \neq \mathrm{e}(g,g)^{b/a}) = 1]$$
$$= \frac{1}{2} + Adv^{\text{SIG}}$$

综上，根据假设及敌手 $\mathcal{A}$ 的优势定义：

$$| \Pr[\mathcal{B}(g, g^{1/a}, g^a, g^{a^2}, g^b, \mathcal{Q} = \mathrm{e}(g,g)^{b/a}) = 1] -$$
$$- \Pr[\mathcal{B}(g, g^{1/a}, g^a, g^{a^2}, g^b, \mathcal{Q} \neq \mathrm{e}(g,g)^{b/a}) = 1] |$$
$$= \left| \frac{1}{2} \cdot \Pr[\text{Abort}] + \Pr[b = b' | \neg \text{Abort}] \cdot \Pr[\neg \text{Abort}] - \left(\frac{1}{2} + Adv^{\text{SIG}}\right) \right|$$
$$= \left| \frac{1}{2} - \frac{1}{2}\Pr[\neg \text{Abort}] + \Pr[b = b' | \neg \text{Abort}] \cdot \Pr[\neg \text{Abort}] - \left(\frac{1}{2} + Adv^{\text{SIG}}\right) \right|$$
$$= \left| \left(\Pr[b = b' | \neg \text{Abort}] - \frac{1}{2}\right) \cdot \Pr[\neg \text{Abort}] - Adv^{\text{SIG}} \right|$$
$$\geq \left| \left(\pm \varepsilon + \frac{1}{2} - \frac{1}{2}\right) \cdot \Pr[\neg \text{Abort}] - Adv^{\text{SIG}} \right|$$
$$\geq \left| \pm \varepsilon \left(\frac{1}{\mathrm{e}(1 + q_{sk} + q_{rk})} \cdot \left(1 - \frac{q_{\text{ReEnc}} + q_{\text{Dec}}}{p}\right)\right) - Adv^{\text{SIG}} \right|$$

时间复杂度：挑战者 $\mathcal{B}$ 与敌手 $\mathcal{A}$ 的交互过程中，其主要的计算代价是在回答 $\mathcal{A}$ 的重加密和第 1 层密文解密查询所需的双线性映射运算和模指数运算。假设一次双线性映射运算所需的时间为 t_p，一次模指数运算所需的时间为 t_e，那么可得
$$t' \leq t + q_{\text{ReEnc}}(3t_p + 3t_e) + q_{\text{Dec}_1}(t_p + 3t_e)$$

证毕。

定理 2 假设 Sig 是一个不可伪造的一次强签名函数，并且群 ($\mathbb{Z}_1, \mathbb{Z}_2$) 的 3-wDBDHI 假设成立，那么，本方案是 Uni-PRE1-CCA 安全的。

证明 假设 Sig 是一个不可伪造的一次强签名函数，如果存在一个敌手 $\mathcal{A}$ 可以攻破本文所提方案的 $(t, q_{pk}, q_{sk}, q_{\text{ReKeyGen}}, q_{\text{Dec}_1}, \varepsilon)$-Uni-PRE1-CCA 安全性，则存在一个挑战者 $\mathcal{B}$ 可以攻破群 ($\mathbb{Z}_1, \mathbb{Z}_2$) 的 (t', ε')-3-wDBDHI 假设，其中，ε', t' 满足

$$\varepsilon' \geq \left| \pm \varepsilon \left(\frac{1}{\mathrm{e}(1 + q_{sk})} \cdot \left(1 - \frac{q_{\text{Dec}_1}}{p}\right)\right) - Adv^{\text{SIG}} \right|$$
$$t' \leq t + q_{\text{Dec}_1}(t_p + 3t_e)$$

给定 3-wDBDHI 输入实例 $(g, A_{-1} = g^{1/a}, A_1 = g^a, A_2 = g^{a^2}, B = g^b, \mathcal{Q})$，其中，$a, b \in Z_p^*$ 且未知。挑战者 $\mathcal{B}$ 的目标是判断 $\mathcal{Q} = \mathrm{e}(g,g)^{b/a^2}$ 是否成立。挑战者 $\mathcal{B}$ 为 $\mathcal{A}$ 建立如下的公开参数：$\mathcal{B}$ 执行 $\mathcal{G}(1^k) \rightarrow (svk^*, ssk^*)$，然后，随机选择 α_0、α_1 和 α_2 ($\alpha_0, \alpha_1, \alpha_2 \in \mathbb{Z}_p^*$)，设置 $g_1 = A_2^{\alpha_0}$，$u = A_1^{\alpha_1}$，并且 $v = A_1^{-\alpha_1 \cdot svk^*} A_2^{\alpha_2}$。挑战者 $\mathcal{B}$ 和敌手 $\mathcal{A}$ 按照如下的方式进行交互。

阶段1 $\mathcal{B}$ 构造如下预言机。

公钥预言机 $\mathcal{O}_{pk}$ (i)：挑战者 $\mathcal{B}$ 随机选取 $x_i \in \mathbb{Z}_p^*$，然后选择一个随机数 $c_i \in \{0, 1\}$，其中，$\Pr[c_i = 1] = \theta$，$\Pr[c_i = 0] = 1 - \theta$。如果 $c_i = 1$，设定 $pk_i = g^{x_i}$；否则设定 $pk_i = A_1^{x_i}$。最后，挑战者 $\mathcal{B}$ 将元组 (pk_i, x_i, c_i) 加入列表 T_{PK}，并将 pk_i 返回给敌手 $\mathcal{A}$。

私钥产生预言机 $\mathcal{O}_{sk}$ (pk_i)：挑战者 $\mathcal{B}$ 从列表 T_{PK} 中找出元组 (pk_i, x_i, c_i)。如果 $c_i = 1$，将 $sk_i = x_i$ 返回给敌手 $\mathcal{A}$，并把 pk_i 记录在列表 T_{SK} 中；否则 $\mathcal{B}$ 输出 Abort 并终止游戏。

重加密密钥产生预言机 $\mathcal{O}_{\text{ReKeyGen}}$ (pk_i, pk_j)：$\mathcal{B}$ 从列表 T_{PK} 中找出元组 (pk_i, x_i, c_i) 和 (pk_j, x_j, c_j)，根据如下情况为敌手 $\mathcal{A}$ 产生重加密密钥 $rk_{i \to j}$。

（1）若 $c_i = 1$：挑战者 $\mathcal{B}$ 设定 $rk_{i \to j} = pk_j^{1/x_i}$ 并将结果返回给敌手 $\mathcal{A}$，并把 (pk_i, pk_j) 记录在列表 T_{RK} 中。

（2）若 $c_i = c_j = 0$：挑战者 $\mathcal{B}$ 设定 $rk_{i \to j} = g^{x_j/x_i}$ 并将结果返回给敌手 $\mathcal{A}$ 并把 (pk_i, pk_j) 记录在列表 T_{RK} 中。

（3）若 $c_i = 0 \wedge c_j = 1$：挑战者 $\mathcal{B}$ 设定 $rk_{i \to j} = A_{-1}^{x_j/x_i}$ 并将结果返回给敌手 $\mathcal{A}$，并把 (pk_i, pk_j) 记录在列表 T_{RK} 中。

第1层解密预言机 $\mathcal{O}_{\text{Dec}_1}$ (pk_j, $\mathbf{C}_j$)：挑战者首先检查 pk_j 是否都在列表 T_{PK} 中。如果不存在，挑战者输出 $\perp$ 并终止游戏。否则挑战者 $\mathcal{B}$ 解析 $\mathbf{C}_j = (C_1, C_2, C_3', C_4, C_5, C_6, \sigma)$，若 $C_1 = svk^*$，$\mathcal{B}$ 输出 Abort 并终止游戏，否则进行如下操作。

（1）若 $c_j = 1$，由于 $sk_j = x_j$，$\mathcal{B}$ 运行 Dec_1 ($\mathbf{C}_j$, sk_j) 并将结果返回给敌手 $\mathcal{A}$。

（2）若 $c_j = 0$，验证式（1）是否成立，如果不成立，输出 $\perp$ 并退出游戏，否则，由式（4）得到 A_1^r，再计算 $e(A_1^r, A_{-1}) = e(g^{ar}, g^{1/a}) = e(g, g)^r$，则 $m' = \dfrac{C_4}{e(A_1^r, A_{-1})}$，解析 m' 为 ($m \parallel r_1$)，验证 $C_6 = H(m' \parallel C_5) \cdot C_5^{r_1}$ 是否成立，如果不成立，输出 $\perp$ 并退出游戏，否则，输出 m。

挑战阶段：一旦敌手 $\mathcal{A}$ 决定阶段1可以结束，就会输出2个等长的明文 m_0 和 m_1 及要挑战的公钥 pk_i^*。如果 pk_i^* 所对应的 $c_i^* = 1$，$\mathcal{B}$ 输出 Abort 并终止游戏。否则，$\mathcal{B}$ 选择随机数 $b \in \{0, 1\}$ 并计算

$$C_1^* = svk^*$$

$$C_2^* = B^{\alpha_0} = (g^{a^2})^{\alpha_0 \cdot \frac{b}{a^2}} = (A_2^{\alpha_0})^{r^*} = g_1^{r^*}$$

$$C_3'^* = e(A_{-1}, B)^{x_i^*} = e(g^{1/a}, g^b)^{x_i^*} = e(g^{a \cdot x_i^*}, g)^{\frac{b}{a^2}}$$

$$= e(pk_{i^*}, g)^{r^*}$$

$$C_4^* = (m_b \parallel r_1^*) \mathcal{Q}$$

$$C_5^* = B^{\alpha_2} = (g^b)^{\alpha_2} = (g^{a^2 \cdot \alpha_2})^{\frac{b}{a^2}}$$

$$= (g^{a \cdot \alpha_1(svk^* - svk^*)} \cdot g^{a^2 \cdot \alpha_2})^{\frac{b}{a^2}}$$

$$= (g^{a \cdot \alpha_1 svk^*} \cdot g^{-a \cdot \alpha_1 svk^*} \cdot g^{a^2 \cdot \alpha_2})^{\frac{b}{a^2}}$$

$$= (A_1^{\alpha_1 svk^*} \cdot A_1^{-\alpha_1 svk^*} A_2^{\alpha_2})^{\frac{b}{a^2}}$$

$$= (u^{svk^*} \cdot v)^{\frac{b}{a^2}} = (u^{svk^*} \cdot v)^{r^*}$$

$$C_6^* = H(m_b \parallel r_1^* \parallel B^{\alpha_2}) \cdot (B^{\alpha_2})^{r_1^*}$$
$$= H(m_b \parallel r_1^* \parallel C_5^*) \cdot (C_5^*)^{r_1^*}$$
$$\sigma^* = \mathcal{S}(ssk^*, (C_2^*, C_4^*, C_5^*, C_6^*))$$

将挑战密文 $C_{i^*} = (C_1^*, C_2^*, C'^*_3, C_4^*, C_5^*, C_6^*, \sigma^*)$ 返回给 $\mathcal{A}$。显然，若 $r^* = \frac{b}{a^2}$，当 $\mathcal{Q} = e(g,g)^{\frac{b}{a^2}}$ 成立时，C_i^* 必是一个针对 pk_i^* 的有效密文。

阶段 2 $\mathcal{B}$ 构造如下的预言机。

公钥预言机 $\mathcal{O}_{pk}(i)$：和阶段 1 的回答一样。

私钥产生预言机 $\mathcal{O}_{sk}(pk_j)$：如果 $pk_j = pk_i^*$ 或者 (pk_i^*, pk_j) 在列表 T_{RK} 中，则 $\mathcal{B}$ 输出 $\perp$ 并退出游戏；否则和阶段 1 回答一样。

重加密密钥产生预言机 $\mathcal{O}_{\text{ReKeyGen}}(pk_i, pk_j)$：如果 $pk_i = pk_i^*$ 并且 pk_j 在列表 T_{SK} 中，则 $\mathcal{B}$ 输出 $\perp$ 并退出游戏。否则和阶段 1 的回答一样。

第 1 层解密预言机 $\mathcal{O}_{\text{Dec}_1}(pk_j, C_j)$：如果 $C_j = \text{ReEnc}(rk_{i \to j}^*, C_i^*)$，$\mathcal{B}$ 输出 $\perp$，否则挑战者和阶段 1 的回答一样。

猜测阶段：最后，$\mathcal{A}$ 输出一个猜测 $b' \in \{0,1\}$。如果 $b = b'$，那么 $\mathcal{B}$ 输出 1 作为其针对 3-wDBDHI 实例的回答；否则，$\mathcal{B}$ 输出 0。

概率分析：定义 Abort 为敌手 $\mathcal{A}$ 在与挑战者 $\mathcal{B}$ 交互时发生的中断事件。假设 $\mathcal{A}$ 最多进行了 q_{sk}，q_{Dec_1} 次查询。在阶段 1 和阶段 2 对预言机 $\mathcal{O}_{sk}$ 查询中关于 c_i 的 Abort 不会发生的概率为 $\theta^{q_{sk}}$。由于在进行 $\mathcal{O}_{\text{Dec}_1}$ 查询中，出现 $C_1 = svk^*$ 的概率为 $1/p$，因此查询 O_{Dec_1} 中 Abort 不会发生的概率为 $\left(1 - \frac{q_{\text{Dec}_1}}{p}\right)$。在挑战阶段关于 c_i 的 Abort 不会发生的概率为 $(1-\theta)$。因此，在模拟中，关于 coin 的 Abort 不会发生的概率为

$$\Pr[\neg \text{Abort}] = \theta^{q_{sk}}(1-\theta)\left(1 - \frac{q_{\text{Dec}_1}}{p}\right)$$

当 $\theta = \frac{q_{sk}}{1+q_{sk}}$ 时，$\theta^{q_{sk}}(1-\theta)$ 取得最大值，最大值为 $\frac{1}{e(1+q_{sk})}$，即 $\Pr[\neg \text{Abort}] \geq \frac{1}{e(1+q_{sk})}\left(1 - \frac{q_{\text{Dec}_1}}{p}\right)$。

与定理 1 的证明同理，根据假设及敌手 $\mathcal{A}$ 的优势定义可得

$$|\Pr[\mathcal{B}(g, g^{1/a}, g^a, g^{a^2} \cdot g^b, \mathcal{Q} = e(g,g)^{b/a^2}) = 1]$$
$$- \Pr[\mathcal{B}(g, g^{1/a}, g^a, g^{a^2}, g^b, \mathcal{Q} \neq e(g,g)^{b/a^2}) = 1]|$$
$$\geq \left|\pm \varepsilon \cdot \left(\frac{1}{e(1+q_{sk})}\left(1 - \frac{q_{\text{Dec}_1}}{p}\right)\right) - Adv^{\text{SIG}}\right|$$

时间复杂度：假设一次双线性映射运算所需的时间为 t_p，一次模指数运算运算所需的时间为 t_e，可得

$$t' \leq t + q_{\text{Dec}_1}(t_p + 3t_e)$$

证毕。

4.3 方案比较

本文方案与 LV 方案[10]和 WJ 方案[11]都是单向单跳的 PRE 方案。表 1 为本文方案与 LV 方案和 WJ 方案的比较。表 1 中，$|\mathbb{Z}_p|$ 和 l 分别表示 WJ 方案中密文元素 t 和安全参数位长度。$|\mathbb{Z}_1|$ 和 $|\mathbb{Z}_2|$ 分别表示 3 种方案中群 $\mathbb{Z}_1$ 和 $\mathbb{Z}_2$ 中一个元素的位长度。$|svk|$ 和 $|\sigma|$ 分别表示 LV 方案和本文方案中所采用的一次强签名函数的验证密钥位长度和签名位长度。t_p 表示一个双线性配对运算时间，t_e 表示一个模指数运算时间，t_s 表示一次签名运算时间，t_v 表示一次签名验证运算所需的时间。

表 1 本文方案与 LV 方案及 WJ 方案的比较

方案指标		WJ 方案	LV 方案	本文方案
密文长度	第 1 层	$|\mathbb{Z}_p|+2|G_1|+|G_2|+l$	$|svk|+4|G_1|+|G_2|+|\sigma|$	$|svk|+3|G_1|+2|G_2|+|\sigma|$
	第 2 层	$|\mathbb{Z}_p|+3|G_1|+l$	$|svk|+2|G_1|+|G_2|+|\sigma|$	$|svk|+4|G_1|+|G_2|+|\sigma|$
运算代价	Enc_1	$6t_e$	$6t_e+t_s$	$6t_e+t_s$
	Enc_2	$6t_e$	$4t_e+t_s$	$6t_e+t_s$
	ReEnc	$3t_p+6t_e$	$2t_p+4t_e+t_v$	$3t_p+t_e+t_v$
	Dec_1	$2t_p+2t_e$	$5t_p+2t_e+t_v$	$2t_e+t_v$
	Dec_2	$3t_p+7t_e$	$3t_p+2t_e+t_v$	$3t_p+2t_e+t_v$
	总运算代价	$8t_p+27t_e$	$10t_p+18t_e+2t_s+3t_v$	$6t_p+17t_e+2t_s+3t_v$
PRE 类型		单向单跳	单向单跳	单向单跳
随机预言机		无需	无需	无需
困难假设		3-wBDHI	3-wBDHI	3-wBDHI
安全性		CCA	RCCA	CCA
攻陷模型		自适应	非自适应	自适应

假设本文方案和 LV 方案的一次强签名函数都是采用 1 024 bit 的 RSA。3 种方案采用的双线性配对都是 Tate 双线性配对。要达到 1 024 bit RSA 的安全级别，需要 512 bit 的 Tate 双线性配对操作[22]。根据文献 [22] 的实验结果，执行一次 Tate 双线性操作需要 20.04 ms，一次模指数运算为 5.31 ms。而 RSA 的签名时间约为执行一次模指数运算的时间，RSA 的验证时间相对于签名时间可忽略。因此，可分别估算 WJ 方案、LV 方案和本文方案的总运算时间为 303.69 ms，306.6 ms 和 221.13 ms，由此得出本文方案总运算时间分别是 WJ 方案的 72.81%，是 LV 方案的 72.12%。

表 1 的比较结果还表明，本文方案是 CCA 安全的，而 LV 方案只能达到 RCCA 安全，并且在同等困难假设、同样无需随机预言模型下进行证明方案安全性时，本文方案是自适应攻陷模型下 CCA 安全的，而 LV 方案是非自适应攻陷模型下 RCCA 安全的。与 WJ 方案相比，本文方案与 WJ 方案所达到的安全级别相同，但具有更高的运算效率。

5 结束语

针对实际应用中需要高效的标准模型下 CCA 安全的单向 PRE 方案，本文使用 CHK 技术和随机填充技术构造了一种新的高效的单向、单跳的 PRE 方案，并且在无需借助随机预言机的模型下证明了方案的 CCA 安全性。

构造单跳单向 PRE 方案的进一步研究工作主要是：①在保证同等安全级别的情况下如何有效减少密文的长度；②如何实现第 1 层密文完整性的公开验证。

参考文献

［1］BLAZE M, BLEUMER G, STRAUSS M. Divertible protocols and atomic proxy cryptography［A］. EUROCRYPT'98, International Conference on the Theory and Application of Cryptographic Techniques［C］. Espoo, Finland, 1998. 127-144.

［2］ATENIESE G, FU K, GREEN M, et al. Improved proxy re-encryption schemes with applications to secure distributed storage［J］. ACM Transactions on Information System Security, 2006, （9）: 1-30.

［3］SHAO J, LIU P, ZHOU Y. Achieving key privacy without losing CCA security in proxy re-encryption［J］. The Journal of Systems and Software, 2012, 85: 655-665.

［4］TABAN G, CÁRDENAS A A, GLIGOR V D. Towards a secure and interoperable DRM architecture［A］. Proceedings of the ACM Workshop on Digital Rights Management［C］. New York, USA, 2006. 69-78.

［5］LEE S, HEEJIN P, JONG K. A secure and mutual-profitable DRM interoperability scheme［A］. Proceedings of the IEEE Symposium on Computers and Communications［C］. Riccione, Italy, 2010. 75-80.

［6］SHAO J, CAO Z, LIANG X H, et al. Proxy re-encryption with key-word search［J］. Information Sciences, 2010, 180 （4）: 2576-2587.

［7］WANG X A, HUANG X Y, YANG X Y, et al. Further observation on proxy re-encryption with key-word search［J］. The Journal of Systems and Software, 2012, 85: 643-654.

［8］CANETTI R, HOHENBERGER S. Chosen-ciphertext secure proxy re-encryption［A］. Proceedings of the 14th ACM Conference on Computer and Communications Security［C］. Alexandria, VA, USA, 2007. 185-194.

［9］CANETTI R, HALEVI S, KATZ J. Chosen-ciphertext security from identity-based encryption［A］. EUROCRYPT'04［C］. Alexandria, VA, USA, 2007. 185-194.

［10］LIBERT B, VERGNAUD D. Unidirectional chosen-ciphertext secure proxy re-encryption［J］. IEEE transactions on Information theory, 2011, 57 （3）: 1786-1802.

［11］WENG J, CHEN M R, YANG Y J, et al. CCA-secure unidirectional proxy re-encryption in the adaptive corruption model without random oracles［J］. Science China （Information Sciences）, 2010, 53 （3）: 593-606.

［12］HOHENBERGER S, WATERS B. Realizing hash-and-sign signatures under standard assumptions［A］. EUROCRYPT'09［C］. 2009. 333-350.

［13］CHEN L, CHENG Z, SMART N P. Identity-based key agreement protocols from pairings［J］. Journal of Information Security, 2007, 6 （4）: 213-241.

［14］SHAO J, CAO Z F. CCA-secure proxy re-encryption without pairings［A］. PKC 2009［C］. California, USA, 2009. 357-376.

［15］WENG J, DENG R H, LIU S L, et al. Chosen-ciphertext secure bidi-rectional proxy re-encryption schemes without pairings［J］. Information Sciences, 2010, 180: 5077-5089.

[16] CANETTI R, GOLDREICH O, HALEVI S. The random oracle methodology, revisited [J]. Journal of the ACM, 2004, 51 (4): 557-594.

[17] SHAO J, CAO Z F. Multi-use unidirectional identity-based proxy re-encryption from hierarchical identity-based encryption [J]. Information Sciences, 2012, 206 (5): 83-95.

[18] WANG H B, CAO Z F, WANG L C. Multi-use and unidirectional identity-based proxy re-encryption schemes [J]. Information Sciences, 2010, 180: 4042-4059.

[19] BELLARE M, ROGAWAY P. Optimal asymmetric encryption [A]. EUROCRYPT'94 [C]. Perugia, Italy, 1995. 92-111.

[20] BONEH D. Simplified OAEP for the RSA and Rabin functions [A]. CRYPTO 2001 [C]. California, USA, 2001. 275-291.

[21] BELLARE M, ROGAWAY P. The exact security of digital signatures: How to sign with RSA and rabin [A]. EUROCRYPT' 96 [C]. Zaragoza, Spain, 1996. 399-416.

[22] HE D B, CHEN J H, HU J. An ID-based proxy signature schemes without bilinear pairings [J]. Ann Telecommun, 2011, 66: 657-662.

新型通用格式多媒体数字版权管理系统设计与实现

黄勤龙 马兆丰 莫佳 钮心忻 杨义先

1 引言

随着 Internet 技术的快速发展，数字多媒体内容的分发、复制和编辑变得越来越普遍，移动互联网的飞速发展使得多媒体内容的制作、分享和下载越来越简单，由此带来的大量多媒体内容盗链、盗版以及不规范使用行为对数字媒体产业造成巨大的冲击。数字多媒体内容的非法复制和传播损害了版权所有人和内容运营商的合法权益，如何防止数字多媒体内容的非法复制与扩散，保护多媒体内容的版权是数字内容产业发展所面临的关键问题，数字版权管理技术正是为了解决这一关键问题而产生的。

数字版权管理（DRM，digital rights management）是通过数字内容的制作、发行、安全许可和计费等一系列手段防止数字内容的非法误用，确保数字内容在公平、合理、安全许可框架下的条件使用和消费[1]。

2 相关工作

随着 DRM 技术的应用越来越广泛，学术界和工业界进行了大量的研究和实践[2~11]。

马兆丰等人提出了一种新的支持时空约束的数字版权管理安全许可协议[2]，将内容对象与版权对象相分离，通过内容加密密钥 CEK 保护数字内容本身，在用户与许可证中心之间采用动态实时密钥协商算法实现双向认证和动态许可申请。

针对 P2P 网络，Jung-Shian Li 等人提出了一个新的端对端音乐内容分发的 DRM 框架[8]，内容分发的顽健性通过使用基于拉格朗日插值法的网络编码方法来实现，不会对音频质量产生影响，但该框架分发到用户的内容将不受控制。针对 IPTV 内容，Boseung Kim 等人提出了一种采用帧加密的内容保护的方法[9]，该方法使用一种干扰加密方法，即使用散列函数而不是复杂的加密过程，通过改变像素值来重新排列每帧的图像，从而实现简单而又比较有效的 IPTV 内容保护，然而该方法安全性较低，缺少密钥管理和许可证管理。Yeonjeong Jeong 等人提出了一种在不同音频 DRM 系统之间可以互相转换的方法[10]，目前音频内容受多种 DRM 系统，每个采用不同的 DRM 技术，DRM 内容也不相同，该方法使得已经受 DRM 保护的音频内容可以在其他 DRM 兼容的设备上使用，但该方法适用范围有限。钟勇等人提出了一种面向 DRM 的责任授权模型及其实施框架[11]，该模型基于分布式时态逻辑和 Active-U-Datalog 语法规则，具有表达事件驱动、事件驱动和责任补偿等各种责任授权的语义能力，具有良好的可实施性，提高了 DRM 系统对数据使用控制的灵活性和能力。

工业界目前有多种 DRM 解决方案，如 OMA DRM[12]、Marlin DRM[13]、苹果的 FairPlay 系统[14]、微软的 Media DRM 系统[15]和 Adobe 的 Flash Access 系统[16]等，推动了 DRM 的发展和应用，但 OMA DRM 不支持版权对象[17]的重新发行，FairPlay、Media DRM 和 Flash Access 等均只支持有限的几种格式。

现有针对多媒体内容的 DRM 系统存在如下一些问题和局限性。

（1）现有基于内容格式加密或者帧结构加密的多媒体 DRM 系统，其加密过程复杂，内容解密播放时处理性能较低，如 Boseung Kim 等人[9]提出的一种干扰的帧加密方法，其加密速率比采用 AES 算法的非结构化加密方法要低。

（2）现有的音视频等多媒体 DRM 系统，多与音视频的格式相关，一般只支持少数的几种视频格式，如微软的 Media DRM[15]只支持 WMV、WMA 和 ASF 3 种格式，Adobe 的 Flash Access[16]只支持 FLV 和 F4V 2 种格式，目前，DRM 系统未能支持通用格式的多媒体，不同格式之间的多媒体无法统一订购和使用，无法满足不同内容提供商提供的不同多媒体内容保护需求。

（3）现有的多媒体 DRM 系统存在权利许可无法重新发行或者转让的不足，当权利许可丢失或损坏时，用户无法继续使用版权内容，如 OMA DRM，同时用户也不能将自己购买的权利许可转让给他人，如微软的 Media DRM 和 Adobe 的 Flash Access 等。

因此，本文在支持时空约束的数字版权管理安全许可协议[2]的基础上，广泛参考国内外 DRM 标准和规范，综合考虑现有 DRM 系统存在的问题以及多媒体内容消费的需求，设计了一种新型通用格式多媒体数字版权管理模型（CPSec media DRM, content protection security），该模型通过非结构化加密方法，不依赖多媒体内容格式，支持通用格式多媒体内容。另外，为了解决许可证重新发行和转让的问题，采用许可证提取码作为下载许可证的凭证，并支持细粒度使用控制[18]方式。

在此模型的基础上，本文实现了基于固定与移动融合（FMC, fixed mobile convergence）[19]业务的多媒体数字版权管理系统，该系统与运营商业务平台结合，综合了内容加密与打包、许可证管理与分发和 DRM 客户端等重要功能，运营商在运营版权内容的同时，保护内容提供商的权益，同时用户在订购获取内容并下载许可证后可以按需使用内容。

3 CPSec Media DRM 模型技术目标

3.1 支持通用音视频多媒体格式

为了支持不同业务，内容平台包含了大量不同格式的音视频多媒体，包括 H263、

H264、MPEG-4、MPEG-2、MP3 和 AC3 等，CPSec Media DRM 设计时同时支持以上通用的音视频格式和未来的新格式，支持不同内容提供商提供的不同格式的版权内容，为 DRM 系统的融合、流通和推广奠定了基础。

3.2 支持许可证重新发行和转让

为了解决许可证丢失无法使用内容和许可证无法转让的问题，CPSec Media DRM 系统设计了随机的许可证提取码，每个许可证对应一个提取码，用户在 DRM 客户端通过许可证提取码下载许可证，并可将许可证提取码转让给其他人，许可证丢失时可以重新通过许可证提取码下载许可证。

3.3 支持细粒度使用控制方式

DRM 许可证描述了用户使用内容时的各项权利，CPSec Media DRM 设计时支持细粒度使用控制方式，包括使用时间、使用次数、用户绑定、设备绑定等，通过不同权利的动态组合满足试用、包月和赠送等使用场景。

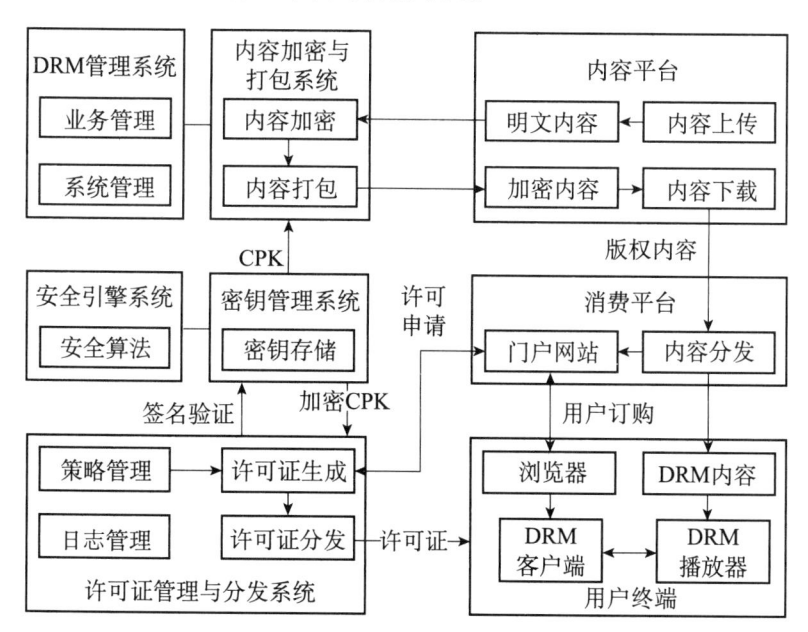

4 CPSec Media DRM 模型设计方案

CPSec Media DRM 同消费平台和内容平台等进行业务、内容和用户数据的交互，完成内容的加密与打包，同时向用户提供控制内容使用的许可证。CPSec Media DRM 功能架构如图1所示，包括内容加密与打包系统、密钥管理系统、安全引擎系统、许可证管理与分发系统、DRM 客户端和 DRM 管理系统等功能单元。

图1 CPSec Media DRM 模型

（1）内容加密与打包系统

内容加密与打包系统接收内容平台需要进行 DRM 保护的内容，使用密钥管理系统提供的内容加密密钥对内容按照非结构化加密方法进行加密。内容打包系统按照 DRM 系统相关规范对加密后的内容打包，然后将受 DRM 保护的内容传送到内容平台，供用户下载使用。

(2) 密钥管理系统

密钥管理系统负责管理 DRM 系统中使用的各种密钥，并维护媒体文件与内容主控密钥的映射关系。内容加密系统从密钥管理系统申请用于加密媒体文件的内容主控密钥；许可证管理与分发系统根据内容标识从密钥管理系统申请对应的内容主控密钥，以加密形式封装到许可证中。

(3) 安全引擎系统

安全引擎系统向密钥管理系统提供以下服务：内容及其主控密钥的加解密、许可证的签名与验证、生成内容主控密钥、对指定内容计算散列值。

(4) 许可证管理与分发系统

许可证管理与分发系统主要负责许可证的生成、分发和管理，包括许可证生成、许可证分发和许可证策略管理等模块。许可证生成模块接收业务系统的许可证创建请求，根据权利信息为用户创建许可证，同时向密钥管理系统申请相应的内容主控密钥，以密文形式封装到许可证；许可证分发模块实现许可证的分发和下载功能；许可证策略管理模块实现许可证策略的管理功能。

(5) DRM 客户端

DRM 客户端执行与媒体文件使用相关的许可和约束，控制用户对媒体文件的使用。用户播放受 DRM 保护的媒体文件时，如果终端没有相应的许可证，媒体播放器会提示用户需要相应的权限才能使用，并通过浏览器将用户重定向到业务系统进行订购，获取许可证下载信息。DRM 客户端获取许可证后，利用内容主控密钥对媒体文件密文进行解密，并根据许可证中的权利信息控制用户对媒体文件的播放及使用。

(6) DRM 管理系统

DRM 管理系统负责内容加密情况、许可证分发与使用情况的统计、分析工作。系统管理负责 DRM 系统角色管理、权限管理和工作状态的检测。

4.1 内容加密与打包系统

4.1.1 内容加密与打包格式

在 CPSec Media DRM 中，通用媒体文件加密后打包成 CPSec Media DRM 内容格式（DCF），定义如下。

(1) 媒体文件头

媒体文件头长度为 20 字节。其中，预留 4 字节，即（'CDRM'）；文件类型 4 字节；CPSec DCF 整体标记 4 字节；CPSec DCF 规范版本标识 4 字节；CPSec DCF 兼容性标记 4 字节。图 2 是文件类型、标记、版本与其他媒体文件内容之间的关系。

(2) 媒体文件体

图 3 是对媒体文件格式的全面描述。DCF 文件体由若干个 CPSec DCF 容器组成，每个 CPSec DCF 容器只包含一个 DCF 头和一个 DRM 内容对象容器。

(3) 非结构化内容加密

内容加密与打包系统使用分组加密算法（如使用 CBC 模式或者 CTR 模式的 AES 算

```
|—4字节—|—4字节—|—4字节—|—4字节—|—4字节—|
```

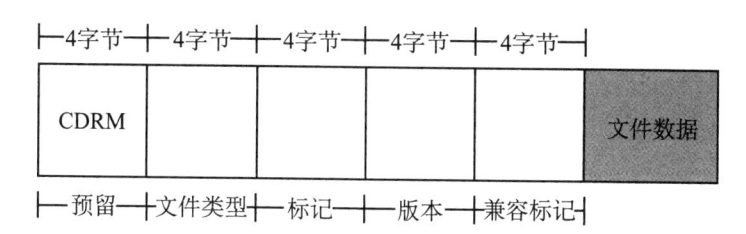

```
| CDRM |      |      |      |      | 文件数据 |
```

```
|—预留—|—文件类型—|—标记—|—版本—|—兼容标记—|
```

图 2　CPSec DCF 媒体头格式

```
|—20字节—|—20字节—|
```

| 文件头 | 容器 | DCF头 | 通用头 | DRM加密内容 |

```
        |————————DRM头————————|——内容容器——|
```

图 3　CPSec DCF 整体格式

法）将不同格式媒体文件按照分块加密，并按照 DCF 整体格式打包。该方法克服了基于内容格式加密方法的局限性，将媒体文件当作整体分块加密，不依赖于多媒体内容的编码格式，因此支持通用格式媒体文件的加密。

4.1.2　内容加密与打包系统工作流程

内容加密与打包系统接收到 DRM 管理系统或内容平台的媒体文件加密请求后，对需要加密的媒体文件按照非结构化加密方法进行加密，同时按照规定的 DCF 对加密后的媒体文件进行打包，内容加密与打包系统参数如表 1 所示。

表 1　内容加密与打包系统参数

参数名称	含义
CP	content provider
CID	content identity
PCD	plain content data
ECD	encrypted content data
ECH	encrypted content hash
DCD	DRM content data
CPK	content provider key
CRK	content random key
CEK	content encryption key
AID	algorithm identity
RID	retrieval identity

内容加密与打包系统工作流程如图 4 所示。

step1　内容加密与打包引擎获取内容主控密钥 CPK 及内容辅助密钥 CRK，安全引擎产生内容加密密钥 CEK，该密钥用于加密媒体内容

$$CEK = E_{CPK}(CRK)$$

step2　内容加密与打包引擎获取加密和打包参数，包括 AID 和 RID 等。

step3　内容加密与打包引擎对 CP 提供的原始媒体文件进行加密，并计算加密内容散

列值 ECH。

$$ECD = E_{CEK}（PCD,AID,RID）$$
$$ECH = Hash（ECD）$$

step4 内容加密与打包引擎对加密后的数据按照规定的 DCF 进行打包，DCD 即是受 DRM 保护的媒体内容。

$$DCD = \{CID \| CRK \| ECD\}$$

step5 所有加密打包过程的参数都保存到数据库中，加密打包后的内容 DCD 提供用户使用。

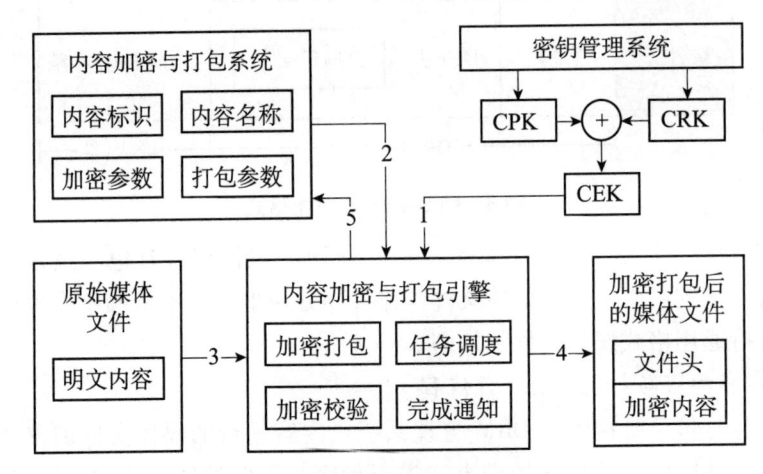

图 4　内容加密与打包系统工作流程

4.2　密钥管理系统

密钥管理系统负责内容主控密钥 CPK 的生成和管理、加密后内容散列值 ECH 的存储和管理等，包括密钥生成、密钥分发、密钥存储和密钥更新等。

密钥管理系统参数如表 2 所示。

表 2　密钥管理系统参数

参数名称	含义
MK	master key
EPK	encrypted provider key
UEK	user encryption key
PRK	private key
PUK	public key

step1 密钥管理系统产生内容主控密钥 CPK，并使用密钥保护 MK 加密存储在数据库中

$$EPK = E_{MK}（CPK）$$

step2 接受内容加密与打包系统的请求，使用密钥保护密钥 MK 解密存储在数据库中加密的内容主控密钥 EPK，返回内容主控密钥 CPK

$$CPK = D_{MK}（EPK）$$

step3 接受许可证管理与分发系统的请求，返回使用用户的公钥 PUK 加密的内容主控密钥 CPK 得到的 UEK 和内容散列值 ECH

$$CPK = D_{MK}（EPK）$$
$$UEK = E_{PUK}（CPK）$$

4.3 安全引擎系统

安全引擎系统为密钥管理系统提供安全计算，主要包括对称加密算法、公钥算法和散列算法等，并支持证书的操作。

4.4 许可证管理与分发系统

许可证管理与分发系统主要包括许可证生成和分发等功能。

（1）许可证生成

许可证生成模块负责根据从业务平台接收的订购信息和用户许可证请求信息生成许可证。

（2）许可证分发

许可证分发模块接收和响应 DRM 客户端的许可证下载请求，将相应的许可证分发到 DRM 客户端。

4.4.1 许可证生成流程

许可证管理与分发系统负责根据从业务平台接收的订购信息，包括用户标识、内容标识以及权限信息等，生成许可证，并返回给业务平台。许可证管理与分发系统参数如表 3 所示。

表 3 许可证管理与分发系统参数

参数名称	含义
UID	user identity
DID	device identity
REX	rights expression
LCQ	license request
LQS	license request signature
LCC	license content
LCS	license signature
LIC	license

许可证管理与分发系统流程如图 5 所示。

step1 业务平台处理用户的订购请求，将订购信息（包括用户标识 UID、内容标识 CID 和权限信息 REX 等）发送到许可证管理与分发系统，许可证管理与分发系统创建该许可证信息。

step2 许可证管理与分发系统根据订购信息中的内容标识从内容加密与打包系统中查询加密内容信息，并保存到许可证信息中。

step3 许可证管理与分发系统将完整的权限信息保存到许可证数据库。

step4 许可证管理与分发系统将许可证下载信息返回给业务平台，业务平台将许可证下载信息返回给用户浏览器，供用户下载许可证。

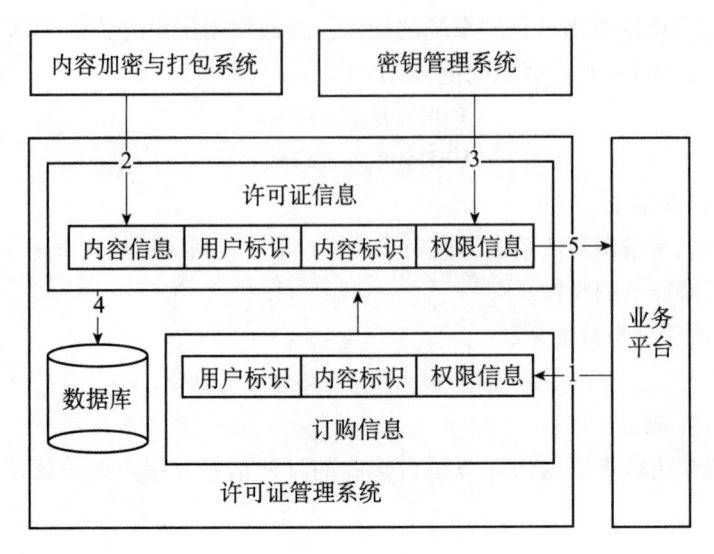

图5 许可证生成流程

4.4.2 许可证分发流程

许可证分发模块接收 DRM 客户端的许可证下载请求,包含设备标识 DID、用户的公钥证书及下载请求签名信息,并将上述信息发送到许可证生成模块,许可证生成模块将最终的许可证内容返回到许可证分发模块,许可证分发模块将许可证分发到 DRM 客户端,如图6所示。

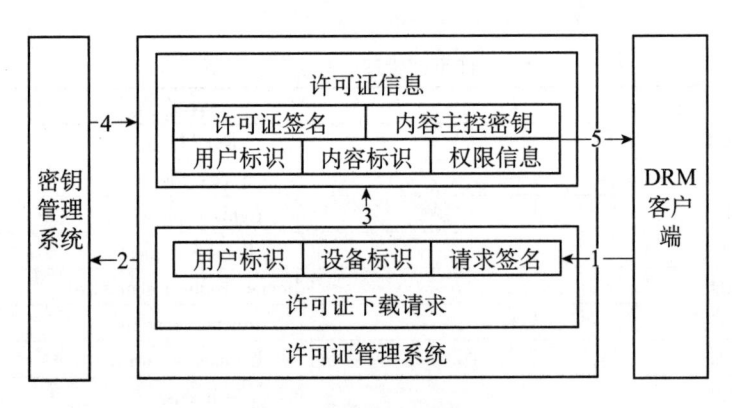

图6 许可证分发流程

step1 许可证管理与分发系统收到 DRM 客户端发起的许可证下载请求,包含许可证下载信息 URL,用户标识 UID,设备标识 DID、用户的公钥 PUK 及下载请求签名信息 LQS 等

$$LCQ = \{URL \parallel UID \parallel DID \parallel PUK \parallel LQS\}$$

step2 许可证管理与分发系统将用户的公钥及下载请求签名信息发送到密钥管理服务器请求验证下载请求和用户身份

$$LQS' = D_{PUK}(URL \parallel UID \parallel DID)$$

验证以下等式是否成立

$$LQS' = LQS$$

step3 许可证管理与分发系统根据下载请求查找到内容标识 CID 和许可证信息，然后将内容标识 CID 发送给密钥管理服务器，获得密钥管理服务器返回的经过加密后的内容主控密钥 UEK 和内容散列值 ECH。

step4 许可证管理与分发系统将权限信息 REX 基于许可证权利描述语言生成待签名的许可证 LCC

$$LCC = \{CID \| UEK \| ECH \| REX \| UID \| DID\}$$

step5 许可证管理与分发系统将待签名的许可证发送给密钥管理服务器请求签名得到 LCS

$$LCS = E_{PRK}（LCC）$$

step6 许可证管理与分发系统在得到密钥管理服务器返回的签名信息 LCS 后，生成最终的许可证文件 LIC

$$LIC = \{LCC \| LCS\}$$

4.5 DRM 客户端

DRM 客户端负责管理包括加密媒体解析和解密、安全引擎调用、许可证下载和管理、客户端管理等。

DRM 客户端的基本工作流程包括：许可证下载和媒体文件解密播放等。

（1）许可证下载

用户订购完成后获取许可证下载信息，通过许

可证下载代理模块完成许可证的下载。用户也可以在 DRM 客户端管理提供的许可证下载界面上输入许可证提取码，发起许可证下载请求。

如图 7 所示，在下载许可证之前，客户端需要向许可证管理与分发服务器提供用户的公钥，在这里，用户的公私钥对由客户端产生和维护。许可证管理与分发服务器和密钥管理服务器协作完成许可证的封装，并把许可证下发到客户端。

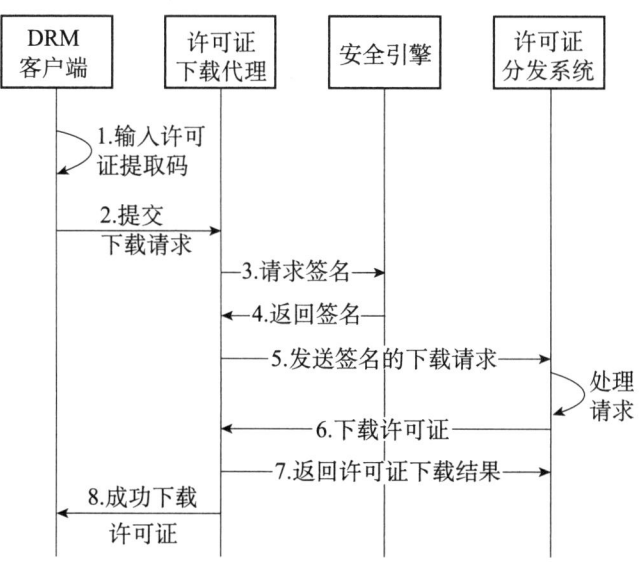

图 7 DRM 客户端下载许可证时序

（2）媒体文件解密播放

DRM 客户端获取许可证后，使用 DRM 播放器按照许可证描述播放内容，时序如图 8 所示。

DRM 客户端使用许可证管理与分发服务器的公钥来验证许可证签名，许可证和设备的绑定是通过用户的公钥加密内容主控密钥 UEK 和用户设备标识 DID 实现，在判断绑定关系正确后，DRM 客户端使用用户的私钥从许可证解密出内容主控密钥 CPK，然后和 DRM 头中的内容辅助密钥 CRK 导出 CEK

$$CPK = D_{PRK}（UEK）$$

$$CEK = E_{CPK}（CRK）$$

DRM 客户端使用 CEK 调用安全引擎解密受保护的媒体内容 ECD，将待播放的明文数据 PCD 交给播放器进行播放

$$PCD = D_{CEK}（ECD，AID，RID）$$

5　CPSec Media DRM 系统实现方案

5.1　内容加密与打包系统

内容加密与打包系统以任务的形式提供服务，支持单个和批量任务的提交，系统后台自动伺服对内容按照指定参数进行加密和打包，任务完成后通知用户和系统。系统支持高、较高、一般、较低、低等 5 个优先级，管理员可根据内容要求动态调整任务优先级。

5.2　密钥管理系统

密钥管理系统采用 3 层密钥管理模型，其中第一层负责媒体内容加密，采用分组密码算法；第二层负责内容密钥保护，所用密钥称为内容主控密钥，采用分组密码算法；第三层负责将内容主控密钥分发给授权用户，采用非对称算法。

5.3　安全引擎系统

安全引擎系统基于 OpenSSL 算法库，提供相关加解密算法，支持对称加密算法、非对称加密算法、散列算法和 X.509 证书操作等，实现公私钥对的生成、数字签名、身份认证、散列值计算、解密内容主控密钥 CMK 等功能。

5.4　许可证管理与分发系统

许可证管理与分发系统负责根据从业务平台接收的订购信息，生成许可证提取码，并返回给业务平台，用户获取许可证提取码后在终端输入许可证提取码下载许可证，系统根据许可证提取码分发许可证到客户端。

CPSec Media DRM 系统定义的权利表达语言 REL（rights expression language）规定的是基于 ODRL[20] 控制 DRM 内容使用权利的语法和语义，即权利表达语言是用于规范定义权利对象的语法和语义，包括基础模板、协议模板、背景模板、许可模板、约束模板、继承模板和安全模板，约束模板包括的细粒度使用控制如表 4 所示。

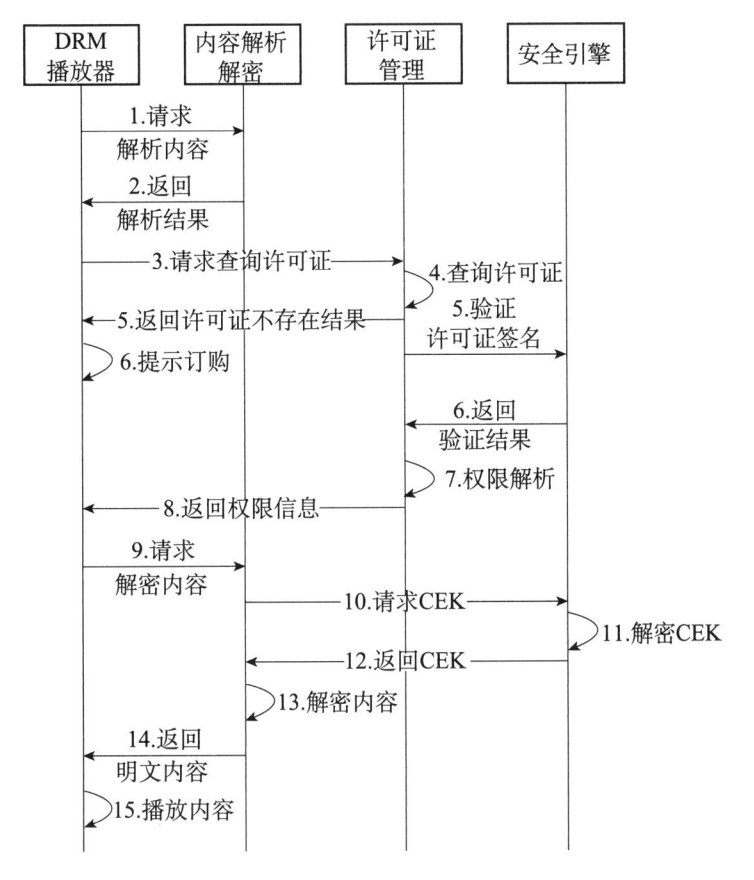

图 8　DRM 媒体解密播放时序

表 4　许可证约束模板中细粒度使用控制

元素	描述
count	计次元素规定一个许可对 DRM 内容可授权使用的次数
timed-count	定时计次元素可视为增加了一个可选择的定时器属性的计次元素
datetime	日期时间元素定义时间的范围，对包含的许可分别表示时间的限制
start	开始元素规定开始的时间或日期
end	结束元素规定结束的时间或日期
interval	间隔时间元素规定许可能够在 DRM 内容上执行的时间周期
accumulated	累计时间元素规定权利作用于 DRM 内容的累计时间的最大值
individual	个体元素规定与 DRM 内容所绑定的个体
system	系统元素规定 DRM 内容和权利对象可以输出到的目标系统

5.5　DRM 客户端

DRM 客户端包括加密文件解析解密、安全引擎、许可证下载代理、许可证管理、本地许可证库、客户端管理、播放器插件和浏览器插件等单元。

6 CPSec Media DRM 实验结果分析

通过实验对比 CPSec Media DRM 系统加密的性能，同时对比原始内容和受 DRM 保护后的内容播放的资源占用等性能，验证本文方案的性能和实时性。

6.1 实验1

比较 CPSec Media DRM 系统采用的非结构化加密和帧加密的加密性能。实验数据选取水平分辨率分别为 320p、480p、720p 和 1 080p 的不同媒体，实验环境为 IBMX3650 服务器，非结构化加密算法采用 AES 算法。

实验过程中分别对上述 4 组 DRM 媒体进行加密处理，并统计其加密时间。

实验中本文的非结构化加密结果和文献[9]的帧加密进行了对比测试，结果如表 5 所示。实验结果表显示非结构化加密平均速度为 10Mbit/s，而帧加密平均速度为 8.4Mbit/s。与帧加密相比，非结构化加密速度平均高出 15%~20%，并且非结构化加密速度符合线性关系，而帧加密随着媒体内容大小和帧数量的不断增多，其速度呈逐渐降低趋势。

表5 非结构化加密结果

内容分辨率	内容大小/MB	加密时间/s 本文	加密时间/s 文献[9]	加密速度/(Mbit·s^{-1}) 本文	加密速度/(Mbit·s^{-1}) 文献[9]
320p	109	11.0	12.6	9.91	8.65
480p	157	15.9	18.2	9.87	8.63
720p	321	32.2	38.3	9.97	8.38
1 080p	648	63.9	80.5	10.14	8.05

与非结构化加密相比，帧加密需要耗费时间在多媒体内容帧结构的解析上，并且帧加密后的媒体依然能够播放，只不过画面出现错乱，而非结构化加密方法将媒体结构信息等全部加密，用户无法播放加密后的媒体，安全性较高。

实验结果表明非结构化加密方法有着较高的加密效率和较好的实用性，并且能够支持不同格式和大小的多媒体内容的加密处理。

6.2 实验2

比较 CPSec Media DRM 系统播放的性能。实验数据选取水平分辨率分别为 320p、480p、720p 和 1 080p 的同一媒体，实验环境 CPU 主频大小为双核 2.2GHz，内存大小为 2GB。

实验过程中分别对上述 4 组 DRM 视频进行下载播放，并统计其 CPU 平均占用率。

实验中 CPU 平均占用率如图 9 所示。实验结果表显示多媒体比特率越高，受 DRM 保护的多媒体播放时 CPU 平均占用率比原始媒体播放时高出越多。

总体来看，DRM 保护的媒体使用时资源占用平均高出 3%~5%，在不影响多媒体质量的前提下，保持着较低的资源占用，能够支持不同硬件性能的终端。

7 CPSec Media DRM 对比分析

目前，主流的多媒体 DRM 方案包括 OMA DRM2.0、Adobe Flash Access 和微软 Media

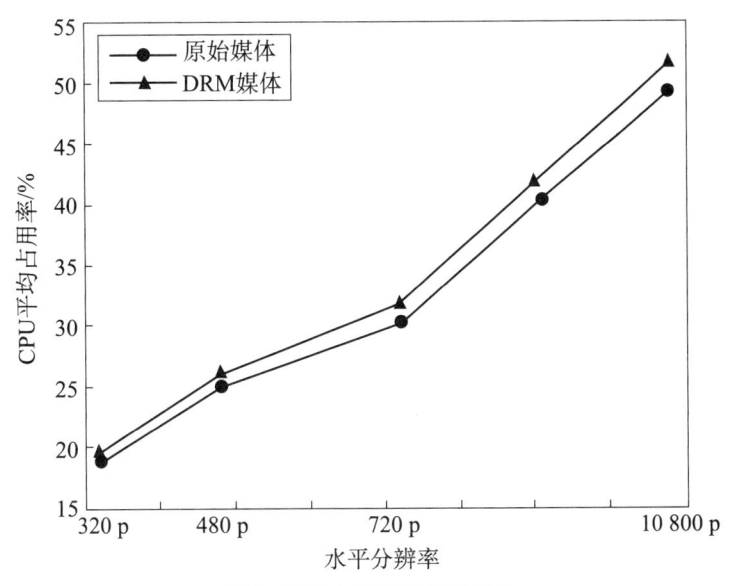

图 9 资源占用实验结果对比

DRM 等，CPSec Media DRM 在支持的媒体格式、内容加密方法、支持的终端平台、许可证重新发行、许可证转让、许可证用户绑定、许可证设备绑定和许可证离线使用等方面与这些方案的对比分析如表 6 所示。本文所提的方案支持通用媒体格式，许可证支持重新发行、转让、用户绑定、设备绑定和离线使用。

针对 DRM 的攻击主要包括协议中的客户端和服务器之间缺乏相互认证，转储内容加密密钥或未加密的内容等，本文所提的方案中媒体内容使用内容加密密钥加密，保证内容的安全性，许可证下载时客户端和服务器之间使用 HTTPS 加密协议，保证下载申请和许可证的安全性，同时下载申请使用用户的私钥签名，提供给服务器认证用户身份，下载的许可证使用服务器的私钥签名，保证许可证的完整性，许可证中的内容密钥使用用户的公钥加密，保证内容加密密钥的安全性。

表 6 多媒体 DRM 对比分析

对比特性	CPSec Media DRM	OMA DRM 2.0	Adobe Flash Access	微软 Media DRM
支持的媒体格式	通用媒体格式	移动媒体格式	FLV 和 F4V	WMV、WMA 和 ASF
内容加密方法	非结构化加密	非结构化加密	结构加密	结构加密
支持的终端平台	PC 终端、移动终端和机顶盒终端等	移动终端	PC 终端、移动终端和机顶盒终端等	PC 终端和移动终端等
许可证重新发行	支持	不支持	支持	支持
许可证转让	支持	不支持	不支持	不支持
许可证用户绑定	支持	支持	不支持	不支持
许可证设备绑定	支持	支持	不支持	不支持
许可证离线使用	支持	支持	支持	不支持

目前，多媒体内容逐渐成为互联网主流，为了适应多媒体技术和移动终端的快速发展，本方案下一步重点研究许可证的离线分发和用户域的支持。

8 结束语

本文提出一种新型通用格式多媒体数字版权管理的模型,该模型通过非结构化加密方法以支持通用多媒体格式,支持不同内容提供商提供的不同类型的版权内容。同时,本模型实现中引入了许可证提取码的概念,用户通过许可证提取码下载许可证,解决许可证重新发行和转让的问题,满足试用、赠送等复杂的使用场景。

与现有的多媒体 DRM 方案相比,本文提出的 CPSec Media DRM 方案,支持通用多媒体格式,支持许可证的重新发行和转让,并且支持细粒度使用控制方式,效率及安全性较高,具有较好的实用性。

参考文献

[1] WIPO-world intellectual property organization [EB/OL]. http://www.wipo.int.

[2] 马兆丰,范科峰,陈铭等. 支持时空约束的可信数字版权管理安全许可协议[J]. 通信学报, 2008, 29(10): 153-164.
MA Z F, FAN K F, CHEN M, et al. Trusted digital rights management protocol supporting for time and space constraint [J]. Journal of Communications, 2008, 29(10): 153-164.

[3] 庄超. 一种新型的 Internet 内容版权保护的计算机制[J]. 计算机学报, 2000, 23(10): 1088-1091.
ZHUANG C. A new computing mechanism for Internet content copyright protection [J]. Chinese Journal of Computers, 2000, 23(10): 1088-1091.

[4] 谭建龙,庄超,白硕. 一种实用的 Internet 内容版权保护系统的设计与实现[J]. 计算机研究与发展, 2001, 38(10): 1119-1203.
TAN J L, ZHUANG C, BAI S. Design and implementation of a practical Internet content copyright protection system [J]. Journal of Computer Research and Development, 2001, 38(10): 1119-1203.

[5] 俞银燕,汤帜. 数字版权保护技术研究综述[J]. 计算机学报, 2005, 28(12): 957-968.
YU Y Y, TANG Z. A survey of the research on digital rights management [J]. Chinese Journal of Computers, 2005, 28(12): 957-968.

[6] 马兆丰,冯博琴. 基于动态许可证的信任版权安全认证协议[J]. 软件学报, 2004, 15(1): 131-140.
MA Z F, FENG B Q. Secure authentication protocol for trusted copyright management based on dynamic license [J]. Journal of Software, 2004, 15(1): 131-140.

[7] 范科峰,莫玮,曹山等. 数字版权管理技术及应用研究进展[J]. 电子学报, 2007, 35(6): 1139-1147.
FAN K F, MO W, CAO S, et al. Advances in digital rights management technology and application [J]. Acta Electronica Sinica, 2007, 35(6): 1139-1147.

[8] LI J S, HSIEH C J, HUNG C F. A novel DRM framework for peer-to-peer music content delivery [J]. Journal of Systems and Soft-ware, 2010, 83(10): 1689-1700.

［9］ KIM B, CHOI J, KIM J, et al. A study on frame encryption for protecting IPTV contents［A］. Advanced Communication Technology (ICACT)［C］. 2011. 1484-1488.

［10］ JEONG Y, KIM J, YOON K. Consumer electronics［A］. Audio DRM Conversion between Different DRM Content Formats［C］. 2008. 1-2.

［11］ 钟勇, 秦小麟, 刘凤玉. 一种面向 DRM 的责任授权模型及其实施框架［J］. 软件学报, 2010, 21（8）: 2059-2069.
ZHONG Y, QIN X L, LIU F Y. Obligation authorization model and its implementation framework for DRM［J］. Journal of Software, 2010, 21（8）: 2059-2069.

［12］ OMA DRM［EB/OL］. http://www.openmobilealliance.org.

［13］ Marlin DRM［EB/OL］. http://www.marlin-community.com.

［14］ Apple Inc. Thoughts on music［EB/OL］. http://www.apple.com/hotnews/thoughtsonmusic.

［15］ Microsoft media rights server. microsoft corp［EB/OL］. http://www.microsoft.com/windows/windowsmedia/drm/default.aspx.

［16］ Adobe flash access［EB/OL］. http://www.adobe.com/products/adobeaccess.html.

［17］ 魏景芝, 杨义先, 钮心忻. OMA DRM 技术体系研究综述［J］. 电子与信息学报, 2008, 30（3）: 746-751.
WEI J Z, YANG Y X, NIU X X. Overview of study on the technical architecture of OMA DRM［J］. Journal of Electronics & Information Technology, 2008, 30（3）: 746-751.

［18］ SANDHU R, PARK J. Usage control: a vision for next generation access control［A］. Proc of the MMM-ACNS-2003［C］. Heidelberg: Springer-Verlag, 2003. 17-31.

［19］ WONG C C, LOW A L Y, HIEW P L. Fixed-mobile convergence: creating values with appropriate business models［A］. Information and Communication Technologies, ICTTA' 06, 2nd［C］. 2006. 17-22.

［20］ ODRL: open digital rights language［EB/OL］. http://www.odrl.net.

基于 UCON 模型的移动数字出版版权保护系统研究与设计*

吕井华 马兆丰 张德栋 闫玺玺

1 引言

移动数字出版是一种以移动通信技术为基础的出版模式，具有移动性、私密性、快捷性、贴身性、智能性、互动性等优势，满足了人们对即时、海量信息的需求。随着移动数据增值业务的蓬勃发展以及智能手机、掌上电脑和电子阅读器等移动终端性能的不断提高，移动数字出版（如移动电视、手机游戏、电子书等）俨然已成为数字出版的一个重要发布环节，产业发展前景广阔。然而，计算机和互联网技术的迅速发展，也使得数字作品的非法制作、存储、分发、复制、修改以及交易越来越容易。因此，移动数字作品的版权保护问题也愈发显得重要。

数字版权管理（Digital Right Management，DRM）是当前对数字作品进行版权保护的主要手段，现已应用到固定数据网络和移动业务领域。OMA DRM 2.0 规范是目前最成熟、参与者最多、影响力最大、最适合应用于移动数据业务的 DRM 方案。该规范最大的创新之处在于逻辑上分离 DRM 内容和版权对象（RO），使内容更适于多应用场景。然而，OMA DRM 2.0 系统复杂，不易于部署和实施；采取把版权对象（RO）和指定设备相绑定的机制，给用户带来了极大的不便[1]。

访问控制是信息安全的基本策略，目的是保证数字作品不被非法访问和使用。访问控制对信息的机密性和完整性起作用。传统访问控制采用前预先授权机制[2]，主要针对的是"服务器端"封闭环境中的数字内容访问控制，不能进行动态授权，也不能对移动终端数字内容使用进行控制，因此不能很好地适应目前以开放式为主的网络环境。针对访问控制模型本身的不足，Ravi Sandhu 教授和 Jaehong Park 博士于 2002 年提出了使用控制（UCON，Usage Control）[3]理论。UCON 模型的授权连续性和属性的可变性，将传统访问控制、信任管理和数字版权管理 3 个领域的问题进行了统一的考虑，它是解决开放式网络环境中的访问控制问题的一种新型的访问控制模型[2-4]。

当前，绝大多数的使用控制实施机制完全以软件为载体，容易受到攻击和监听。鉴于此，在深入研究移动出版的产业链和 UCON 模型的基础上，本文参考 OMA DRM 2.0 标准，引入基于硬件的可信计算技术[5]，设计了基于 UCON 模型的移动数字出版版权保护系统。根据实际应用，验证并分析了该系统的工作流程及其性能。

---

* 本文选自《计算机科学》，第 39 卷第 11A 期，2012 年 11 月，第 6-8 页、44 页

2 移动数字出版产业链分析

移动出版是将图书、报纸、杂志等内容资源进行数字化加工，运用先进的数字版权保护技术（DRM），通过互联网、无线网以及存储设备进行传播，用户在移动阅读设备上通过阅读软件实现阅读和听书等功能，以实现随时随地的阅读[6]。以目前移动数字出版的商业模式来看，移动数字出版的产业链，从内容的提供到最终用户的访问，包括内容提供商（CP）、服务提供商（SP）、平台运营商、移动运营商和移动终端用户5个环节。移动数字出版的产业链模型及各环节功能如图1所示。

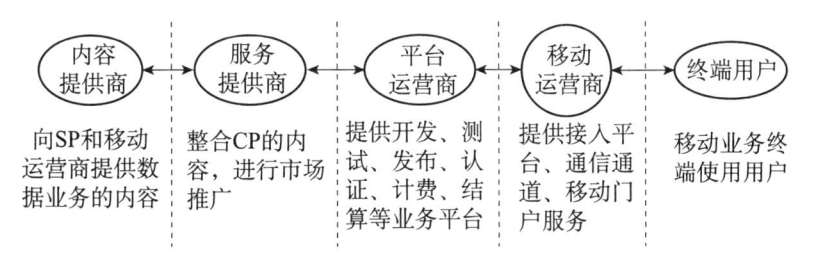

图1 移动数字出版产业链模型及其功能

基于 UCON 模型的移动数字出版版权保护系统作为移动数字出版产业链中的一类业务平台，集移动版权交易分发、移动内容授权控制和移动终端版权保护等服务为一体，旨在实现多移动业务模式和多移动通信方式的移动数字出版的版权保护。

3 基于 UCON 模型的移动数字出版版权保护系统

3.1 系统体系架构

OMA DRM 2.0 是目前使用最为广泛的数字版权保护标准，本系统参考该标准，根据目前移动出版实际运作情况及发展趋势构建基于 UCON 模型的移动出版版权保护系统，其系统体系架构如图2所示。

根据目前移动数字出版多业务多平台应用情况，本系统包括数据提供子系统和数据使用子系统两部分，它们分别采用基于服务器和客户端的使用控制引用监控器结构。基于服务器的引用监控器负责整体的数据服务管理、定制与分发，不允许用户下载客体资源（即使可以下载，服务器端系统和决策等也不会受到影响），允许引用监控器控制外的用户访问客体资源。基于客户端的引用监控器可以全面地控制已分发下载的数字资源在客户端的使用情况，如使用时间、使用方式以及使用次数等。采用基于服务器和客户端的引用监控器结构，本系统支持在线和离线两种方式的访问控制服务，可实现授权数字内容在多用户多设备构成的内容共享域内的正常交换和使用，防止非授权使用和非法扩散，满足新型的内容应用服务模式下的数字版权保护需求。

内容/服务提供者（CP/SP）提供的内容和版权服务器提供的密钥经 DRM 打包工具，生成 DRM 内容和版权对象（RO）。内容发布者发送 DRM 内容，版权发布者（RI）产生

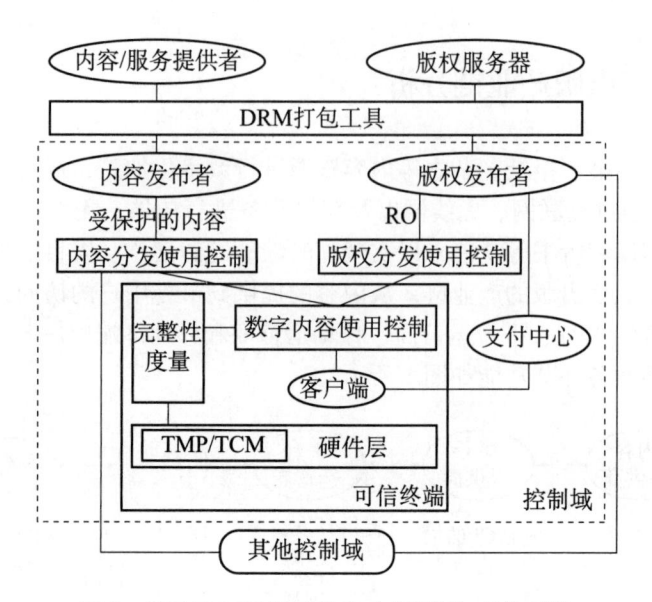

图 2 基于 UCON 模型的移动出版版权保护系统

RO 来控制 DRM 内容的使用。经内容/版权分发使用控制，内容发布者和 RI 将用户申请的内容和 RO 下发到客户端。可信平台（TMP）或可信密码模块（TCP）提供了基于硬件的可信根，用以鉴别用户身份。根据信任度评估，对客户端应用程序的数字内容使用进行控制，实现数字出版内容的版权保护。

3.2 系统工作机制

从数据流的分析来看，基于 UCON 模型的移动出版版权保护系统可包括数字内容传输、数字资源分发控制和移动终端数字内容使用控制 3 部分。

3.2.1 数字内容传输安全

系统沿用 OMA DRM 2.0 标准的内容加密和 DRM 打包、内容加密密钥（CEK）封装过程及 RI 数字签名方式。数字内容传输过程如图 3 所示。

（1）内容提供者把打包加密的内容传送给内容分发者，由内容分发者发送 DRM 内容。用户请求共享数字内容，获取内容访问权。基于 UCON 使用控制模型，授权判定是内容分发者决定是否分发业务给用户。

（2）目前移动出版商业模式是基于支付的访问控制策略，保证内容服务商和移动运营商的经济效益。经支付判断，由 RI 给 DRM 内容分发授权证书。

（3）与 OMA DRM 2.0 标准不同的是，本系统采用 TCG 规范中的签署密钥（Endorsement key，EK）的公钥（PubEK）加密 RO，并用其私钥（PrivEK）在客户端解密 RO。

（4）使用 pull，push 或流传输机制分别发送 DRM 内容和 RO。

3.2.2 数字资源分发控制

基于服务器端的使用控制引用监控器负责整体的数据服务管理、定制与分发。本系统采用的资源分发控制模型如图 4 所示。

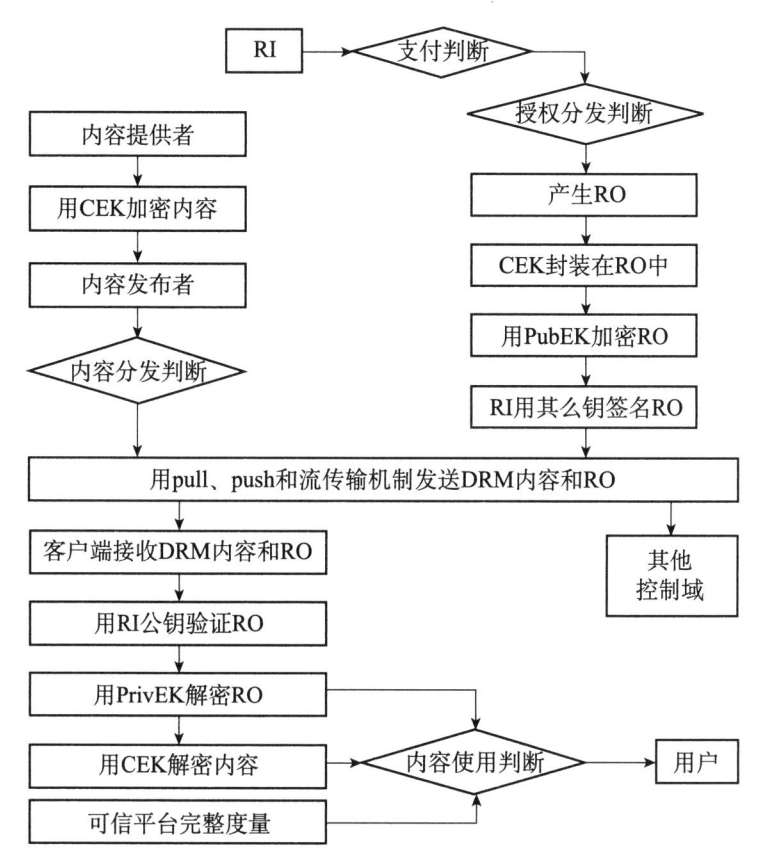

图3 基于UCON模型的移动出版版权保护系统工作流程

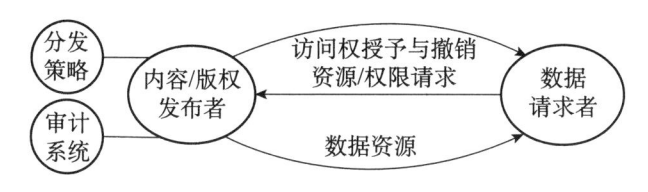

图4 数字资源分发控制

资源分发控制模型形式化描述如下：

S：资源请求者，获取资源访问权或数据资源的主体。

O：资源拥有者，在此内容/版权发布者为访问客体。

R：数据资源或资源访问权。

$ATT(S)$：与内容/版权发布者有关的属性，如RO或DRM内容。

$ATT(O)$：资源请求者的相关属性，如可信度、物理环境信息等。

$Allowed(s, o, r)$：访问控制函数，内容/版权发布者向资源请求者发送DRM内容或RO；

$preUpdate(ATT(s))$：$preUpdate(ATT(o))$：对主客体属性进行更新。

分发策略是资源拥有者发布内容和签发证书的方式；审计系统是用来存储分发的授权证书，以备日后审计、撤销时使用。通常，数字版权管理使用基于支付的安全策略。RI

首先对请求权限进行支付判断，然后实施分发控制。

3.2.3 移动终端数字内容使用控制

数据使用子系统基于可信计算平台，保证用户身份可信。可信计算平台内部各元素之间要对上层进行严密认证，从系统的启动开始，BIOS、操作系统的加载模块、操作系统都要被一一验证，以确保启动链中的软件未被篡改。移动终端数字内容使用控制架构如图5所示。传感器记录了操作系统的物理环境，可供使用控制监控器作为评估依据。完整性度量服务（IMS）的最主要的功能是测量其他包含可信计算基（TCB）且实施使用控制策略的组件。完整性认证服务（IVS）验证相应 IMS 测量的完整值，并为使用控制监控器生成部分实施策略。

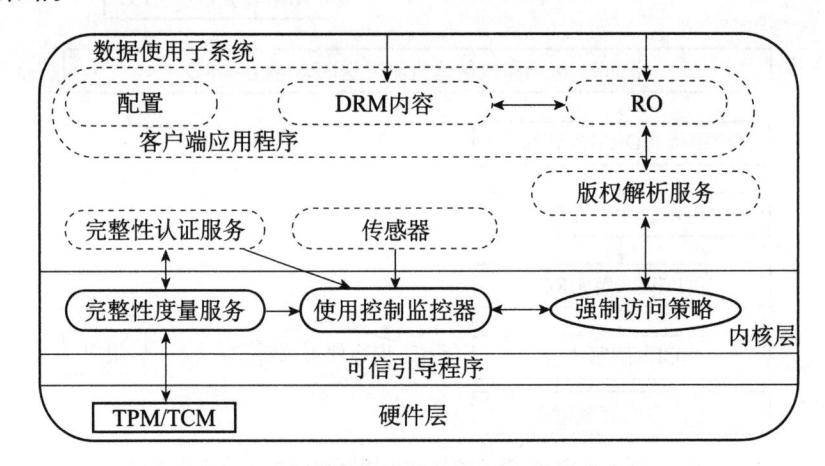

图5　移动终端数字内容使用控制架构

（1）当一个用户登录系统或通过调用客户端应用程序试图访问数据时，基于用户认证的使用控制监控器审核用户属性，如角色和必需的用户授权证书。

（2）当用户调用客户端应用程序，并在内存加载之前 IMS 测量客户端应用程序。

（3）IMS 和 IVS 测量值作为使用控制监控器评估的信任度，传感器监控移动终端设备信息（如系统配置、位置等）。信任度和物理环境可作为使用控制实施的上下文信息。

（4）策略解析服务用于将下载的版权对象解析为策略并转化为服务，作为使用控制监控器的使用规则，包括被授权使用的用户和终端设备、授权使用的方式及使用期限等规则信息。

（5）强制访问控制是系统强制客户端服从访问控制策略，可防止病毒、间谍软件、蠕虫病毒等恶意程序攻击系统漏洞。在本系统中，强制访问控制策略包括使用规则及客户端和整个安全系统的配置信息等。

（6）以上信息作为使用控制监控器的输入，进行请求判定并返回客户端对 DRM 内容访问的结果。

（7）如果允许访问，版权解析服务调用 TPM/TCM 签署密钥的私钥（PrivEK）解封密钥并解密 DRM 内容。如果拒绝访问，则返回出错信息给客户端应用程序。

综上对基于 UCON 模型的移动出版版权保护系统工作机制的分析，现给出一个基于此系统的移动数字出版内容使用流程的简单实例，如图6所示。

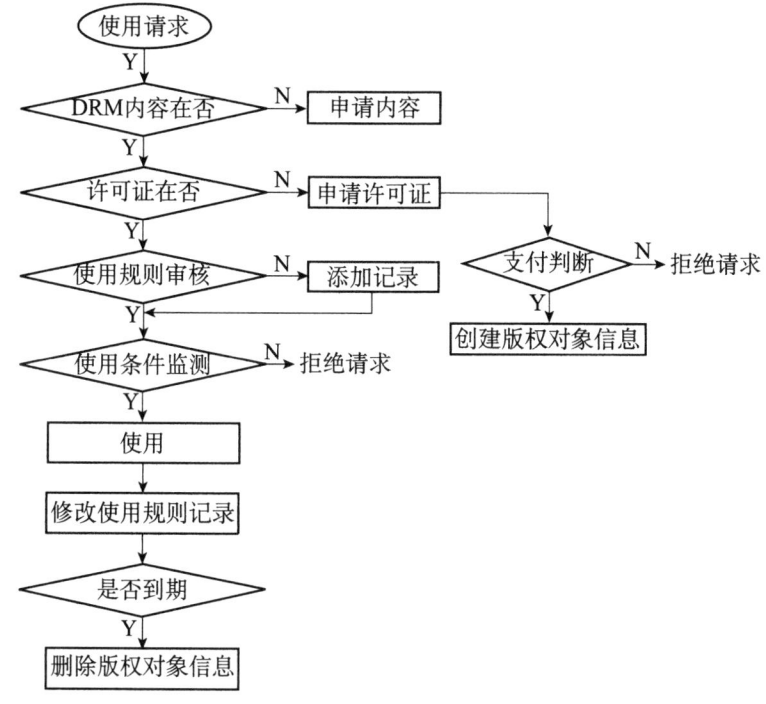

图6 移动数字出版内容使用流程

3.3 系统性能分析

3.3.1 安全性分析

基于UCON模型的移动出版版权保护系统的安全性评测可从抗攻击能力和攻击后防御强度两个方面来分析[7]。

（1）抗攻击能力

抗攻击能力可从加解密方式、权限对象的保护和传输安全3个指标来评测。

加解密方式：本系统服务器端使用128bit的CEK对数字内容进行DRM打包加密，采用RC4算法，安全性依赖于算法。

权限对象的保护：本系统客户端嵌入于可信终端，CEK使用TPM/TCM签署密钥的公钥（PubEK）加密，之后使用服务器端的私钥签名，防止机密数据被非授权用户及非法进程所获取，保护权限对象的完整性。权限对象保护依赖于"PubEK"，我们一致认为PubEK是保密的。

传输安全：本系统包含了在传输权限对象过程中对物理环境进行使用控制验证，因此可以有效地保障数据在传输过程中的安全。

（2）攻击后防御强度

攻击后防御强度可从版权可控性和系统可恢复性两个指标来评测。

版权可控性：签署密钥的私钥（PrivEK）只存在于TPM/TCM中，且一个TPM/TCM对应唯一的EK。强制访问控制策略可有效防止恶意攻击，内核层使用控制监控器可提供用户与终端设备的相互验证及其授权使用的方式及使用期限等使用规则。因此，即使本系统被破解，版权对象也是可控的。

系统可恢复性：本系统包括数据提供子系统和数据使用子系统。在系统被攻破的前提下，数据使用子系统部署在移动终端，较难更新，但是可以采用更新数据提供子系统的方法来恢复，如更换 DRM 加密算法、升级版权服务器和内容服务器。

表 1 给出了基于 UCON 模型的移动出版版权保护系统与 OMA DRM 的安全性能对比情况。由此可见，基于目前移动终端发展，本文提出的系统能够明显地提高移动数字版权保护的完整性和保密性。

表 1 本文系统与 OMA DRM 安全性比较

安全特性指标	OMA DRM	基于 UCON 模型的移动出版版权保护系统
用户与终端验证	无	有
客户端与终端的完整性认证	无	有
客户端数据安全保证	无	有
防恶意攻击	无	有
权限对象的加密保护	客户端公钥	基于可信平台，依赖于"PubEK"
版权可控性	一定范围可控	基于使用控制监管，版权可控
系统可恢复性	难恢复	可恢复

3.3.2 应用分析

目前，OMA DRM 对终端的支持比较滞后且直播流业务的实现方式未确定。在应用方面，OMA DRM 的用户只能在特定的设备上使用已购买的 DRM 内容，而不能带到异地使用，用户也不能将自己购买的 RO 转让给别人，这给用户带来了极大的不便。

基于 UCON 模型的移动出版版权保护系统是在终端可信平台上实现的。移动终端设备先进且可信，客户端应用程序可以采用"终端设备——数字内容使用控制——移动存储"的方式，对 DRM 内容和 RO 进行转移操作。从应用方面来说，基于 UCON 模型的移动出版版权保护系统安全性高、运行速度快，更方便用户使用。

结束语 本文给出了一个适于现代商业模式的基于 UCON 模型的移动出版版权保护系统。在实际应用中内容使用和权力控制关系会更复杂，在此只讨论了系统模型，系统具体实现需进一步完善。希望本文能对移动出版版权保护的深入研究和实施推广提供一定的参考价值。

参考文献

[1] 魏景芝，杨义先，钮心忻. OMA DRM 技术体系研究综述 [J]. 电子与信息学报，2008, 30 (3)：746-751

[2] Park J, Sandhu R. Usage control：A vision for next generation access control [C] // International Workshop on Mathematical Methods, Models and Architectures for Computer Networks Security, 2003：17-31

[3] Park J, Sandhu R. Towards usage control models：beyond traditional access control [C] // Proceedings of the Seventh ACM Symposium on Access Control Models and Technologies. ACM Press, 2002：57-64

[4] Park J, Sandhu R. The UCON$_{ABC}$ Usage Control Model [J]. ACM Transactions on Information and Sys-

tems Security, 2004, 7 (1): 128-174

[5] 阎希光. 可信计算的研究及其发展 [J]. 信息安全与通信保密, 2006 (1): 18-20

[6] 陈晓宏. 传统出版向数字出版转型的思考 [J]. 中共福建省委党校学报, 2009 (1): 87-91

[7] 李润峰, 马兆丰, 杨义先, 等. 数字版权管理安全性评测模型研究 [J]. 计算机科学, 2011, 38 (3): 24-27

[8] Zhang Xin-wen, Seifert J P, Sandhu R. Security Enforcement Model for Distributed Usage Control [C] //Proc. of 2008 IEEE International Conference on Sensor Networks, Ubiquitous, and Trustworthy Computing. Taichung, China: IEEE Computer Society, 2008: 10-18

[9] Park J, Zhang X, Sandhu R. Attribute mutability in usage control [J]. Annual IFIP WG Working Conference on Data and Applications Security, 2004, 11 (3): 1-12

[10] 王斐, 王凤英. 基于使用控制的资源分发模型 [J]. 山东理工大学学报, 2007, 21 (4): 31-34

[11] 聂丽平. 基于UCON访问控制模型的分析与研究 [D]. 合肥: 合肥工业大学, 2006

[12] 初晓博, 秦宇. 一种基于可信计算的分布式使用控制系统 [J]. 计算机学报, 2010, 33 (1): 93-102

基于数字水印的 PDF 完整性认证研究*

支 策　马兆丰　蒋 铭　钮心忻　杨义先

引言

当下，数字水印的研究方向主要针对图像、视频和音频等，针对文本载体进行水印设计研究的进展较慢。但是目前大量的信息处理都由传统的纸质文档向电子文档进行转变，因此，针对文本文档的水印研究依旧有重要价值[1-2]。PDF（Portable Document Format）是一种与设备无关的文档格式，利用这一格式可以使人们以更有效的方式共享、观看和打印文档，目前已经发展成为网络信息传递中的主流文件格式。因此，研究 PDF 文档的数字水印技术具有广泛的应用价值。目前针对 PDF 文档的数字水印研究主要有如下方式：

（1）基于文本格式的水印嵌入。算法通过对 PDF 文档中字体间隔，字体颜色、字体亮度等特征进行微调，实现水印信息的嵌入[3-4]。但其格式统计特征明显，且难以抵抗格式转换攻击，嵌入容量较小，水印隐蔽性较弱。

（2）基于语法和语义的水印嵌入。利用自然语句技术，通过同义词转换、标点处理、句型转换等方式实现水印嵌入[5]，可抵抗格式转换的攻击。但因汉字语言的多义性、复杂性等特点，难以创建语义和逻辑连贯的段落，实现难度大，较难实现大容量的水印嵌入。

文中针对 PDF 作为格式化文件的特点，采用伪造无效输出对象的形式，在完全不改变原始文件显示方式的情况下获取水印冗余空间，并设计提出了一种既可以对 PDF 文档每一页进行完整性认证，同时又包含了版权声明的基于结构的水印算法，具有安全、高效和高冗余空间的特点。

1 PDF 文档结构分析

PDF 文档的组成可从物理构成和逻辑构成两方面描述，物理构成指 PDF 文档在物理上的组织方式，逻辑构成指 PDF 文档的逻辑运作方式。

1.1 PDF 文档的基本组成元素

对象是 PDF 文档的基本组成元素，其主体部分是由一系列这样的对象构成的，这些对

---

* 本文选自《信息安全与通信保密》，第 10 期，2012 年 10 月，第 63－66 页

象代表了文档中的各个组件，如页面、字体和图像等。

1.2 PDF 文档的物理构成

PDF 文档结构可分为 4 个部分[6]，如图 1 所示：

图 1 PDF 文档结构

（1）文件头（Header）。指明了该文件所遵从的 PDF 规范的版本号，文件头一定出现在文件的第一行。

（2）文件体（Body）。PDF 文档的主要部分，由一系列的对象构成，如页面对象、内容对象等。

（3）交叉引用表（Xref）。为了能对文件体中各个对象进行随机存取而设立的一个间接对象的地址索引表，通过交叉引用表可获得文档中各个对象相对文档开始的偏移量，可快速定位对象位置。

（4）文件尾（Trailer）。声明了交叉引用表的地址，并指明了文件体的根对象（Catalog）。根对象是文件体逻辑上开始的地方，通过根对象对其他对象的引用并查询交叉引用表，即可实现对 PDF 文档中所有对象的访问。

1.3 PDF 文档的逻辑构成

如图 2 所示，PDF 文档逻辑构成为：从文件尾所指定的根出发，将所有的对象以页面为模型，联系成一个逻辑上的整体，从而实现了整个文档输出的描述。根是一个容器对象（Document catalog），一个文档只有一个有效的容器，容器包含了页面组（Pages）、大纲等，页面组包含了页面（Page）对象，页面对象由各种基本的内容流对象（文本流、图像流等）组成，这些对象共同完成了页面所有输出结果的描述。

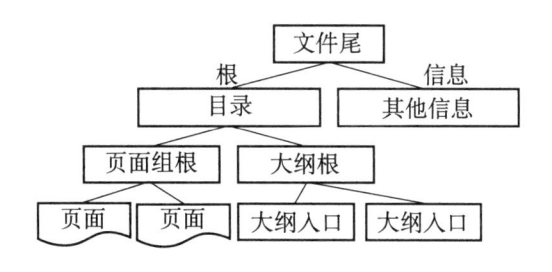

图 2 PDF 逻辑结构

2 PDF 数字水印实施过程

水印实施过程分为 3 个部分：水印生成部分、水印嵌入部分与水印提取部分。

2.1 水印生成

为使数字水印同时达到完整性验证和版权认证的功能，该算法水印信息包含相应的两部分：完整性验证信息和版权验证信息。同时为保证水印的安全性，水印不应以明文形式嵌入 PDF 文档中，需要加入一定的加密算法，保障水印信息的安全。PDF 数字水印生成过程如图 3 所示。

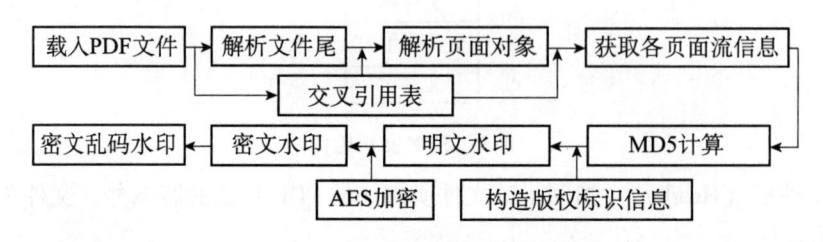

图 3　PDF 数字水印生成过程

2.1.1 完整性验证信息

完整性验证信息实现以页为精度对 PDF 文档进行完整性校验，当文件被非法篡改时，通过对完整性验证内容的分析确定各个页面是否被修改。MD5 的全称是 Message-Digest Algorithm5（信息-摘要算法），它可将一段任意长度报文，即数据文件、文本文件或者二进制文件，通过一系列算法压缩成一段 128 位的信息摘要[7]。该算法通过对原始 PDF 文档各个页面内容流单独进行 MD5 计算，得到各自的长度为 128 位的摘要信息，将其按一定格式构造为完整性验证字符串。完整性验证信息具体生成流程如下：

（1）读取原始 PDF 文档，获取 PDF 文档的文件指针。

（2）将文件指针定位到文件结尾位置，并倒叙上移，获取原始 PDF 文档文件尾和交叉引用表定位信息位置。

（3）根据 PDF 文件结构进行解析，获取各个页面的内容对象，解析内容对象，获取内容流信息，将流信息保存进 Byte [] 变量中，若单独页面存在多个内容对象则进行流拼接，确保每页生成一个 Byte [] 形变量。

（4）对获取到的每页 Byte [] 变量进行 MD5 摘要计算，获取各页面散列值，记录在字符串变量 strMD5_ Num 中，与加密算法不同，摘要算法在理论上是不可逆的，因此可依据散列值完成完整性认证。

（5）根据（4）构造完整性验证字符串如下：STREAM_ INFO：[Count] [strMD5 _1，strMD5_2，…，strMD5_Count]。其中，STREAM_INFO 表征该部分水印为完整性验证信息；Count 为 PDF 文档页面的数量；strMD5_Count 为各对应页面的散列值。

2.1.2 构造版权声明内容

版权声明的部分作用为声明 PDF 文档的版权所有方，在水印中应该包含尽可能详尽的版权信息，在产生版权纠纷时，即使原始文档中作者等版权信息遭到恶意修改，仍可通过水印提取技术提取到版权声明信息，验证版权的归属，确保版权所有方的合法权益。根据实际需要同时为满足通用性，该算法选择版权声明信息组成部分如下：

COPYRIGHT_INFO：

〔Count〕〔FileName，FileID，CopyRightInfo，TimeStamp〕

其中，COPYRIGHT_INFO 表征该字符串版权信息，标识该水印为版权声明部分；Count 为版权标识数量；FileName 为文件名；FileID 为文件唯一 ID 号；CopyRightInfo 为版权相关信息；TimeStamp 为时间戳信息。

2.1.3 明文水印加密处理过程

为增加水印的安全性，同时为保证在构造 PDF 对象时去除水印明显的形式特征，使其更加接近自然 PDF 文档对象的特征，不应该将水印的明文信息直接嵌入到 PDF 文档中，需对明文水印做进一步的处理。AES 是一个迭代的、对称密钥分组的密码，它可以使用 128、192 和 256 位密钥，并且用 128 位（16 字节）分组加密和解密数据[8]。与传统的 DES 加密方式相比，AES 加密具有加密强度高、加密速度快、通用性高和实现便捷灵活的特点。

鉴于 AES 的以上优点，文中采用 AES 加密算法对明文信息进行加密处理。采用 AES 加密的另一好处是，明文字符串经 AES 加密后生成的密文信息特征与原始 PDF 文档内容流特征相似，都为不可识别的乱码形式，提高了密文水印的隐蔽性。

2.2 水印嵌入

水印嵌入的基本思想是：PDF 文档作为结构化文档与顺序化文档不同，其显示方式完全由逻辑控制，与文件中各个对象的顺序无关，经统计观察发现，绝大部分 PDF 文档中各对象的存储是无序的，这就方便伪造形式上合法的对象，然后添加到 PDF 文档中，这样虽然对 PDF 文档进行了修改，但是新加对象没有在其显示逻辑过程中，因此水印添加前后 PDF 文档在显示上完全没有改变，具有良好的隐蔽性。如图 4 所示，数字水印嵌入过程如下：

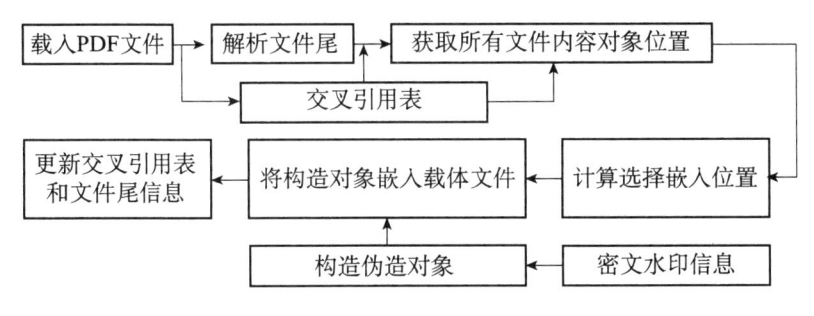

图 4 水印嵌入过程

（1）载入原始 PDF 文档。

（2）获取 PDF 文档的文件尾信息与交叉引用表信息。

（3）利用交叉引用表信息分析 PDF 文档各对象偏移量，选择水印嵌入位置。为增加数字水印的隐蔽性，水印的嵌入位置应该是动态变化的，且不应该出现在文件开始或文件结尾部分，这里假设文件的总对象数为 N，则算法规定嵌入位置为〔N/4〕至〔N/43〕之间。

（4）利用水印生成过程产生的密文水印构造 PDF 文档对象。构造的对象其父对象为页面对象，其结构符合内容流对象的结构，如下：N 0 obj < </Length Num/Filter/FlateDe-

code> >stream＊＊＊endstream endobj。其中 N 为对象号，Num 表示内容流的长度即 stream 与 endstream 之间的长度，＊＊＊号代表流信息，即水印的嵌入位置。/Filter/FlateDecode 代表文件流中的信息是经过过滤器处理过的，以文本显示出来为乱码形式。由于水印加密过程中原本可正常显示的明文被处理成了乱码，与自然文件中内容流的信息在格式上十分相似，可抵抗格式化分析软件。

（5）将伪造的 PDF 文档对象写入（3）中选择的位置，并计算构造对象的大小，更新交叉引用表的信息。由于伪造对象的写入，致使源文件中伪造对象插入位置之后的对象都有了固定大小的偏移，因此需对交叉引用表进行更新，否则交叉引用表中对象偏移量将小于对象实际偏移量。

通过以上 5 步即将密文水印以伪造对象的形式嵌入到 PDF 文档中，效果如图 5 所示。如图 5 所示，上方框中的对象为构造的含水印信息的 PDF 文档对象，下方框中的对象为原始对象，可见二者在形式上没有任何差异，有效保证了嵌入水印的安全性。

图 5　水印嵌入效果

2.3　水印提取

如图 6 所示，水印提取过程为水印嵌入过程的逆过程，通过载入 PDF 进行水印嵌入的逆过程，即通过解析文件尾提取嵌入的水印对象，对加密的水印信息进行解密处理，通过明文水印信息，最终实现对 PDF 文档的完整性认证和版权认证。

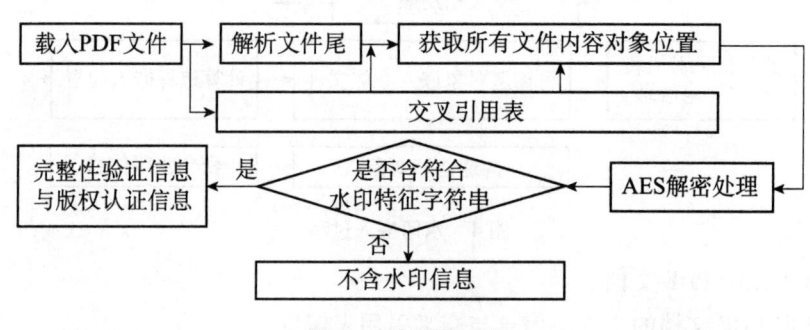

图 6　水印提取过程

3　结果与性能分析

3.1　水印嵌入和提取测试

实验选取包含两个页面的 PDF 文档，对其进行水印嵌入测试。如图 7 所示，（a）和

（b）分别为水印嵌入前后的效果图，可见水印嵌入前后 PDF 显示并没有任何变化，构造的水印对象在 PDF 文档的结构上完全与原始 PDF 文档融合，但是并没有加入到其显示的逻辑过程中，水印嵌入前后 PDF 阅读器对 PDF 文档的解析过程并没有改变，因此水印的添加不会对 PDF 文档显示产生任何影响。

当对测试文档做部分修改，如图 7 中（c）所示，原始 PDF 文档第三行中“工学门类为主体”和“信息技术为特色”两句话被交换了位置，对被修改的 PDF 文档进行逐页 MD5 摘要计算，结果如下：

Page1：96d102f01fe3ec69f3eb5bb39e34cd28

Page2：glf78074efe18d2c33365ebb8b73d05c

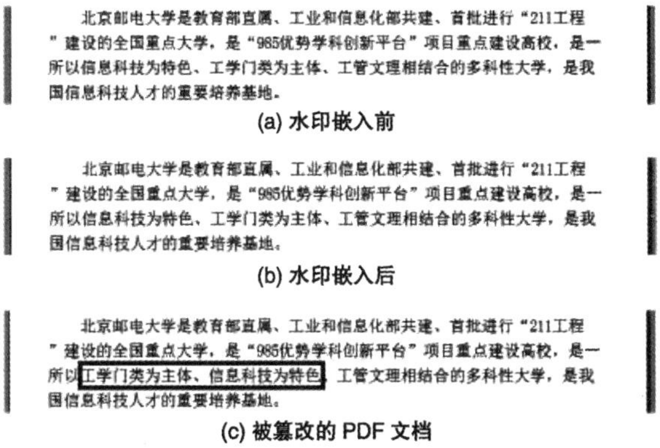

北京邮电大学是教育部直属、工业和信息化部共建、首批进行“211工程”建设的全国重点大学，是“985优势学科创新平台”项目重点建设高校，是一所以信息科技为特色、工学门类为主体、工管文理相结合的多科性大学，是我国信息科技人才的重要培养基地。

(a) 水印嵌入前

北京邮电大学是教育部直属、工业和信息化部共建、首批进行“211工程”建设的全国重点大学，是“985优势学科创新平台”项目重点建设高校，是一所以信息科技为特色、工学门类为主体、工管文理相结合的多科性大学，是我国信息科技人才的重要培养基地。

(b) 水印嵌入后

北京邮电大学是教育部直属、工业和信息化部共建、首批进行“211工程”建设的全国重点大学，是“985优势学科创新平台”项目重点建设高校，是一所以工学门类为主体、信息科技为特色、工管文理相结合的多科性大学，是我国信息科技人才的重要培养基地。

(c) 被篡改的 PDF 文档

图 7　水印效果对比

再经水印提取过程对被篡改的 PDF 文档进行水印提取，提取原始水印如下：

STREAM_INFO：[2][a2622eccc989f3062b09931b98aae259，91f78074efe18d2c33365ebb8b73d05c]

COPYRIGHT_INFO：[2][PDFTestFile，000000001，版权所有（c）*******，2012-3-15]

通过对完整性信息（STREAM_INFO）的比对可发现，页面 1 的 MD5 摘要信息由 a2622eccc989f3062b09931b98aae259 变化为 96d102f01fe3ec69f3eb5bb39e34cd28，说明文档第一页内容遭到了篡改。提取版权认证信息（COPYRIGHT_INFO）获取该 PDF 文档题目为 PDFTestFile，文件编号为 000000001，版权信息为版权所有（c）*******，时间戳为 2012-3-15。即使作者信息遭恶意修改也可通过版权认证信息实现版权的认证。

3.2　水印性能测试

水印嵌入效率为水印嵌入性能之一，由于该算法实现了基于页精度的完整性验证，PDF 文档页面数量的增加在理论上会增加嵌入时长，因此为验证水印的嵌入效率，分别制作了 3 类 PDF，所含页数分别为 25 页、50 页和 100 页，并对其进行水印添加测试效率。

测试机器环境为 CPU：Intel（R）Core（TM）i5 CPU M 540@ 2.53 GHz，内存大小为 4 GB，结果如表 1 所示。

表1 水印性能测试

文档大小/kb	页面数量/页	处理文档个数	嵌入耗时/ms	平均嵌入效率/ms·kb-1
35	50	100	1 242	0.35
67	100	100	1 867	0.28
132	200	100	3 139	0.24

通过测试结果可看出，水印嵌入效率和文件中对象数目成正比，且当文件中对象数目越多时，其添加效率越高，对于普通文本型 PDF 文档，大小集中在 100~1 000 KB 之间，处理时间约为百毫秒级，完全满足应用需求。

该水印算法在视觉上具有良好的透明性，但是水印的嵌入会造成 PDF 文档体积的增加，当体积变化过大时会威胁水印的安全性，因此对 PDF 文档大小变化做了统计，为了反映水印的极端性能情况，测试采用的 PDF 文档具有体积小、页数多的特点，其统计结果如表 2 所示。

表2 嵌入文档体积变化

原始大小/bit	页面数量/页	嵌入后大小/bit	体积变化/bit	体积变化百分比/（%）
35 467	25	36 488	1 032	2.91
68 467	50	70 321	1 854	2.7
134 464	100	137 966	3 502	2.60

由表 2 可知，在采用极端 PDF 文档的基础上，对原始文档体积的影响也限定在 3% 之内，日常应用的 PDF 文档较少可以达到 100 页以上，且相同页数下体积会比试验文档大得多，因此该算法对普通 PDF 文档体积影响会比上述结果小得多，完全满足保证水印安全性的限值。

4 结语

文中提出了一种针对 PDF 文档的数字水印算法，可以完成对 PDF 文档的版权认证和以页为精度的完整性认证，具有高效、高冗余空间的特点。但是由于文本文件的特点，目前无论针对格式化或非格式化的文本文件的水印嵌入都有一定局限性，与静态图像水印算法比较，文本水印在鲁棒性、冗余度等方面依旧有较大差距。同时，该算法对 PDF 标准规范依赖过高，对非线性的 PDF 文档支持有所不足，但是在办公电子化的今天，PDF 文档的应用越来越广泛，针对 PDF 文档数字水印的研究依旧有很大的价值与前景。

参考文献

[1] 杨义先，钮心忻. 多媒体信息伪装综论［J］. 通信学报，2002，23（5）：32-38.

[2] 吴宗灵，李翔，王士林. 基于数字水印的图像完整性保护研究［J］. 通信技术，2010，43（9）：150-152，155.

[3] 唐承亮，肖海青，向华政. 基于文字 RGB 颜色变化的脆弱型文本数字水印技术［J］. 计算机工程与应，2005，41（36）：6-8.

[4] 顾艳春，杨扬. 一种基于 PDF 文档和置乱技术的文本数字水印算法［J］. 佛山科学技术学院学

报,2009,27(2):43-46.

[5] 白剑,徐迎晖,杨榆.利用文本载体的信息隐藏算法研究[J].计算机应用研究,2004,21(12):147-148.

[6] 李针,田学动.PDF文件信息的抽取与分析[J].计算机应用,2003,23(12):145-147.

[7] 陈松,黄炜.MD5算法的FPGA实现[J].信息安全与通信保密,2007(6):129-130.

[8] 吴昌银,岳青松,王元峰,等.AES安全性及其影响研究[J].信息安全与通信保密,2006(11):140-141,144.

第二辑
相关算法研究

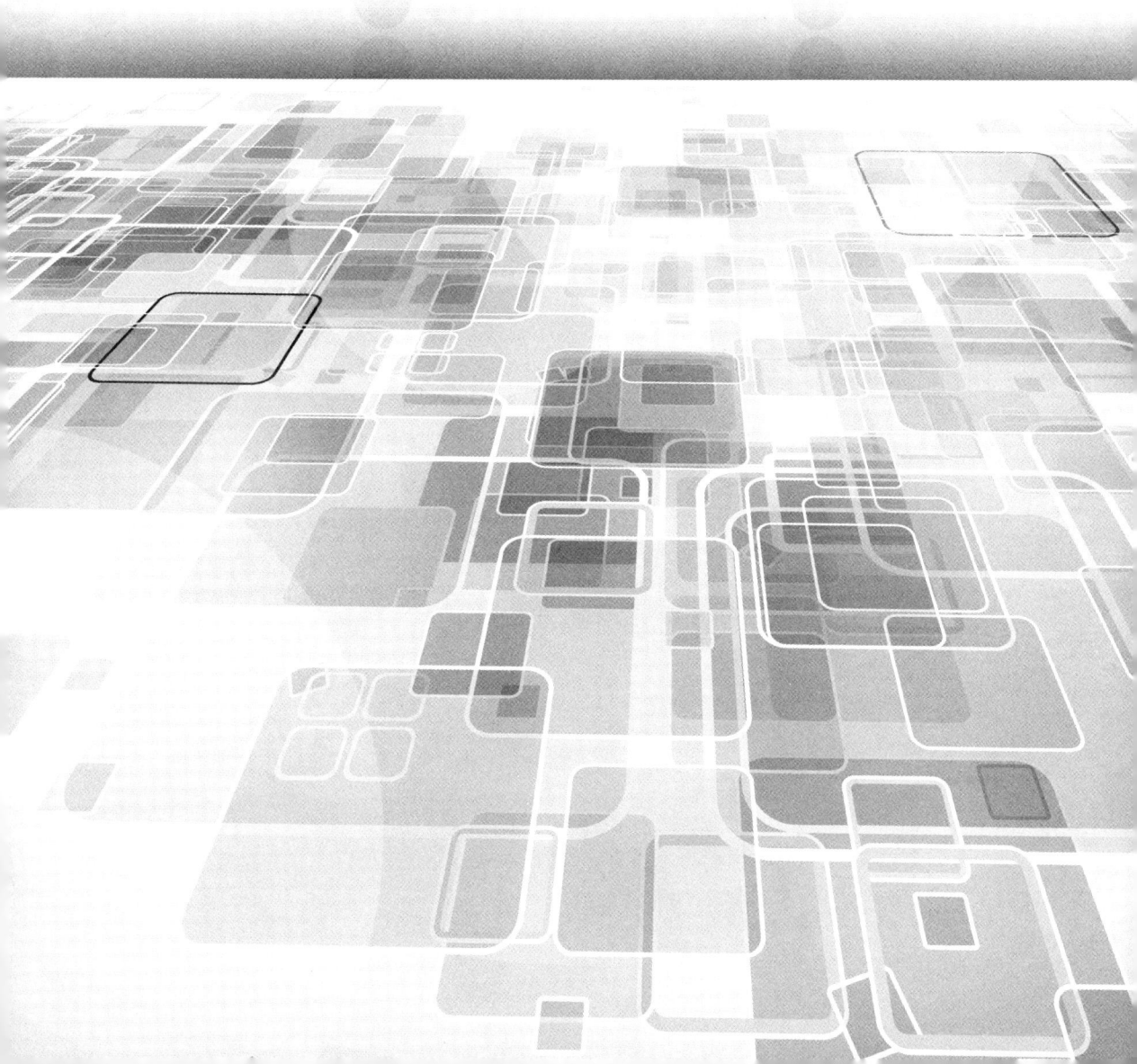

一种基于 H.264/AVC 的视频可逆脆弱水印算法

张维纬　张　茹　刘建毅　伍淳华　钮心忻　杨义先

1　引言

脆弱水印技术的目的是为数字多媒体作品提供完整性和真实性认证并能定位篡改区域和还原原始的内容[1]。在现有的大多数脆弱水印算法中，嵌入脆弱水印对视频质量的影响极小。但是对于某些特殊的场合，比如医疗、军事和司法等领域，即使由于脆弱水印的嵌入导致视觉上微小的感知也是无法接受的。因此，一种称为可逆脆弱水印的技术引起了越来越多的研究与关注。目前作为主流的视频压缩编码标准，H.264/AVC 采用了许多新的技术，编码效率比以往的标准有了很大的提高[2]，其优异的压缩性能和良好的网络适应性在视频产品领域扮演着重要的角色。因此，研究基于 H.264 为压缩编码标准的视频水印技术显得十分迫切[3]。

近年来，已有学者对基于 H.264/AVC 压缩编码标准的视频脆弱水印技术进行了研究。Zhang 等人[4]根据 H.264/AVC 编码时 P 帧和 B 帧编码最佳分块模式选择的脆弱性，提出了一种水印嵌入在模式 8×8 的运动补偿的非零离散余弦变换（Discrete Cosine Transform, DCT）交流系数上的认证方案。Qiu 等人[5]提出把脆弱水印嵌在 1/4 像素运动估计搜索过程中运动矢量预测残差的水平和垂直分量中。Su 等人[6]提出通过计算每帧图像的奇异值分解（Singular Value Decomposition, SVD）值获得特征码，并采用最小可视失真（Just Noticeable Distortion, JND）模型把水印嵌入到 DCT 域中的内容认证方案。该方案只能检测视频的帧数是否被增删，无法检测帧内的内容是否被篡改，并且该方案计算量大，无法适用于实时性要求较高的场合。Wang 等人[7]提出在 H.264/AVC 编码过程中在每个 4×4 的 DCT 块的最后一个量化后的非零系数中嵌入脆弱水印。该算法水印的嵌入容量较大，但对视频的质量影响也较大。Xu 等人[8]提出在嵌入水印过程中首先找出合适的参考帧的指数哥伦布码，然后建立这些码字和水印比特的映射规则。水印的嵌入是通过调制相应的指数哥伦布码字。提取水印时，不必解码视频，而只要通过从比特流中解析指数哥伦布码字。

以上所提出的基于 H.264/AVC 压缩编码标准的视频脆弱水印都是不可逆的，并且这些算法无法实现对篡改区域的定位。其原因是 H.264/AVC 视频编码标准采用的新技术——帧内预测。帧内预测的主要目的是减少帧内图像的空间冗余，提高编码效率。在帧内预测模式下,依据先前编码和重建后的块形成一个预测块 P,当前块减去预测块 P 得到一个差值,然后对这个差值进行块变换、量化和熵编码等操作。每个 4×4 亮度块有 9 种预测模式,每个 16×16 亮度块有 4 种预测模式。在对当前块进行编码时,选择最优的编码模式。

文献[4-8]提出的基于 H.264/AVC 压缩编码标准的视频脆弱水印算法都是采用在 H.264/AVC 编码过程中进行水印的嵌入,这类算法在编码过程中会造成由于嵌入水印后的误差漂移,而且由于嵌入水印造成的误差漂移是不可逆的。再者,这类算法的另一个缺点是嵌入水印需要先完全解码 H.264 码流,然后再在编码的过程中嵌入水印,增加了计算量,这不适用于实时性要求较高的场合。

近年来,脆弱水印方案与可逆信息隐藏技术的结合在原始图像[9]、JPEG 图像[10]、MPEG-4 视频[11]、2 维矢量地图[12]、3 维模型[13]等载体进行应用。在这些应用中,可逆脆弱水印与压缩编码标准的结合首先假设压缩前后的差别视觉上是无法感知的。目前针对 H.264/AVC 标准的可逆信息隐藏算法研究并不多。文献[14-16]将可逆信息隐藏技术运用于 H.264 标准视频的错误隐藏和错误复原技术领域,该类算法在一个宏块中嵌入多比特的其他宏块信息,以在解码时对受损的数据进行恢复或估计。这类算法虽然嵌入信息的容量大,但在没有还原模块的解码器中,解码后对视频质量的影响很大。而即使水印是可逆的,在认证领域也要使由于嵌入水印引起的失真尽可能小[17]。因此该类算法不适用于可逆的脆弱水印认证领域。Huo 等人[18]提出了一种用于版权保护的基于 H.264/AVC 的可逆水印算法。该算法根据 4×4 块的预测模式分布,选择不会因水印嵌入产生误差传播或具有单一误差传播方向的 4×4 块,然后根据其传播方向选择能够消除误差传播的 DCT 系数对,采用"和不变"方法嵌入可逆水印。该算法能消除嵌在 4×4 块水印引起的误差漂移,提高水印的视频质量,但算法首先需要进行完全解码,并且只能选择相邻块满足一定编码模式的 4×4 块嵌入水印,限制了水印的嵌入容量,算法只考虑 4×4 编码模式,这在一定程度上影响了编码效率。Lin 等人[19]提出一种基于 H.264/AVC 的可逆视频水印算法,该算法首先利用相邻宏块的残差值量化后的 DCT 值预测当前块的值,并利用预测差值的直方图平移嵌入水印。算法嵌入的水印容量较大,但没有考虑人眼的视觉特性,对水印视频质量的影响也较大。Liu 等人[20]对水印嵌入导致的帧内误差漂移进行分析,得到耦合系数对,即在一个量化后的 DCT 系数上嵌入水印,需在其耦合的系数上进行补偿,从而达到消除误差漂移的目的。算法对水印视频的影响较小,且嵌入的容量较大。但算法同样需要完全解码获得每个块的编码模式,其次嵌入的条件是选择幅值满足一定条件的系数嵌入水印,这意味着如果当前宏块的系数都为零,则无法进行水印的嵌入,也就无法实现对该宏块的篡改定位。因此不能直接应用于篡改定位的脆弱水印。

针对基于 H.264/AVC 视频脆弱水印算法的不足,本文提出的方案首先对 H.264 码流进行熵解码,得到 I 帧亮度分量残差块量化后的 DCT 系数,先计算当前宏块 DCT 系数的哈希值,再把该哈希值嵌入到下一个相邻宏块中。水印的嵌入考虑人眼的视觉特性,将可逆水印嵌在人眼不敏感的 4×4 亮度块的残差量化 DCT 系数中,水印嵌入后再进行熵编码得到嵌入水印后的码流。在水印嵌入过程中由于没有进行运动补偿,所以由于水印的嵌入造成当前宏块值的改变不会在帧内预测中造成误差漂移。在解码端,先对 H.264 码流进行熵解码得到 DCT 系数,再计算当前宏块 DCT 系数的哈希值及提取下一个相邻宏块中的水印值，通过比较哈希值和提取的水印值是否相同进行视频数据的完整性认证并对遭篡改的区域进行定位。水印提取的同时对当前块进行数据还原，这样在解码端进行运动补偿时就不会造成水印的误差漂移。

2 本文提出的水印方案

2.1 水印的生成

在 H.264/AVC 标准中，编码器是以宏块（16×16）为单位进行编码的，所得的残差系数再进行 4×4 整数 DCT 变换，变换后每个宏块有 16×16 个 DCT 系数。本文提出的算法把当前预测残差宏块量化后的 256 个 DCT 系数的值作为 HASH 函数（本文实验选用 MD5 作为哈希函数）的输入，输出 128 bit 的 HASH 值，然后把这 128 bit 的 HASH 值进行 M 等分，对每一份的 HASH 值分别进行异或操作得到 M bit 的认证码，再把这个认证码作为水印信息嵌入到相邻的下一个编码宏块，水印信息的产生过程如图1所示。当视频的像素值或量化后的 DCT 系数遭到篡改时，HASH 函数的输出值会产生相应的改变，就可以在解码端定位篡改区域。

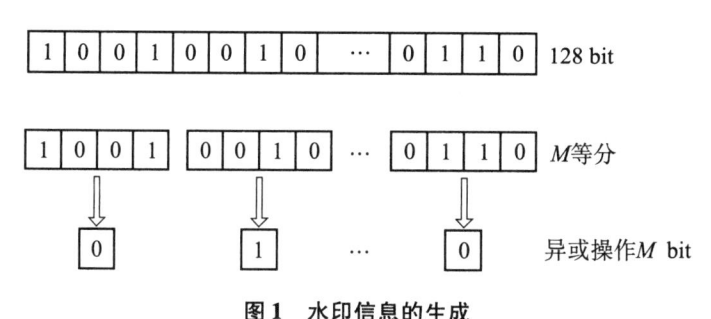

图 1 水印信息的生成

2.2 水印的嵌入

2.2.1 水印嵌入位置的选择

H.264 帧间预测是利用已编码视频帧/场和基于块的运动补偿的预测模式。与以往标准帧间预测的区别在于块尺寸范围更广（从 16×16 到 4×4）、亚像素运动矢量的使用（亮度采用 1/4 像素精度）及多参考帧的运用等。其压缩效率更高，P、B 帧不适合于水印的嵌入，因此采取的算法在 I 帧的宏块中嵌入水印。

视频序列与静止图像的不同在于它包含有运动的部分，具有变化的特性。而人眼在物体发生运动时的空间敏感度有所下降，可以在运动区域嵌入水印信息[21]。在 H.264 编码中，每个宏块中 4×4 子块的非零系数个数代表当前子块的运动活性[22]。本文算法先统计每个宏块中小块的非零系数个数，在个数最多的子块中嵌入水印。Wang 等人[7]提出把水印嵌入到一个宏块中固定的一个 4×4 子块上，而通过实验发现，对非零系数个数最多的 4×4 子块中嵌入水印对视频质量和码率的影响更小。

2.2.2 水印的嵌入算法

H.264 宏块的预测残差经过整数 DCT 变换和量化后，预测残差的能量主要集中在中低频的 DCT 系数中，大部分的高频系数都是零。因此，宏块中的 4×4 子块经过 zigzag 扫描后，1 维分量的后几个系数都为零。图 2 是 Foreman 序列在编码过程中某个宏块的 4×4 子块量化后的 DCT 系数及其 zigzag 扫描图，其扫描后产生的 1 维分量系数为 [-3, 2, 4, -1, -2, 0, 3, 0, -1, 1, 0, 0, 0, 0, 0, 0]。

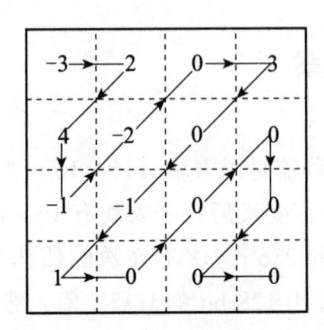

图 2 预测残差 4×4 子块 DCT 系数及 zigzag 扫描顺序

记 zigzag 扫描后的最后一个非零 DCT 系数在 1 维分量中的顺序下标为 LNZ。例如图 2 的 LNZ = 10，当子块所有的系数都为零时，LNZ = 0。记最后一个非零系数为 C_{LNZ-1}。本文提出的可逆水印的嵌入算法为首先把最后一个非零系数 C_{LNZ-1} 的 LSB 信息嵌入在其后的一个零系数上，再把水印信息 w 嵌在 C_{LNZ-1} 的 LSB 上。

具体的嵌入算法可分为以下 3 种情况：

情况 1　LNZ = 0

当宏块中 4×4 子块非零系数最多的子块系数都为零时，直接把水印信息嵌在 zigzag 扫描后的最后一个系数上，这是因为在 H.264 编码过程中，不会出现只有 zigzag 扫描后最后一个系数为非零的情况，这种情况在解码端也易于提取。而 zigzag 扫描后最后一个系数对应于高频区域，人眼比较不敏感。具体算法为

$$C_{15} = \begin{cases} 0, & w = 0 \\ 1, & w = 1 \end{cases} \quad (1)$$

情况 2　1 ≤ LNZ ≤ 15

首先，把最后一个非零系数的 LSB 嵌在其后的零系数上。

$$C'_{LNZ} = \begin{cases} 1, & \mod(C_{LNZ-1}, 2) = 1 \\ -1, & \mod(C_{LNZ-1}, 2) = 0 \end{cases} \quad (2)$$

再把水印信息嵌在最后一个非零系数的 LSB 上。

$$C_{LNZ-1} = C_{LNZ-1} - \mod(C_{LNZ-1}, 2) + w \quad (3)$$

以图 2 预测残差 4×4 子块 DCT 系数嵌入水印为例，其嵌入水印后的 DCT 系数如图 3 所示。

情况 3　LNZ = 16

由情况 2 可知，嵌入水印使嵌入的 4×4 子块 DCT 系数最后一个非零系数由嵌入前的 LNZ = 15 变成 LNZ = 16。在提取水印时，为区别是由情况 2 还是情况 3 嵌入的水印，嵌入水印前 LNZ = 16 的水印嵌入算法如下：

首先，最后一个非零系数 C_{LNZ-1} 嵌入其前一个系数 C_{LNZ-2} 的 LSB 信息，并保证嵌入水印

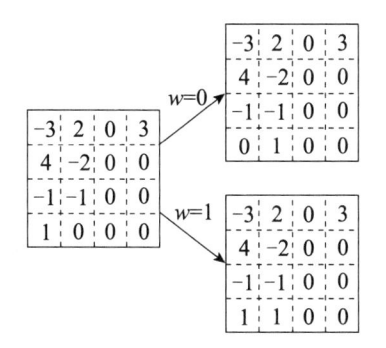

图 3 情况 2 中 4×4 子块 DCT 系数水印嵌入图

后的最后一个非零系数绝对值大于 1：

$$C'_{LNZ-1} = 2C_{LNZ-1} + \mathrm{mod}(C_{LNZ-2}, 2) \tag{4}$$

再把水印信息嵌在 C_{LNZ-2} 系数上：

$$C'_{LNZ-2} = C_{LNZ-2} - \mathrm{mod}(C_{LNZ-2}, 2) + w \tag{5}$$

以 H.264 编码中某个预测残差 4×4 子块量化 DCT 系数嵌入水印为例，其嵌入水印后的 DCT 系数如图 4 所示。

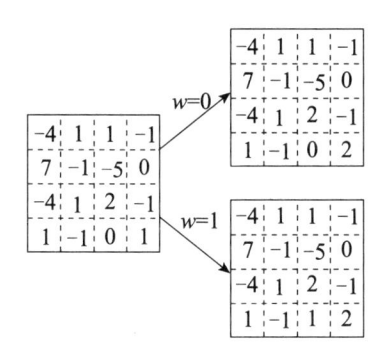

图 4 情况 3 中 4×4 子块 DCT 系数嵌入水印

2.3 水印的提取和视频的还原

根据可逆水印的嵌入算法，水印的提取算法如下：首先对嵌入水印的 H.264 码流进行熵解码，得到每个宏块预测残差的量化 DCT 系数，再统计每个宏块中 4×4 子块 DCT 系数的非零个数，找出非零个数最多的 4×4 子块，并对其进行水印的提取和视频的还原。由于水印的嵌入会使嵌入水印的 4×4 子块 DCT 系数的非零个数增加或者保持不变，因此，只要视频数据没有遭到篡改，水印的嵌入位置和提取位置就会保持同步。记 NZ 为 4×4 子块 DCT 系数的非零个数。水印的提取和视频的还原过程分如下 4 种情况：

（1）LNZ = 0

$$w = 0 \tag{6}$$

（2）LNZ = 16 且 NZ = 1

提取水印：

$$w = 1 \tag{7}$$

还原视频：

$$\hat{C}_{15} = 0 \tag{8}$$

(3) $2 \leqslant LNZ \leqslant 15$

提取水印：

$$w = \begin{pmatrix} 0, & \mathrm{mod}\ (C'_{LNZ-2},\ 2) = 0 \\ 1, & \mathrm{mod}\ (C'_{LNZ-Z},\ 2) = 1 \end{pmatrix} \tag{9}$$

还原视频　由嵌入水印后的最后一个非零系数 C'_{LNZ-1} 判断嵌入水印之前的最后一个非零系数 C_{LNZ-1} 的 LSB 值。

由嵌入算法中的式（2）可知，嵌入水印之前最后一个非零系数 C_{LNZ-1} 的 LSB 值为

$$\mathrm{mod}\ (C_{LNZ-1},\ 2) = \begin{cases} 1, & C'_{LNZ-1} = 1 \\ 0, & C'_{LNZ-1} = -1 \end{cases} \tag{10}$$

还原最后一个非零系数的前一个系数 C'_{LNZ-2}：

$$\hat{C}_{LNZ-2} = C'_{LNZ-2} + \mathrm{mod}\ (C_{LNZ-1},\ 2) - w \tag{11}$$

还原最后一个非零系数 C'_{LNZ-1}：

$$\hat{C}_{LNZ-1} = 0 \tag{12}$$

(4) LNZ = 16 且 NZ > 1　在这种情况下，要首先判断嵌入水印之前 LNZ = 16 还是 LNZ = 15，提取算法如下：

(a) 如果 $|C'_{LNZ-1}| = 1$　这种情况是嵌入水印之前 LNZ = 15。提取水印和还原视频的算法与提取水印的（3）一样，用式（9）提取水印，用式（10）、式（11）、式（12）还原视频数据；

(b) 如果 $|C'_{LNZ-1}| > 1$　这种情况是嵌入水印之前 LNZ = 16。提取水印的算法与式（9）相同。

还原视频　由嵌入算法的式（4）可知：

$$\mathrm{mod}\ (C_{LNZ-2},\ 2) = \mathrm{mod}\ (C'_{LNZ-1},\ 2) \tag{13}$$

还原最后一个非零系数的前一个系数 C'_{LNZ-2}

$$\hat{C}_{LNZ-2} = C'_{LNZ-2} + \mathrm{mod}\ (C_{LNZ-2},\ 2) - w \tag{14}$$

还原最后一个非零系数 C'_{LNZ-1}：

$$\hat{C}_{LNZ-1} = (C'_{LNZ-1} - \mathrm{mod}\ (C_{LNZ-2},\ 2))/2 \tag{15}$$

2.4　认证和定位

认证和定位的流程框图如图 5 所示。

首先对 H.264 码流进行部分解码获得预测残差的量化 DCT 系数，对当前宏块相邻的前一个宏块的 DCT 系数进行 HASH 变换，获取宏块的 HASH 值 H，再提取当前宏块的水印值 w，比较 HASH 值和提取的水印值是否一致，如果一致，则认证通过，如果不一致，则进行篡改定位。

3　实验结果及分析

本实验基于 H.264 参考软件模型 JM18.0，实验所用的序列为 QCIF（176×144）格式

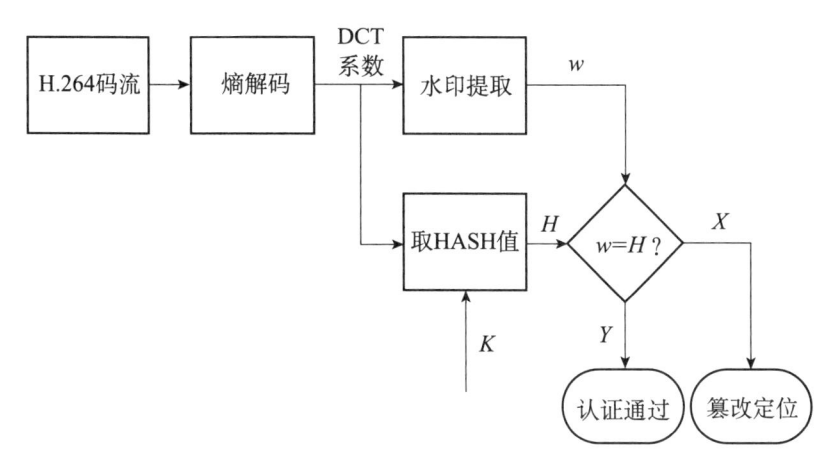

图 5　认证和定位的流程框图

的 Foreman，Carphone，Coastguard，Akiyo，Container，测试视频既包括了动态性较强的视频序列 Carphone，也包括了相对动态性较弱的视频序列 Container。每种序列都是帧率为 30 帧/s，帧数为 100 帧，按 IPPPPPP…的顺序进行编码，每隔 10 帧编码一个 I 帧，在每个 I 帧中嵌入水印，QP 值设为 28。在一个 I 帧中嵌入的水印比特数为 99 bit。

图 6 和图 7 分别为 Foreman 和 Container 序列在嵌入水印前后第 30 帧视频质量的对比。从图中可以看出，无论是 Foreman 序列还是 Container 序列，从主观上判断，嵌入水印之后图像质量都几乎没有下降。虽然水印的嵌入会使 PSNR 值略有降低，但在解码端，可逆水印提取的同时也能获得原始的视频数据。

(a)第30帧原始图像　　(b)第30帧水印图像

图 6　Foreman 测试序列嵌入水印前后的比较

为了全面衡量嵌入视频的视觉效果，本文给出 3 种峰值信噪比实验结果。峰值信噪比值 PSNR 指编码后（未嵌入水印）视频与未编码的原始 YUV 视频文件比较计算而得。峰值信噪比值 PSNR1 指编码嵌入视频与未编码的原始 YUV 视频文件比较计算而得。峰值信噪比值 PSNR2 是指嵌入水印视频与嵌入水印的视频经 H.264 解码的视频比较计算而得，该解码器是普通的解码器，即没有加入提取水印和视频还原模块的解码器。这两种类型的峰值信噪比值的实验结果均为测试视频序列 10 个 I 帧的亮度峰值信噪比的平均值（由于所有操作均在亮度块中进行，对色度块没有任何影响）。表 1 为视频测试序列水印嵌入前后对视频序列质量的影响情况。

(a)第30帧原始图像　　　　　　　(b)第30帧水印图像

图7　Container 测试序列嵌入水印前后的比较

表1　测试序列水印嵌入前后 PSNR 值比较

测试序列	PSNR（dB）	PSNR1（dB）	PSNR2（dB）
Foreman	38.989	38.972	43.940
Carphone	41.388	41.360	43.480
Coastguard	38.763	38.753	51.140
Akiyo	46.877	46.840	45.260
Container	41.236	41.192	52.990

从表1可以看出，PSNR 和 PSNR1 相差极小，这是由于本文算法的水印是在熵解码后嵌入水印再进行熵编码，嵌入水印过程没有进行运动补偿，所以不会对视频质量造成影响。在一般的应用场合，即如果解码器中没有视频数据还原模块，嵌入的水印会在解码运动补偿时造成嵌入水印一定的误差漂移，但表1中 PSNR2 都在 43dB 以上，因此水印算法可以保证解码端视频的质量。在一些特殊的应用场合，要求提取水印后能还原视频，如果解码器中含有本文算法中的水印提取和数据还原模块，则解码端的 PSNR2 值为无穷大，即通过可逆水印会得到原始的视频。

表2为嵌入水印前后不同图像码率的变化情况。可以看到水印前后码率的变化并不大，满足码率稳定的要求。

表2　测试序列水印嵌入前后码率的变化

测试序列	水印前码率（kbit/s）	水印后码率（kbit/s）	码率增量（kbit/s）
Foreman	270.94	272.98	2.04
Carphone	258.77	258.88	0.11
Coastguard	356.45	356.90	0.45
Akiyo	128.19	128.23	0.04
Container	257.50	257.73	0.23

当篡改者解码已嵌入水印的 H.264 码流，通过改变敏感数据后再进行编码后，通过本文的算法，可以定位到篡改的区域。图8为篡改区域的定位结果。从图中可以看出，本文算法能有效定位遭篡改的区域。

表3为本文算法与文献[7,19]在同一个实验平台上的比较结果。所选的测试序列是 Foreman 序列。

(a) 第1帧图像　　　　　　(b) 遭篡改图像　　　　　　(c) 对篡改区域的定位

图 8　Stefan 序列篡改区域定位

表 3　本文算法与文献 [7, 19] 的比较

算法	PSNR1（dB）	PSNR2（dB）	码率增量（kbit/s）	是否可逆	是否定位
本文	38.972	43.94	2.04	是	是
文献 [7]	38.981	44.75	1.46	否	否
文献 [19]	38.543	43.01	1.97	是	否

实验中，3 种算法嵌入的水印比特数是相同的，即 1 个宏块中嵌入 1 bit 的水印信息。从表 3 可以看出，本文算法水印嵌入前后对视频质量的影响与文献 [7] 相比，PSNR1 相差不大，PSNR2 值及码率的影响比参考文献 [7] 大。与文献 [19] 相比，本文算法的 PSNR1 值和 PSNR2 值较大，即对视频质量的影响较小，但码率略大。这是由于文献 [7] 中的水印是不可逆的，采用的算法是在一个宏块的固定位置嵌入 1bit 的水印信息，因此其对视频质量和码率影响较小。文献 [19] 是可逆水印，其水印的嵌入方法是利用预测差值的直方图平移嵌入水印，由水印的嵌入算法可知，无论嵌入的水印信息是"0"还是"1"，4×4 子块的最后一个非零系数都要增"1"或者减"1"，这导致对视频质量的影响较大，特别是当前块的最后一个非零系数是低频系数时，嵌入水印对当前块的影响更明显。本文提出的算法在宏块中嵌入 1 bit 的水印信息和 1 bit 的被嵌入 DCT 系数的 LSB 值，每个宏块比文献 [7, 19] 多嵌入 1 bit 信息，但本文算法在宏块中活性最大的子块中嵌入水印，在视觉上可以减少水印的可见性。虽然码率有所增加，但本文算法是可逆水印，即解码端可以得到原始视频数据，并可以对遭到篡改的区域进行定位。

4　结束语

针对已有算法的不足，本文根据人眼的视觉特性，结合 H.264 编码标准的特性，通过在一个宏块中选取活性最大的子块，自适应修改 I 帧每个宏块亮度分量量化后的最后一个非零系数，并把最后一个非零系数的 LSB 系数嵌在其后的一个系数，达到嵌入可逆脆弱水印的目的。算法嵌入水印不必进行完全解码，从而减少计算复杂度；考虑人眼视觉特性，增加水印的不可见性。提取端能实现水印的盲提取，而且不需要再输入水印的位置信息，提取水印的同时能实现视频数据的还原。实验结果表明，嵌入的可逆脆弱水印对视频质量和码率的影响较小，而且能有效定位遭篡改的区域。

存在的不足及下一步的工作：①进一步降低对视频质量的影响，主要是减少或者去除嵌入的水印在解码端造成误差的漂移；②对视频残差系数 DCT 改变从而嵌入可逆的数据，对视频的码率也造成一定的影响；③定位的精度不够高。接下来的工作主要是考虑如何控制误差漂移，把水印嵌入造成的视频质量的影响降到最低。另外，本文算法篡改区域的定位是宏块级别的，如何提高定位精度也是今后的工作之一。

参考文献

[1] Vleeschouwer C D, Delaigle J F, and Macq B. Invisibility and application functionalities in perceptual watermarkingan—anoverview [J]. *Proceedings of IEEE*, 2002, 90 (1): 64-77.

[2] Kwon S K, Tamhankar A, and Rao K R. An overview of H.264/MPEG-4 part 10 [J]. *Journal of Visual Communication and Image Representation*, 2003, 17 (2): 186-216.

[3] Kim D W, Choi Y G, Kim H S, et al. the problems in digital watermarking into intra-frames of H.264/AVC [J]. *Image and Vision Computing*, 2010, 28(8): 1220-1228.

[4] Zhang J and Ho A T S. An efficient authentication method for H.264/AVC [C]. 2nd European Workshop on the Integration of Knowledge, Semantics and Digital Media Technology, London, 2005: 157-164.

[5] Qiu G, Marziliano, Ho A T S, et al. A hybrid watermarking scheme for H.264/AVC video [C]. Proceedings of the 17th International Conference on Pattern Recognition, Cambridge, 2004: 865-869.

[6] Su P C, Wu C S, Chen I F, et al. A practical design of digital video watermarking in H.264/AVC for content authentication [J]. *Signal Processing: Image Communication*, 2011, 26 (8-9): 413-426.

[7] Wang C C and Hsu Y C. Fragile watermarking scheme for H.264 video authentication [J]. *Optical Engineering*, 2010, 49(2): 027003.

[8] Xu D W and Wang R D. Watermarking in H.264/AVC compressed domain using Exp-Golomb code words mapping [J]. *Optical Engineering*, 2011, 50(9): 097402.

[9] Qin C, Chang C C, and Chen, P Y. Self-embedding fragile watermarking with restoration capability based on adaptive bit allocation mechanism [J]. *Signal Processing*, 2012, 92 (4): 1137-1150.

[10] Zhang X P, Wang S Z, Qian Z X, et al. Reversible fragile watermarking for locating tampered blocks in JPEG images [J]. *Signal Processing*, 2010, 90(12): 3026-3036.

[11] Chen H, Chen Z Y, Zeng X, et al. A novel reversible semi-fragile watermarking algorithm of MPEG-4 video for content authentication [C]. Proceedings of the Second International Symposium on Intelligent Information Technology Application, Shanghai, 2008, 3: 37-41.

[12] Wang N N and Men C G. Reversible fragile watermarking for 2-D vector map authentication with localization [J]. *Computer-Aided Design*, 2012, 44 (4): 320-330.

[13] Wang J T, Yang Y W, Chang Y T, et al. A high verification capacity reversible fragile watermarking scheme for 3D models [J]. *International Journal of Innovative Computing, Information and Control*, 2011, 7 (1): 365-378.

[14] Chung K L, Huang Y H, Chang P C, et al. Reversible datahiding-based approach for intra-frame error concealment in H.264/AVC [J]. *IEEE Transactions on Circuits and System for Video Technology*, 2010, 20 (11): 1643-1647.

[15] Lie W N, Lin T C, T sai D C, et al. Error resilient coding based on reversible data embedding tech-

nique for H. 264/AVC video [C]. Proceedings of IEEE International Conference on Multimedia & Expo, ICME 2005, Amsterdam, 2005: 1174-1177.

[16] Lin S D, Meng H C, and Su Y L. A novel error resilience using reversible data embedding in H. 264/AVC [C]. International Conference on Information, Communications and Signal Processing, Singapore, 2007: 1-5.

[17] Fridrich J, Goljan M, and Du R. Invertible authentication watermark for JPEG images [C]. IEEE International Conference on Information Technology: Coding and Computing (ITCC), Las Vegas, 2001: 223-227.

[18] Huo W J and Zhu Y S. Areversible watermarking algorithm with error-drift elimination in H. 264/AVC stream [C]. Proceedings of International Conference on Consumer Electronics, Communications and Networks, Xianning, 2011, 4: 2893-2896.

[19] Lin Y C and Li J H. Reversible watermarking for H. 264/AVC videos [C]. International Scientific Research and Experimental Development. VII. International University Conference 2011, Paris, 2011, 78: 828-831.

[20] Liu Y X, Li Z T, and Ma X J. Reversible data hiding scheme based on H. 264/AVC without distortion drift [J]. *Journal of Software*, 2012, 7(5): 1059-1065.

[21] 刘红梅, 黄继武, 肖自美. 一种小波变换域的自适应视频水印算法 [J]. 电子学报, 2001, 29(12): 1656-1660.
Liu H M, Huang J W, Xiao Z M. An adaptive video watermarking algorithm in wavelet domain [J]. *Acta Electronica Sinica*, 2001, 29(12): 1656-1660.

[22] Mansouria A, Znaveh A M, Torkamani-azar F, *et al*. A low complexity video watermarking in H. 264 compressed domain [J]. *IEEE Transactions on Information Forensics and Security*, 2010, 5(4): 649-657.

A Video Watermarking Algorithm of H. 264/AVC for Content Authentication

Weiwei ZHANG   Ru ZHANG   Xianyi LIU   Chunhua WU   Xinxin NIU

I. Introduction

In recent years, digital videos achieve more and more applications, such as DVD, VCD, video conference, video-on-demand, etc. With the rapid development of multimedia processing technologies, digital videos can be easily tampered, altered or forged by unauthorized users with video editing tools. Under these circumstances, authenticity and integrity verification of digital video becomes an important research topic nowadays [1]. Video watermarking technology provides useful solution for such problems by embedding the watermark information behind a cover [2, 3, 4, 5].

Because most digital videos are stored and distributed in compressed format in the internet, compressed-domain video watermarking is especially attractive [1]. H. 264 [6] is the most recent video coding standard from the ITU-T Video Coding Experts Group and the ISO/IEC Moving Pictures Experts Group. It is expected that it will become one of the most popular video coding standard for broadcast on wireless channels and internet media [7]. However, difference from other image/video compression techniques, it is not easy to find a successful watermarking scheme for H. 264/AVC [8].

In recent years, a few watermarking algorithms for H. 264/AVC based video authentication have been proposed in the open literature. Pröfock et al. [9] proposed a fragile, blind and erasable watermarking algorithm. In their algorithm, watermark is embedded into some skipped macroblocks of the H. 264. The algorithm achieves low video quality degradations and low data rate, but it has low watermark payload. Zhang et al. [10] proposed a new scheme which makes an accurate usage of the tree-structured motion compensation, motion estimation and lagrangian optimization of the standard. The watermark is embedded based on the best mode decision strategy in the sense that if undergone any spatial and temporal attacks, the scheme can detect the tampering by the sensitive mode change. Kim et al. [11] proposed a video authentication scheme which inserts a watermark bit on the motion vectors for inter-coded macroblocks or on the mode number for intra-coded macroblocks. The scheme has high watermark payload with small image quality and compression power degradation.

Those above proposed digital video watermarking algorithm [9-11] for authentication based on H.264/AVC are sensitive to even any little modification. However, most digital videos are stored and distributed in compressed format. It is difficult to distinguish common video processing from malicious tampering with fragile watermarking. Semi-fragile watermarking allows acceptable content-preserving manipulations such as H.264/AVC compression, Gaussian low-pass filtering, median filtering, and salt and peppers noise attacks, while it can detect content-altering malicious manipulations such as removal, addition, and modification of objects.

Semi-fragile watermark based on H.264/AVC had been studied in recent years. Chen et al. [12] proposed a video authentication system, watermark authentication code is used Block Subband Index and Coefficient Modulation to embed in the quantized AC coefficient of I frame. Their system can locate the tampered locations. However, the method requires extra computation to employ Index/Coefficient Modulation. Xu et al. [1] proposed a semi-fragile watermark for H.264/AVC algorithm which embeds watermark into the DCT coefficients in diagonal positions using a modulation method. The algorithm can detect both spatial and temporal tampering. Su et al. [13] proposed a semi-fragile video watermarking, in their scheme, the watermark signals, which represent the serial numbers of video segments, are embedded into nonzero quantization indices of frames to achieve both the effectiveness of watermarking and the compact data size. However, their scheme can just locate the edited segments in the tampered video. Besides, the method needs to compute the Just Noticeable Difference (JND) which is time consuming.

In this paper, we propose a semi-fragile watermarking scheme for H.264/AVC video authentication. Our scheme requires little extra computation. The content-based authentication code is generated according to the invariance of the relation between DCT DC coefficients. Then, the authentication code is embedded into the DCT coefficients in diagonal positions in I frames. The tampered areas can be located by comparing the extracted watermarking and the content-based authentication code.

II. The Proposed Scheme

A. Content – based watermark generation

In content-based authentication watermarking, extract robust content feature is very important. Lin et al. [14, 15] found and proved that after repetitive JPEG or MPEG-2 compression, the magnitude relationship between the two DCT coefficients at the same position in separate blocks of an image remains invariance. However, unlike JPEG or MPEG-2 compression, only the resulting prediction residue is transformed using an integer transform in the H. 264/AVC encoding process. The invariant features in JPEG or MPEG-2 cannot be applied directly to H. 264/AVC video[1].

Inspired by reference [14, 15], after repetitive experiments, we found that most of the relationship between DCT DC coefficients at the same position in the two 4 × 4 sub-blocks remains invariance after H. 264/AVC compression. Taking sequence "foreman" (cif 352 × 288) as example, there are total 6336 subblocks (4 × 4) in the first frame. After H. 264 recompression, the number of the changing magnitude relationship between integer DCT DC coefficients of the two adjacent sub-blocks is 634. It accounts for about 10%. Obviously, it cannot satisfy the requirement for constructing the content-based authentication code. We propose an algorithm which can reduce the number of changing magnitude relationship after H. 264 recompression.

In H. 264/AVC, each frame consists of macroblocks (16 × 16) which may be divided into sub-block partition for motion prediction. The prediction residuals will be processed by an 4 × 4 integer Discrete Cosine Transform. And each macroblock contains 16 sub-blocks (4 × 4). These sub-blocks are scanned according to the predetermined order, as illustrated in Fig. 1.

0	1	4	5
2	3	6	7
8	9	12	13
10	11	14	15

Fig. 1 Scan for 4 × 4 sub-blocks

Taking sequence "foreman" (cif 352 × 288) as example, after H. 264/AVC recompression, DCT DC coefficients of the sixteen 4 × 4 sub-blocks in the third macroblock in the first I frame is shown as equation (1)

$$\begin{bmatrix} DC_0 & DC_1 & DC_4 & DC_5 \\ DC_2 & DC_3 & DC_6 & DC_7 \\ DC_8 & DC_9 & DC_{12} & DC_{13} \\ DC_{10} & DC_{11} & DC_{14} & DC_{15} \end{bmatrix} = \begin{bmatrix} 896 & 896 & 896 & 896 \\ 896 & 896 & 896 & 832.5 \\ 896 & 816 & 682.25 & 659.5 \\ 671.5 & 689 & 756 & 839 \end{bmatrix} \quad (1)$$

Transform it into one-dimensional array:

$$[DC_0 \ DC_1 \ DC_2 \ DC_3 \ DC_4 \ DC_5 \ DC_6 \ DC_7 \ DC_8$$
$$DC_9 \ DC_{10} \ DC_{11} \ DC_{12} \ DC_{13} \ DC_{14} \ DC_{15}]$$
$$= [896 \ 896 \ 896 \ 896 \ 896 \ 896 \ 896 \ 832.5 \ 896$$
$$816 \ 671.5 \ 689 \ 682.25 \ 659.5 \ 756 \ 839]$$

The content-based authentication code is defined as:

$$w_n = \begin{cases} 1, & if \ DC_k \geqslant DC_{k-1} \\ 0, & else \end{cases} \quad (2)$$

Where w_n is the authentication code, DC is the DCT DC coefficients in a 4×4 sub-blocks, k is the position of a 4×4 sub-blocks in a macroblock.

The third macroblock authentication code can begenerated as following:

$$[1\ 1\ 1\ 1\ 1\ 1\ 0\ 1\ 0\ 0\ 1\ ⓪\ 0\ 1\ 1] \quad (3)$$

After H.264 recompression, the DCT DC coefficients of the sixteen 4×4 sub-blocks in the third macroblock in the first I frame is showed as following:

$$\begin{bmatrix} DC_0 & DC_1 & DC_4 & DC_5 \\ DC_2 & DC_3 & DC_6 & DC_7 \\ DC_8 & DC_9 & DC_{12} & DC_{13} \\ DC_{10} & DC_{11} & DC_{14} & DC_{15} \end{bmatrix} = \begin{bmatrix} 896 & 896 & 896 & 896 \\ 896 & 896 & 896 & 832.5 \\ 896 & 816 & 682.25 & 659.5 \\ 679.5 & ⓖ81 & 754.5 & 838.75 \end{bmatrix} \quad (4)$$

Transform it into one-dimensional array:

$$[DC_0\ DC_1\ DC_2\ DC_3\ DC_4\ DC_5\ DC_6\ DC_7\ DC_8$$
$$DC_9\ DC_{10}\ DC_{11}\ DC_{12}\ DC_{13}\ DC_{14}\ DC_{15}]$$
$$= [896\ 896\ 896\ 896\ 896\ 896\ 896\ 832.5\ 896$$
$$816\ 671.5\ 681\ 682.25\ 659.5\ 756\ 839]$$

The third macroblock authentication code is generated as following:

$$[1\ 1\ 1\ 1\ 1\ 1\ 0\ 1\ 0\ 0\ 1\ ①\ 0\ 1\ 1] \quad (5)$$

According to Equation (3) and (5), After H.264 recompression, one of the authentication code is changed, for example, "0" in Equation (3) is changed into "1" in Equation (5) The reason of changing is that "689" in Equation (1) is changed into "681" in Equation (4), which changes the magnitude relationship between the current DC coefficient and its adjacent.

The reason why the magnitude relationship between in teger DCT DC coefficients of the two adjacent subblocks is changed is that the adjacent pixels of natural images have certain correlation. Because of the correlation, some of the integer DCT DC coefficients of the two adjacent sub-blocks are very closely even equation, which causes the robustness of the authentication code low.

In order to improve the robustness of the authentication code, the correlation of some of the integer DCT DC coefficients must be removed. Taking the first frame of sequence "foreman" (cif 352×288) as example, there are 6336 integer DCT DC coefficients, we scramble the position of these coefficients according to the following rule:

$$[DC_0\ DC_{6335}\ DC_1\ DC_{6334}\ DC_2\ DC_{6333}\ \cdots\ DC_{3167}\ DC_{3166}\ DC_{3168}\ DC_{3167}]$$

Authentication code generation   Authentication code generation

Fig. 2 Authentication code generation

After scrambling the position of the coefficients, the difference of the adjacent integer DCT DC coefficients increases. So it improves the robustness of the authentication code.

Adopting the scrambling method, after H. 264 recompression, the number of the changing magnitude relationship between integer DCT DC coefficients of the two adjacent sub – blocks of the sequence "foreman" is 81. It accounts for about 1. 28%.

Table 1 shows the number of the changing magnitude relationship between integer DCT DC coefficients of the two adjacent sub – blocks of the four test sequences. N1 denotes the number of the changing magnitude relationship without scrambling, N2 denotes after scrambling.

TABLE 1　THE NUMBER OF THE CHANGING MAGNITUDE RELATIONSHIP OF THE TWO ADJACENT SUB – BLOCKS WITHOUT SCRAMBLING AND AFTER SCRAMBLING

	Without scrambling (N1)	scrambling (N2)
Akiyo	605	57
Bus	379	99
Traffic	545	50
Coastguard	476	25

Table 1 shows that after scrambling the position of the integer DCT DC coefficients, the method can improve the robustness of the authentication code obviously.

B. Watermark embedding

The proposed watermark embedding scheme in H. 264/AVC encoder is as following. The authentication code is embedded into the DCT coefficients in diagonal positions of the high frequency quantized coefficients. If the authentication code is "1", let the high frequency coefficients be zero, else let them higher than zero. The watermark is embedded in the block as follows:

$$X'_{level} \begin{cases} X_{level}, & if\ X_{level} > 1\ and\ w_n = 1; \\ X_{level} + 2, & if\ X_{level} \leqslant 1\ and\ w_n = 1; \\ 0 & if\ w_n = 0 \end{cases} \quad (6)$$

Where w_n is the authentication code, X_{level} is quantized DCT coefficients, X'_{level} is the watermarked DCT coefficients.

C. Watermark extraction

Watermark extraction is very simple. First, the decoder selects the embedded sub – block. Then the algorithm exacts the watermark as follows:

$$w'_n = \begin{cases} 0 & if\ X_{level} = 0 \\ 1 & if\ X_{level} > 0 \end{cases} \quad (7)$$

Where w'_n is the extracted watermark, X_{level} is the watermarked DCT coefficients.

D. Video authentication

In the decoder side, the authentication codes can be extracted from the current I frame, and the watermarks are extracted from the next I frame. The algorithm can detect the tampering areas by mismatch between the authentication codes with watermark.

• Authentication process

Firstly, the difference of the authentication codes and extracted watermark is transform to a two dimension difference image.

$$D_{ij} = | w_{ij} - w'_{ij} | \qquad (8)$$

Where w_{ij} is the authentication codes, W'_{ij} is extracted watermark.

The difference image denotes the difference between the authentication codes and the extracted watermarks. If the pixel in the difference image is "0", it denotes the authentication codes and the extracted watermarks, vice versa. So the areas are tampered or not can be justified according to the distribution of the "1" in the difference image.

Secondly, the dense and sparse points are defined as followed:

If a pixel "1" in the difference image has at least one "1" pixel in its eight neighborhood, and it is defined the dense point. Otherwise, it is defined the sparse point.

The malicious manipulation or content-based manipulation can be justified according to equation (9) and (10)

$$r = \frac{N_d}{N_s + N_d} \qquad (9)$$

$$\begin{cases} content\text{-}based\ manipulation, & if\ r < T \\ malicious\ manipulation, & if\ r \geq T \end{cases} \qquad (10)$$

Where N_s denotes the number of the sparse point, N_s is the number of the dense point. T is the threshold according to the experiment.

• Tampered areas location

If the manipulation is content-based, then the authentication passes, otherwise, locates the malicious manipulation areas.

If a pirel in the diffcerence tmage is the dense point, then define the four neighborhoods as dease points. Then locate the areas of 4×4 sub-block corresponding to the dense point.

III. Experiment Results

The proposed digital video watermarking scheme is implemented in H.264/AVC JM-12.4 reference software. Six standard video sequences (Foreman, Stefan, Coastguard, Flower Garden, Container Ship, Traffic) in CIF format (288×352) are used for our simulation. There are 100 frames of the test video to be encoded and decoded. The GOP size is set as 15 with one I frame followed by 14 P frames. The frame rate of the video is 30 fps. The value of QP is set to 20, there are 6336 bit watermarks to be embedded into one I frame.

A. Imperceptibility test

To evaluate the imperceptibility of the proposed scheme, the test sequence "Traffic" is shown in Figure 3.

(a)Original frame (the 6th frame)   (b) Watermarked frame (the 6th frame)

Fig. 3   Original and watermarked frame (QP = 26)

In the experiment, figure 3 (a) is the 6th original frame of test sequence "Traffic", figure 3 (b) is the watermarked frame, as we can see, no visible artifacts can be observed in the Figure 3.

(a)the PSNR degradation at frame rate 1M bit/s (b)the PSNR degradation at frame rate 768k bit/s

(c)the PSNR degradation at frame rate 512k bit/s

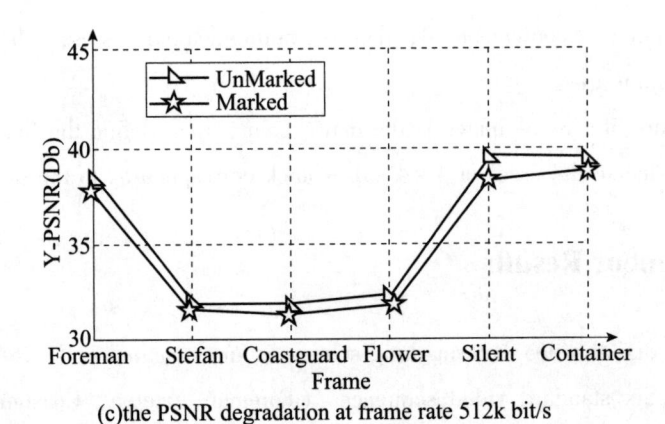

Fig. 4   PSNR degradation of six test video at difference frame rates

Figure 4 shows that at different frame rate, the six test video sequences have little PSNR degradation after watermark.

B. Robustness to common signal processing

Semi-fragile watermark should be robustness to common signal processing. Table 2 shows that the proposed watermark scheme can robust to some common signal processing.

	Gaussian noise (0, 0.0005)	Salt and pepper noise 0.05	Gaussian low pass filter (5*5)	Contrast enhance ment
(ρ')	0.89	0.94	0.74	0.94

Where ρ' is the ratio of difference between theauthentication codes and the exacted watermark and the otal number of the extracted watermark.

C. Tampering areas location

Figure 5 shows the proposed watermark scheme can detect and locate the malicious areas.

(a) The tampered frame (the 6th frame) (b) Tampered area location

Fig. 5　Tempered area location

IV. Conclusions

A semi-fragile watermarking scheme for H. 264/AVC is proposed in this paper to detect the spatial tampering. The robust video features extracted from video frame are used to form the authentication code. Then the authentication code is embedded into the DCT coefficients in diagonal positions in I frames. Spatial tampering can be located by comparing the extracted watermarking and the content-based authentication code. Experiment results show that the proposed semi-fragile watermarking scheme can justify the malicious manipulation and content-based manipulation.

Acknowledgment

This work is supported by the National Natural Science Foundation of China (61003284), National Natural Science Foundation of China (61170271), Beijing Municipal Natural Science Foundation (4122053), the Fundamental Research Funds for the Central Universities (BUPT2011RC0210), Press and publication of major science and technology research and development projects "Digital rights protection technology research and development project" (GXTC-CZ-1015004/09、GXTC-CZ-1015004/15-1).

References

[1] D. Xu, R. D. Wang, J. C. Wang, "A novel watermarking scheme for H. 264/AVC video authentication," Signal processing: Image Communication, vol. 26, pp. 267-279, 2011.

[2] M. P. Queluz, "Authentication of digital images and video: generic models and a new contribution," Signal Processing: Image Communication, vol. 16 (5) pp. 461-475, 2001.

[3] S. Chen, H. Leung, "Chaotic watermarking for video authentication in surveillance applications," IEEE Transactions on Circuits and Systems for Video Technology, vol. 18, pp. 704-709, 2008.

[4] H. B. Bi, Y. B. Zhang, X. M. Li, "Video watermarking robust against spatio-temporal attacks," Journal of Networks, vol. 6, 2011, pp. 932-936.

[5] S. C. Chu, L. H. C. Jain, H. C. Huang, et al, "Error-resilient triple-watermarking with multiple description coding," Journal of Networks, vol. 5, 2010, pp. 267-274.

[6] T. Wiegand, G. J. Sullivan, G. Bjntegaard, A. Luthra, "Overview of the H. 264/AVC video coding standard," IEEE Transactions on Circuits and Systems for Video Technology vol. 13, pp. 560 – 576, 2003.

[7] G. B. Yang, J. J. Li, Y. L. He, "An information hiding algorithm based on intra-prediction modes and matrix coding for H. 264/AVC video stream," AEU-International Journal of Electronics and Communications, vol. 65, pp. 331-337, 2011.

[8] D. W. Kim, Y. G. Choi, H. S. Kim, et al, "The problems in digital watermarking into intra-frames of H. 264/AVC,", Image and Vision Computing, vol. 28, 2010, pp. 1220-1228.

[9] D. Pröfock, H. Richter, M. Schlauweg, "H. 264/AVC video authentication using skipped macroblocks for an erasable watermark", VCIP 2005. Beijing, 2005, pp. 1480-1489.

[10] J. Zhang, A. T. S. Ho, "An efficient authentication method for H. 264/AVC", EWIMT 2005, London, 2005, pp. 157-164.

[11] T. Kim, K. Park, Y. Hong, "Video watermarking technique for H. 264/AVC," Optical Engineering, vol. 51, 2012.

[12] T. Y. Chen, T. H. Chen, Y. T. Lin, et al, "H. 264 video authentication based on semi-fragile watermarking," International Conference on Intelligent Information Hiding and Multimedia Signal Processing, Harbin, 2008, pp. 659-662.

[13] P. C. Su, C. S. Wu, I. F. Chen, et al, "A practical design of digital video watermarking in H. 264/AVC for content authentication," Signal Processing: Image Communication, vol. 26, 2011, pp. 413-426.

[14] C. Y. Lin, S. F. Chang, "A robust image authentication method distinguishing JPEG compression from malicious manipulation," IEEE Transaction on Circuits and Systems of Video technology, vol. 11, 2011, pp. 153-168.

[15] C. Y. Lin, S. F. Chang, "Issues and solutions for authenticating MPEG video," Proceedings of the SPIE Security and Watermarking of Multimedia Contents, vol. 3657, 1999, pp. 54-65.

An Audio Zero-watermarking Algorithm Based on Wavelet and Cepstrum Coefficients Mean Comparison*

Hu Tenga Zhang rub Liu Jianyic

Introduction

As the digital audio products are unceasingly produced and issued, the requirement on the quality of audio products gradually becomes higher. However, there is no ideal method to satisfy the need of copyrights protection and the requirement for higher audio quality at the same time. Audio watermark serves as an appropriate way to protect audio products, with multiple research results that can effectively protect products from music piracy.[1,2,3]

The auditory sensation system of human beings is more sensitive than their visual system.[4] Thus, the focal point of research is to satisfy the two most important features of audio watermark: robustness and imperceptibility. According to these problems, some people proposed the audio zero-watermarking algorithm which can utilize instead of changing the important characteristics[5] of the audio to compose the information of the watermark. The audio zero-watermarking algorithm can well solve the conflicts between the robustness and imperceptibility of the invisible digital watermark.

Based on the previous research results, this essay proposed an audio zero-watermarking algorithm based on wavelet transform and cepstrum transform. This algorithm first used wavelet transform to extract low frequency coefficients of the audio signal, segmented the low frequency coefficients with specified length, conducted cepstrum transform of every segments, and composed zero-watermark according to the two neighboring mean value relation.

Propossed Zero-watermarking scheme

The embedding scheme and decoding scheme are displayed in Figure 1.

Embedding Scheme. The zero-watermarking algorithm proposed by this essay does not need the original audio in watermark extraction, which means it can realize the blind detection of watermark.

Step 1: As this essay chose a binary image as the watermark information, it had to transform

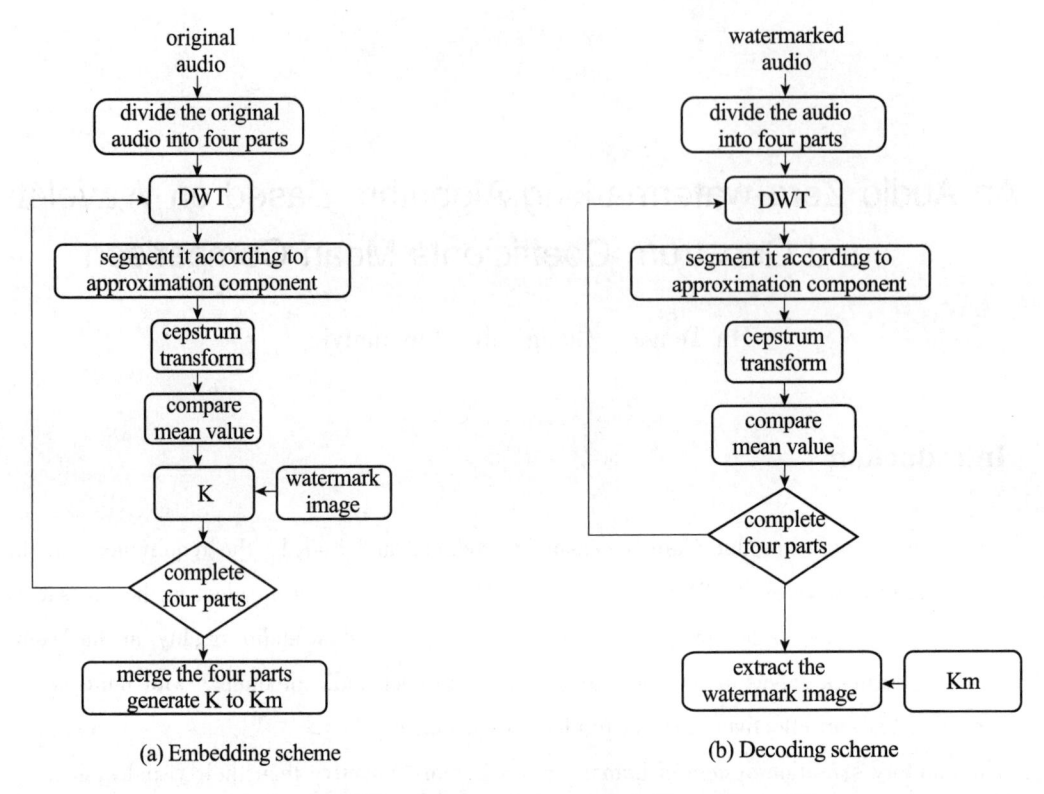

Fig. 1 Embedding scheme (a) and Decoding scheme (b)

the two-dimensional watermark information into one-dimensional sequence before composing the watermark:

$$W = \{w(k) = v(i, j), 0 \leq i, j < M, k = m \times m\}, v(i, j) \in \{0, 1\} \quad (1)$$

Then we can get the one-dimensional watermark information sequence $W(k)$ which would be embedded.

Step 2: Suppose the original audio signal is A, then divide it into four parts (A1, A2, A3, A4). Use the "db4" wavelet to conduct 3-level DWT in every part, extract the third level low frequency wavelet coefficients Ca3 and get the length "L" of Ca3.

Step 3: Choose the appropriate fixed length M to segment the third level low frequency wavelet coefficients Ca3, then we get:

$$Ca3 = ca(1) + ca(2) + ca(3) + \cdots + ca(N) \quad (2)$$

The sum of segments $N = L/M$.

Step 4: conduct cepstrum transform in every low frequency coefficients, the equation of cepstrum transforms:

$$C = \text{REAL}(\text{IFFT}(\log(\text{FFT}(ca(n))))) \quad (3)$$

Then we get real cepstrum coefficients C. Get rid of the parts in the two ends with large fluctuation, select the stable middle part to generate the cepstrum sequence $C(k)$ to compose watermark.

Step 5: Calculate the mean value of the cepstrum coefficients C (k) and compose the audio characteristic sequence U (i). Compare the mean value Mm, Mm + 1 of every segment of cepstrum coefficients.

(1) If $M_m \geq M_{m+1}$, then U (m) = 1;
(2) If $M_m < M_{m+1}$, then U (m) = 0;

Carry out XOR in audio characteristic sequence U (i) and W (k) to get a group of one-dimensional sequence V(i). Repeat step 2 to 5 to process A2, A3, A4 to get V1(i), V2(i), V3(i), V4(i) respectively.

Step 6: Merge V1(i), V2(i), V3(i), and V4(i) into Vm (i) which would be stored as the audio key. If the watermark extraction is needed, it can use Vm(i) and the watermarked audio to extract the watermark, thus the copyright of the owner can be proved.

Decoding Scheme. The audio information with embedded watermark would go through some kinds of attacks after being copied and processed. Thus the original watermarked audio may be an audio signal which has been attacked. Suppose the watermarked audio is A_1, the steps of decoding scheme are as follows:

Step 1: Divide the watermarked audio signal into four parts, use the "db4" wavelet to conduct 3-level DWT in every part, extract the third level low frequency wavelet coefficients Ca3 and get the length "L" of Ca3. Use Equation 2 to segment Ca3.

Step 2: conduct cepstrum transform in every segment of low frequency coefficients according to Equation 3, cut off the parts in the two ends with large fluctuation, select the stable middle part.

Step 3: Calculate the mean value of every cepstrum coefficients respectively, compare it of every neighboring segments, and extract the characteristic coefficients of the audio signal which would be tested. Then we get characteristic sequence Uc(i).

(1) If $M_m \geq M_{m+1}$, then $U_c(m)$ = 1;
(2) If $M_m < M_{m+1}$, then $U_c(m)$ = 0;

Step 4: After processing the four parts of the signal according to step 1 to 3, we can get four groups of Uc(i); divide Vm(i) into four equal parts, and conduct XOR in them with corresponding Uc(i) to get four groups of sequences of one-dimensional watermark information; then carry out bitwise addition in the four groups of sequences of the watermark information and calculate the mean value M' of every bit. It is processed according to the following equation:

(1) If $M' \geq 0.5$, then $U_c(m)$ = 1;
(2) If $M' < 0.5$, then $U_c(m)$ = 0;

Raise the final watermark information Uc(m) from one-dimensional to two dimensions, then we can get the extracted watermark image.

Experiment Simulation and Results

Simulation Experiments Environment. The algorithm went through simulation experiments in matlab7.8 (2009a). A common piece of song was adopted (mono, 44.1 kHz, 16 bit, with 40s time duration) as the sample for experiment. The waveform of the audio is as Figure 2. We adopted "db4" wavelet to conduct 3-level wavelet decomposition in the original audio. The embedded watermark was the self-made 64 * 64 binary image, as in the Figure 3.

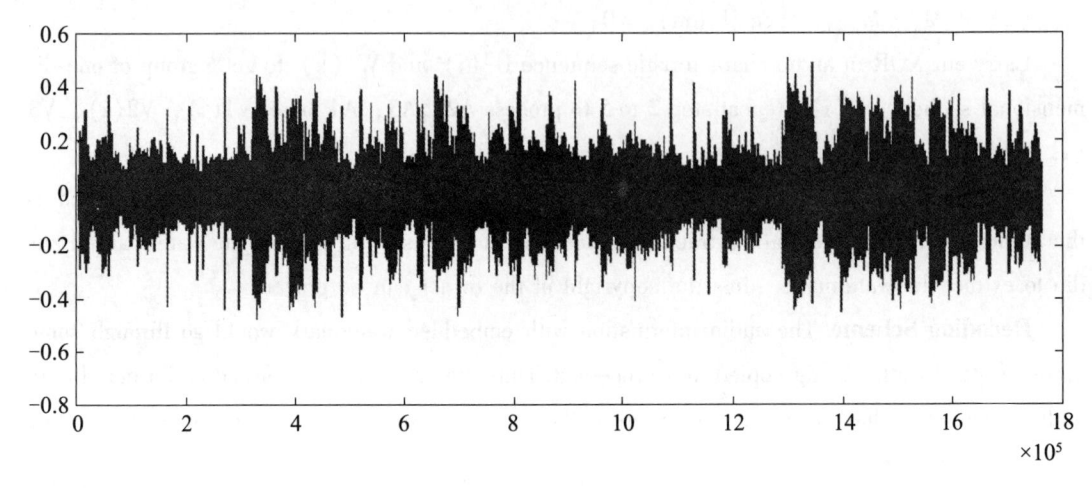

Fig. 2　Original Audio

BUPT
HT

Fig. 3　Watermark Image

This essay adopted NC (normalized cross-correlation) and BER (bit error rate) to testify and evaluate this simulation. The definitions of them are as equation 4 and 5.

$$NC = \frac{\sum_{i=0}^{M-1}\sum_{j=0}^{N-1} w(i,j)\tilde{w}(i,j)}{\sqrt{\sum_{i=0}^{M-1}\sum_{j=0}^{N-1} w^2(i,j)}\sqrt{\sum_{i=0}^{M-1}\sum_{j=0}^{N-1} \tilde{w}^2(i,j)}} \tag{4}$$

$$BRE = \frac{B}{M \times N} \times 100\% \tag{5}$$

The Results and Comparing with the Efficiency of Other Algorithms. At present, there are some problems in every mainstream audio algorithm. The time-domain algorithm has large embedding capacity and easy implementation, but its robustness is poor and the watermark information can be easily removed; while the frequency-domain algorithm (DWT, DCT) cannot take robustness and imperceptibility into account at the same time, and its embedding capacity could be restricted. The algorithm in reference [7] well solved the problem of embedding capacity, but it could not effectively combat the low-pass filter attacks; the algorithm in reference [8] settled the conflicts between robustness and imperceptibility to some degree, but it could not achieve ideal results in low-pass filter attacks and it could not combat against synchronized attacks.

As depicted in Table 1, these are the simulation results of our algorithm comparing with those in reference [7] and [8]. These can demonstrate that every attack has some influence on zero-watermarking algorithm, but it has better robustness under various attacks than algorithms proposed in reference [7] and [8] did.

Table 1 Compared with the Reference [7] and Reference [8]

Type of Attack	Reference [7]		Reference [8]		Our		Extracted Watermark
	NC	BER	NC	BER	NC	BER	
No Attack	1	0	1	0	1	0	BUPT HT
Gaussian white noise-(0, 0.01)	0.998	0.005	0.996 9	0.003 1	1	0	BUPT HT
Gaussian white noise-(0, 0.02)	—	—	0.992 3	0.006 3	0.999	0.000 4	BUPT HT
Low-pass filtering-(11kHz)	0.824	0.500	0.984 6	0.008 6	0.99 6	0.00 7	BUPT HT
Low-pass filtering-(8kHz)	—	—	0.879 8	0.094 5	0.993	0.013	BUPT HT
Resampling (up)	0.981	0.054	—	—	1	0	BUPT HT
Resampling (down)	0.997	0.001	1	0	1	0	BUPT HT
Requantization (16→32→16 bits)	0.998	0.002	1	0	1	0	BUPT HT
Requantization (16→8→16 bits)	0.998	0.002	0.993 8	0.003 9	1	0	BUPT HT
MP3 compression (320Kbps)	0.999	0.001	—	—	1	0	BUPT HT
MP3 compression (256Kbps)	—	—	1	0	1	0	BUPT HT
MP3 compression (160Kbps)	—	—	1	0	1	0	BUPT HT
Wavelet denoising	—	—	—	—	1	0	BUPT HT
Echo Attack (500ms)	—	—	—	—	0.996	0.017	BUPT HT

From Table 1, it can be testified that the watermark can be extracted completely if it was under no attack, with BER being 0, NC 1.

Extract watermarks after the watermarked audio having gone through following attacks:

(1) *Resampling*. Carry out upsampling and downsampling in the audio signal. The upsampling sampled the original audio from 44.1kHz to 88.2kHz, then back to 44.1kHz; the downsampling sampled the original audio from 44.1kHz to 22.05kHz, then back to 44.1kHz.

(2) *Requantization*. Proceed requantization in the audio signal. It adopted requantization (16→32→16bits) and requantization (16→8→16bits) in the audio signal.

(3) *MP3 Compression*. Compress the original audio into MP3 file, according to the three common code rates: 320Kbps, 256Kbps and 160Kbps. Then recover them to wav file.

(4) *Adding Gaussian white noise*. Add noise with different intensities (with 0 mean value,

standard deviation being 0.01, 0.02 respectively) into the original audio.

(5) *Low-pass filtering*. Adopt the 6-order Low Pass Butterworth Filter, with 11 025 Hz and 8 000 Hz as the cut-off frequency.

(6) *Wavelet denoising*. Use the 1-d signal wavelet denoising processing function of Matlab to denoise the signal with Heuristic soft threshold selection method, which chooses sym6 wavelet basis to conduct 5-level decomposition in the signal.

(7) *Echo attack*. Conduct 500ms delay in the audio signal, and stack it in the original signal to generate echo of which the volume is 10% of the original audio volume.

Conclusions

This essay proposed a method to compose zero-watermarking based on wavelet and cepstrum coefficients mean value. It first conducted 3-level wavelet decomposition of the audio, extracted approximation component of the third layer wavelet, segmented the approximation component, and conducted cepstrum transform of every segments, removed the part with high fluctuation in cepstrum coefficients, and selected the stable middle part to calculate the mean value, then construct a binary audio characteristic sequence based on the two neighboring mean value relation. After that, it used this characteristic sequence and the meaningful binary watermark image to conduct XOR, to finally get a sequence that can be preserved in registration organizations to complete the embedding of the zero-watermarking. The simulation results showed that the algorithm has very good robustness under common attacks like resampling, requantization, MP3 compression, Gaussian white noise, low-pass filtering and wavelet denoising. As depicted in Table 1, the algorithm proposed by this essay is superior to those in reference [7] and [8].

Acknowledgements

The work was supported by:

(1) Beijing Natural Science Foundation's project (90604022) (4122053).

(2) National Natural Science Foundation's project (61003284).

(3) Fundamental Research Funds for the Central Universities (2013RC0310).

(4) Press Publication Major Science and Technology Engineering Project (GXTC-CZ-1015004/09) (GXTC-CZ-1015004/15-1).

(5) National Key Technology Research and Development Program (2012BAH08B02).

(6) National 863 Program (2012AA012606).

References

[1] WANG Jianhui, LI Lijuan. An Audio Watermarking Algorithm with Self-Synchronization Based on Complex Cepstrum Domain [J]. Computer Engineering & Science. 2009, 31 (12): 41-43.

[2] BAI Yubao, BAI Sen, LIU Chenghao. Digital Audio Watermarking Algorithm Basedon Wavelet and Cepstrum Domain [J]. Computer Engineering & Science. 2012, 29 (3): 163-167.

[3] LI Yueqiang, SUN Xingming, HOU Fazhong. An Audio Watermarking Algorithm Based on Complex Cepstrum Coefficient Mean Comparison [J]. Microcomputer Information. 2006, 22 (8-3): 250-253.

[4] WU Guohua, WU Qinhan, ZHOU Xiaodong. An Audio Zero-watermarking Algorithm Based on DWT [J]. Mechanical & Electrical Engineering Magazine. 2009, 26 (9): 16-19.

[5] WEN Quan, SUN Tanfeng, WANG Shuxun. Concept and Application of Zero-Watermark [J]. Acta Electronica Sinica, 2003, 31 (2): 1-3.

[6] Bo-Lin Kuo, Chih-Cheng Lo, Chi-Hua Liu, Bin-Yih Liao, and Jeng-Shyang Pan. Audio Watermarking with HOS-Based Cepstrum Feature [J]. Lecture Notes in Computer Science. v6422LNAI, nPART 2, 2010. 316-323

[7] TAN Liang, WU Bo, LIU Zhen, ZHOU Mingtian. An Audio Information Hiding Algorithm with High-Capacity Which Based on Chaotic and Wavelet Transform [J]. Acta Electronica Sinica. 2010, 38 (8): 1812-1818.

[8] Zhaoyang Ma, Xueying Zhang, and JinxiaYang. A Novel Dual Watermarking Schemefor Audio Copyright Protectionand Content Authentication [J]. Lecture Notes in Computer Science. Volume 6146, 2010: 149-156.

An Algorithm to Control Watermarking Capacity Using PSNR[*]

Yong Xing Daoshun Wang

1 Introduction

The purpose of watermarking capacity research is to evaluate how much information can be hidden into a digital cover image while satisfying watermarking invisibility and robustness [1-2]. There are many related works for calculating watermarking capacity. Moulin et al. regarded watermarking as information channel between encoders and decoders and studied optimal watermarking strategies under constrained resources [3]. Zhang et al. used Noise Visibility Function (NVF) to compute the allowable distortion of each pixel by its neighbors' values [2]. Based on this, Yaghamee et al. defined NVF as the depth of each pixel in the quadtree decomposition of the cover image [4]. They also proposed a new method to estimate image complexity based on the concept of ROI and used ROI to calculate capacity [5]. In addition, Caciula et al. [6] and Pei et al. [7] researched the capacity of adaptive reversible watermarking.

However, these existing methods have ignored the quality issues [8]. When the number of embedded bits reaches the upper bound, the quality of stego-image becomes poor. To solve this problem, we see image quality as a parameter when calculating capacity. Then, watermarking capacity is the maximum number of bits that can be hidden in terms of particular quality requirements.

2 Background and Motivation

Zhang et al. used NVF to analyze watermarking capacity [2]. NVF is a function characterizes local image properties, identifying textured and edge regions where watermark should be more strongly embedded. The NVF at each pixe (r, c) is written as

$$\text{NVF}(r, c) = \frac{1}{1 + \delta_x^2(r, c)} \qquad (2\text{-}1)$$

where $\delta_x^2(r, c)$ is the local variance in a window centered on the pixel (x, c). Yaghmaee et

---

[*] 本文选自 Advanced Materials Research Vols. 989–994 (2014), 第 2368–2372 页

al. [4] partitioned $N \times N$ cover image and redefined NVF at each pixel (r, c) with its level $L(r, c)$ in the quadtree as

$$\text{NVF}(r, c) = \frac{L(r, c)}{\log_2 N} \tag{2-2}$$

In both of these two methods, the allowable distortion of each pixel (r, c) is

$$\Delta(r, c) = (1 - \text{NVF}(r, c)) \cdot \Delta_0 + \text{NVF}(r, c) \cdot \Delta_1 \tag{2-3}$$

where Δ_0 and Δ_1 are the maximum allowable pixel distortions in textured and flat region respectively. All the watermark amplitudes bulid an image named Maximum Watermark Image (MWI).

In order to investigate the quality of stego-images when the number of embedded bits reaches the estimated capacity, we do experiment on 2180 images with Zhang's method and Yaghmaee's method respectively, and compute the PSNR's of their MWT's. The result is presented in Table 1. Most PSNR's are no more than 22, with the Zhang's method, and are between 22 and 28, with the Yaghmaee's method. This shows that these two methods have ignored the trade-off between capacity and quality and thus over-estimated the capacity. If taking the quality of stego-image as a parameter, we can ensure the stego-image can achieve the desired quality requirements.

Table 1 Distrbution of the PSNR of Stego-images

Range of PSNR	Zhang et al. [2] method		Yaghmaee et al. [4] method	
	Number	Ratio	Number	Ratio
$[30, +\infty)$	14	0.64%	72	3.30%
$[28, 30)$	9	0.41%	45	2.06%
$[26, 28)$	22	1.01%	227	10.41%
$[24, 26)$	65	2.98%	721	33.07%
$[22, 24)$	180	8.26%	994	45.60%
$[20, 22)$	911	41.79%	119	5.46%
$[0, 20)$	979	44.91%	2	0.09%
Total	2 180	100%	2 180	100%

3 The Proposed Algorithm

Yaghmaee et al. proposed the ROI model to measure image complexity [5]. They divided cover image into 16 blocks, computed *Intensity*, *Contrast*, *Location*, *Edge* and *Texture* for each block, and imtegrated the five parameters into *Importance Measure* (IM), a real number between 0 and 1, to represent the image content. For there is direct relation between watermarking capacity and image complexity, capacity is closely associated with IM. Taking into consideration the quality of stego-image, which is usually measured by PSNR, we estimate capacity based on the ROI model.

Let $P_{expected}$ be the expected PSNR or stego-image, $P_{expected}$ is controlled by watemerk encoder and expresses the expected quality of stego-image. This requires that the actual PSNR of stego-image should no less than Pexpected. We propose an algorithm to calcalate the copacity of a gray-level image as following.

Algorithm: Computing the capacity of cover image

Input: A cover image S and the expected PSNR $P_{expected}$ of its stego-image S'
Output: Capacity C of the cover image
Steps: 1. Based on the ROI mode [5], divide the cover image S into blocks and calculate IM (S_i) for each block S_i.

2. Obtain the assumed PSNR of each block S_i in stego-image by computing

$$P_i = \frac{P_{expected}}{[\text{IM}(S_i)]^{1/2N_b}} \tag{3-1}$$

where N_b is the number of blocks. In the ROI model, $N_b = 16$.

3. Estimate the maximum distortions of the pixels in block S_i as

$$\Delta_i = \frac{255}{\sqrt{t_i}} \tag{3-2}$$

where $t_i = 10^{P_i/10}$ is a parameter dictated by P_i.

4. Let $\delta_x^2(r, c)$ be the local variance of block S_i in the 3×2 window centered on the pixel (r, c). The tolerable distortion of pixel (r, c) is

$$\Delta(r, c) = \left(1 - \frac{1}{\sqrt{1 + \delta_x^2(r, c)}}\right) \cdot \Delta_i \tag{3-3}$$

5. All pixel distortions make a new image named MWI. Assume σ_{iw}^2 denotes the variance of the corresponding MWI block and σ_n^2 denotes the variance of noise. The watermarking capacity of the whole cover image is

$$C = \sum_i C_i = \sum_i W_i \log\left(1 + \frac{\sigma_{iw}^2}{\sigma_n^2}\right) \tag{3-4}$$

There are some explanations essential for us to understanding this algorithm. First, a larger IM (S_i) means more distortion in S_i is acceptable. Second, if we partiton the cover image into substantially uniform blocks of different sizes by quadtree decomposition [4], the number of blocks is usually more than 16 and all allowable distortions of the pixels in block S_i are approximately the same as (3-2). Third, as NVF does in [2], the different textures around different pixels result in different tolerable distortions. (3-3) indicates richer texture can tolerate more distortions. Fourth, watermarking can be considered as a form of communication [3]. So watermarking capacity problem can be solved using traditional information theory [2]. We treat the whole image block S_i as one AWGN channel and assume every block suffers from the same channel attack. Then the capacity of the whole image is the sum of those for each block in (3-4).

4 Analysis on Stego-image Quality

We analyze the quality of stego-image when the number of embedded bits reaches the estimated capacity. Let P_{actual} be the actual PSNR of stego-image. According to the definition of PSNR,

$$P_{actual} = 10 \cdot \log_{10} \frac{m \cdot n \cdot 255^2}{\sum_{r,c} (S'(r,c) - S(r,c))^2} \quad (4\text{-}1)$$

Considering $\Delta(r, c) = S'(r, c) - S(r, c)$, according to (3-2) and (3-3),

$$P_{actual} = 10 \cdot \log_{10} \frac{m \cdot n}{\sum \left[\left(1 - \frac{1}{\sqrt{1+\delta_x^2(r,c)}}\right) \cdot \frac{1}{10^{P_i/10}} \right]} \quad (4\text{-}2)$$

Let $IM_{max} = \max_i \{IM(S_i)\}$. Applying (3-1) to (4-2), we get

$$P_{actual} \geq 10 \cdot \log_{10} \frac{m \cdot n \cdot 10^{P_{min}/10}}{\sum_{r,c} \left[\left(1 - \frac{1}{\sqrt{1+\delta_x^2(r,c)}}\right)^2 \right]} \quad (4\text{-}3)$$

Obviously, $1 - \frac{1}{\sqrt{1+\delta_x^2(r,c)}} < 1$. Then

$$P_{actual} > 10 \cdot \log_{10} 10^{\frac{P^{min}}{10}} = P_{min} = \frac{P_{expected}}{(IM_{max})^{1/(2N_b)}} \quad (4\text{-}4)$$

Because of $IM(S_i) \in (0, 1)$, we have $IM_{max} < 1$ and $(IM_{max})^{1/(2N_b)} < 1$. Thus (4-5)

$$P_{actual} > P_{expected} \quad (4\text{-}5)$$

It indicates that stego-image S' can satisfy the quality requirements. But this does not means stego-images always have good quality when the number of hiding bits is below the upper bound of formula (3-4). A sufficient condition for good quality is that the modification of each pixel in cover images should not exceed its corresponding gray level of MWI. If the distortions of some regions go beyond the limit, although formula (4-4) is satisfied, the quality of stego-images may be poor. However, for our method is somewhat conservative in computing capacity, stego-images may be still good in vision even if the actual embedding capacity slightly exceeds formula (3-4).

5 Experiments

The quality of an image is generally considered to be good when its PSNR is no less than 28. So we set the expected PSNR is 28 and compute the distortions of the MWI's of 2 180 cover images obtained by the proposed method in Section 3. The experimental result shows that 90.09% PSNR's are between 28 and 30, and the rest are more than 30. Take Lena image for example. Fig. 1 is the MWI and stego-images of Lena. The MWI showed in Fig. 1 (b) is almost pure black because of its low gray values. Fig. 1 (c) amplifies its gray values by 8 times and clearly displays the contour of Lena. This shows that our algorithm has good adaptability. Fig. 1 (d) ~ (f) display three stego-images obtained by three different embedding methods. These stego-images have no visual difference from the cover image [Fig. 1 (a)]. Reviewing Table 1 in Section 2, we can see that the proposed algorithm can guarantee the quality of stego-images to be good.

(a) Cover image (b) MWI of Lena (c) Amplify MWI by 8

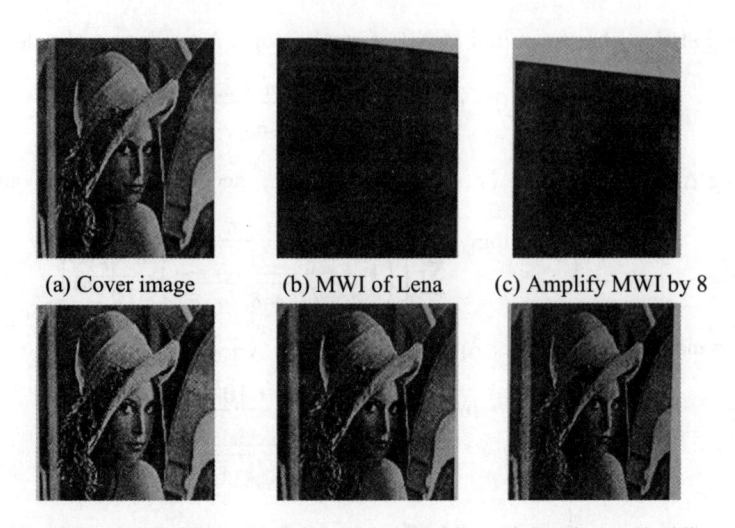

(d) Additive embedding (e) Subtractive embedding (f) Random embedding

Fig. 1: MWI and stego-images of Lena (PSNR = 28.70)

In Fig. 2, we draw the curve of watermarking capacities of four experimental images. With the rucease of PSNR, the quality requirements become higher, thus less modification on cover images raluces embedding capacity. When PSNR is More than 40, cover images are almost not modifiable and watermarking capacity tends to 0. In terms of any specific PSNR, the relationship of the capacities of different images is determined. It indicates that watermarking capacity depends on the self-characteristics of cover images.

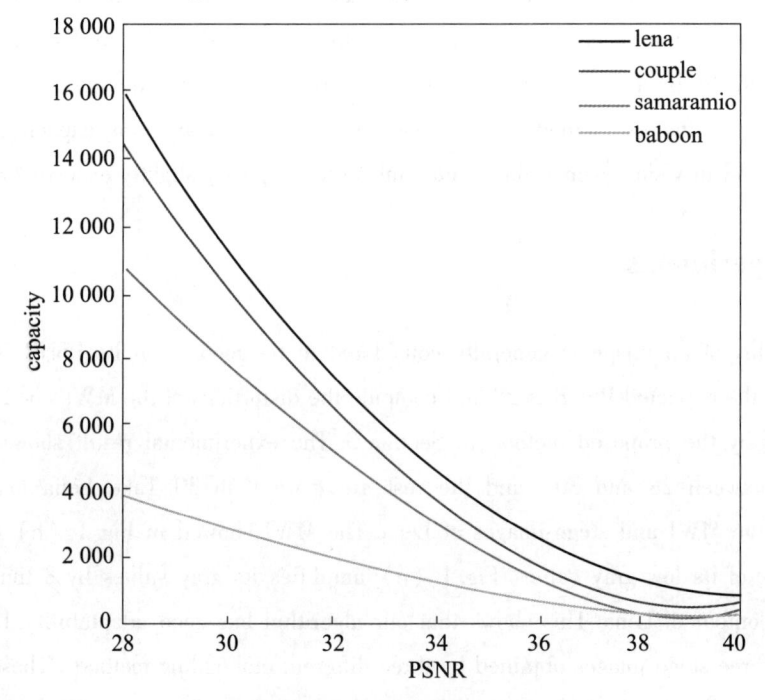

Fig. 2: Curve of watermarking capacity

6 Conclusions

In this paper, we regard image quality as one parameter and research the watermarking capacity problem closely associated with quality issues. Based on the ROI model, our method estimates the allowable distortion, the potential for embedding watermark, for each pixel in spatial domain in teins of the specific PSNR of stego-image. Experimental results show that our method can meet the quility requirements without introducing artifacts.

Acknowledgements

This research was supported in part by the National Natural Science Foundation of China (Grant Nieas. 61170032 and 61373020), and in part by the Project of General Administration of Press and Peadlication of China (GAPP-ZDKJ-BQ/15-2).

References

[1] P. H. Wong, O. C. Au, A Capacity Estimation Technique for Jpeg-to-JPEG Image Watemarking, IEEE Tran. Circuits and Systems for Video Technology, 2003, 13 (8), pp. 746-863.
[2] F. Zhang, H. B. Zhang, Digital Watermarking Capacity Analysis in Wavelet Domain, International Conference on Signal Processing, 2004, 3, pp. 2278-2281.
[3] P. Moulin, M. K. Mihcak, The Parallel Gaussian Watermarking Game, IEEE Trans. Information Theory, 2004, 50 (2), pp. 272-289.
[4] F. Yaghmaee, M. Jamzad, Computing Watermark Capcity in Images According to Their Quad Tree, International Symposium on Signal Processing and Information Technology, 2005: 823-826.
[5] F. Yaghmaee, M. Jamzad, Estimating Watermarking Capacity in Gray Scale Images Based on Image Complexity, EURASIP J. on Advances in Signal Processing, 2010, 2010, pp. 1-9.
[6] I. Caciula, D. Coltuc, Capacity Control of Reversible Watermarking by Two-Thresholds Embedding: Further Results, International Symposium on Signals, Circuits and Systems, 2013: 1-4.
[7] Q. Pei, X. Wang, Y. Li, et al., Adaptive Reversible Watermarking with Improved Embedding Capacity, J. Systems and Software, 2013, 86 (11), pp. 2941-2848.
[8] F. Yaghmaee, M. Jamzad, Introducing a Two Dimensional Measure for Watermarking Capacity in Images, Image Analysis and Recognition, Springer Berlin Heidelberg, 2008, pp. 213-220.

A New Echo Hiding Algorithm with High Robustness[*]

Mo Zhou Shun-Dong Li Xiang-Yang Luo Dao-Shun Wang

Introduction

Echo hiding method was described for the first time in [1]. An echo can be considered as a delayed version of the signal itself. The delay can be made small so that the echo is not audible. Many algorithms based on echo hiding have been developed, such as single echo, double echo, forward backward echo and time spread echo hiding [2, 3, 4, 5] and their improvements. Yousof Erfani et al. [6] proposed three methods based on single and double echo hiding. Foo Say Wei et al. [7] embedded watermark bit 0 and 1 into different channels to achieve higher robustness. Duan et al. [8] introduced a developed cepstrum method which improved the accuracy by making use of the cepstral value of the original signal. Experimental results in [8] show that Echo hiding method has high watermark capacity without high robustness.

The Modulated Lapped Transform (MLT) is commonly used to implement block transform coding in video and audio compression. It allows for perfect reconstruction, has almost optimal performance for transform coding of a wide variety of signals with no blocking artifacts [9]. In [10] the modulated complex lapped transform (MCLT) was given as a simple extension to the MLT and preserved the advantages of it. After that, some research has been done to improve the speed of MCLT algorithm [11-15]. We use MCLT to improve the robustness of echo hiding method in [1].

The outline of the paper is as follows. We propose a new echo hiding method for stereo signals in Section 2 and combine MCLT with our echo hiding method to improve robustness. The evaluation results and discussions are presented in Section 3. Finally the conclusions are given in Section 4.

Capacity Enlargement-Combining Echo Hiding with Spread Spectrum

Echo hiding method boasts a relatively large data capacity. The spread spectrum method embeds watermarks in the frequency domain while the echo hiding method works in the time do-

---

[*] 本文选自 International Journal of Automation and Power Engineering (IJAPE) Volume 2 Issue 4, May 2013, 第240-246页

main. What's more, both methods process audio sequences block by block. Based on [1], we propose a new stereo echo hiding method below. Then, we try to combine it with the spread spectrum method in MCLT domain to improve robustness.

Our Improved Echo Hiding Method

We propose a new echo hiding scheme for stereo signals. Both channels are used to encode a watermark bit with different delay values. To encode watermark bit 0, echoes with delay value d_0 are embedded in the left channel and echoes with delay value d_1 are embedded in the right channel. To encode watermark bit 1, echoes with delay value d_1 are embedded in the left channel and echoes with delay value d_0 are embedded in the right channel.

When extracting the embedded watermark, we compare the difference of cepstrum value in two delay points of both channels.

The embedding procedure in our method based on [1] is as follows.

Input: an stereo audio signal portion $x_i(n)$, echo bit e, initial echo amplitude a, n varies from 0 to $M-1$, $e \in \{0, 1\}$, M is the number of samples in the block

---

Watermark embedding procedure:

(1) Divide the stereo audio signal portion $x_i(n)$ into left channel portion $x_i^l(p)$ and
$$x_i^r(q), p \text{ and } q \text{ vary from 0 to } \frac{M}{2} - 1$$

(2) Embed the echo bit into both channels of the block and get the resulted sequence (see [1])
$$y_i^l(p) = x_i^l(p) + a^* x_i^l(p - d_e)$$
$$y_i^r(q) = x_i^r(q) + a^* x_i^r(q - d_{1-e})$$

(3) Recombine the left portion and the right portion and get the watermarked audio portion $y_i(n)$

Output: an processed audio signal block $y_i(n)$

The extracting procedure in our method is as follows.

Input: an processed audio signal block $y_i(n)$

Watermark extracting procedure:

(1) Divide the stereo audio signal portion $y_i(n)$ into left channel portion $y_i^l(P)$ and
$$y_i^r(q), p \text{ and } q \text{ vary from 0 to } \frac{M}{2} - 1$$

(2) Compute the cepstrum of both channels (see [1])
$$c_l(p) = F^{-1}(\log F(y_i^l(p)))$$
$$c_r(q) = F^{-1}(\log F(y_i^r(q)))$$

(3) Decide the echo hiding bit e
$$e = \begin{cases} 0 & \text{if } c_l(d_0) - c_l(d_1) > c_r(d_0) - c_r(d_1) \\ 1 & \text{if } c_l(d_0) - c_l(d_1) < c_r(d_0) - c_r(d_1) \end{cases}$$

Output: extracted echo bit e

TABLE 1 CORRECT BIT RATE (CBR) AND SIGNAL-TO-NOISE-RATIO (SNR) OF SINGLE ECHO HIDING METHOD AND OUR PROPOSED ECHO HIDING METHOD

audio sequence	single echo hiding [1]		our proposed echo hiding	
	CBR	SNR	CBR	SNR
clip 1-10	76.09%	16.008	79.53%	17.693
clip 11-20	75.78%	17.540	78.13%	18.784
clip 21-30	76.72%	18.653	78.59%	20.118
clip 31-40	75.16%	20.927	76.09%	22.147
clip 41-50	74.22%	17.406	81.09%	18.749
clip 51-60	80.16%	15.564	85.78%	17.249
clip 61-70	84.69%	20.686	84.84%	22.019
average	77.54%	18.112	80.58%	19.537

TABLE 2 CBR OF SINGLE ECHO HIDING METHOD AND OUR PROPOSED ECHO HIDING METHOD UNDER VARIOUS ATTACKS

Attacks	single echo hiding [1]	our proposed echo hiding
Re-sampling (22.05kHz)	66.75%	82.83%
MP3 compression	56.50%	56.47%
Noise attack	62.70%	65.11%
Low-pass filtering	61.56%	73.37%
High-pass filtering	63.39%	64.15%

We use Sound Quality Assessment Material (SQAM) audio [16] as test material to compare our echo hiding method with the original single echo hiding.

Table 1 shows that our proposed method has higher extracting rate and better conceptual transparency compared to the single echo hiding method. Table 2 shows that our proposed echo hiding method is more robust than single echo hiding under various attacks except MP3 compression.

It is necessary to point out that the comparison betwween single echo hiding and our proposed echo hiding are based on the same embedding capacity of one watermark bit in 2048 samples of two channels, the same decay rate of 0.5 and initial amplitude of 0.1 and 0.08 respectively. Note that our method is computationally more complex than the method in [1].

Watermark Embedding Procedures of the Proposed Approach

Next we will combine the echo hiding method proposed above the spread spectrum method in MCLT domain and get a new scheme that works both in the time domain and the transform domain. In the encoder side, we've tried two combining orders and find out that echoes embedded after the MCLT transform will result in better performance in robustness. In the decoder side, since both methods just read the audio sequence rather than modify it, the order doesn't matter.

The embedding procedure is as follows with step 1-3 comes from [17].

Watermark Extracting Procedures of the Proposed Approach

The extracting procedure in is as follows with step 1-3 comes from [17].

Let $p \cdot q$ denote the normalized inner product of vector p and q, i.e., $p \cdot q \equiv N^{-1} \sum_i p_i q_i$

Input: audio signal blocks $x_i(k)$, magnitude change a, permutated watermark chip $chip_s(k)$, k varies from 0 to $M-1$, s varies from 0 to $c-1$, c is the number of all possible watermark characters, echo bit e, $e \in \{0, 1\}$, M is the number of samples in the block

Watermark embectd procedure:

(1) Compute the analysis window $h_a(n)$ (see [10])

(2) Perform MCLT transform on $x_i(k)$ and get MCLT coefficients

$$X_i(k) \sum_{n=0}^{M-1} x_{i-1}(n) p_a(n,k) + \sum_{m=M}^{2M-1} x_i(n-M) p_a(n,k)$$

(3) Modify $X_i(k)$ according to the corresponding watermark bit $chip(k)$ and get

$$X_i^{'}(k) = \begin{cases} X_i(k) \cdot a & if\ chip_s(k) = 1 \\ X_i(k) \cdot (1/a) & if\ chip_s(k) = 0 \end{cases}$$

(4) Perform inverse MCLT transform on $X_i^{'}(k)$ and get $x_i^{'}(k)$

$$x_i^{'}(k) = \sum_{n=0}^{M-1} X_i^{'}(n) p_s(k,n)$$

(5) Divide the stereo audio signal portion $x_i^{'}(k)$ into left channel portion $x_i^{'}(p)$ and $x_i^{r}(q)$, p and q varies from 0 to $\frac{M}{2} - 1$

(6) Embed the echoes into both channels of the block (see [1]) and get the resulted sequence

$$y_i^l(p) = x_i^l(p) + a^* x_i^l(p - d_e)$$
$$y_i^r(q) = x_i^r(q) + a^* x_i^r(q - d_{1-e})$$

(7) Recombine the left portion and the right portion and get the watermarked audio portion $y_i(k)$

Output: processed audio signal blocks $y_i(k)$

Input: watermarked audio signal blocks $y_i(k)$, k varies from 0 to $M-1$, M is the number of samples in the block

Watermark extracting procedure:

(1) Compute the analysis window $h_s(n)$ (see [10])

(2) Perform MCLT transform on $y_i(k)$ and get MCLT coefficients

$$Y_i(k) = \sum_{n=0}^{M-1} y_{i-1}(n) p_s(n, k) + \sum_{n=M}^{2M-1} y_i(n-M) p_s(n, k)$$

(3) Compute the correlations of $Y_i(k)$ with all possible watermark chips in the pool and get the extracted watermark chips $chip_s(k)$

$$Correlation\ (Y_i, chip_s) = Y_i \cdot chip_s = \mathrm{Max}\ \{Y_i \cdot chip_t\}\ for\ all\ possible\ t$$

(4) Divide the stereo audio signal portion $y_i(k)$ into left channel portion $y_i^l(p)$ and $y_i^r(q)$, p and q varies from 0 to $\frac{M}{2} - 1$

(5) Compute the cepstrum of both channels (see [1])

$$c_l(p) = F^{-1}(\log F(y_i^l(p)))$$
$$c_l(q) = F^{-1}(\log F(y_i^r(q)))$$

(6) Decide the echo hiding bit e

$$e = \begin{cases} 0 & if\ c_l(d_0) - c_l(d_1) > c_r(d_0) - c_r(d_1) \\ 1 & if\ c_l(d_0) - c_l(d_1) < c_r(d_0) - c_r(d_1) \end{cases}$$

Output: extracted watermark chip $chip_s(k)$ and echo bit e

Experiment Results

We use Sound Quality Assessment Material (SQAM) audio [16] as test material, all 70 audio clips having a sampling frequency of 44100 Hz, 2 channels and a quantization of 16 bits. Various attacks are performed using Adobe Audition 3.0 and Audacity 1.3.6, which are both popular tool-sets for professional audio processing and editing.

Transparency Evaluation

SNR (Signal-to-Noise Ratio) [18] is a statistical difference metric which is used to measure the perceptual similarity between the undistorted original audio signal and the distorted watermarked audio signal.

Robustness Evaluation

Since an extracted watermark is taken as a proof of authorship, the embedded watermark should withstand attemps at removing or damaging it. We have simulated five kinds of attemps, namely resampling, MP3 compression, white noise addition, low-pass filtering and high-pass filtering with audio processing software Adobe Audition 3.0 and Audacity, which can be freely downloaded from the Internet. The simulation results are listed below.

Another important criterion of watermarking algorithms is their minimum error rate of watermark detection or extraction. Therefore, we have used the CBR (Correct Bit Rate).

The correct bit rate in Table 7 are the averages of the correct bit rates obtained for 70 audio clips. The correct bit rate for each clip is defined as: $CBR = \dfrac{Number\ of\ rightly\ extracted\ bits}{Number\ of\ embedded\ bits\ for\ the\ clip}$

TABLE 3 SNR OF ECHO HIDING AND ECHO HIDING WITH MCLT

audio sequence	SNR of our echo hiding method in Section 2.1	SNR of echo hiding with MCLT
clip 1-10	17.693	18.810
clip 11-20	18.784	22.810
clip 21-30	20.118	23.473
clip 31-40	22.147	15.650
clip 41-50	18.749	19.163
clip 51-60	17.249	19.358
clip 61-70	22.019	18.354
average	19.537	19.660

TABLE 4 CBR OF ECHO HIDING AND ECHO HIDING WITH MCLT UNDER VARIOUS ATTACKS

Attacks	Proposed echo hiding in Section 2.1	Our echo hiding with MCLT
No attacks	80.58%	94.71%
Re-sampling (22.05kHz)	82.83%	95.71%
MP3 compression	56.47%	86.30%
Noise attack	65.11%	77.86%
Low-pass filtering	73.37%	92.92%
High-pass filtering	64.15%	88.80%

Various options of the attacks above are defined as follows:

No attacks: closed loop (immediately decoding after encoding)

Re-sampling: sampling the watermarked signal with 22.05kHz sampling rate

MP3 compression: compressing the watermarked signal by MPEG-1 layer 3 and reverting it again to the original wave file

Noise attack: adding white noise with zero mean and Gaussian power density function to the watermarked signal

Low-pass filtering: a first order low-pass filter with cut-off frequency 1600Hz is used

High-pass filtering: a first order high-pass filter with cut-off frequency 1600Hz is used

Table 3 and Table 4 show that combined with MCLT method, the robustness of echo hiding method is improved at the cost of lower embedding capacity and higher computational complexity.

According to some previous work [8], the correct bit rate of the echo method is no higher than 83%, which is verified by our own tests. We take advantage of the majority vote to lower the bit error rate. We embed all the watermark bits $2*k+1$ times and then extract them. If no less than $k+1$ bits corresponding to one bit is 0, we decide that the bit is 0. If no less than $k+1$ bits corresponding to one bit is 1, we decide that the bit is 1. Our experimental results show that majority vote improves the bit correct rate and robustness of echo hiding method at the cost of lower capacity.

Conclusions

We first propose a new echo hiding method based on single echo hiding in [1], which is better than single echo hiding in both robustness and transparency with the same watermark capacity. Then, we have also improved the robustness of echo hiding method through combining it with the spread spectrum algorithm in MCLT domain [17]. Experimental results show that our two methods have high robustness.

Acknowledgements

This research was supported in part by the National Natural Science Foundation of China (Grant Nos. 61070189, 61170032, and 61272435), Project of General Administration of press and publication of China under Grant GAPP-ZDKJ-BQ/15-2, and was also supported by the national postdoctoral foundation of China (Grand Nos. 201003111, 20110491838, and 2012T50842).

References

[1] Bender W, Gruhl D, Morimoto N. Techniques for data hiding. IBM Systems Journal, 1996, vol. 35, pp. 313-336.

[2] Byeong-Seob Ko, Ryouichi Nishimura, Yoiti Suzuki. Time-spread echo method for digital audio watermarking. IEEE Transactions on Multimedia, 2005, vol. 7 (2), pp. 212-221.

[3] Daniel Gruhl, Anthony Lu, Walter Bender. Echo hiding. IBM Systems Journal, 1996, vol. 35, pp. 328-332.

[4] Darko Kirovski, Henrique S. Malvar. Spread-spectrum watermarking of audio signals. IEEE Transactions on Signal Processing, 2003, vol. 51 (4), pp. 1020-1033.

[5] Foo Say Wei, Dong Qi. Audio watermarking of stereo signals based on echo-hiding method. Conference Proceedings of the 7th International Conference on Information, Communications and Signal Processing, 2009.

[6] H. S. Malvar. A modulated complex lapped transform and its applications to audio processing. IEEE International Conference on Acoustic, Speech, and Signal Processing, 1999, vol. 3, pp. 1421-1424.

[7] H. S. Malvar. Fast algorithm for the modulated complex lapped transform. IEEE Signal Processing Letters, 2003, vol. 10, pp. 8-10.

[8] Hyen O Oht, Jong Won Seoktt, Jin Woo Hongtt, Dae Hee Yount. New echo embedding technique for robust and imperceptible audio watermarking. International Conference on Acoustics, Speech, and Signal Processing, 2001, vol. 3, pp. 1341-1344.

[9] Hyoung Joong Kim, Yong Hee Choi. A novel echo-hiding scheme with backward and forward kernels. IEEE Transactions on Circuits and Systems for Video Technology, 2003, vol. 13 (8), pp. 885-889.

[10] Jingchang Chen, Ruimin Hu, Haojun Ai, Weiping Tu. DCT-II based fast algorithm for MCLT. Signal Processing, 2005, vol. 21 (1), pp. 63-66.

[11] Liuyun Duan, Jiebao Zong, Ying Wang, Hongfei Cheng, Zhong Yin. Developed cepstrum method for data extraction based on echo hiding. Electronic Design Engineering, 2010, vol. 18 (7), pp. 77-79.

[12] Qionghai Dai, Xinjian Chen. New algorithm for modulated complex lapped transform with symmetrical window function. IEEE Signal Processing Letters, 2004, vol. 11 (12), pp. 925-928.

[13] Quackenbush, S. R., Barnwell III, T. P., Clements, M. A.: "Objective measures of speech quality" (Prentice-Hall, 1988).

[14] Seymour Shlien. The modulated lapped transform, its time-varying forms, and its Applications to audio coding standards, IEEE Transactions on Speech and Audio Processing, 1997, vol. 5 (4), pp. 359-366.

[15] SQAM-Sound Quality Assessment Material, http://tech.ebu.cn/publications/sqamcd Xinjian Chen, Qionghai Dai. A novel DCT-based algorithm for computing the modulated complex lapped transform. IEEE Transaction on Signal Processing, 2006, vol. 54 (11), pp. 4480-4484.

[16] Yousof Erfani, M. Shahram Moin, Mehdi Parviz. New methods for transparent and accurate echo hiding by using the original audio cepstral content. 6th IEEE/ACIS International Conference on Computer and Information Science, 2007, pp. 1087-1092.

[17] Yun Ge, Dong Zhang. New Fast Algorithm for Modulated Complex Lapped Transform with Arbitrary Windowing Function. Journal of Electronics & Information Technology, 2010, vol. 32 (3), pp. 747-749.

A Visual Hiding Algorithm Based on Human Visual System

Rui Dong Daoshun Wang

1 Introduction

The human visual system has less sensitivity on redundancy of the whole image, partial or slight changes of the image. By taking the advantage of these features, image information hiding embeds the secret into carrier image under the condition that not affecting the transmission quality of the carrier image. Naor and Shamir [1] first proposed the scheme of visual cryptography in 1994. The secret information can be retrieved by a simple superposition. Lee et al. [2] hided information within meaning stego images based on HVS with no pixel expansion. Yamaguchi [3] proposed a continuous hue based scheme using parallel error spread and optimum hue mapping. Both of the two schemes have no pixel expansion, but the cover image can be seen partially in the background of recovered image during recovering. Refs. [4-6] use the digital halftoning to achieve the goals of no pixel expansion. Hou [7] proposed the asymmetric watermarking scheme based on HVS.

In this paper, we propose an visual hiding algorithm scheme based on HVS. A pair of invert images is used as the cover images in this algorithm, and the background color of the recovered image is black, which greatly improves the visual quality the secret image.

2 Related Work

Visual Cryptography is an effective method of information hiding. Hou [7] proposed the asymmetric watermark algorithm based on HVS, and the complementary matrixes Naor and Shamir used are shown as follow:

$$\begin{bmatrix}1&0\\1&0\end{bmatrix}\begin{bmatrix}0&1\\0&1\end{bmatrix}\begin{bmatrix}1&1\\0&0\end{bmatrix}\begin{bmatrix}0&0\\1&1\end{bmatrix}\begin{bmatrix}1&0\\0&1\end{bmatrix}\begin{bmatrix}1&0\\1&0\end{bmatrix}$$

$$\qquad\text{Vertical}\qquad\text{Horizontal}\qquad\text{Cross}$$

Hou's algorithm is shown as follow, and an example is given in Figure 1:

Input: $2^{c-1} \times 2^{c-1}$ secret image S, cover image C
Output: stego image S_1, S_2, cover image C
Construction:

Step 1: if $S(i, j) = 0$, randomly fill the 2×2 blocks of S_1, S_2 into the above matrixes; else if $S(i, j) = 1$, randomly fill the 2×2 of S_1 into the above matrix, and fill S_2's blocks into S_1's complementary matrix, until S_1, S_2 are constructed.

Step 2: if $S_1(i, j) = 1$, decrease the gray scale $C(i, j)$ by 8, until C is constructed.

Fig. 1 (a) Cover image, (b) original secret image, (c) (d) stego image 1 and 2, (e) recovered image

In image information hiding, the visual quality of the stego image is an important measurement, PSNR is widely used for measuring visual quality of stego image [9, 10]. PSNR's definition is shown as follow:

$$\text{PSNR} = 10 \cdot \log_{10} \frac{(255)^2}{\text{MSE}} dB \quad (1)$$

MSE represents the mean square error between the cover image and stego image:

$$\text{MSE} = \frac{1}{M \times N} \sum_{i=1}^{M} \sum_{j=1}^{N} (x_{i,j} - y_{i,j})^2 \quad (2)$$

where $x_{i,j}$ and $y_{i,j}$ represent the pixel value of cover and stego image respectively, $M \times N$ represent the size of image. Generally, MSE can be used to evaluate the quality of binary image.

In Hou et al. 's algorithm, the PSNR of the stego image is 26.144dB, and we can see that the stego image has serious artifacts comparing with the original cover image.

3 Proposed Visual Hiding Algorithm

In this section, the detail of the proposed algorithm will be shown. Our algorithm is similar to Hou's algorithm [8], both of them are based on HVS. Firstly, the cover image is halftone processed with error diffusion algorithm. Then embed the secret image into the texture and less visual sensitive regions of the cover image.

3.1 Texture and Edge

According to the HVS characters, the process strength of the stego image is affected by the texture complexity, the more complex the texture is, the higher the available process strength is, correspondingly, the higher the recovered image quality is. So it is effective to use the edge and texture to decide the embedding region and strength.

The entropy [9] of image represents the image's average information amount, and it can be used to evaluate texture's complexity. Variance is a measure for edge in images, and generally, the variance around edge is much bigger. Based on the relation between entropy and variance, we can divide the region feature into the following four categories:

Table 1　Feature categories based on entropy and variance

	Smooth	Edge	Texture	Others
Entropy (H)	small	big	large	small
Variance (Var)	small	big	small	large

Through the above, we can conclude that regions with complex textures and less edges are the ideal regions for embedding. Secret embedding needs regions that contain a lot of textures, so the entropy will be taken into consideration firstly.

3.2 Construction of the Algorithm

The cover images used in this algorithm are two halftoned images with invert color to each other. The pixels of the input secret image S are black, and the recovered image has the invert color, which greatly increases the contrast.

Let secret image be S, let cover image 1 and cover image 2 be I and I' respectively. Let stego image 1 and 2 be S_1 and S_2 respectively, and T be the threshold of detection. Let M_1 (M_2) be the modification degree of the first (second) pixel in the 1×2 block of stego image 1. Let $M'1$ ($M'2$) be the modification degree of the first (second) pixel in the 1×2 block of stego image 2. The algorithm use T to constraint the modification of the current pixel. Table 2 give the detail criterion for modification:

Table 2　Criterion for pixel modification

S	I	I'	condition	S_1	S_2
[1　1] [1　0] [0　1]	[1　0]	[0　1]	Probability: 1/2	[1　0]	[1　0]
	[0　1]	[1　0]		[0　1]	[0　1]
	[0　0]	[1　1]	$M'_1 \geq T$	[0　0]	[1　0]
			$M'_1 < T \ M'_2 \geq T$	[0　0]	[0　1]
	[1　1]	[0　0]	$M_1 \geq T$	[1　0]	[0　0]
			$M_1 < T \ M_2 \geq T$	[0　1]	[0　0]
[0　0]	without any modification				

In the modification criterion is based on the connected region's white pixels. And the modification degree is to avoid adhesion. A pending pixel has 8 neighbor black pixels in continuous 3×3 connected region. In this paper, we set weight for the other 8 pixels in the connected region to decide the modification degree $M(i, j)$. Let function $B(x, y)$ return 0 on $x = y$, return 1 on $x \neq y$, then the modification degree of $A(i, j)$ is:

$$M(i,j) = \sum_{r=-1}^{1}\sum_{t=-1}^{1} w(A(i,j), A(i+t, j+t)) B(A(i,j), A(i+t, j+t)) \quad (3)$$

where $w(x, y)$ represents the weight of the pixel on coordinate (x, y), and the weight assigning criterion is shown as following:

(a) 5 for pixel with no modifications.

(b) For modified pixels: 3 for pixels in diagonal direction, 2 for pixels in horizontal and vertical directions.

Assigning different weights for pixels with and without modifications is to decrease the possibility of adhesion caused by modifying neighbor pixels. Treating horizontal and vertical pixels differently is for the reason that human eyes are more sensitive to horizontal and vertical pixels than the diagonal ones. The detail algorithm is given as fellow.

Input: original secret image S, grayscale image C
Output: stego image S_1, S_2
Construction:

Step 1: Halftone process C to get cover image I and the invert image I', let $S_1 = I$, $S_2 = I'$.

Step 2: Decide the start coordinate of the stego region: X, Y.

(1) Define a new structure "D", which contains the elements of coordinate, entropy and variance.

(2) Scan C pixel by pixel with a sliding window is size S, and record the entropy, MSE and start coordinate of the region to an array Arr with D as element and in size N.

(3) Sort the array Arr in entropy descending order. Get the element with the biggest MSE as$_{DE}$ from the first $\lceil \partial N \rceil$ elements in Arr ($0 < \partial < 1$), record its coordinate as X, Y.

Step 3: Scan S with row step size 1 and column step size 2 to get neighbor pixels $S(i, j)$, $S(i, j+1)$, and the corresponding cover image $I(i+X-1, j+Y-1)$ and $I(i+X-1, j+Y)$.

Step 4: Calculate the modification degree for $S(i, j)$, $S(i, j+1)$, $I(i+X-1, j+Y-1)$ and $I(i+X-1, j+Y)$.

Step 5: According to the table 2, then modify S_1 and S_2 according to the modification degree and detection threshold T.

Example 1: original secret image S: [1 0 1 1 0 0], cover image I:

$$\begin{bmatrix} 1 & 0 & 1 & 0 & 1 & 1 & 0 & 0 \\ 1 & 1 & 0 & 1 & 1 & 0 & 0 & 1 \\ 1 & 0 & 1 & 0 & 1 & 1 & 0 & 0 \end{bmatrix}$$, set all the initial weights to 5, ideal embedding position: $X = 2$, $Y = 2$. Sequentially scan two consecutive pixels of the original secret image, detection threshold $T = 20$, the stego image is constructed as follows:

1. $S = [1 \ 0]$, $I = [0 \ 0]$, $I' = [1 \ 1]$. The modification degree of the first pixel of S_2: $M'_1 = 3 \times 5 = 15 < T$, then this pixel cannot be modified. The modification degree of the first pixel of S_2: $M'_2 = 4 \times 5 = 20 \geq T$, then this pixel can be modified. Modify the corresponding block of S_2 to $[0 \ 1]$, and mark this pixel as "modified". The recovered result: $R = [0 \ 1]$.

2. $S = [1 \ 1]$, $I = [1 \ 0]$, $I' = [0 \ 1]$. Permute the two consecutive pixels values of the S_1 or S_2 with probability 0.5, in this process modify the corresponding block of S_2 to $[1 \ 0]$, and mark the pixel as "modified". The recovered result: $R = [1 \ 0]$.

3. $S = [0 \ 0]$. No need to modify.

4 Comparison and Discussion

4.1 Experimental Results

By observing Figure 2, it is convenient to see that as T differences. The quality of the stego images and the recovered image changes. Figure 2 is the experimental results by different T. By observing experimental results, when $T = 0$, the stego image will leak the information for the secret image. So the appropriate value for T is important. As T increases, the quality of stego images increase while the quality of recovered image decreases.

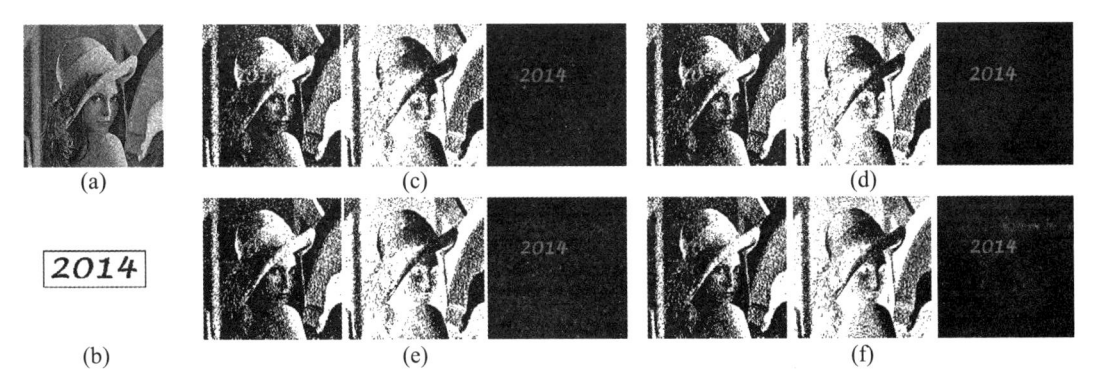

Fig. 2 Experimental results. (a) cover image, (b) secret image, (c) ~ (f) stego images and recoverd image are generated with $T = 0$, 10, 21, 25

MSE can be used to evaluate the quality of binary image. The smaller the MSE, the better the quality of stego images. The secret have the number of black pixels is 2838. This paper defines the number of the meaningful pixels as information amount, which can be counted to describe the quality of the recovered image. The comparison result is summarized as Table 3.

Table 3 MES for stego images with different T

T	Stego 1	Stego 2	Information amount
0	300.1413	239.5167	1553
10	260.7013	235.6482	1345
21	174.6277	170.1628	843
25	156.5200	159.0005	729

By observing Table 3, it is convenient to see that as T increases. The MSE of the stego images increase and the information amount of the recovered image increase (Because of the stego 2 is inverse, when calculating the MSE of the stego 2, we should use the inverted cover image). By the experimented results, different texture complexity of image result in different embedded effect. So the ideal value of t is variable in different cases. By observing the experimental results, when t = 21, the experimental result is ideal.

4.2 Comparison with Hou's Algorithm

In this section, we compare the proposed algorithm with Hou's algorithm in four typical aspects: ①the type of cover image, ②whether require extra pixel expansion or not, ③whether require the stego images meaningful or not, and ④ the quality of recovered image.

Table 4 Comparison of the proposed algorithm and Hou's algorithm

Algorithms	Cover images	Pixel expansion	Meaningful		The quality
			S_1	S_2	
Hou's algorithm	Gray	$m = 4$	Yes	No	Less poor
Our algorithm	Halftone	$m = 1$	Yes	Yes	Good

From Table 4, the cover image in Hou's algorithm is grayscale image, the stego image 2 is random lattice, and the recovered image has the problem of pixel expansion (m = 4). In case of minor modification, it may be low chromatic aberration between the secret regions and others, so, identifying the secret information through human vision is difficult in this case. This paper's algorithm has no pixel expansion, and all the two stego images are meaningful. All the non-secret information regions of recovered image are formed by black pixels, so the recovered image has better visual effect. Combined with the grey-level modification method in Hou's algorithm, this paper's algorithm can extends to the grayscale stego image algorithm, and the recovered image could also have high visual effect.

5 Conclusions

This paper proposes a visual Hiding method based on visual cryptography. This algorithm chooses the ideal embedding region for secret image based on the HVS characters, which can decrease the possibility of the meaningful neighbor pixels adhesion of the secret image, and decrease the phenomenon of the exposing of the secret. While inversing the cover images, it improves the contrasts of the recovered image.

Acknowledgement

This research was supported in part by the National Natural Science Foundation of China (Grant Nos. 61170032 and 61373020), and in part by the Project of General Administration of press and publication of China (GAPP-ZDKJ-BQ/15-2).

References

[1] M. Naor, A. Sharmir. Visual Cryptography [C] //Preproceeding of Eurocrypt 94. BerLin: Springer, 1994: 1-12.

[2] K. H. Lee, P. L. Chiu. An extended visual cryptography algorithm for general access structures, IEEE Transactions on Information Forensics and Security, 2012, 7 (1): 219-229.

[3] Y. Yamaguchi, An extended visual cryptography algorithm for continuous-tone images, Lecture Notes in Computer Science (LNCS), 2012, 7128: 228-242.

[4] Y. C. Hou, S. F. Du. Visual Cryptography Techniques for Color Images without Pixel Expansion [J]. Journal of Information. Technology and Society, 2004 (4): 95-110.

[5] M. Nakajima, Y. Yamaguchi. "Extended visual cryptography for natural images," in Proc. WSCG Conf. 2002, 2002: 303-412.

[6] Y. C. Hou, C. F. Lin, C. Y. Chang. Visual cryptography for color images without pixel expansion. Journal of Technology. 2001, 16 (4): 595-603.

[7] Y. C. Hou, P. M. Chen. An asymmetric watermarking scheme based on visual cryptography. Proc. of ICSP, 2000, 2: 992-995.

[8] R. W. Floyd. An adaptive algorithm for spatial gray-scale [C] //Proc. Soc. Inf. Disp. 1976, 17: 75-77.

[9] C. I. Podilchuk, E. J. Delp. Digital watermarking: algorithms and applications [J]. IEEE Signal Processing Magazine, 2001, 18 (4): 33-46.

[10] I. J. Cox, M. L. Miller. The first 50 years of electronic watermarking [J]. Journal of Applied Signal Processing, 2002 (2): 126-132.

Reversible Data Hiding based on Histogram Technique*

Dao-Shun Wang Yi Liu Song Liu Xing-Fu Xu Shun-Dong Li

1 Introduction

Reversible data hiding (RDH), also referred to as lossless, distortion-free, or invertible data hiding, is a technique that the cover-media can be exactly recovered after the hidden data have been extracted out from Stego-media [1~2]. In some applications, such as medical diagnosis and law enforcement, it is critical to reverse the marked media back to the original Cover-media after the hidden data are retrieved for legal considerations. In other applications that require high-precision, such as remote sensing and high-energy particle physical experimental investigation, it is also desirable that the original cover media can be recovered as exact as possible [1~2]. Ni et al. [1~2] first employed the peak-zero points (or maximum-minimum points or peak-valley pairs) in the histogram of the Cover-image to embed the secret message (hidden information, or watermark) by modifying the gray values between the peak values and zero values; the embedding capacity is equal to frequency of the peak points. Note that the peak and zero points must be transmitted to the receiver as auxiliary information for hidden data retrieval. In Section 2, we review the method by Ni et al. [1-2].

Reversibility is no doubt the most basic requirement of reversible data hiding. In addition, the performance of a reversible data hiding algorithm can be measured by payload capacity limit, visual quality, and complexity [3-4].

To maintain high image quality, and increase embedding payload capacity, some methods attempt to make the auxiliary information as small as possible, other methods have to use the auxiliary information as big as possible [1-8]. In Section 3, we present some typical algorithms to adjust the information.

For a histogram-shifting based reversible data hiding technique, the capacity is determined by the peak height of the histogram of the Cover-image. Generally speaking, the higher the peak height of a histogram is, the higher the capacity can achieve. This can be seen in Ni et al.'s method [1-2]. In section 4, we introduce four typical algorithms to increase capacity for RDH based on histogram modification.

---

* 本文选自 Steganography and Watermarking, 第131-162页

When hidden data are embedded, a distortion (pixel value difference) between the Cover-image and the Stego-image occurs. Several methods have been proposed attempted to reduce this type of distortion [20 - 25] in RDH algorithms. Three such methods are presented in Section 5.

2 RDH Using Histogram-shifting

The algorithm proposed in Ni *et al.* [1 - 2] identifies the zero or the minimum points of the histogram of a Cover-image and slightly modified the pixel grayscale values to embed data into the Cover-image. The embedding and extracting procedure are given as Tables 2.1 and 2.2, respectively.

Table 2.1 The embedding procedure of Ni *et al.* 's algorithm

Input: The $M \times N$ Cover-image I, the hidden data W.
Output: The Stego-image I'', auxiliary parameters: zero point (minimum point) min, maximum point MAX, where $MAX, min \in [0, 255]$.
Step 1: Generate the histogram H of I;
Step 2: In H, find a maximum point MAX and a minimum point min, those pixel are MAX, min, respectively.
Step 3: Assume $MAX < min$. Scan I,
   If $I(i, j) \in (MAX, min)$, then $I'(i, j) = I(i, j) + 1$;
   Else $I'(i, j) = I(i, j)$.
   Where $i \in [0, M-1]$, $j \in [0, N-1]$
Step 4: Scan I'.
   If $I(i, j) = MAX$, then $I''(i, j) = I'(i, j) + w$;
   Else $I''(i, j) = I'(i, j)$.
   Where $i \in [0, M-1]$, $j \in [0, N-1]$, w represent a bit of W.

Table 2.2 The extracting procedure of Ni *et al.* 's algorithm

Input: This $M \times N$ Stego-image I'', auxiliary parameters: zero point $H(min)$, maximum point $H(MAX)$, and overhead bookkeeping information.
Output: The hidden data W, the Cover-image I.
Step 1: Scan I'' in the same sequential order as used in embedding procedure.
   If $I''(i, j) = MAX$ or $I''(i, j) = MAX + 1$, then
   $w = I''(i, j) - MAX$ and $I''(i, j) = MAX$.
   Where $i \in [0, M-1]$, $j \in [0, N-1]$, w represent a bit of W.
Step 2: Scan I'' again.
   If $I''(i, j) \in (MAX, min]$, then $I'(i, j) = I''(i, j) - 1$.
   Else $I'(i, j) = I''(i, j)$.
   Where $i \in [0, M-1]$, $j \in [0, N-1]$
Step 3: $I(i, j) = I'(i, j)$, $i \in [0, M-1]$, $j \in [0, N-1]$

The following example demonstrates the above embedding and extracting procedures.

Example 2
Embedding procedure:
Step 1: Take a 512×512 Lena image (Fig. 2.1) as the Cover-image I. The histogram H of image I is shown in Fig 2.2. Denote the secret message as $w \in \{0, 1\}$ and the Stego-image as I''.

Fig. 2. 1 The cover-image I

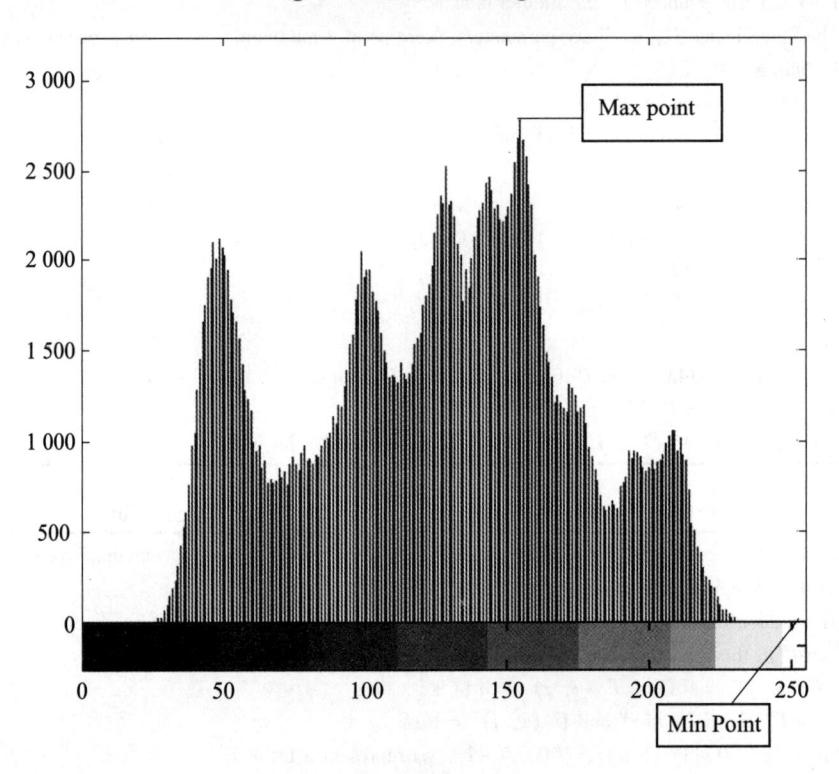

Fig. 2. 2 The histogram H of I

Step 2: Find a peak point ($MAX = 150$) and a zero point ($min = 255$) in H. We use $I(i, j)$ to represent a pixel value of I, where $i \in [0, 511]$, $j \in [0, 511]$.

Step 3: Scan I, if $I(i, j) \in (150, 255)$, then $I'(i, j) = I(i, j) + 1$.

(E. g. If $I(i, j) = 155$, then $I'(i, j) = I(i, j) + 1 = 155 + 1 = 156$.)

Else $I'(i, j) = I(i, j)$.

Step 4: Scan I'

If $I'(i, j) = 150$, then $I''(i, j) = I'(i, j) + w$;

(E. g. For $w = 0$, $I''(i, j) = I'(i, j) + w = 150 + 0 = 150$.

For $w = 1$, $I''(i, j) = I'(i, j) + w = 150 + 1 = 151$.)

Else $I''(i,j) = I'(i,j)$

Output: Stego-image I''

Extracting procedure:

Suppose that the receiver has obtained the auxiliary information: the peak point (maximum point) is 150 and zero point (minimum point) is 255, namely $MAX = 150$ and $min = 255$.

Step 1: Scan I'' to obtain hidden message w.

If $I''(i,j) = MAX$ or $I''(i,j) = MAX + 1$, then
$w = I''(i,j) - MAX$ and $I''(i,j) = MAX$
(E. g. If $I''(i,j) = 150$, then $w = I''(i,j) - MAX = 150 - 150 = 0$.
If $I''(i,j) = 151$, then $w = I''(i,j) - MAX = 151 - 150 = 1$.)

Step 2: Scan I'' to recover the cover-image.

If $I''(i,j) \in (MAX, min)$, then $I'(i,j) = I''(i,j) - 1$
Else $I'(i,j) = I''(i,j)$.
[E. g. If $I''(i,j) = 156$, then $I'(i,j) = I''(i,j) - 1 = 156 - 1 = 155$.
If $I''(i,j) = 147 \notin (150, 255)$, then $I'(i,j) = I''(i,j) = 147$.)

Output: w, I''.

It is easy to verify that $I(i,j) = I''(i,j)$, thus we can recover the Cover-image without any data loss.

Ni et al. [1-2] utilized the zero or the minimum points of the histogram of a Cover-image and slightly modified the pixel grayscale values to embed data into the Cover-image. However, Ni et al.'s scheme needs to save the maximum and minimum points as auxiliary information and transmit the auxiliary information to the receiving side for data retrieval. The handling of the auxiliary information is discussed in the next section.

3 RDH by Adjusting the Auxiliary Information

This section introduces four schemes, which are Hwang et al.'s [5], Kuo et al.'s [6], Tai et al.'s [7], and Hong et al.'s [8], aiming at removing or reducing the amount of auxiliary information to be saved and transmitted.

3.1 Hwang et al.'s and Kuo et al.'s scheme without any auxiliary information transmitted to receiving side

The method proposed by Hwang et al. [5] modifies Ni et al.'s method by combining the auxiliary information and embed message into the secret message. They utilize a peak point of image histogram and the location map and modify pixel values slightly to embed data. Tables 3.1-1 and 3.1-2 shows the embedding and extracting procedure.

Table 3.1-1 The embedding procedure of Hwang *et al.*'s algorithm

Input: The Cover-image I, the hidden data W.
Output: The Stego-image I''.
Step 1: Generate the histogram H of the Cover-image I.
Step 2: In H, find a maximum point MAX, then find a left minimum point $min(L)$ and a right minimum point $min(R)$.
Step 3: Scan I.

$$I'(i,j) = \begin{cases} I(i,j), & if\ I(i,j) = MAX \\ I(i,j) - 1, & if\ min(L) < I(i,j) < MAX \\ I(i,j) - 1, & if\ MAX < I(i,j) < min(R) \end{cases} \quad (1)$$

Step 4: Create a location map LM (Fig. 6.3.1-1 depicts structure of location map), consisting of minimum point, number of pixels of minimum point when the value of the minimum point is not "0", coordinates of X and Y where the value of the minimum point is not "0".
Step 5: Obtain $P = L \cup W = p_1 p_2 \cdots p_l$, l is bits length of P;
Step 6: Scan I'.

$$I''(i,j) = \begin{cases} I'(i,j) + 1, & if\ I'(i,j) = MAX - 2\ and\ P = 1 \\ I'(i,j) - 1, & if\ I'(i,j) = MAX + 2\ and\ P = 1 \\ I'(i,j), & otherwise \end{cases} \quad (2)$$

Table 6.3.1-2 The extracting procedure of Hwang *et al.*'s algorithm

Input: The Stego-image I''.
Output: The hidden data W, the Cover-image I.
Step 1: Generate the histogram H of the cover-image I'', and find a maximum point MAX in H.
Step 2: Scan I''.

$$P = \begin{cases} 0, & if\ I''(i,j) = MAX - 2\ or\ I''(i,j) = MAX + 2 \\ 1, & if\ I''(i,j) = MAX - 1\ or\ I''(i,j) = MAX + 1 \end{cases} \quad (3)$$

Step 3: Scan I'' again

$$I'(i,j) = \begin{cases} MAX, & if\ I''(i,j) = MAX - 1\ or\ I''(i,j) = MAX + 1 \\ MAX, & if\ I''(i,j) = MAX - 2\ or\ I''(i,j) = MAX + 2 \\ I''(i,j), & otherwise \end{cases} \quad (4)$$

Step 4: Using the structure of location map, disassemble P into location map LM and hidden data W.
Step 5: Use LM to recover the cover-image I,

$$I(i,j) = \begin{cases} I'(i,j) + 1, & if\ min(L) \leq I'(i,j) < MAX - 1 \\ I'(i,j) - 1, & if\ MAX + 1 < I'(i,j) \leq min(R) \\ I'(i,j), & otherwise \end{cases} \quad (5)$$

| Min Point | Count Of Min Point | Min Value1 (X, Y) | Min Value2 (X, Y) | ... | Watermark |

Fig. 3.1-1 Structure of Location Map *LM*

Compared with Ni *et al.*'s scheme, as the location map is portion of the secret message, there is no need to save and transmit the auxiliary information. However, this scheme will waste the storage quantity and decrease the original data hiding capacity.

To enhance the data hiding capacity and keep the quality of reversible data, Kuo *et al.* [5] construct an efficient location map by using only one bit to record the change of the selected minimum point to improve the data hiding capacity.

The embedding process and extracting process in Kuo *et al.*'s scheme are similar to the processes in Hwang *et al.*'s scheme, but the methods of setting up the location map is different. In Kuo *et al.*'s scheme, they utilize one bit to record the primitive position instead of recording the coordinates of minimum points in the original image. Hence, it will reduce the size of storage quantity effectively and then increase the fact capacity of embedded information in Kuo *et al.*'s scheme. Fig. 3.1-2 depicts structure of location map.

Min1	Min2	Reversible bit total	Reversible bit	Watermark

Fig. 3.1-2　Structure of Location Map *LM*

3.2　Tai *et al.*'s and Hong's scheme using binary tree structure

Ni *et al.* [1~2] use one pair or two pairs of peak and zero points of an equal histogram. However multiple pairs of peak and minimum points can be used for embedding. Moreover, the histogram modification technique carries with it an unsolved issue in that multiple pairs of peak and minimum points must be transmitted to the recipient via a side channel to ensure successful restoration.

Tai *et al.* [7] use an auxiliary binary tree structure for solving the issue of communication of multiple peak points, and each element of the binary tree denotes a peak point.

Assume that the number of peak points used to embed messages is 2^L, where L is the level of the binary tree. Once a pixel difference d_i, that satisfies $d_i < 2^L$ is encountered, if the message bit to be embedded is "0", the left child of the node d_i is visited; otherwise, the right child of the node d_i is visited. All the recipient needs to share with the sender is the tree level L, because they propose an auxiliary binary tree that predetermines multiple peak points which are used to embed messages. Tables 3.2-1, and 3.2-2 respectively shows the embedding and extracting procedure and Fig. 3.2-1 (see Fig. 2 in [7]) is an auxiliary binary tree of Tai *et al.*'s scheme.

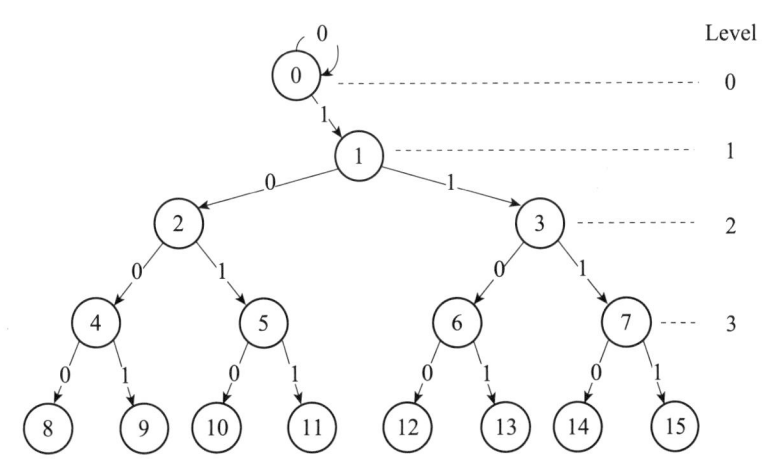

Fig. 3.2-1　Auxiliary binary tree of Tai *et al.*'s scheme

Table 3.2-1 The embedding procedure of Tai et al. 's algorithm

Input: The Cover-image I the hidden data W.
Output: The Stego-image I', maximum point MAX.
Step 1: Generate the histogram H of I.
Step 2: Determine the level L of the binary tree.
Step 3: Shift H from both sides by 2^L units. The histogram shifting information is recorded as overhead bookkeeping information that will be embedded into the cover-image with payload.
Step 4: Scan H in an inverse s-order. Calculate the pixel difference d_i between pixel x_{i-1} and x_i

$$d_i = \begin{cases} x_i, & if\ i=0 \\ |\ x_i - x_{i-1}\ |, & otherwise \end{cases} \qquad (6)$$

Step 5: Scan the whole Cover-image in same inverse s-order. If $d_i \geq 2^L$, shift x_i by 2^L units, and the Stego-image pixel value y_i is

$$y_i = \begin{cases} x_i, & if\ i=0 \\ x_i + 2^L, & if\ d_i \geq 2^L\ and\ x_i \geq x_{i-1} \\ x_i - 2^L, & if\ d_i \geq 2^L\ and\ x_i < x_{i-1} \end{cases} \qquad (7)$$

Step 6: If $d_i < 2^L$, modify x_i according to the message bit

$$y_i = \begin{cases} x_i + (d_i + w), & if\ x_i \geq x_{i-1} \\ x_i - (d_i + w), & if\ x_i < x_{i-1} \end{cases} \qquad (8)$$

Where w is a message bit of the hidden data W and $w \in \{0, 1\}$

Table 3.2-2 The extracting procedure of Tai et al. 's algorithm

Input: The Stego-image I', auxiliary parameters: maximum point MAX.
Output: The hidden data W, the Cover-image I.
Step 1: Scan I' in an inverse s-order.
Step 2: If $|\ y_i - x_{i-1}\ | < 2^{L+1}$, extract message bit

$$w = \begin{cases} 0, & if\ |\ y_i - x_{i-1}\ |\ is\ even \\ 1, & if\ |\ y_i - x_{i-1}\ |\ is\ odd \end{cases} \qquad (9)$$

Where x_{i-1} denotes the restored value of y_{i-1}.

Step 3: Restore the original value of host pixel x_i by

$$x_i = \begin{cases} y_i + \left[\dfrac{y_i - x_{i-1}}{2}\right], & if\ |\ y_i - x_{i-1}\ | < 2^{L+1}\ and\ y_i < x_{i-1} \\ y_i - \left[\dfrac{y_i - x_{i-1}}{2}\right], & if\ |\ y_i - x_{i-1}\ | < 2^{L+1}\ and\ y_i > x_{i-1} \\ y_i + 2^L, & if\ |\ y_i - x_{i-1}\ | \geq 2^{L+1}\ and\ y_i < x_{i-1} \\ y_i - 2^L, & if\ |\ y_i - x_{i-1}\ | \geq 2^{L+1}\ and\ y_i > x_{i-1} \\ y_i, & otherwise \end{cases} \qquad (10)$$

Step 4: Repeat Step 2 until the embedded message is completely extracted.
Step 5: Extract the overhead information from the extracted message. If a value "1" is assigned in the location i, restore x_i to its original state by shifting it by 2^L units; otherwise, no shifting is required.

Tai et al. use a binary tree structure to solve the problem of communicating pairs of peak points, so their method does not need to record the peak point of each embedding level. However, their method unnecessarily shifts some differences that are likely embeddable at low embedding level, and provides no selective mechanism to exclude those likely un-embeddable differences from being shifted. Therefore, some unnecessary image degradation might exist in the method by Tai *et al.* [7].

Inspired by Tai *et al.*'s work, Hong's scheme [8] introduces a dual binary tree for data embedding to significantly increase the payload of Tai *et al.*'s method at low embedding level. The contribution of the Hong's method is that the embedding efficiency is greatly enhanced. The algorithm of Hong *et al.*'s scheme is similar to the algorithm of Tai *et al.*'s scheme. Dual binary tree of Hong's scheme is shown in Fig. 3.2-2 (see Fig. 3 in [8]).

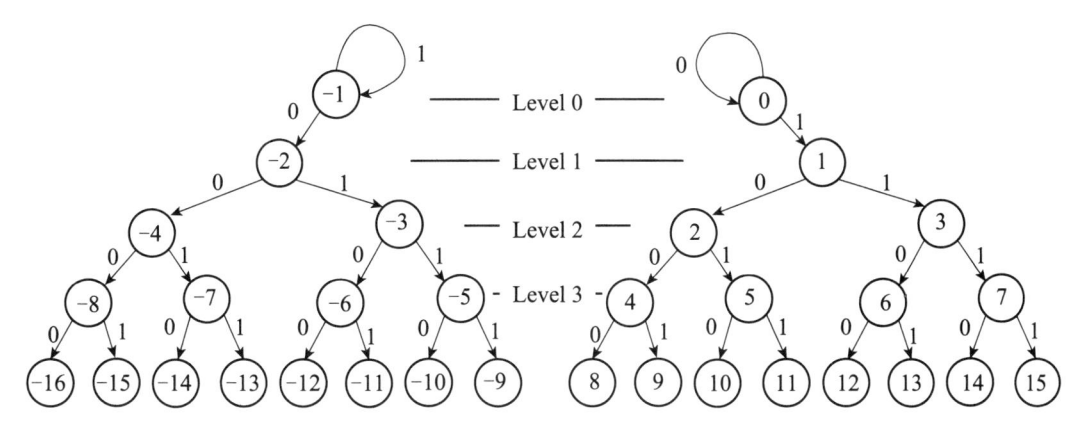

Fig. 3.2-2 Dual binary tree of Hong's scheme

4 High-capacity RDH Based on Histogram Modification

Most of the RDH methods in the previous sections have a low capacity of hidden data. For this reason, a lot of methods focusing on improving the capacity emerged [9~19]. Four of such methods are considered typical and will be discussed below.

Tsai *et al.* [9] [Tsai 2009] proposed a scheme which explores the similarity of neighboring pixels in the images by using the prediction technique and uses the residual histogram of the predicted errors of the host image to hide secret data, and the capacity of this method is approximately as three times as that of the original histogram-based method. Hong *et al.* [10] analyzed and further improved on Tsai *el al.*'s method. In Hong *et al.*'s method a better prediction and a sharper prediction error histogram are used to embed data, and a higher capacity can be achieved. Zeng *et al.* [12] proposed a method based on pixel difference shifting to spare space for data hiding and multi-layer embedding. The capacity of Zeng *et al.*'s method is 1.08 bits per pixel. Zhao *et al.*'s method [13] used a histogram based on difference statistics and employed a multilevel histogram modification mechanism to increase the capacity. Among all these methods, histogram of image block and multi-level embedding are used to improve capacity.

4.1 RDH using predictive coding and histogram shifting (Tsai)

In Ref. [9], Tsai *et al.* proposed a method based on predictive coding to increase the capacity. They calculated the similarity of neighboring pixels in the images using the prediction technique, and used the residual histogram of the predicted errors of the host image to hide secret data. In their method, the overlapping between peak and zero pairs was used to increase the hiding capacity further. A higher capacity was obtained and a good quality Stego-image was preserved in the proposed scheme. In Tsai et al.'s method, they employed a simple predictor to transform pixels in the spatial domain to error values in the prediction domain. After constructing the error histogram, the histogram-shifting technique is then employed to conceal data.

The detailed embedding, extraction and restoration procedures of their method are described as follows.

Embedding procedure:

To embed data, the Cover-image I of size $M \times M$ is partitioned into N blocks $\{B_i\}_{i=1}^{N}$. Each block is composed of $m \times m$ pixels, and in the description of the theme we choose $m = 3$ as this setting will achieve the best results. Let c_i be the center pixel of block B_i, and $\{b_{i,j}\}_{j=1}^{8}$ be the pixels in B_i excluding c_i. The center pixel c_i is termed of the basic pixel of B_i, and $\{b_{i,j}\}_{j=1}^{8}$ are termed the non-basic pixels of block B_i. Then the embedding procedure is shown as follows.

Table 4.1-1 The embedding procedure (Tsai)

Input: A Cover-image I and information to be embedded.
Output: A Stego-image I' and extra information of peaks.
Step 1: Obtain the prediction errors $\{e_{i,j}\}_{j=1}^{8}$ by subtracting the corresponding values of $\{b_{i,j}\}_{j=1}^{8}$ from c_i, $1 \leq i \leq N$. A prediction error histogram E is then constructed.
Step 2: Let $E_p = \{E \mid e_{i,j} \geq 0\}$ and $E_n = \{E \mid e_{i,j} \leq 0\}$, for $1 \leq i \leq N$ and $1 \leq j \leq 8$. Two peak points P_p and P_n can be calculated from the histograms E_p and E_n, respectively. Similarly, two zero points Z_p and Z_n are also calculated.
Step 3: For each block B_i, the histogram-shifting technique with two pairs of peak and zero points (P_p, Z_p) and (P_n, Z_n) is employed. During the embedding, the prediction errors are modified. The modified prediction errors are denoted by $\{e'_{i,j}\}_{j=1}^{8}$, $1 \leq i \leq N$.
Step 4: The Stego-image block B'_i is then constructed by adding up $\{e'_{i,j}\}_{j=1}^{8}$ and c_i, $1 \leq i \leq N$. The Stego-image can be obtained by grouping these stego blocks, and the peaks (P_p, Z_p) and (P_n, Z_n) are recoded and served as a key for decoding.

Extraction and image recovery procedures:

The data extraction and image recovery procedures are similar to that of data embedding procedure. The Stego-image I' is preprocessed as in the embedding phase: I' of size $M \times M$ is partitioned into N blocks $\{B'_i\}_{i=1}^{N}$ with 3×3. Let c'_i be the basic pixel of block B'_i, $1 \leq i \leq N$. Since the basic pixel c_i is not modified during the embedding phase, c_i is equal to c'_i. The detailed data extraction and the original image recovery procedure are shown as Table 4.1-2.

Table 4.1-2 The extracting procedure (Tsai)

Input: A Stego-image I' and extra information of peaks.
Output: An original image I and extracted information.
Step 1: Obtain the prediction errors $\{e'_{i,j}\}_{j=1}^{8}$ by subtracting the corresponding values of $\{b'_{i,j}\}_{j=1}^{8}$ from c'_i, $1 \leq i \leq N$. The modified prediction error histogram E' is then constructed.
Step 2: Let $E'_p = \{e'_{i,j} \geq 0\}$ and $E'_n = \{e'_{i,j} \leq 0\}$, for $1 \leq i \leq N$ and $1 \leq j \leq 8$.
Step 3: The embedded data can be extracted by applying the histogram-shifting technique using the parameters (P_p, Z_p) and (P_n, Z_n) recorded in the embedding phase. In this stem the original prediction errors $\{e_{i,j}\}_{j=1}^{8}$, $1 \leq i \leq N$, are then recovered.
Step 4: The original image block B_i can be reconstructed by adding up $\{e_{i,j}\}_{j=1}^{8}$ and c_i. The original image I can then be recovered by grouping the blocks B_i, $1 \leq i \leq N$.

The hiding capacity of Tsai *et al.*'s method is approximately as three times as that of the original histogram-based method. Compared to the histogram-based method, the quality of the Stego-image improved about 1.5dB when the same amounts of secret data were embedded. In Tsai *et al.*'s method, the nearest prediction technique is employed for which pixel values are predicted by the nearest basic pixel. For the histogram based reversible data hiding technique, the peak height of the prediction error histogram determines the capacity. Although the capacity of Tsai *et al.*'s method is higher than that of Ni *et al.*'s method, some useful information provided by the adjacent basic pixels of the current basic pixel are not fully explored. Since the values of basic pixels in the Cover-image are preserved after data embedding, the adjacent basic pixels of the current basic pixels should provide rich clues to have the prediction more accurate.

Besides, Tsai *et al.*'s method doesn't take the block variance into account, that is all the blocks have equally probability to join the embedding process. However, high-variance blocks should be embedded less information due to the inaccurate prediction. Hong *et al.* [10] analyzed the problem and showed that embedding data into low-variance blocks often results in a higher capacity and smooth blocks possess more embeddable bits than those complex blocks.

4.2 A local variance-controlled RDH using predictive coding and histogram shifting (Hong)

Hong *et al.* [10] proposed a new method. They exploited the information provided by a set of five basic pixels to give a more precise prediction of the values of non-basic pixels. With a better prediction and a sharper prediction error histogram, a higher capacity can be achieved. The proposed method also provides a local variance-controlled mechanism in which high-variance blocks will not join the embedding process to prevent quality loss. A detailed description of Hong et al.'s method is presented below.

The prediction rule:

In the proposed method, the Cover-image I of size $M \times M$ is partitioned into N blocks $\{B_i\}_{i=1}^{N}$ of $m \times m$ pixels where N is the total number of blocks. Normally, we set $m = 3$ for the best results. For each block B_i, the center pixel c_i is selected as the basic pixel, and other pixels are the non-basic pixels. For a non-border block B_i with basic pixel c_i, there are four other basic pixels c_i^L, c_i^R, c_i^T and c_i^B directly located on the left, right, top and bottom of c_i, respectively. These four basic pixels are termed satellite basic pixels of c_i. Fig. 4.2 (see Fig. 3 in [10]) shows an image block B_i with the basic pixel c_i and non-basic pixels $b_{i,1}$, $b_{i,2}$, $b_{i,3}$, $b_{i,4}$, $b_{i,5}$, $b_{i,6}$, $b_{i,7}$ and $b_{i,8}$. Pixels c_i^L, c_i^R, c_i^T and c_i^B are the corresponding satellite basic pixels.

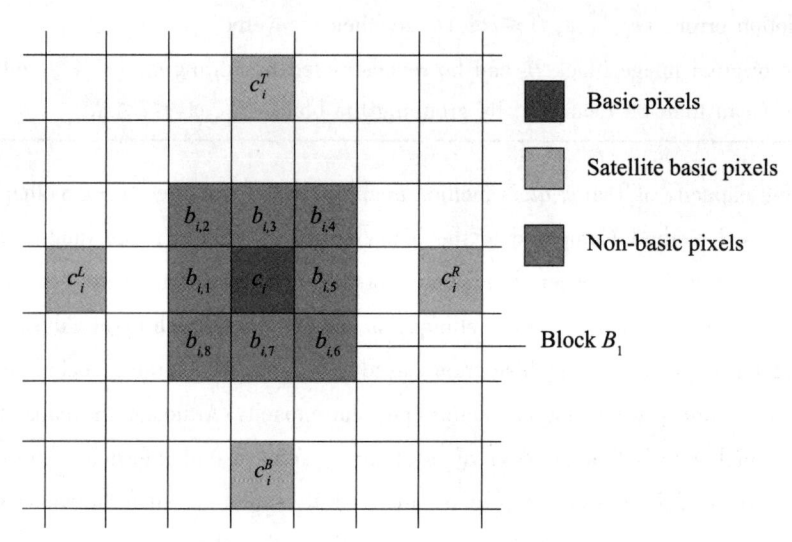

Fig. 4.2 Example of basic pixels, non-basic pixels and satellite basic pixels

The values of the eight non-basic pixels associated with each basic pixel are the values that should be predicted. Instead of predicting these values by the nearest basic points as in Tsai *et al.*'s method, Hong *et al.* predicted them by referencing the values of satellite basic pixels of the current basic pixel. The prediction values $p_{i,1}$, $p_{i,2}$ and $p_{i,3}$ of non-basic pixel $b_{i,1}$, $b_{i,2}$ and $b_{i,3}$ can be calculated as follows, respectively:

$$\begin{cases} p_{i,1} = round\left(\frac{1}{3}(2c_i + c_i^L)\right) \\ p_{i,2} = round\left(\frac{1}{3}(c_i + c_i^L + c_i^T)\right) \\ p_{i,3} = round\left(\frac{1}{3}(2c_i + c_i^T)\right) \end{cases} \quad (11)$$

where $round(x)$ is a function that rounds x to the nearest integer. And the other five prediction value can also be predicted like this. For blocks located in the border of the Cover-image, the prediction rules for each non-basic pixel can be modified according to the location of the border blocks and can also be left along without embedding any data.

Local variance-controlled mechanism:

For those basic pixels located in a complex region, the prediction of the corresponding non-basic pixels is less accurate; therefore, modifying the prediction errors of these non-basic pixels contributes fewer payloads than those pixels located in a smooth area while preserving the same distortion. Hong et al. choose the smooth region to embed data, and calculate the variance of the current basic pixel and the corresponding satellite basic pixels to determine whether a basic pixel locates in a smooth region or a complex region by:

$$\text{var}(c_i) = \frac{1}{5}((c_i - c_m)^2 + (c_i^L + c_m)^2 + (c_i^R - c_m)^2 + (c_i^T - c_m)^2 + (c_i^B - c_m)^2). \tag{12}$$

where c_m is the average value of c_i, c_i^L, c_i^R, c_i^T and c_i^B. If $\text{var}(c_i) > TH$, where TH is a predefined threshold, then the basic pixel c_i is classified as within a complex region; otherwise, within a smooth region is classified.

Embedment of assistant information:

The assistant information which includes the compressed location map and other side information must be known before extracting the embedded data. So Hong et al. divide the Cover-image I into two parts which are I_L and I_M. I_L is used for embedding the assistant information and I_M is used for embedding the data bits and LBSs of I_L. The detail data embedding and extracting procedures are shown as the following Table 4.2-1, and 4.2-2.

Table 4.2-1 The embedding procedure (Hong)

Input: A Cover-image I of size $M \times M$ and encrypted data bits S.
Output: A Stego-image I'.
Step 1: Record pixels valued 0 and 255 in the Cover-image I in a location map, and compress the location map to result L. Concatenate the encrypted data bits S and the auxiliary information to form a new bit string S_C.
Step 2: Divide the Cover-image into two sub-images I_L and I_M. The number of pixels in I_L must be larger than or equal to $|S_C|$.
Step 3: Set $TH = 0$ and partition the sub-image into blocks $\{B_i\}_{i=1}^N$ of size 3×3 and determine the basic pixel, non-basic pixel and satellite pixels of each block.
Step 4: Classify blocks $\{B_i\}_{i=1}^N$ into smooth blocks SB and complex blocks CB using the method as mentioned above.
Step 5: For each block B_i in SB, predict the non-basic pixels in B_i and calculate the prediction errors by

$$e_{i,j} = b_{i,j} - p_{i,j}. \tag{13}$$

where $b_{i,j}$ represents the non-basic pixels in B_i and $p_{i,j}$ represents the corresponding prediction value of $b_{i,j}$, $1 \leq j \leq 8$.
Step 6: Construct the histogram E of prediction errors. Obtain the two pairs (P_+, Z_+) and (P_-, Z_-) of peaks and zeros of histogram.
Step 7: If the summation of the number of the prediction errors valued P_+ and P_- is smaller than $|S_C|$, repeat Steps 4~6 and use the binary searching technique to find a minimum threshold TH such that the summation is larger than or equal to $|S_C|$.
Step 8: For $1 \leq i \leq 8$, $1 \leq j \leq 8$, the prediction errors $e_{i,j}$s are sequentially scanned and a bit s of S_C is embedded by modifying the scanned prediction error $e_{i,j}$ according to the following rules:
(a) If the scanned prediction error $e_{i,j} = P_+$ or $e_{i,j} = P_-$, a bit s can be embedded by modifying $e_{i,j}$ to $e'_{i,j}$ using the rule:

$$e'_{i,j} = \begin{cases} e_{i,j}, & if\ s = 0 \\ e_{i,j} + 1, & if\ s = 1\ and\ e_{i,j} = P_+ \\ e_{i,j} - 1, & if\ s = 1\ and\ e_{i,j} = P_- \end{cases} \quad (14)$$

(b) Otherwise, no bit can be embedded and the scanned prediction error $e_{i,j}$ should be modified to $e'_{i,j}$ using the rule:

$$e'_{i,j} = \begin{cases} e_{i,j} + 1, & if\ P_+ < e_{i,j} < Z_+ \\ e_{i,j} - 1, & if\ Z_- < e_{i,j} < P_- \\ e_{i,j} & otherwise \end{cases} \quad (15)$$

Step 9: Repeat Step 8 until bits in S_C are all embedded.

Step 10: Construct the stego block B'_i by adding up $e'_{i,j}$ and $p_{i,j}$ and get sub-image I'_M.

Step 11: Convert the auxiliary information including location map and its size, two pairs of peaks and zeros, a threshold and the length of the data bits into binary form A_{info}. And embed it into the sub-image I_L using the LSB replacement method.

Table 4.2-2 The data extraction and original image recovery procedure (Hong)

Input: The Stego-image I' of size $M \times M$.
Output: The encrypted data bits S and the recovered original image I.
Step 1: Divide the Stego-image I' into two sub-images I'_L and I'_M. Extract the first $|A_{info}|$ LSBs of I'_L and the embedded assistant information.
Step 2: Partition the stego sub-image I'_M into blocks in the same way as in the embedding procedure.
Step 3: Classify blocks $\{B_i\}_{i=1}^N$ into smooth blocks SB and complex blocks CB using the method as mentioned above.
Step 4: For each block B'_i in SB, predict the non-basic pixels in B'_i and calculate the prediction errors by

$$e'_{i,j} = b'_{i,j} - p'_{i,j}. \quad (16)$$

where $b'_{i,j}$ represents the non-basic pixels in B'_i and $p'_{i,j}$ represents the corresponding prediction value of $b'_{i,j}$, $1 \leq j \leq 8$.

Step 5: Scan the predication errors $e'_{i,j}$ s sequentially using the same order as in the embedding phase. If the scanned position is in L, then skip $e'_{i,j}$ and proceed to the next one. Otherwise, a bit s can be extracted according to the following rules:

$$s = \begin{cases} 0 & if\ e'_{i,j} = P_+\ or\ e'_{i,j} = P_- \\ 1 & if\ e'_{i,j} = P_+ + 1\ or\ e'_{i,j} = P_- - 1 \end{cases} \quad (17)$$

The original prediction error $e_{i,j}$ can be recovered using the rules:

$$e_{i,j} = \begin{cases} e'_{i,j} - 1 & if\ P_+ < e'_{i,j} \leq Z_+ \\ e'_{i,j} + & if\ Z_- < e'_{i,j} \leq P_- \\ e'_{i,j} & otherwise \end{cases} \quad (18)$$

Step 6: Repeat Step 4 until all the embedded bits have been extracted.
Step 7: Construct the original image block B_i by adding up $e_{i,j}$ and $p'_{i,j}$.

Hong et al.'s method has better performance than other state-of-art reversible data hiding methods in terms of Stego-image quality.

4.3 RDH using predictive coding and histogram shifting (Zeng)

In Ref. [12], Zeng et al. proposed another method using pixel difference shifting for data hiding. The pixel differences are generated between a reference pixel and its neighbors in a pre-assigned block. Then the difference histogram is shifted and a large number of data can be embedded into the cover-image. They also used multi-layer embedding to improve the hiding capacity. Their method has a big difference from other histogram shifting based methods, which can extract the hidden data and recover the exact original Cover-image with no extra information except the length of the hidden data and the Stego-image itself. The capacity of Zeng et al.'s method is 1.08 bits per pixel. The detailed description of the method is shown as follows.

In Zeng et al.'s method they calculate the pixel differences first. For each block with a series of pixel values p_1, p_2, p_3, $\cdots p_k$, sort them in ascending order and choose the middle pixel as the reference pixel p_r. Then compute the $k-1$ differences between p_r and the other $k-1$ pixels and get the differences d_1, d_2, d_3, $\cdots d_{r-1}$, d_{r+1}, $\cdots d_k$. With these pixel differences, the pixel difference histogram can be got. Zeng et al. introduced a threshold δ which is a nonnegative integer and used the pixel differences whose absolute values are equal to δ to embed data. The difference histogram shifting rule is below.

If the pixel differences with value 0 (i.e., $\delta = 0$) will be used to embed data, then

$$d_i = \begin{cases} d_i + 1 & if\ d_i > 0 \\ d_i & if\ d_i \leq 0 \end{cases} \quad (19)$$

where $1 \leq i \leq k$ and $i \neq r$. (i.e, $\delta \neq 0$) will be used to embed data.

$$d_i = \begin{cases} d_i + 1 & if\ d_i > \delta \\ d_i - 1 & if\ d_i < -\delta \\ d_i & if\ |d_i| \leq \delta \end{cases} \quad (20)$$

where $1 \leq i \leq k$ and $i \neq r$.

The difference histogram shifting can be reserved according to the following rule.

If $\delta = 0$ then

$$d_i = \begin{cases} d_i - 1 & if\ d_i > 1 \\ d_i & if\ d_i \leq 1 \end{cases} \quad (21)$$

If $\delta \neq 0$ then

$$d_i = \begin{cases} d_i - 1 & if\ d_i > (\delta + 1) \\ d_i + 1 & if\ d_i < -(\delta + 1) \\ d_i & if\ |d_i| \leq (\delta + 1) \end{cases} \quad (22)$$

With these the embedding procedure is given by Zeng et al. as follows.

Table 4.3-1 The embedding procedure (Zeng)

Input: Cover-image, secret data bit stream, threshold δ used to embed data and block size.
Output: Stego-image.
Step 1: Find the reference pixel and compute the pixel difference.
Step 2: Shift the pixel difference histogram and get the redundant space using the above rules.

(续表)

Step 3: Embed data into each block using the following equation:

$$d_i = \begin{cases} d_i + 1 & \text{if } d_i = \delta \text{ and } b = 1 \\ d_i - 1 & \text{if } \delta \neq 0 \text{ and } d_i = -\delta \text{ and } b = 1 \\ d_i & \text{otherwise} \end{cases} \quad (23)$$

where $1 \leq i \leq k$, $i \neq r$ and b is the to-be-embedded bit.

Step 4: Produce the stego-block by

$$p_i^s = \begin{cases} p_r - d_i & \text{if } i \neq r \\ p_r & \text{otherwise} \end{cases} \quad (24)$$

where $1 \leq i \leq k$.

The data extraction is a reverse process, and the detail is shown as follows:

Table 4.3-2 The data extraction and original image recovery procedure (Zeng)

Input: Stego-image, the threshold δ, the length of the secret data and block size.
Output: Secret data and the restored cover-image.
Step 1: Generate the pixel differences in the same way as in the embedding procedure.
Step 2: Scan the pixel differences in the same order as used in the embedding phase. If a pixel difference with value δ (or $-\delta$) is encountered, a it "0" is extracted, and if a pixel difference with $\delta + 1$ (or $-(\delta+1)$ when $\delta \neq 0$) is encountered, a bit "1" is extracted.
Step 3: Restore the original pixel differences by

$$d_i = \begin{cases} d_i - 1 & \text{if } d_i = (\delta + 1) \\ d_i + 1 & \text{if } \delta \neq 0 \text{ and } d_i = -(\delta + 1) \\ d_i & \text{otherwise} \end{cases} \quad (25)$$

where $1 \leq i \leq k$, $i \neq r$.
Step 4: Apply the reverse difference histogram shifting.

To increase the embedding capacity Zeng et al. also used a multi-layer embedding. The original pixel values are modified at most by 1 during data embedding, so the reversible embedding process can be applied to the Cover-image once again as long as there is no pixel with value less than 1 or larger than 254 after the data embedding procedure. Zeng et al. chose a 13-layer embedding to enhance the embedding capacity and keep low distortion, and they found 12-layer embedding can be another good choice. The dynamic reference pixel and multi-layer embedding method proposed by Zeng et al. can offer very high embedding capacity and low image degradation, and the method can restore the exact original Cover-image after data extraction with no extra information except message length and the Stego-image itself.

4.4 RDH based on multilevel histogram modification and sequential recovery (Zhao)

Zhao et al. [13] proposed a RDH method based on difference statistics and multilevel histogram. In Zhao's method, they used the histogram of neighbor pixel differences instead of Cover-image histogram to hide data. A multilevel histogram modification mechanism is used to further increase the capacity of hidden data, as there are more peak points. The embedding algorithm and extracting algorithm are given as follows.

In this scheme, an integer parameter called embedding level EL is involved to control the hiding capacity. A larger EL indicates more secret data can be embedded. As the embedding operations for $EL > 0$ are more complicated than those of $EL = 0$, we describe them for $EL = 0$ and $EL > 0$ separately. The Embedding and extracting algorithms are listed as below (see Table 4.4-1, 4.4-2).

Table 4.4-1 The data embedding procedure of Zhao et al. 's algorithm

Input: The Cover-image I and the secret message W.
Output: The Stego-image I'.
Step 1: Inverse "S" scan I into a pixel sequence P_1, P_2, P_3, $\cdots$, $P_{M \times N}$.
Step 2: Compute the differences d_i ($1 \leq i \leq M \times N$) as follows

$$d_i = \begin{cases} p_1 & i = 1 \\ p_{i-1} - p_i & 2 \leq i \leq M \times N \end{cases} \tag{26}$$

Step 3: Select an EL
(a) If $EL = 0$, execute Step 4.
(b) If $EL > 0$, go to Step 5.
Step 4: Data embedding for $EL = 0$.
(a) Shift the right bins of $b(0)$ rightward one level as:

$$d'_i = \begin{cases} p_1 & if\ i = 1 \\ d'_i & if\ d_i \leq 0,\ 2 \leq i \leq M \times N \\ d_i + 1 & if\ d_i > 0,\ 2 \leq i \leq M \times N \end{cases} \tag{27}$$

(b) Examine $d'_i = 0$ ($2 \leq i \leq M \times N$) one by one. Each difference equaling 0 can be used to hide one secret bit. The operation is as:

$$d'_i = \begin{cases} p_1 & if\ i = 1 \\ d'_i + w & if\ d'_i = 0,\ 2 \leq i \leq M \times N \\ d'_i + 1 & if\ d'_i \neq 0,\ 2 \leq i \leq M \times N \end{cases} \tag{28}$$

After that, go to Step 6.
Step 5: Data embedding for $EL > 0$
(a) Shift the right bins of $b(EL)$ rightward $EL + 1$ levels, and shift the left bins of $b(-EL)$ leftward EL levels as:

$$d'_i = \begin{cases} p_1 & if\ i = 1 \\ d_i & if\ |d_i| \leq EL,\ 2 \leq i \leq M \times N \\ d_i + EL + 1 & if\ d_i > EL,\ 2 \leq i \leq M \times N \\ d_i - EL & if\ d_i < -EL,\ 2 \leq i \leq M \times N \end{cases} \tag{29}$$

(b) Examine $d'_i = 0$ ($2 \leq i \leq M \times N$) in the range of $[-EL, EL]$ one by one. The multilevel data embedding strategy is described as follows.
(i) Embed the secret data as:

$$d''_i = \begin{cases} p_1 & if\ i = 1 \\ d'_i & if\ |d'_i| \leq EL,\ 2 \leq i \leq M \times N \\ 2 \times EL + w & if\ d'_i = EL,\ 2 \leq i \leq M \times N \\ -2 \times EL - w + 1 & if\ d'_i = -EL,\ 2 \leq i \leq M \times N \end{cases} \tag{30}$$

(ii) EL is decreased by 1.

(iii) If $EL \neq 0$, execute (i) and (ii) repeatedly. If $EL = 0$, execute as follows and then go to Step 6:

$$d''_i = \begin{cases} p_1 & if\ i = 1 \\ d'_i + w & if\ d'_i = 0,\ 2 \leqslant i \leqslant M \times N \\ d'_i & if\ d'_i \neq 0,\ 2 \leqslant i \leqslant M \times N \\ d'_i & if\ d'_i \neq 0,\ 2 \leqslant i \leqslant M \times N \end{cases} \quad (31)$$

Step 6: Generate the marked pixels sequence p'_i as:

$$p'_i = \begin{cases} p_1 & i = 1 \\ p_{i-1} - d''_i & 2 \leqslant i \leqslant M \times N \end{cases} \quad (32)$$

Step 7: Rearrange p' and the marked image I' is obtained.

Table 4.4-2　The data extracting procedure of Zhao et al.'s algorithm

Input: The Stego-image I', the embedding levels (EL).
Output: the Cover-image I, the secret message W.
Step 1: Inverse "S" scan I' into a pixel sequence $p'_i (1 \leqslant i \leqslant M \times N)$.
Step 2: Receive the EL parameter from the encoder via a secure channel. If $EL = 0$, then execute Step 3 and Step 4. If $EL > 0$, execute Step 5 and Step 6.
Step 3: For $EL = 0$, the Cover-image pixels are recovered as:

$$p_i = \begin{cases} p'_1 & if\ i = 1 \\ p'_i & if\ p_{i-1} - p'_i \leqslant 0,\ 2 \leqslant i \leqslant M \times N \\ p'_i + 1 & if\ p_{i-1} - p'_i \geqslant 1,\ 2 \leqslant i \leqslant M \times N \end{cases} \quad (33)$$

Step 4: For $EL = 0$, the secret message is extracted as:

$$w = \begin{cases} 0, & if\ p_{i-1} - p'_i = 0,\ 2 \leqslant i \leqslant M \times N \\ 1, & if\ p_{i-1} - p'_i = 1,\ 2 \leqslant i \leqslant M \times N \end{cases} \quad (34)$$

Rearrange these extracted bits and the original secret sequence is obtained. After that, go to Step 7.
Step 5: For $EL > 0$, obtain the first host pixel as $p_1 = p'_1$. The marked differences are computed as:

$$d''_i = \begin{cases} p'_1, & i = 1 \\ p_{i-1} - p'_i, & 2 \leqslant i \leqslant M \times N \end{cases} \quad (35)$$

Then the original differences are obtained as:

$$d_i = \begin{cases} d''_i - EL - 1, & if\ d''_i > 2 \times EL + 1,\ 2 \leqslant i \leqslant M \times N \\ d''_i + EL & if\ d''_i < -2 \times EL,\ 2 \leqslant i \leqslant M \times N \\ r & if\ d''_i \in (2r, 2r+1),\ r = 0, 1, \cdots EL,\ 2 \leqslant i \leqslant M \times N \\ -r & if\ d''_i \in (-2r, -2r+1),\ r = 0, 1, \cdots EL,\ 2 \leqslant i \leqslant M \times N \end{cases} \quad (36)$$

Next the host pixel sequence is recovered as:

$$p_i = \begin{cases} p'_1 & i = 1 \\ p'_{i-1} - d_i & 2 \leqslant i \leqslant M \times N \end{cases} \quad (37)$$

A sequential recovery strategy is utilized.
Step 6: For $EL > 0$, the secret data extraction is associated with $EL + 1$ rounds. First set the round index $R = 1$.
(a) Extract the data as:

$$w_R = \begin{cases} 0 & if\ d''_i = 2 \times EL,\ 2 \leqslant i \leqslant M \times N \\ 0 & if\ d''_i = -2 \times EL + 1,\ 2 \leqslant i \leqslant M \times N \\ 1 & if\ d''_i = 2 \times EL + 1,\ 2 \leqslant i \leqslant M \times N \\ 1 & if\ d''_i = -2 \times EL,\ 2 \leqslant i \leqslant M \times N \end{cases} \quad (38)$$

（续表）

(b) EL is decreased by 1 and R is increased by 1.
(c) If $EL \neq 0$, execute (a) and (b) repeatedly. If $EL = 0$,

$$w_R = \begin{cases} 0, & d''_i = 0, \ 2 \leq i \leq M \times N \\ 1, & d''_i = 0, \ 2 \leq i \leq M \times N \end{cases} \quad (39)$$

In equation above, R is increased as $EL + 1$.
(d) Rearrange and concatenate the extracted data w_R $(1 \leq R \leq EL + 1)$ as:

$$w = cat(w_1, w_2, \cdots, w_{EL+1}). \quad (40)$$

Hence, the hidden secret bits are obtained, and then go to Step 7.
Step 7: Rearrange the recovered sequence p_i $(1 \leq i \leq M \times N)$ into I.

As Zhao et al.'s method employed the multi-level histogram modification for embedding data, their method can achieve higher capacity than one or two level histogram modification based methods. As the secret data is embedded in the differences of adjacent pixels values, the quality of the stego-image is improved compared with that in previous multi-level histogram modification based work.

From the methods that we introduced above, we can see that traditional methods based on one or two level histogram modification cannot offer a high capacity. But the methods which divide the Cover-image into blocks and use the prediction error or pixel differences histogram to embed data can obtain a higher embedding capacity. Multi-level or multi-layer embedding can increase the embedding capacity greatly.

5 Histogram-based RDH With Minor Distortion

In most data hiding techniques, the cover-image is inevitably distorted due to data embedding itself. Typically, this distortion cannot be removed completely due to quantization, bit replacement, or truncation at the gray level 0 and 255. Although the distortion is often quite small, it may be unacceptable for medical or legal imagery or images with a high strategic importance in certain military applications [20]. Thus, it is desired to reverse the watermarked image back to the Cover-image after the embedded data are extracted. Data embedding satisfying this requirement is referred to as lossless data hiding. In this section, we will introduce three schemes to reduce the distortion by Lee et al. [21], Jung et al. [23] and Chung et al. [24] in sections 5.1, 5.2, and 5.3, respectively.

5.1 Lee et al.'s scheme

Lee et al. [21] utilize characteristics of the difference image and modify pixel values slightly to embed the data. It is unnecessary to transmit any additional information to the receiving side for data retrieval.

Assume that the size of Cover-image I is $M \times N$, and the secret message is a binary sequence. The embedding procedure of Lee's scheme is shown as Table 5.1-1.

Table 5.1-1 The embedding procedure (Lee)

Input: The Cover-image I, the secret message W.
Output: The Stego-image I'.
Step 1: Form the difference image D:

$$D(i,j) = I(i, 2j+1) - I(i, 2j), \quad 0 \leq i \leq M-1, \quad 0 \leq j \leq \frac{N}{2}-1. \tag{41}$$

Step 2: Obtain the modified difference image $\tilde{D}$:

$$\tilde{D}(i,j) = \begin{cases} D(i,j) + 1 & \text{if } D(i,j) \geq 2 \\ D(i,j) - 1 & \text{if } D(i,j) \leq -2 \\ D(i,j) & \text{otherwise.} \end{cases} \tag{42}$$

Step 3: Form the $\tilde{I}(i, 2j+1)$ as:

$$\tilde{I}(i, 2j+1) = \tilde{D}(i,j) - I(i, 2j). \tag{43}$$

Step 4: Obtain I':

$$I'(i, 2j+1) = \begin{cases} \tilde{I}(i, 2j+1) + 1 & \text{if } \tilde{D}(i,j) = 1 \text{ and } w = 1 \\ \tilde{I}(i, 2j+1) - 1 & \text{if } \tilde{D}(i,j) = -1 \text{ and } w = 1 \\ \tilde{I}(i, 2j+1) & \text{otherwise.} \end{cases} \tag{44}$$

$$I'(i, 2j) = I(i, 2j). \tag{45}$$

In this process, we extract the secret message and recover the Stego-image by calculating the difference image from the Stego-image, which is shown in Table 5.1-2.

Table 5.1-2 The secret image extraction procedure and cover-image recovery

Input: The Stego-image I'.
Output: The recover image I_e, the recover secret message W_e.
Step 1: Calculate the difference image D_e from I':

$$D_e(i,j) = I'(i, 2j+1) - I'(i, 2j), \quad 0 \leq i \leq M-1, \quad 0 \leq j \leq \frac{N}{2}-1. \tag{46}$$

Step 2: Scan D_e, then

$$W_e = \begin{cases} 0, & \text{if } D_e(i,j) = -1 \text{ or } 1 \\ 1, & \text{if } D_e(i,j) = -2 \text{ or } 2 \end{cases} \tag{47}$$

Step 3: Scan D_e again, then

$$I_e(i, 2j+1) = \begin{cases} I'(i, 2j+1) + 1 & \text{if } D_e(i,j) \geq 2 \\ I'(i, 2j+1) - 1 & \text{if } D_e(i,j) \leq -2 \\ I'(i, 2j+1) & \text{otherwise.} \end{cases} \tag{48}$$

$$I_e(i, 2j) = I'(i, 2j). \tag{49}$$

The data recovering in the above scheme is not completely lossless because of the loss of information occurs during addition and subtraction at the boundaries of the grayscale range (at the gray level 0 and 255).

In order to prevent this problem, Lee adopt modulo arithmetic for secret message addition and subtraction. They have defined the addition modulo c as $I(i, 2j+1) +_c 1 = (I(i, 2j+1) + 1) \bmod c$, and the subtraction modulo c as $I(i, 2j+1) -_c 1 = (I(i, 2j+1) - 1) \bmod c$, where c is the cycle length.

The reversibility problem arises from pixels with truncation due to overflow or underflow. Therefore, Lee uses $+_c$ and $-_c$ instead of $+$ and-only when truncation (due to overflow or underflow) occurs. In other words, we have only to consider $255 +_c 1$ and $0 -_c 1$.

In the receiving side, it is necessary to distinguish between the cases when, for example, $I'(i, 2j+1) = 255$ was obtained as $I(i, 2j+1) + 1$ and $I(i, 2j+1) -_{256} 1$.

Assume that no abrupt change between two adjacent pixels occurs. If there is a significant difference between $I'(i, 2j+1)$ and $I'(i, 2j)$, Lee estimates that $I(i, 2j+1)$ is manipulated by modulo arithmetic

$$\begin{cases} I(i, 2j+1) & if \ |I'(i, 2j+1) - I'(i, 2j)| \leq \tau \\ I'(i, 2j+1) +_{256} 1 & otherwise. \end{cases} \quad (50)$$

Lee et al. [21] proposed a scheme giving about 3dB improvement in PSNR for typical images as compared to Ni's scheme [1~2]. Moreover, it is unnecessary to transmit any side information to the receiving side for data retrieval. Experimental results in Ref. [21] showed that the proposed scheme above provides high embedding capacity while keeping the embedding distortion as small as possible.

5.2 Jung et al.'s scheme

In Jung et al.'s [23] algorithm, the data embedding level is adaptively adjusted for each pixel with a consideration of the human visual system (HVS) characteristics.

To solve overflow and under flow problem, the Cover-image histogram is shrunk from both sides by 2^L, where L is the embedding level. To realize reversible data embedding, the overhead information describing this preprocessing as losslessly compressed and embedded together with pure payload data. Detailed description for preprocessing can be found in [7].

In this scheme, $\Omega_{i,j}$ represents a causal window surrounding $I(i, j)$ and $N(\Omega_{i,j})$ returns a cardinality of the set $\Omega_{i,j}$; var$(\Omega_{i,j})$ represents the variance of pixel values in $\Omega_{i,j}$, T_e is an edge threshold; T_l and T_a are two thresholds representing the luminance adaptation and the activity masking of the HVS characteristics, respectively, and $\lambda = 0.5$ [7].

Tables 5.2-1 and 5.2-2 show the embedding and extracting procedure of Jung et al.'s algorithm, respectively.

Table 5.2-1 The embedding procedure of Jung et al.'s scheme

Input: The Cover-image I, the secret message W, the embedding level L.
Output: The Stego-image I'.
Step 1: Scan I, obtain the predicted value as follows

$$\hat{I}(i,j) = \frac{1}{N(\Omega_{i,j})} \sum_{(m,n) \in \Omega_{i,j}} I(m,n). \quad (51)$$

Step 2: Calculate the pixel difference:

$$d(i,j) = |I(i,j) - \hat{I}(i,j)|. \quad (52)$$

Step 3: Estimate the edge for each pixels as follows:

$$E(i,j) = \begin{cases} 1 & if \ \text{var}(\Omega_{i,j}) > T_e \\ 0 & if \ \text{var}(\Omega_{i,j}) \leq T_e \end{cases} \quad (53)$$

(续表)

Step 4: Estimate the JND values:
$$jnd(i,j) = T_l(i,j) + \lambda \frac{T_a(i,j)}{T_l(i,j)}. \tag{54}$$

Step 5: Adaptively adjust the embedding finally level for each pixel as follows
If $E(i,j) = 0$,
$$K_{i,j} = \arg\max 2^k, \ 2^k < jnd(i,j), \ k \leq L. \tag{55}$$
If $E(i,j) = 1$,
$$K_{i,j} = \arg\min 2^k, \ 2^k > jnd(i,j), \ k \leq L. \tag{56}$$

Step 6: Obtain the I' obeying the rules as:
If $d(i,j) < 2^{k_{i,j}}$, then
$$I'(i,j) = \begin{cases} I(i,j) + d(i,j) + w, & if\ I(i,j) \geq \hat{I}(i,j) \\ I(i,j) - d(i,j) - w, & if\ I(i,j) < \hat{I}(i,j) \end{cases} \tag{57}$$
Else
$$I'(i,j) = \begin{cases} I(i,j) + 2^{k_{i,j}}, & if\ I(i,j) \geq \hat{I}(i,j) \\ I(i,j) - 2^{k_{i,j}}, & if\ I(i,j) < \hat{I}(i,j) \end{cases} \tag{58}$$

Table 5.2-2 The extracting procedure of Jung et al.'s scheme

Input: The Stego-image I', the embedding level L.
Output: The recover image I_e, the recover secret message W_e.
Step 1: Obtain the pixel value prediction, edge and JND and embedding level by using the causal window.
Step 2: Scan I'
If $|I'(i,j) - \hat{I}(i,j)| < 2^{k_{i,j}+1}$, then
$$w_e = \begin{cases} 0, & if\ |I'(i,j) - \hat{I}(i,j)|\ is\ even \\ 1, & if\ |I'(i,j) - \hat{I}(i,j)|\ is\ odd \end{cases} \tag{59}$$
$$I_e(i,j) = \begin{cases} I'(i,j) + \left[\frac{|I'(i,j) - \hat{I}(i,j)|}{2}\right], & if\ I'(i,j) < \hat{I}(i,j) \\ I'(i,j) - \left[\frac{|I'(i,j) - \hat{I}(i,j)|}{2}\right], & if\ I'(i,j) \geq \hat{I}(i,j) \end{cases} \tag{60}$$
Else
$$I_e(i,j) = \begin{cases} I'(i,j) + 2^{k_{i,j}}, & if\ I'(i,j) < \hat{I}(i,j) \\ I'(i,j) - 2^{k_{i,j}}, & if\ I'(i,j) > \hat{I}(i,j) \end{cases} \tag{61}$$

Given only the Stego-image and the embedding level, the Cover-image is recovered and the embedded bits are obtained in the data extraction process. Because we can obtain the pixel value prediction, edge and JND, and embedding level in the extracting process by using the causal window.

Since the overhead information bits describing the preprocessing are also extracted, the Cover-image is finally recovered by shifting back the image histogram.

The conventional histogram modification methods embed a message bit into the histogram of pixel values [1~2] or the histogram of the pixel differences [7]. Since Tai et al.'s method

[7] outperforms Ni et al.'s method [1~2], Tai et al.'s method is chosen as Jung et al.'s basic framework.

Compared to Tai et al.'s work, Jung et al. [23] used a causal window to predict a pixel value, an edge, and the just noticeable difference (JND) and exploit these predicted values when performing data embedding.

The experimental results of Jung et al.'s scheme demonstrated that this pixel level adaptive embedding method could provide the superior visual quality of the embedded images.

5.3 Chung et al.'s scheme

The histogram modification method proposed by Ni et al. is very efficient for reversible data hiding. Besides the excellent execution-time performance, Ni et al.'s method has a high PSNR lower bound of marked images.

In Chung et al.'s algorithm, an observation on Ni et al.'s reversible data hiding method is pointed out that the distortion of the marked image from Ni et al.'s method is dependent on the number of 1's in the secret message. From this observation, Chung et al. [24] first present a secret message complement scheme to reduce the distortion occurred in Ni et al.'s method. Later, combinatorial analysis for average distortion ratio of the proposed scheme is provided.

5.3.1 Observation on Ni et al.'s scheme

Given a 512×512 Lena image I where the peak value is $P = 154$ and its frequency is 2787; it yields $f_p(154) = 2787$, the valley value $P = 154$ and its frequency is zero. Suppose an n-bits secret message denoted by $W = w_1 w_2 w_3 \cdots w_n$, where $w_i \in \{0, 1\}$ and $n = 2787$, and it meets the frequency of the peak value.

Based on Ni et al.'s method, Chung et al. first modify those pixel values in the range $(P, V)(= (154, 235))$ by performing shift operations: $I(x, y) = I(x, y) + 1$ for $P < I(x, y) < V$ where $I(x, y)$ denotes the gray value at location (x, y). Note that if the valley value whose frequency is not zero, we must record the relevant positions for the valley value before performing. After completing the shift operations, for embedding the watermark W, the peak value P with frequency 2787 is modified by the following rule:

$$I'(x, y) = \begin{cases} I(x, y) + 1 & if\ I(x, y) = P \\ I(x, y) & otherwise \end{cases} \quad (62)$$

For $0 \leq x, y \leq 511$, where $w_i \in \{0, 1\}$ denotes the currently embedded bit in W.

Observation: Suppose the number of 1's in the secret message W is k, $0 \leq k \leq n - 1$. After performing the histogram modification-based secret message process in (62), the frequency of the gray value $P + 1$ ($= 155$) in the marked image I becomes k and the frequency of the gray value P ($= 154$) in I' becomes $n - k$, where P denotes the peak value.

Reconsidering the histogram, it is known that $n = 2787$; From observation 1, for example, assume $k = 2000$; after performing the above histogram modification-based watermarking, in these

2787 peak values for $P = 154$, there are 2000 peak values being changed from 154 ($= P$) to 155 ($= P + 1$) and 787 ($= 2787 - 2000$) peak values retain the same.

This example reveals that using the Ni, *et al.*'s process, the number of distorted peak values is equal to the number of 1's in the hidden data W i. e. the parameter k.

To relax the distortion problem, a simple secret message complement scheme is presented in next subsection.

Proposed secret complement scheme and the average analysis of distortion ratio:

Let the numbers of 1's and 0's in the secret W be denoted by $|W_1|$ and $|W_0|$, respectively, and it satisfies $|W| = |W_1| + |W_0|$, where S denotes the length of the binary string $S \in \{W, W_1, W_0\}$; Let the complement of W be denoted by $\overline{W}$, the proposed secret message complement scheme obeys the follow rule:

$$W = \begin{cases} \overline{W} & if \ |W_1| > |W_0| \\ W & otherwise \end{cases} \tag{63}$$

For example, assume that the secret message is given by $W = 110111011101$, then we have $|W| = 12$, $|W_1| = 9$, $|W_0| = 3$, and $\overline{W} = 001000100010$, since $|W_1|$ ($= 9$) is much larger than $|W_0|$ ($= 3$), by (63), the original secret message W ($= 001000100010$) as a new secret message; after performing (62), only three peak values, instead of nine, are added to one. On the other hand, instead of nine gray values, only three gray values, 154's are changed to 155's. We have the following average distortion ratio for the peak values by using the above secret message complement scheme.

Theorem 1[24]. Given a watermark W with $|W| = n$, the proposed watermark complement scheme yields the average distortion ratio is:

$$R_d = \begin{cases} 1/2 - \binom{n-1}{n/2}/2^n & if \ n \ is \ even \\ 1/2 - \binom{n-1}{(n-1)/2}/2^n & if \ n \ is \ odd \end{cases} \tag{64}$$

5.3.2 Block-based secret message complement scheme

It is a tradeoff between the block size and the overhead for recording whether the watermark complement scheme is used for each block or not.

In this scheme, W represents the original secret message, b represents the number of blocks, $f_{n_1}(W_i)$ and $f_{n_0}(W_i)$ denote the number 1's and the number of 0's in the i-th block of W, respectively; $\overline{W}_i$ denotes the complement of the i-th block of W. The block-based watermark scheme is presented as Table 5.3-1.

The overhead of the above block-based watermark scheme in (66) is $b + \lceil \log_2 b \rceil$ bits where $\lceil \log_2 b \rceil$ bits are used to denote the size of each block and each bit of these b bits is used to specify whether the relevant block has been complemented or not.

Table 5.3-1 Block-based watermark complement scheme

Input: The original secret message W, the number of partitioned blocks b.
Output: The new secret message W', overhead.
Step 1: Partition W into b blocks: $W_1 W_2 W_3 \cdots W_b$ as
$$W_i = W_{i1} W_{i2} W_{i3} \cdots W_{i(n/b)}. \tag{65}$$
$i = 1, 2, 3, \cdots, b$, assuming n/b is an integer.
Step 2: Obtain W_i' according to (63):
$$W_i' = \begin{cases} \overline{W}_i & if f_{n_1}(W_i) > f_{n_0}(W_i) \\ W_i & otherwise \end{cases} \tag{66}$$
Step 3: Generate W' by cascading these b blocks
$$W' = W_1' W_2' \cdots W_b'. \tag{67}$$

It is a tradeoff between the number of partitioned blocks and the overhead for recording whether the watermark complement scheme is used for each block or not. Thus, the best choice for the number of partitioned blocks, saying as b^*, can be determined by

$$b^* = \arg \min[f_{n_1}(W') + f_{n_1}(h_b)], 1 \leq b \leq |W|. \tag{68}$$

Where $h_b = b + [\log_2 b]$ denotes the overhead associated with the number of partitioned blocks, say b; $f_n(h_b)$ denotes the number of 1's in h_b; $f_{n_1}(W')$ denotes the number of 1's in the number of 1's in the new watermark W'. Note that W' and b must satisfy the following condition:

$$|W'| + b + [\log_2^b] \leq C. \tag{69}$$

Where C denotes the embedding capacity of the cover-image.

After embedding the overhead with $b^* + [\log_2 b^*]$ bits and the new secret message W' into the cover-image, it is easy to extract the overhead and W' from the stego-image completely. According to the first b^* bits of the overhead, W' is thus partitioned into b^* blocks and then from the last $[\log_2 b^*]$ of the overhead, each partitioned block can be recovered to the original one. Finally, these cascaded recovered blocks constitute the original watermark W.

The distortion reduction ratio R_r is calculated by R_d^{Ni} and R_d^{Chung}.

Where R_d^{Ni} and R_d^{Chung} denote the distortion ratios of Ni, et al.'s method and Chung et al.'s method, respectively.

$$R_r = \frac{R_d^{Ni} - R_d^{Chung}}{R_d^{Ni}}. \tag{70}$$

Some experimental results in Ref. [24] are carried out to demonstrate the distortion reduction effect and higher PSNR lower bound advantages of our proposed method when compared to Ni et al.'s reversible data hiding method.

6 Conclusions

In this chapter, we first introduce an RDH algorithm proposed by Ni *et al.* Then we present four methods that improved on Ni's algorithm by adjusting auxiliary information and increase capacity. Finally we propose some approaches to reduce the distortion of RDH. We notice that reversible data hiding methods usually fail to recover the secret message exactly when the Stego-image is attacked (such as lossless compression). Therefore, developing robust reversible data hiding method [25~33] that can resistant to these attacks should be an interesting topic.

Actual data embedding is performed by increasing the difference value and finding the extra space that can contain to-be-embedded bits. Thus, the overflow and under flow problem can happen when the embedded value exceeds a pixel value bound (0 to 255 in 8 bit images). Detailed description for preprocessing can be found in [3, 34~37].

Acknowledgments

This research was supported in part by the National Natural Science Foundation of China (Grant Nos. 60873249, 60902102, 61070189, and 61170032), Project of General Administration of press and publication of China under Grant GAPP-ZDKJ-BQ/15-2, and was also the postdoctor foundation of China (Grand No. 201003111).

References

[1] Z. Ni, Y. Q. Shi, N. Ansari, and W. Su, "Reversible data hiding," *Proc. IEEE International Symposium on Circuits and Systems (ISCAS 2003)*, Thailand, vol. 2, pp. II 912 – II 915, May 2003.

[2] Z. Ni, Y. Q. Shi, N. Ansari, and W. Su, "Reversible data hiding," *IEEE Transactions on Circuits and Systems for Video Technology*, vol. 16, no. 3, pp. 354-362, March 2006.

[3] J. Tian, "Reversible data embedding using a difference expansion," *IEEE Transactions on Circuits and Systems for Video Technology*, vol. 13, no. 8, pp. 890-896, August 2003.

[4] Y. Hu, H. K. Lee, and J. Li, "De-based reversible data hiding improved overflow location map," *IEEE Transactions on Circuits and Systems for Video Technology*, vol. 19, no. 2, pp. 250-260, Feb. 2009.

[5] J. H. Hwang, J. W. Kim, and J. U. Choi, "A Reversible Watermarking Based on Histogram Shifting," *International Workshop on Digital Watermarking*, Lecture Notes in Computer Science, vol. 4283, 2006, pp. 348-361, doi: 10.1007/11922841_28.

[6] W. C. Kuo, D. J. Jiang, and Y. C. Huang, "Reversible data hiding based on histogram," *International Conference on Intelligent Computing*, Lecture Notes in Artificial Intelligence, vol. 4682, 2007, pp. 1152-1161, doi: 10.1007/978-3-540-74205-0_119.

[7] W. L. Tai, C. M. Yeh, and C. C. Chang, "Reversible data hiding based on histogram modification of pixel differences," *IEEE Transactions on Circuits and systems for video technology*, vol. 19, no. 6, pp. 906-910, June 2009.

[8] W. Hong, "Adaptive reversible data hiding method based on error energy control and histogram shifting," *Optics Communications*, vol. 285, no. 2, Jan. 2012, pp. 101-108, doi: 10.1016/j.optcom.2011.09.005.

[9] P. Tsai, Y. C. Hu, and H. L. Yeh, "Reversible image hiding scheme using predictive coding and histo-

gram shifting," *Signal Processing*, vol. 89, no. 6, June 2009, pp. 1129-1143, doi: 10.1016/j.sigpro.2008.12.017.

[10] W. Hong and T. S. Chen, "A local variance-controlled reversible data Hiding method using prediction and histogram-shifting," *The Journal of Systems and Software*, vol. 83, no. 12, Dec. 2010, pp. 2653-2663, doi: 10.1016/j.jss.2010.08.047.

[11] W. Hong, "An efficient prediction-and-shifting embedding technique for high quality reversible data hiding," *Eurasip Journal on Advances in Signal Processing*, vol. 2010, Feb. 2010, Article ID 104835, 12pages, doi: 10.1155/2010/104835.

[12] X. T. Zeng, Z. Li, Ping, and L. D. Ping, "Reversible data hiding scheme using reference pixel and multi-layer embedding," *International Journal of Electronics and Communications (AEU)*, vol. 66, no. 7, July 2012, pp. 532-539, doi: 10.1016/j.aeue.2011.11.004.

[13] Z. Zhao, H. Luo, Z. M. Lu, and J. S. Pan. Jeng-Shyang, "Reversible data hiding based on multilevel histogram modification and sequential recovery," *International Journal of Electronics and Communications (AEU)*, vol. 66, no. 10, Oct. 2012, pp. 814-826, doi: 10.1016/j.aeue.2011.01.014.

[14] M. Fallahpour, D. Megias, and M. Ghanbari, "Reversible and high-capacity data hiding in medical images," *IET Image Process*, vol. 5, no. 2, March 2011, pp. 190-197, doi: 10.1049/iet-ipr.2009.0226.

[15] H. W. Yang, I. E. Liao, and C. C. Chen, "Reversible data hiding based on median difference histogram," *Journal of Information Science and Engineering*, vol. 27, pp. 577-593, May 2011.

[16] C. W. Lee and W. H. Tsai, "A lossless large-volume data hiding method based on histogram shifting using an optimal hierarchical block division Scheme," *Journal of Information Science and Engineering*, vol. 27, pp. 1265-1282, 2011.

[17] Y. C. Lin and T. S. Li, "Reversible image data hiding using quad-tree segmentation and histogram shifting," *Journal of Multimedia*, vol. 6, no. 4, pp. 349-358, August 2011.

[18] C-F. Lee and H-L. Chen, "Reversible data hiding based on histogram modification of prediction-error," *The Imaging Science Journal*, vol. 59, no. 5, pp. 278-292 (15), Oct. 2011.

[19] B. M. Irany, X. C. Guo, and D. Hatzinakos, "A high capacity reversible multiple watermarking scheme for medical images," *17th International Conference on Digital Signal Processing (DSP 2011)*, pp. 1-6, July 2011.

[20] J. Fridrich, M. Goljan, and R. Du, "Invertible authentication," *Proc. SPIE*, *Security and Watermarking of Multimedia Contents* Ⅲ, vol. 4314, pp. 197-208, 2001.

[21] S. K. Lee, Y. H. Suh, and Y. S. Ho, "Lossless data hiding based on histogram modification of difference images," *Advances in Multimedia Information Processing (PCM 2004)*, *Lecture Notes in Computer Science*, vol. 3333, 2005, pp. 340-347, doi: 10.1007/978-3-540-30543-9_43.

[22] W. Lin, L. Dong, and P. Xue, "Visual distortion gauge based on discrimination of noticeable contrast changes," *IEEE Transactions on Circuits and Systems for Video Technology*, vol. 15, no. 7, pp. 900-909, July 2005.

[23] S. W. Jung, L. T. Ha, and S. J. Ko, "A new histogram modification based reversible data hiding algorithm considering the human visual system," *IEEE Signal Processing Letters*, vol. 18, no. 2, pp. 95-98, Feb. 2011.

[24] K. L. Chung, Y. H. Huang, W. M. Yan, and W. C. Teng, "Distortion reduction for histogram modification-based reversible data hiding," *Applied Mathematics and Computation* (*AMC* 2012), vol. 218, no. 9, Jan. 2012, pp. 5819-5826, doi: 10.1016/j. amc. 2011. 10. 056.

[25] G. Xuan, J. Chen, J. Zhu, Y. Q. Shi, Z. Ni, and W. Su, "Lossless data hiding based on integer wavelet transform," *IEEE Workshop on Multimedia Signal Processing* (*MMSP* 02), pp. 312-315, Dec. 2002.

[26] E. Varsaki, V. Fotopoulos, and A. N. Skodras, "A reversible data hiding technique embedding in the image histogram," unpublished.

[27] E. Chrysochos, V. Fotopoulos, A. N. Skodras, and M. Xenos, "Reversible image watermarking based on histogram modification," 11*th Panhellenic Conference on Informatics with international participation* (*PCI* 2007), vol. B, pp. 93-10, May 2007.

[28] M. Fallahpour and M. H. Sedaaghi, "High capacity lossless data hiding based on histogram modification," *Electronics Express* (*IEICE* 2007), vol. 4, no. 7, pp. 205-210, April 2007.

[29] S. L. V. Krishna, B. A. Rahim, F. Shaik, and K. S. Rajan, "Lossless embedding using pixel differences and histogram shifting technique," *Recent Advances in Space Technology Services and Climate Change* (*RSTSCC* 2010), Nov. 2010, pp. 213-216, doi: 10. 1109/RSTSCC. 2010. 5712850.

[30] M. A. M. Abadi, H. Danyali, M. S. Helfroush, "Reversible watermarking based on interpolation error histogram shifting," 5*th International Symposium on Telecommunications* (*IST* 2010), Dec. 2010, pp. 840-845, doi: 10. 1109/ISTEL. 2010. 5734139.

[31] X. Gao, L. An, Y. Yuan, D. Tao, and X. Li, "Lossless data embedding using generalized statistical quantity histogram," *IEEE Transactions on Circuits and Systems for Video Technology*, vol. 21, no. 8, August 2011, pp. 1061-1070, doi: 10. 1109/TCSVT. 2011. 2130410.

[32] H. C. Huang, Y. H. Chen, and Y. Y. Lu, "Histogram-based difference expansion for reversible data hiding with content statistics," 7*th Intelligent Information Hiding and Multimedia Signal Processing* (*IIH-MSP* 2011), Oct. 2011, pp. 37-40, doi: 10. 1109/IIHMSP. 2011. 38.

[33] L. An, X. Gao, Y. Yuan, and D. Tao, "Robust lossless data hiding using clustering and statistical quantity histogram," *Neurocomputing*, vol. 77, no. 1, pp. 1-11, Feb. 2012.

[34] A. M. Alattar, "Reversible watermark using the difference expansion of a generalized integer transform," *IEEE Transactions on Image Processing*, vol. 13, no. 8, pp. 1147-1156, August 2004.

[35] D. M. Thodi and J. J. Rodriguez, "Expansion embedding techniques for reversible watermarking," *IEEE Transactions on Image Processing*, vol. 16, no. 3, pp. 721-730, Mach 2007.

[36] Y. Hu, H. K. Lee and J. Li, "DE-based reversible data hiding with improved overflow location map," *IEEE Transactions on Circuits and Systems for Video Technology*, vol. 19, no. 2, pp. 250-260, 2009.

[37] L. An, X. Gao, C. Deng, and F. Ji, "Reversible watermarking based on statistical quantity histogram," *Advances in Multimedia Information Processing* (*PCM* 2009), *Lecture Notes in Computer Science*, vol. 5879, 2009, pp. 1300-1305, doi: 10. 1007/978-3-642-10467-1_135.

Ciphertext Query Algorithm for Character Data Based on DAS Model*

ZHANG Meng-Yi   CAO Chen-Lei   ZHANG Ru   LIU Jian-Yi

I. Introduction

With the booming development of emerging network services, such as e-commerce, social network and online storage, all kinds of business data surge continuously, which leads to more maintenance cost. To reduce the data storage and maintenance cost effectively for small or medium sized network service providers, many cloud service providers offer database as service (DAS)[1]. But in such a service mode, the user can not limit the data access of the database service provider (DSP) and DSP can easily access the user's data stored in the cloud. To address these problems, the user stores the ciphertext of the data in database cloud to keep the data secure. But how to query the ciphertext quickly and accurately becomes a new research focus on ciphertext storage. Existing solutions can be divided into three categories: ①the ciphertext-only query method based on homomorphism and order-maintained encryption; ②the fast decryption query method based on sub-keys and smart cards; ③the twice query method based on filtering and indexing. The designing idea of the last method can be explained as follows. Firstly, create index for the ciphertext using filtering and indexing, which can reduce the query range of the ciphertext. Then the ciphertext is decrypted for precise queries. In this paper we combine the DAS model with the principle of the twice query method based on filtering and indexing, and propose a new query algorithm for the ciphertext in database.

II. Related Works

On the basis of DAS model, H. Hacıgümüş first proposes a bucket partition method[2] for the numeric data, and implements the twice query algorithm based on filtering and indexing. In subsequent, homomorphism[3] and optimization[4] are adopted by H. Hacıgümüş to improve the twice query algorithm for numeric data. After that, researchers propose a variety of ciphertext storage and query models.

---

* 本文选自 2nd International Conference on Computer Science and Network Technology (ICCSNT 2012), 第 816－821 页

Among the models, R. Agrawal[5] proposes an order-maintained encryption algorithm, and implements the ciphertext query according to the range of the numeric data. Z. F. Wang[6] proposes a new ciphertext query algorithm for numeric data. In this algorithm, Z. F. Wang uses B + tree to work with the plaintext which is to be encrypted, and obtains the index tree of the ciphertext. Z. F. Wang also proposes a fast query algorithm for the ciphertext of character data based on dual code[7], but it is difficult for this algorithm to resist dictionary attacks and brute – force attacks. Besides the vulnerability, the algorithm is invalid for single character. On the basis of the feature matrix encoding, H. Zhu proposes a ciphertext query algorithm[8] and introduces a compression algorithm for the character code to reduce the space of index storage. This algorithm greatly guarantees the security and improves the efficiency of ciphertext query. In the algorithm proposed by Y. Zhang, the plaintext is divided into groups and the grouping result is encoded[9]. Then Y. Zhang uses the encoding result to create index for the data to finish the corresponding ciphertext query. Y. Zhang improves his algorithm by introducing Hash function[10], but the algorithm still cannot resist dictionary attacks and brute-force attacks. Besides security problems, if parameters in the algorithm are inappropriate, different codes may produce the same index code, which leads to high rate of preliminary index misjudgment.

In recent years, N. Liu et al. introduce homomorphism into DAS model to create index for the ciphertext, and design a ciphertext query algorithm based on dual filter model[11]. Although the algorithm has high rate of data filtering, the calculation process is very complex due to numbers of keys, which causes key management inconvenience. Y. C. Lin proposes storage and query algorithm for ciphertext in database based on optimal bucket partition[14]. Her algorithm improves the query speed of the original algorithm[15], but does not solve the security problems. Y. Cao. et al. improve the algorithm in [7], and propose a fast query algorithm for the encrypted strings in database[16], but the analysis of the algorithm shows that the security problems still exist. On the basis of characteristic matrix encoding algorithm[7,8], Z. D. Wu further proposes $n \times n$ reachable matrix encoding algorithm[12], which has expansion characteristics, and the user can determine the length of matrix code and the security level as needed.

According to the research mentioned above, we can come to the conclusion that ciphertext query mainly consists of two parts: extract the feature of the plaintext to generate index code, and store the index code in the database as an additional attribute; in the query process, transform original query statement into the query based on the index code and make preliminary query to filter out irrelevant ciphertext.

III. System Model and Algorithm Design

A. Database Encryption and Query Model

Based on the characteristics of DAS model, database encryption and query model in this paper is shown in Figure 1.

The model is constituted by the client and the server service modules, including the service contents of encrypted data storage and ciphertext query. The client is responsible for the encryption of confidential data and the generation of the corresponding ciphertext index code; the database server is responsible for storing the ciphertext data and its index code.

When user performs data query operation, the client extracts metadata and generates query index code according to the user-specified keywords. Then the client transforms the original query statement entered by the user to an encrypted one; the server searches the ciphertext according to the index code and the encrypted query statement, and then sends the query results back to the client. On receiving the preliminary results, the client decrypts them and saves the plaintext. For the second query, the user's original query statement is executed on the plaintext. Finally, the client shows precise query results to the user.

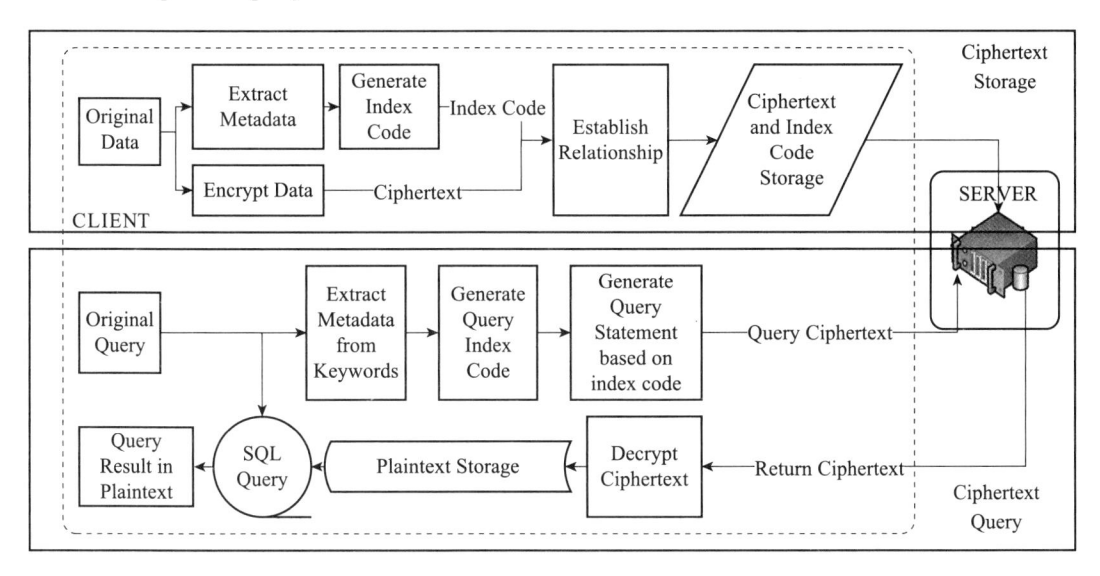

Figure 1 Database Encryption and Query Model

B. Ciphertext Storage Model

In order to introduce the algorithm we design, we give the following definitions in reference to the model in [2]:

Definition 1. Correlative Relationship.

$R(A_1, A_2, \cdots, A_n)$ represents the relationship between the correlative fields in database.

Definition 2. Ciphertext. A_i^E represents the result of encrypting the data stored in field A_i using symmetric cryptography $(1 \leq i \leq n)$.

Definition 3. Ciphertext Index Code. Use ciphertext index code generating algorithm to process the data stored in field A_i, the result of which is defined as Ciphertext Index Code A_i^S $(1 \leq i \leq n)$.

Based on Definition 1 to 3, the database ciphertext storage model used in this paper is de-

fined as:
$$R(A_1, A_2, \cdots, A_i^E, \cdots, A_j^E, \cdots A_n, A_i^S, \cdots, A_j^S), 1 \leq i \leq j \leq n. \quad (1)$$

C. Metadata and Metadata Set

Definition 4. Metadata and Metadata Set. In the case that the character data input by the user can be reconstructed by the elements in collection $U = \{a_1, a_2, \cdots a_n\}$, elements in U are defined as metadata and collection $U = \{a_1, a_2, \cdots a_n\}$ is defined as metadata set.

Example 1. Metadata set for English is ASC Ⅱ code set. Metadata set for Chinese characters is Unicode code set. For the text data made of characters, metadata set is the thesaurus obtained by word splitting.

Defination 5. Reconstructed Metadata Set. In the case that arbitrary character data D input by the user can be reconstructed by metadata stream $c_1 c_2 \cdots c_m$, in which the elements are from U, we remove duplicate metadata in $c_1 c_2 \cdots c_m$. The reconstructed metadata set of D on set U is defined as $\{c_1, c_2, \cdots c_l\}_{l \leq m}$. If $1 \leq i, j \leq l$, then $i \neq j \Leftrightarrow c_i \neq c_j$.

Example 2. According to Definition 4, the composition of characters "Google" is the data stream "G—o—o—g—l—e" and the corresponding reconstructed metadata set is $\{G, o, g, l, e\}$.

Before extracting the metadata, the client first determines metadata set according to the concrete data input by the user, and then splits the data on the basis of the elements in the metadata set, and generates the reconstructed metadata set for character data according to the splitting results. This paper proposes an extraction algorithm for the reconstructed metadata set of character data, as follows:

Algorithm 1. The extraction algorithm for reconstructed metadata set.

Input: character data entered by the user and metadata set U.

Output: reconstructed metadata set.

Step 1. Split the character data according to the elements in U and use metadata stream $c_1 c_2 \cdots c_m$ ($c_i \in U$) to express character data D.

Step 2. Remove duplicate elements within the metadata stream and generate the reconstructed metadata set of D: $\{c_1, c_2, \cdots c_l\}_{l \leq m}$.

D. Split Metadata Set

Before index code generating algorithm encodes the plaintext of character data, the client should split the metadata set to ensure that different users get different encoding results, which can guarantee the security of encoding.

Algorithm 2. Splitting algorithm for metadata set.

Input: metadata set and symmetric key.

Output: splitting result of set U and subset numbers.

Step 1. Use MAC algorithm with the symmetric key entered by the user to compute MAC codes of the elements in U.

Step 2. Transform the MAC codes into numbers, and rank the elements in U from small to large according to the number values.

Step 3. Divide the ordered set U into several subsets. Assume that $\{U_1, U_2, \cdots U_n\}$ is the ordered splitting result, and U_i $(1 \leq i \leq n)$ is one of the subsets of U. The subsets of U need to satisfy the following conditions:
$$U_1 \cap U_2 \cap U_3 \cdots \cap U_n = \Phi, \ U_1 \cup U_2 \cup U_3 \cdots \cup U_n = U.$$

Step 4. $f: \{U_1, U_2, \cdots U_n\} \rightarrow \{1, 2, \cdots n\}$ is a bijective function. Number the subsets in Step 3 by mapping them to natural numbers, and save the splitting result with the numbers of the subsets.

Example 3. In the case that the key is 0x 672D-4E18-5EA4-5F9E-A6BB-FAD5-830F-BCF6-D2D9-E50E, use HMAC-SHA1 to compute MAC codes of the elements in metadata set $U = \{a, b, c, d, e, f, g, h, i, j, k, l\}$:

a: 0x 2554-06F4-E261-3280-3B06-C48E-161A-48FC-1C4B-9A44

b: 0x 7633-B9B3-322E-04AC-D436-6E83-33DD-D553-D7A0-DC95

c: 0x BDD1-CA24-5544-68BC-4E8D-3DF0-6885-3102-841F-1D1E

d: 0x 0530-D335-34CE-7EE9-A132-4E4C-0599-AA61-68F3-432B

e: 0x 851B-FC5C-4E43-E670-FF9D-A721-D855-1916-2DEF-0F97

f: 0x 98AD-5786-4B0D-C17F-C54C-C8E6-A965-C72A-9362-4F66

g: 0x CFEB-A108-40AC-0B17-0217-1307-C2A9-12C7-808C-6780

h: 0x 888C-2FAF-C908-EDBC-FC95-85C1-DDD1-B3D4-849D-931C

i: 0x E2E0-9B59-3671-A21C-4DDB-3C67-06CC-7DB0-AB0E-5C80

j: 0x C136-0AE9-2A09-8762-B798-5D7B-CB41-501B-88F9-9DF9

k: 0x E08D-000A-F141-DFFA-884C-3CCE-B650-FB0F-00FE-2D40

l: 0x 5CE2-FD9A-4BEC-F2B5-043A-2FF3-4A4D-2C60-5EF5-02E9.

After that, transform MAC codes of the elements into numbers and rank the elements from small to large according to the number values. The new placement can be obtained as: $U = \{d, a, l, b, e, h, f, c, j, g, k, i\}$. Finally, make three adjacent elements in $U = \{d, a, l, b, e, h, f, c, j, g, k, i\}$ as a unit and split the set as: $U_1 = \{d, a, l\}$, $U_2 = \{b, e, h\}$, $U_3 = \{f, c, j\}$ and $U_4 = \{g, k, i\}$. The splitting result satisfies the condition $U = \{U_1, U_2, U_3, U_4\}$, and we make $f(U_i) = i$.

E. Index Code Generation

According to the splitting result of the metadata set, numbers of the subsets and the reconstructed metadata set, index code generating algorithm encodes the plaintext entered by the user to generate the index code for ciphertext query.

Algorithm 3. Ciphertext index code generating algorithm

Input: the splitting result of metadata set, numbers of the subsets and the reconstructed metadata set of character data.

Output: ciphertext index code.

Step 1. Bind the two adjacent elements in the reconstructed metadata set $\{c_1, c_2, \cdots c_l\}$ together and generate the duplet sets of metadata $\{(c_1, c_2), (c_2, c_3), \cdots (c_{l-1}, c_l)\}$.

Step 2. According to the splitting result of metadata set and numbers of the subsets, encode the elements in $\{(c_1, c_2), (c_2, c_3), \cdots (c_{l-1}, c_l)\}$. The pseudo-code of the algorithm is as follows:

```
boolean code[l][n];
for(int i=1;i<=l-1;i++){
for(int j=1;j<=n;j++){
if({c_i,c_{i+1}}∩U_j≠Φ)
code[i-1][j-1]=1;
else
code[i-1][j-1]=0;}}
```

$U = \{U_1, U_2, \cdots U_n\}$ is the splitting result of the metadata set. In this algorithm we select arbitrary i and j from appropriate ranges: $1 \leq i \leq l-1$ and $1 \leq j \leq n$. If $\{c_i, c_{i+1}\} \cap U_j \neq \Phi$, then the jth position in the code of (c_i, c_{i+1}) is 1 (e.g. ($\underbrace{00\cdots0}_{j-1}00\underbrace{0\cdots0}_{n-j}$)) and the code length is equal to the number of subsets of U. The combination of binary calculation results stored in array $code[l][n]$ is the ciphertext index code for character data.

The length of ciphertext index code is proportional to the length of splitting result and the length of character data. Assume that the splitting result of the metadata set contains n subsets, and the to-be-processed character data consists of m metadata. Then the length of the corresponding ciphertext index code is $l = (m-1) * n$.

Example 4. According to Step 1 in Algorithm 3, split the reconstructed metadata set of character data "black". The splitting result is $\{(b, l), (l, a), (a, c), (c, k)\}$.

After that, according to the splitting result of the metadata set and the encoding result of subsets in Example 3, we use Step 2 in Algorithm 3 to encode $\{(b, l), (l, a), (a, c), (c, k)\}$ and get the ciphertext index code of "black" as 0x C8A3.

Theorem 1. Assume the reconstructed metadata set of character data D_1 is S_1 and the reconstructed metadata set of D_2 is S_2. In the case that other input parameters are the same, the ciphertext index codes generated by Algorithm 3 are D_1: $code_1$ and D_2: $code_2$ respectively. In this condition, if $code_1 \& code_2 = code_2$ is established, we can conclude $S_2 \subset S_1$, and vice versa.

F. Data Encryption Storage

In the process of data encryption and storage[13], the client first encodes the sensitive data entered by the user and generates the corresponding ciphertext index code. Then the client uses symmetric cryptography to encrypt the sensitive data and generates the ciphertext. The database stores the ciphertext and the corresponding index code in accordance with the storage model defined in (1).

G. Ciphertext Query

In the DAS mode, when the user needs to perform keyword query in the ciphertext segment, the client first encodes the plaintext keywords, and generates the index code for query. Then the client transforms the original query statement into the ciphertext one based on the query index code. According to the correlative relationship in (1), the server returns the corresponding ciphertext back to the client. Finally the client decrypts the ciphertext and performs precise query using the plaintext query statement.

Algorithm 4. Ciphertext query algorithm

Input: query statement containing query keywords.

Output: the ciphertext.

Step 1. Extract query keywords, and based on the existing metadata set exclude the special symbols for fuzzy query, such as " % " " * ". Then use Algorithm 1 to extract the reconstructed metadata set of query keywords.

Step 2. Make the three parameters: the splitting result of the metadata set, numbers of the subsets and the reconstructed metadata set in Step 1 as the input of Algorithm 3, and generate the query index code.

Step 3. According to Theorem 1, transform the original query statement into the ciphertext query based on the query index code. The transformation rules are as follows: ①In the case that the original plaintext query statement is in the form of $A_t = $ '$character$', the ciphertext query should be transformed into $A_t^S = code$. $code$ is the query index code of the keyword $character$; ②In the case that the original plaintext query statement is in the form of A_t $LIKE$ '% $character$ %', the ciphertext query should be transformed into A_t^S & $code = code$.

Step 4. Based on the correlative structure in①, send the query results which meet the ciphertext query statement back to the client to finish the ciphertext query operation.

With Algorithm 1 to 4 proposed above, we describe how to create ciphertext index code for sensitive data and how to use the index code to perform ciphertext query.

IV. Implementation and Statistics Analysis

A. System Implementation

We design and implement a test system for ciphertext-storage in database according to Figure 1 and Algorithm 1 to 4.

In the test system, the server-side hardware runtime environment is as follows: Intel Core (TM) 2 Quad Processor dual-core CPU and DDR2 4G memory. The server-side software operating environment is: Windows 7, Oracle 11g, Oracle JRE 1.7.1 and Web-logic 12C. Development languages are Java and SQL. Development environment: Spring 3.1, Oracle JDK 1.7.1 and part of open source architecture from the third party.

The client-side implements the encryption of sensitive data and the extraction of ciphertext index code on user-specified needs. In the process of implementation, we adopt AES-128 as the encryption algorithm and HMAC-SHA1 as MAC algorithm. The client communicates with the database server through the Http request. The server filters and parses the request sent from the client through the Servlet interface, and then connects multiple Oracle databases in different places through the JNDI interface provided by Web-logic 12C. On receiving the ciphertext query statement sent from the client, the server only needs to perform the ciphertext query as specified in the statement. We also guarantee the transparency in the process of ciphertext storage and query in database, to simulate the ciphertext storage service based on DAS model.

B. Statistics Analysis

In the algorithm testing process, in order to eliminate interference factors, we only test the ciphertext query for data in a single table, not data in cascade tables. In addition, we select English words as the test set of character data to control the size of the metadata set. To illustrate the performance of the algorithm, we give the following definition:

Definition 4. Filtration Efficiency R_f. Assume we get N_1 data for the preliminary ciphertext query, and N_2 data for the second plaintext query. We define $R_f = N_2/N_1$.

Definition 5. Detection Rate R_t. Assume we get N_1 data after the second plaintext query and there are N_2 data expressly stored in the database, which should be found. We define $R_t = N_1/N_2$.

Definition 6. Algorithm Execution Time T_e. From the moment that the user performs data query to the time the server returns the preliminary query results to the client.

In order to test the performance of the algorithms according to Definition 4 to 6, we use variety kinds of query statements for our experiment. The concrete content is shown in Table 1. C_1 and C_2 represent the query keywords entered by the user and A_i^S is the ciphertext index code corresponding to field A_i.

TABLE I. QUERY STATEMENT IN THE TEST

Curve Name	Query Statement	Ciphertext Attribute
T1	$A_i = \,'C_1\,'$	A_i^S
T2	A_i LIKE $'\%C_1\%\,'$	A_i^S
T3	A_i LIKE $'C_1\,'$ OR $'C_2\,'$	A_i^S
T4	A_i LIKE $'C_1\,'$ AND $'C_2\,'$	A_i^S

Since the number of subsets of the metadata set directly affects the length of index code and the performance of the algorithm, in the test process we select 52 English letters (26 capital and 26 small) as the metadata set, and get six kinds of splitting results of the subsets according to Algorithm 2 (the number of subsets is from minimum 11 to maximum 26, with an increase of 3). In this paper, we choose 1 000 000 data in English for test, and the statistical results are shown in Figure 2 and Figure 3. The abscissa in Figure 2 represents the number of subsets of the metadata set, and the ordinate is the filtration efficiency R_f. The abscissa in Figure 3 represents the number of subsets of the metadata set and the ordinate is execution time of the algorithm T_e.

Figure 2 shows that the more subsets the metadata set is split into, the more closer R_f is to 1, and the higher filtration efficiency is; the less subsets the metadata set is split into, the lower filtration efficiency is. In the case that the number of subsets is the same, different query statements have different filtration efficiency: the more precise the query statement is (e.g. T4), the higher R_f is; the blurrier the query statement is (e.g. T2), the lower R_f is.

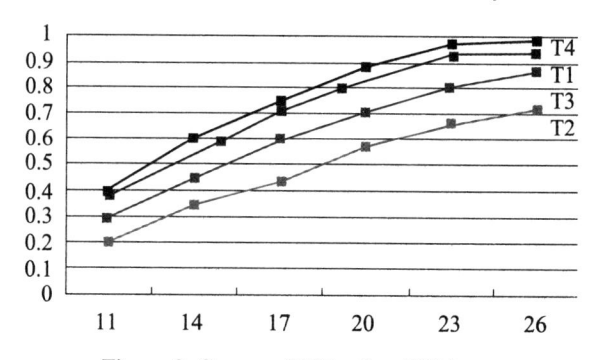

Figure 2. Curves of Filtration Efficiency

In Figure 3, the number of the subsets distributes in the [11, 26] interval and the execution time of the algorithm under different query statements is different: for the slightly complex query statement (e.g. T3), execution time is longer; for the simple query (e.g. T1), execution time is shorter.

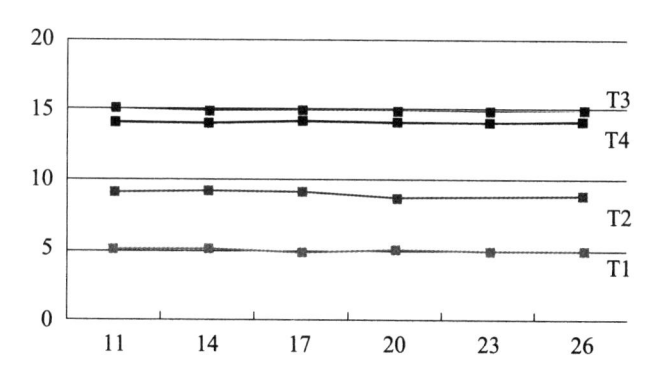

Figure 3. Curves of Algorithm Execution Time

We test and compare the execution time of our algorithm (Algorithm 1) with the algorithm in [11] (Algorithm 2) under the same experimental environment. We choose 100, 1000, 10000, 100000 data respectively as the test samples. The statistics are shown in Table 2.

TABLE II. EXECUTION TIME COMPARATION

Name Number	Algorithm 1	Algorithm 2
100	50ms	55ms
1000	60ms	80ms
10000	90ms	120ms
100000	160ms	200ms

R_t is always 1 in repeated experiments, which supports the conclusion in Theorem 1. The experimental statistics verify the design of the algorithm. Therefore, the user can find his data as needed with no omissions by using the ciphertext query algorithm in this paper. Compared with the algorithm in [11], our algorithm has better execution efficiency.

Ⅴ. Conclusions

The ciphertext query algorithm we design in this paper consists of two parts: the generation and storage of the ciphertext index code, and ciphertext-only query based on the index code. The user can generate the metadata set and determine the splitting pattern of the set according to actual requirement. The more subsets the metadata set is divided into, the higher filtration efficiency the algorithm has; the less subsets the metadata set is divided into, the lower filtration efficiency the algorithm has. The execution efficiency of the algorithm has nothing to do with the length of the index code, only related to the complexity of the query statement. The more complex the query statement is, the longer the algorithm executes. The detection rate of the algorithm is constant 1, which means the user can find any stored data without omission.

With the increasement of the length of ciphertext index code, the filtration efficiency of the algorithm has been significantly improved, but how to balance the length of the index code and the query efficiency, how to further improve filtration efficiency in the case of relatively short code length—these problems will be solved in later research work.

References

[1] H. Hacıgümüş, B. Iyer, S. Mehrotra, "Providing database as a service," in Proceedings of ICDE' 02, San Jose, Canada, 26 February-1 March 2002. IEEE Computer Society, Los Alamitos, CA, 2002, pp. 29-38.

[2] H. Hacıgümüş, B. Iyer, L. Chen, S. Mehrotra, "Executing SQL over encrypted data in the database service provider model," in: Proceedings of SIGMOD'02, Madison, Wisconsin, 3-6 June 2002, ACM Press, New York, 2002, pp. 216-227.

[3] H. Hacıgümüş, B. Iyer, S. Mehrotra, "Efficient execution of aggregation queries over encrypted relational databases," in: Proceedings of DASFAA'04, Jeju Island, South Korea, 17-19 March 2004, Springer-Verlag, Berlin, 2004, pp. 125-136.

[4] H. Hacıgümüş, B. Iyer, L. Chen, "Query optimization in encrypted database systems," in: Proceedings of DASFAA' 05, Beijing, China, 17-20 April 2005, Springer-Verlag, Berlin, 2005, pp. 43-55.

[5] R. Agrawal, J. Kiernan, R. Srikant, and Y. Xu. "Order preserving encryption for numeric data," ACM SIGMOD June 13-18, 2004, Paris, France.

[6] Z. F. Wang, W. Wang, B. L. Shi. "Storage and Query over Encrypted Character and Numerical Data in Database," The Fifth International Conference on Computer and Information Technology (CIT'05).

Shanghai, China, 2005. pp. 82-87.

[7] Z. F. Wang, J. Dai, W. Wang, B. L. Shi. "Fast Query Over Encrypted Character Data in Database," Computational and Information Science, Proceedings, Shanghai, China, 2004, vol. 4, pp. 289-300.

[8] H. Zhu, J. Cheng, R. Jin. "Executing Query over Encrypted Character Strings in Databases," Proceedings-2007 Japan-China Joint Workshop on Frontier of Computer Science and Technology, FCST 2007, pp. 90-97.

[9] Y. Zhang, W. X. Li, X. M. Niu. "A Method of Bucket Index over Encrypted Character Data in Database," Proceedings-3rd International Conference on Intelligent Information Hiding and Multimedia Signal Processing, IIHMSP 2007. vol. 1, pp. 186-189.

[10] Y. Zhang, W. X. Li, X. M. Niu. "A secure cipher index over encrypted character data in database," The Seventh International Conference on Machine Learning and Cybernetics, Kunming, 12-15 July 2008. vol. 2 pp. 1111-1116.

[11] N. Liu, Y. J. Zhou, X. X. Niu, Y. X. Yang. "Querying Encrypted Character Data in DAS Model," International Conference on Networking and Digital Society, 2010. vol. 2, pp. 402-405.

[12] Z. D. Wu, G. D. Xu, Z. Yu, X. Yi, E. H. Chen, Y. C. Zhang. "Executing SQL queries over encrypted character strings in the Database-As-Service model," Knowledge-Based Systems, 2012, in press.

[13] Erez Shmueli, Ronen Vaisenberg, Yuval Elovici, Chanan Glezer. "Database encryption-an overview of contemporary challenges and design considerations," SIGMOD Record, September 2009. vol. 38, No. 3.

[14] Y. C. Lin, X. M. Wang. "Database encryption storage and query based on optimal bucket partition," Computer Engineering, 2011, vol. 37. pp. 105-110.

[15] B. G. Cui, D. X. Liu, T. Wang. "Practical Techniques for Fast Searches on Encrypted String Data in Databases [J]," Computer Science, 2006, vol. 33, pp. 115-118.

[16] Y. Cao, D. K. He. "Practical techniques for fast query over encrypted character data in database," Application Research of Computers, 2009, vol 26, pp. 736-738.

第三辑
其他相关研究

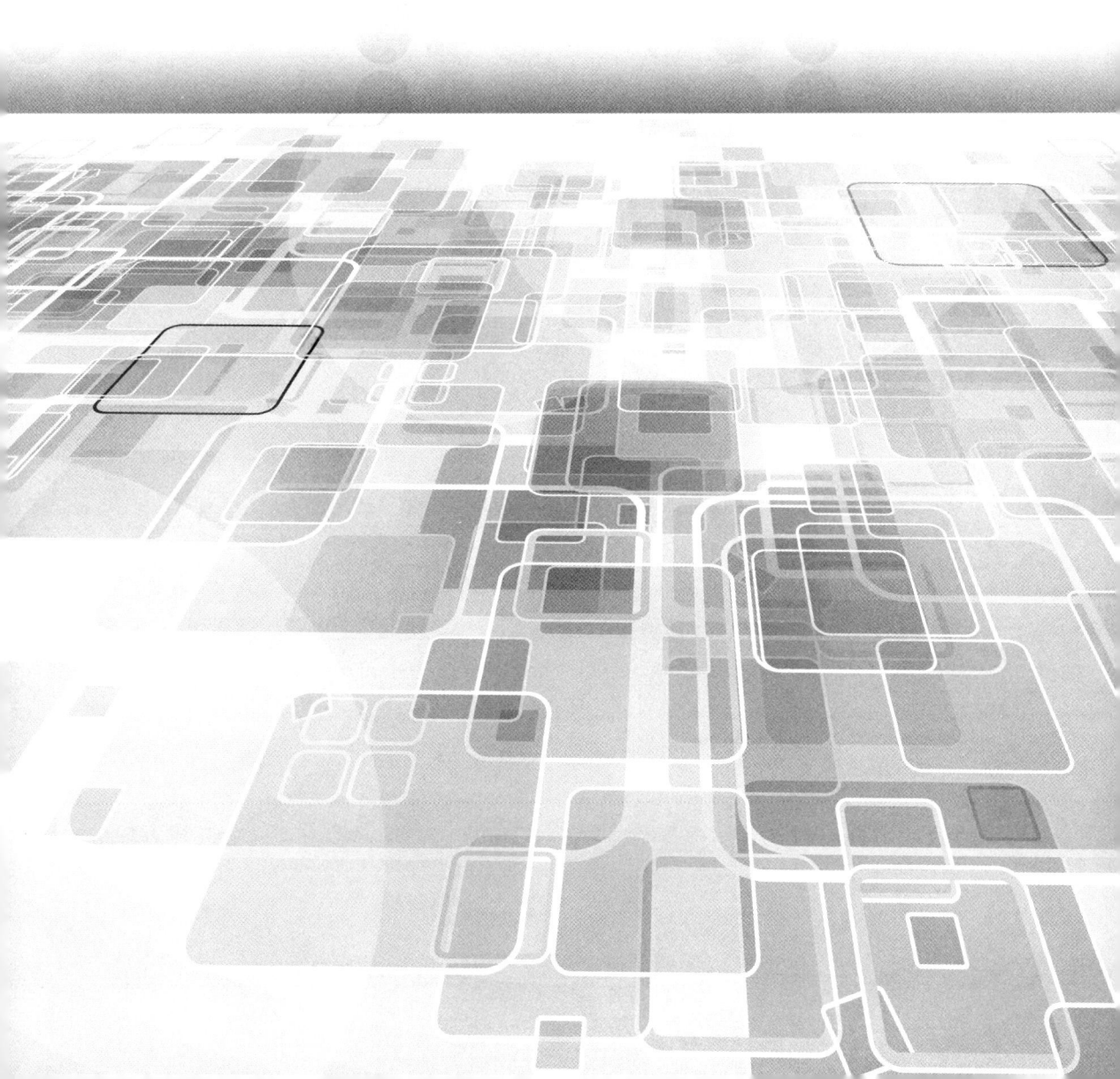

第二章

黄花蒿的研究

数字版权保护技术带来的变化*

李嘉俊

随着互联网技术的快速发展,在网上交易和传播的电子书、视频、图片、PPT、DOC等格式的文件越来越多,图书的网络版和传统图书的数字化是不可避免的。但是这些在网络上传播的数字化内容,很容易就被人们复制粘贴下来,上传到网盘里、文库里进行共享,不断地传递,所以目前传统图书的电子版以及网络出版图书都十分需要的就是版权的保护。如何做好版权的保护是近几年来IT技术行业以及国家有关部门工作的重点和难点。

在进入21世纪以前,版权的纠纷相对较少,对图书等传统作品的保护都是通过相关的法律和一定的管理机构来实行。[1] 之后慢慢地有了P2P技术,网络传播的东西就越来越多,许多的电影、小说在网络上基本上都可以免费地找到,盗版现象也逐渐多了起来。传统的保护方式已经不能满足数字化内容的要求。所以版权的保护工作就越来越受到各界的认可。电影、视频、音频的版权保护已经做得日益成熟了,基本上现在已经不能在网盘上下载到侵权的电影视频了。而像我们百科全书这样的工具书目前正需要扩大其影响力。为了适应时代的发展,我们需要把传统图书网络化,自然不可避免版权保护这样的问题。近几年来,国家新闻出版广电总局的数字版权保护技术研发工程的成果在一些出版社进行了应用的示范。基于方正Apabi的数字版权保护技术,本文就将对应用示范过程中,数字版权保护技术的介绍和对出版社传统工具书的影响和改变进行论述。

1. 数字版权保护技术国内外研究发展现状

在美国的数字出版领域,大概分在线课堂、电子书、在线课外辅导、在线测试、家庭作业管理等几种出版模式。数字加密技术、电子签名技术、指纹技术在数字出版保护的过程中应用得比较广泛。其中使用比较成熟的就是DRM技术。传统的DRM技术主要是数字加密、身份的认证、硬件许可和许可的管理。亚马逊2007年发布了kindle,让电子书有了一定的保护。用户在亚马逊官网购买下载电子书后只能在kindle上面进行阅读,比较有效地保护了电子书的版权。在当今美国市场,各种各样的电子阅读器供消费者去选择,有多功能书写板、平板电脑、跨平台电子阅读器、专用阅读器。亚马逊采用专用格式的电子书文件格式,通过唯一方法编辑。这样电子书就仅能给自定义的用户使用,这个文件格式就

---

* 本文选自《现代国企研究》,第2期,2016年1月(下),第207页、第209页

是 .azw 文件。Apple 也在电子书的市场占据一定的份额，随着 iPhone 和 iPad 销量的增加，苹果推出了一些电子书的 APP，用户可以通过 APP 阅读电子书。

国内的数字版权保护技术发展得还不是特别的好，目前方正 Apabi 的 DRM 技术对出版领域有很大的帮助。Apabi 的 DRM 技术实现了对数字内容的制作、加密、发布、销售，相比于国外对电子书单一的形式有很大优势。21 世纪以来，Apabi 的版权保护技术不断地走向成熟，在出版领域已经有了不少成功的实例。方正 Apabi 有着本土优势，对中文的支持基本达到了完善程度，个别少数民族文字还在完善。

2. 数字版权保护技术对传统工具书的加工流程

数字版权保护技术主要为了防止网络上的数字内容被非法地复制传播的一种技术。这种技术能有效地使没有授权的用户不能正常地访问被保护的数字内容。将传统工具书制作成能在网络销售的电子版这个过程是版权保护的基础。我们首先通过转换工具把 pdf 格式的工具书转换成 cebx 格式，然后再利用数字出版研发工程研发的图书元数据加工工具，对图书的元数据进行智能化加工。利用该工具可以自定义要添加的元素，例如价格、作者、出版时间、图书分类等等。让传统的工具书更容易更准确地加工成数字内容产品。数字版权保护工作需要从最基础的加工开始，为保护工程打下坚实的基础。

3. 数字版权保护技术对图书进行版权保护号的注册管理

经过加工后的图书，根据其 ISBN 和作者、出版地等信息，可以在数字版权保护工程的数字内容注册管理平台上进行 DRMI 号的注册。然后由版权保护机构的机构管理员进行（具体给出机构名称或性质）审核，通过后获得注册成功的 DRMI 号。消费者购买了成功注册的图书之后可以在数字内容注册管理平台上去查询图书的真伪。数字内容注册管理平台也可以批量注册，方便了出版社用户更快地完成注册工作。

4. 数字内容版权保护技术的加密发布和阅读

注册过 DRIM 号的数字图书，通过数字内容版权保护工程的发布工具进行发布，发布时需要输入从数字内容注册管理平台注册来的 DRMI 号，选择发布的销售平台进行加密发布。购买者用户可以在销售网站的帮助中心，下载数字内容版权保护工程的专用阅读软件，安装完成后在自己账户下，输入阅读工具的硬件信息码之后就可以对购买的图书进行下载阅读了。通过这种方式，如果用户所下载的图书被复制到另外的电脑上是不能进行阅读的。数字版权保护工程正是通过专用的阅读软件、唯一的设备信息、加密的特殊格式的图书来保护版权的。

5. 数字版权保护技术对传统工具书的影响和改变

数字版权保护技术使传统工具书的传播途径更丰富，不再单一地通过纸书的方式。数字版权保护技术通过加密技术保证了数字资源的安全性，对工具书的二次传播加以了限制，传统工具书不再会随意地被复制、传播。数字版权保护技术的出现是数字出版发展的一个必然产物，给传统工具书带来了新的希望，让传统的工具书既享受到了对版权的保护，也充分享受了数字化和物联网带来的便利。使传统的工具书更跟得上信息化时代文化发展的步伐，能加速传统媒体和新媒体的融合。

6. 数字版权保护技术存在的风险和不足之处

在电子书数字版权管理系统中，许可证通过将电子书内容和用户绑定实现许可用户阅读该电子书内容，该许可证会定义有效时间以支持各种可能的商业模式。当许可证到期时如果没有本地时钟安全，一个攻击者可以通过修改本地时钟来继续阅读该电子书。秘钥的存储也存在风险，电子数字版权管理客户端需要存储一些敏感的数据，包括公钥密码的私钥、对称密码的密钥、设备密钥，如果一个攻击者获得用户或者设备的公钥密码，就可以解密整个电子书。同时也存在软硬件环境的风险问题。

数字版权保护技术对数字内容的版权有了一定程度的保护，但是它也带来了一些其他方面的问题。例如，版权保护技术会使读者读书的步骤更繁琐，需要下载单独的阅读软件，输入设备信息码等等，会使得有些读者因为麻烦而不选择购买这些图书，会对图书的销售量产生一定的影响。数字版权保护技术的阅读软件对于多设备的支持还不完善，对一些用户量不是特别大的移动终端还不能很好地兼容。用户的体验也相对较差，用起来不方便，操作很繁琐。

7. 数字版权保护技术的未来展望

数字版权保护技术为数字内容所有者的版权和收入提供了安全保障，其研究已经越来越受到关注。数字版权保护技术是我国信息化建设的重要内容，也是电子书产业可持续发展的关键。数字版权保护技术的不断推广和不断地创新进一步保障了出版商、各大运营商和用户的相关利益，从而使电子书内容向着良性循环的方向发展。数字版权保护技术正在走向成熟。目前DRM技术已经在电子书、音乐、电影、软件等领域得到了一定的应用，但还存在一些难点问题有待解决。相信未来数字版权保护技术一定可以支持各种复杂的软硬件环境，支持多种满足市场的服务方式（搜索、订阅、借阅、阅读、章节等），支持更多种格式文件的保护。数字版权保护技术也一定会不断地优化，使保护过程更简单，让版权所有者和读者更方便。

参考文献

[1] 吕志军. 数字出版对传统出版业务流程的影响[J]. 大学出版. 2007（2）.

[2] 王艾. DRM：数字出版的攻与守[J]. 出版广角. 2012（7）：35-37.

[3] 岳建光. 科技出版社传统专业工具书的数字化转型探索[J]. 科技与出版. 2013（6）：22-24.

[4] 余银燕，汤帜. 一种具有硬件适应性的数字版权保护机制[J]. 北京大学学报. 2005（5）：800-808.

[5] 范科峰，莫玮，曹山，赵新华. 裴庆祺. 数字版权管理技术及应勇研究进展[J]. 电子学报. 2007（6）.

[6] 汪保友，王俊杰. 数字水印与版权保护［J］. 计算机应用与软件. 2004（1）.

[7] 胡梦云. 数字环境下版权保护模式研究［D］. 北京：中国政法大学. 2011.

[8] 司端峰. 王益冬. 多媒体数字版权保护系统的研究与实现[J]. 北京大学学报. 2005（5）.

访问控制模型研究进展及发展趋势*

李凤华　苏铓　史国振　马建峰

1　引言

访问控制技术是信息系统安全的核心技术之一,通过对用户访问资源的活动进行有效监控,使合法的用户在合法的时间内获得有效的系统访问权限,防止非授权用户访问系统资源。该技术兴起于20世纪70年代,最初是为了解决大型主机上共享数据授权访问的管理问题。根据访问控制策略类型的差异,早期的安全策略分为自主访问控制(Discretionary Access Control,DAC)和强制访问控制(Mandatory Access Control,MAC)两种类型。但是,随着计算机和网络技术的发展,DAC、MAC已经不能满足实际应用的需求,为此出现了基于角色的访问控制模型(Role-Based Access Control,RBAC)[1,2]。RBAC将用户映射到角色,用户通过角色享有许可。该模型通过定义不同的角色、角色的继承关系、角色之间的联系以及相应的限制,动态或静态地规范用户的行为。作为现在访问控制模型研究的基石,RBAC一直是访问控制领域的研究热点,先后出现了RBAC96[2]、ARBAC97(Administrative RBAC97)[3]、ARBAC99[4]、ARBAC02[5]和NIST RBAC(National Institute of Standards and Technology RBAC)[6]等一系列更加完善的基于角色的访问控制模型。RBAC的出现基本解决了DAC由于灵活性造成的安全问题和MAC不支持完整性保护所导致的局限性问题,此后的数年间,访问控制模型的发展呈现出相对稳定的态势。访问控制技术迅速应用于信息系统的各个领域,与信息加密、身份认证、安全审计、入侵检测、系统恢复、风险分析和安全保障等理论与技术有机结合,实现了信息系统安全可靠的存储访问与传输,有效防止了非授权的信息访问和信息泄密[7,8]。随着信息技术的发展以及分布式计算的出现,信息的交互从局域网逐渐转向广域网,各种信息系统通过因特网互联、互接的趋势越来越明显。单纯的RBAC模型已经不能适应这种新型网络环境的要求,为了保证信息访问的合法性、安全性以及可控性,访问控制模型需要考虑环境和时态等多种因素。在开放式网络环境下,信息系统要求对用户和信息资源进行分级的访问控制和管理,"域"的概念被引入了访问控制模型的研究中,先后出现了基于任务的访问控制模型、面向分布式的访问控制模型和与时空相关的访问控制模型。

---

* 本文选自《电子学报》,第4期,2012年4月,第805–813页

泛在计算、移动计算、云计算等新型计算模式的出现推动了互联网的进步，同时也为访问控制模型的研究提出了新的挑战。在具有异构性和多样性特征的网络环境下，访问控制技术向细粒度、分层次的方向发展，授权依据开始逐渐面向主、客体的安全属性，出现了基于信任、基于属性和基于行为等一系列基于安全属性的新型访问控制模型及其管理模型。

2　基于任务的访问控制模型

随着数据库、网络和分布式计算的发展，组织任务进一步自动化，这促使人们将安全问题方面的注意力从独立的计算机系统中静止的主体和客体保护转移到随着任务的执行而进行动态授权的保护上。

1997 年 Thomas 等人采用"面向任务"的观点，提出了基于任务的访问控制模型（Task-Based Access Control, TBAC），从任务的角度来建立安全模型和实现安全机制，在任务处理的过程中提供了动态实时的安全管理[9~11]。该模型能够对不同工作流实行不同的访问控制策略，并且能够对同一工作流的不同任务实例实行不同的访问控制策略，适用于工作流、分布式、多点访问控制的信息处理以及安全工作流的管理。

2003 年，为了满足大型企业对安全信息管理的需求，出现了将 TBAC 和 RBAC 融合的基于任务—角色的访问控制模型（Task-Role Based Access Control, TRBAC）[12]。随后，文献[13]在 RBAC 模型的基础上深入分析了转授权问题，提出了基于角色和任务的转授权模型 TRBDM（Task and Role-Based Delegation Model），但文献[13]仅是从概念角度引入了转授权的静态责任分离约束和动态责任分离约束，并未给出具体分析和相应的形式化表达。

从 20 世纪 90 年代开始，工作流技术引起了计算机安全领域研究人员的普遍关注。工作流是为完成某一目标而由多个相关任务构成的业务流程，它根据一系列定义的规则，使数据在不同的执行用户间进行传递与执行[14]。当数据在工作流中流动时，执行操作的用户在不断改变，用户的权限也在改变，采用传统的访问控制技术已经不能满足动态授权的安全需求。2000 年 Knorr 在研究 Petri 网中工作流的动态访问控制的基础上，提出了利用工作流动态构建访问控制矩阵的方法[15]。随后，文献[16]研究了工作流访问控制模型中用户的层次，设计了一种构建典型用户层次的方法，该方法可以直接应用于支持用户层次的 RBAC；文献[17]将 RBAC 应用于可扩展的工作流系统中，在确保工作流系统可扩展的前提下，该模型能够有效增强对授权访问工作流系统用户的安全控制。但是，这些文献缺乏对权责分离问题和工作流访问控制转授权问题的论述。

3　面向分布式和跨域的访问控制模型

随着分布式技术的飞速发展和普遍应用，出现了多种不同形式的分布式系统，协同工作和跨域访问是分布式系统中的两大特点，为此出现了基于团队的访问控制模型等针对分布式系统的访问控制模型。

3.1 基于团队的访问控制模型

基于团队的访问控制（Team-based access control，TMAC）[18]提供了一种以团队为核心，将 RBAC 用于团队协作环境的解决方法。TMAC 旨在解决协作环境中的两个安全需求，首先是混合访问控制模型的需求，该混合模型具有跨对象基于角色的权限，但需要对具有某些角色的个人用户和对象实施基于身份的细粒度访问控制。其次需要区分权限分配的被动概念和基于上下文授权激活的主动概念。Alotaiby 等人对该模型进行了扩展，提出 TMAC04 模型[19]，该模型允许特定用户在上下文有限和新权限组织中现有角色的基础上加入团队执行所需的操作。

3.2 分布式基于角色的访问控制模型

一个分布式管理系统有多个不同的管理域，每个域中包含客户、服务器、域安全管理器和外域安全管理器。目标导向类访问控制模型（Object oriented RBAC，ORBAC）[20]建立在分布式管理系统的基础上，能够完整地实现原始 RBAC 模型，并且实现了多域访问控制。文献[21]基于 RBAC 提出了分布式基于角色的访问控制模型（Distributed Role-Based Access Control，dRBAC）。该模型利用 PKI 识别信任敏感操作实体的身份和验证委托证书，在跨多个管理域的动态协作环境中实现了资源的访问控制，为域间协作提供了一种可扩展的分布式信任管理和访问控制机制。文献[22]针对在分布式协同操作环境中基于角色的访问控制在利用角色映射的方式时可能存在的安全问题，提出了一种适用于分布式协同操作环境的 RBAC 模型（Role-Based Access Control model for distributed cooperation environment，RBAC-DC），但是该文献并未对模型中的角色层次和角色约束进行论述。为此，文献[23]提出的可约束的分布式 RBAC 模型，定义了适用于分布式远程资源共享服务的主体、角色、分布式角色、权限以及自组织的概念。该模型支持时态约束、势约束和上下文约束，从而能够支持访问控制更多的语义表达，并允许资源提供者和签署机构确定更高级别的安全组织策略。

3.3 基于开放式系统的访问控制模型

文献[24]提出的基于开放式系统的访问控制模型（Open Architecture for Securely Interworking Services RBAC，OASIS RBAC）是一种在开放的分布式环境中用于实现安全互操作的访问控制模型。该模型旨在使自主管理域指定其自身的访问控制策略，为了支持优先级管理，该模型引入了委派的概念，具有特定角色的用户能够利用委派证书授权其他用户。

3.4 基于域的访问控制模型

基于域的访问控制模型也是用于分布式系统间协同工作的模型，主要用于分散的多个管理者之间进行协同工作的多域应用环境。Shafiq 等人提出了基于域的访问控制模型，该模型是一种可以将多域间异构的 RBAC 策略统一应用于全局 RBAC 策略，并在不同的域之间实现资源安全共享的整合框架[25]。该整合方法包括混合和消除冲突两个过程，首先将各个协作域的访问控制策略在全局系统中进行综合；之后以一种优化的方法在全局系统中对冲突的部分加以消除。文献[26]通过分析跨域计算网格、P2P 系统以及 WEB 服务等典型的分布式系统，提出了一种策略域访问控制模型（Policy Domain Access Control，

PDAC），将分布式系统的节点抽象为一个域，并且为这个定义的域添加策略选择机制，从而使该域能够进行访问控制。但是文献［26］并未对PDAC模型的信任评估进行定义和论述。

3.5 使用控制模型

文献［27］提出的使用控制模型（Usage Control，U-CON），主要研究传统的访问控制、信任管理、数字版权保护等问题。Park等人将认证、职责和条件整合到U-CON中，提出了一种扩展的UCON，即$UCON_{ABC}$模型[28]。随后，文献［29］利用Lamport时序逻辑研究了UCON以及$UCON_{ABC}$的逻辑规范；文献［30］对UCON模型进行了形式化分析，提出了使用现行时序逻辑进行UCON模型检测的方法；文献［31］通过构造形式化模型的方法得出一些使用控制模型的安全结论，并且分析了关于授权中使用控制模型（$UCON_{onA}$）的安全性；文献［32］针对跨域访问过程中的协调性问题，提出了基于UCON的跨域访问模型（xDUCON）；文献［33］通过对Web服务中使用访问控制的研究，将信任的概念引入跨域使用控制模型中；文献［34］将风险评估的方法引入UCON的授权机制中，提高了使用访问控制模型的灵活性和安全性。使用控制模型的提出主要是面向分布式环境的访问控制需求，文献［35］提出了一种分布式计算环境下使用控制的实施方案。虽然UCON模型在分布式、跨域环境下具有明显的优势，但是该模型的授权管理较为复杂。

4 与时空相关的访问控制模型

4.1 上下文相关的访问控制模型

传统的访问控制模型都是非上下文敏感的，需要复杂而静态的认证基础设施。此外，在某些应用中，与用户的标识相比，访问控制更加依赖于用户的上下文，上下文敏感的访问控制模型[36]应运而生。上下文相关的访问控制模型主要包含基于空间上下文的访问控制模型[37]、Location-aware RBAC[38~40]模型和GEO-RBAC[41,42]模型。

在无线和移动网络中，有许多基于位置的服务和基于位置的移动应用程序，因而需要位置感知访问控制系统的支持。空间信息在这些模型中被看成是一个关键的上下文信息。文献［40］提出了一个形式化的访问控制模型SC-RBAC来保证位置感知应用程序的安全，通过引入空间角色的概念将空间上下文集成到角色中，并引入了逻辑位置域的概念来说明角色的空间边界，可根据用户的当前位置来判断会话中哪些角色是有效的，并为受限的SC-RBAC模型确定空间职责隔离限制、基于位置的基数限制和基于位置的时序限制。

Ardagna提出的基于位置的访问控制模型（Location-Based Access Control）旨在将位置信息整合到普通的访问控制模型中，在进行访问授权时能够考虑用户的位置因素[41]。在位置感知的应用程序中，用户经常被分为不同的类别，因此可以对RBAC模型加以改进和扩展，使其支持基于位置和空间的访问控制。Ray等人提出了一种位置感知的RBAC模型，将RBAC中的组件和位置信息联系起来，并根据位置信息确定一个主体对客体是否具有访问权限[42,43]。该模型讨论了RBAC中不同组件与位置的关系，但没有考虑到时态和环境对访问控制的影响。

为了给实际的移动应用提供一种完整的可扩展的空间上下文访问控制模型框架，Bertino 等人对基于空间和位置的 RBAC 模型进行扩展，提出了 GEO-RBAC 访问控制模型[41,42]，该模型具有两个显著特征：一是利用空间实体来描述客体、用户位置和基于地理位置的角色，角色通过用户的位置进行激活；二是支持物理位置和逻辑位置。针对以往空间数据的访问控制中不能同时支持矢量数据和栅格数据，并且效率较低的问题，文献[43]提出一种面向空间索引树的访问控制模型，该模型为栅格数据和矢量数据提供了更为有效的访问控制方法。

4.2 基于时态的访问控制模型

现有的 RBAC 等访问控制模型对时间约束的支持功能相对简单，对时态对象的存取控制建模能力弱。在绝大多数信息系统中，时间因素无处不在，用户仅在特定的时间段具有特定的角色，因此迫切需要 RBAC 模型能够支持复杂的时间约束建模。

文献[44]提出了一种基于时态特性的访问控制模型（Temporal Role-Based Access Control，TRBAC），将时态约束加入到 RBAC 中。该模型带有时态约束，但是没有考虑对用户—角色分配和角色—权限分配的时态因素。文献[45]提出的时态模型把模型要素及其关系上的时态约束嵌入到模型中，通过定义新的时态继承机制实现动态基于角色的存取控制，该模型能够有效减少约束规则库中的规则数量，提高存取控制效率；文献[46]将基于时态特征的访问控制模型中的单一主体扩展为多主体，使其更适合现有的复杂网络环境。TRBAC 模型仅对角色增加了时态约束，并未对其他要素增加约束。Joshi 等人提出的通用基于时态的访问控制模型（Generalized Temporal Role-Based Access Control，GTRBAC）是对 TRBAC 的扩展[47]，该模型提供了更加广泛的时态约束，并且支持细粒度的基于时态的访问控制策略。文献[48,49]分别提出了基于时态特征的位置感知 RBAC 模型（Temporal and Location-based RBAC，TLRBAC）和基于尺度的时空 RBAC 模型（Role-Based Access Control Model Based on Space, Time and Scale STS-RBAC）。

5 基于安全属性的访问控制模型

5.1 基于信任的访问控制模型

Sudip Chakrabony 等在文献[50]中提出了基于信任的访问控制模型 TrustBAC（Trust based access control model）。该模型首先为用户划分信任级，然后通过信任级别决定角色。文献[51]将时态的概念引入 TrustBAC 模型中，为诸如在线应用等细粒度访问控制规则的制定提供了更为灵活的方法。文献[52]针对信任的主观性、模糊性与不确定性，建立了包括信任综合评价与信任计算的信任度量化模型。

5.2 基于属性的访问控制模型

基于属性的访问控制（Attribute-Based Access Control，ABAC）针对目前复杂信息系统中的细粒度访问控制和大规模用户动态扩展问题，将实体属性（组）的概念贯穿于访问控制策略、模型和实现机制三个层次，通过对主体、客体、权限和环境属性的统一建模，描述授权和访问控制约束，使其具有足够的灵活性和可扩展性。该机制广泛应用于大型分布式环境[53,54]、Web 服务系统[55~57]、网格计算[58]以及消息共享和管理[59,60]中。文献［61］针对云计算存储服务中服务提供者信任域不同的特点，提出了一种基于属性的细粒度分层访问控制机制 HBAE（Hierarchical Attribute-Based Encryption），并且对约束条件进行了描述。文献［62］则针对云存储基于密文的访问控制问题，提出了一种云存储密文访问控制方法 AB-ACCS，通过控制数据的密文属性进行权限管理，有效地降低了权限管理的难度。

5.3 基于行为的访问控制模型

随着移动互联网和移动计算的广泛应用，多网融合的通信网络系统已是一个异构的、开放的、分布式的和支持移动计算的网络系统。各种网络、信息系统通过 Internet 互联的趋势越来越明显，从而满足了人们日益增长的开放互联的个性化服务需求，这决定了在开放网络环境下传播信息的方式是多样化的。虽然上述部分模型中已考虑了与访问控制相关的时态因素和位置因素，但现有的模型都没有对移动计算下角色所处环境（各种客观因素组成的环境要素，如场所物理位置、网络位置、逻辑位置、硬件平台、软件平台等）对访问控制的影响进行详细分析，故上述模型无法支持开放网络环境下的移动计算。为此，文献［63］提出了"行为"的概念，综合角色、时态状态和环境状态等相关安全信息，提出了基于行为的访问控制模型（Action-Based Access Control，ABAC），文献［64］讨论了该模型中角色、时态状态和环境状态之间的相互关系，并且对行为状态管理函数进行了形式化描述。通过将角色、时间和环境综合考虑，可以使 ABAC 灵活地处理各种信息系统中的访问控制问题。文献［65］基于 ABAC 模型，针对协作信息系统面临的资源授权决策问题，提出了协作信息系统访问控制机制的流程，并给出了相应的安全关联及其产生方法，以及一种安全认证协议。文献［66］给出了一种基于 ABAC 应用于 Web 服务的安全体系结构。

该 ABAC 模型继承了传统访问控制中角色和角色控制的理念，综合考虑了时态和环境约束，而且支持移动计算中接入用户、接入位置、接入的具体业务以及接入平台随机和不可预知的特点，具有更为广泛的应用范围，该模型能够更加有效地解决网络环境下支持移动计算的信息系统中的访问控制问题。但是行为中角色、时态、环境三者之间的约束关系和管理策略问题还有待进一步研究。

6 策略冲突检测与消解

由于不同信息系统之间的差异，相应的安全策略存在策略不一致、语义不同或相互矛盾的问题，指定的措施或给定的结论之间也存在着相互抵触的情况。这些都有可能造成访问控制的错误裁决，因此，消解访问控制策略的冲突至关重要。访问控制技术的研究提出了大量的检测与消除方法[67,68]。文献［68］提出了一种基于 ponder 语言的角色、域和元素的策略冲突检测与消解方法；访问控制策略标记语言 XACML[69,70]基于属性匹配机制定义了策略规则，在传统的分布式环境的访问控制策略的执行中得到了广泛应用。XACML 标准包含了冲突检测算法，能够减少策略冲突对访问请求的影响。文献［71］分析了 XACML 中属性层次操作关联引发的各种规则冲突类型，给出了基于属性层次操作关联的冲突检测算法和基于状态相关性的其他类型冲突检测算法。Bonatti 等[72]针对基于属性的访问控制,将访问控制策略形式化为主体、客体和行为三元组授权集合,用合成代数组合安全策略,利用逻辑设计和局部评估技术来评估代数表达式,从而实现冲突的检测与消解。文献[73]则提出了基于逻辑编程的策略冲突检测与消解方法;文献[74]通过对分布式系统中元素之间的关系进行研究,统一抽象出有向无环图,提出了一种基于有向图的冲突检测方法。文献[75]以有限自动机理论为基础,提出了相应的冲突检测方法。但是上述方法仅仅针对某种特定的安全策略,缺乏扩展性,而且算法复杂度较大。

针对分布式系统节点内的冲突检测问题,文献[76]提出了通过状态转换方式进行冲突检测的方案。为了解决冲突检测机制依赖于管理员的问题,文献[77]提了一种应用于可信可控网络的冲突检测机制。多级安全策略冲突与消除技术由于等级保护环境下信息系统多级、分布的特征而变得更为复杂,国内外在该方面的研究较少。如何在泛在网络环境下结合新型的访问控制策略进行冲突的检测与消解仍需进一步研究。

7 发展趋势

经过了近五十年的发展,访问控制模型的研究取得了丰硕成果。结构化文档[78]等新型网络信息表现方式的出现,加速了信息传播速度,也带来了对象化、细粒度的安全分级数据管理问题;泛在计算、移动计算、云计算满足了人们日益增长的开放互联的个性服务需求,也带来了新的访问控制问题。面向信息物理社会的泛在网络互联环境,基于分布式、不确定、动态交互的分布式计算、移动计算、云计算和泛在计算等计算模式的信息传播与访问方式,现有的访问控制模型不能解决结构化文档的实时动态重组、多级安全和细粒度控制而引起的策略可伸缩调整、策略冲突与消解、结构化文档内容变更轨迹的过程追踪与回溯等新的访问控制安全问题。现有的访问控制模型虽然已逐步考虑了与安全相关的时空因素和环境因素,但是仍然有许多尚待解决的问题。访问控制技术的发展将呈现如下趋势:

(1) 如何面向信息物理社会的泛在网络互联环境中分布式计算、移动计算、云计算和泛在计算等计算模式的信息传播与多模式访问方式,研究细粒度多级安全的访问控制模型及其策略;

(2) 针对用户移动办公时跨域、跨终端显现/处理设备等环境状态改变和时间状态变更时,研究访问权限的可伸缩性动态调整方法;

(3) 研究区域网络边界内部策略和多级互联外部策略冲突与消解方法,研究多级安全策略冲突检测与消解模型;

(4) 研究结构化文档内容变更轨迹或访问授权的过程追踪与回溯方法。

参考文献

[1] D F Ferraiolo, D R Kuhn. Role-based access control [A]. In Proceedings of the 15th National Computer Security Conference [C]. Baltimore, USA, 1992, 08.554 – 563.

[2] R Sandhu, E Coyne, H Feinstein, et al. Role-based access control models [J]. IEEE Computer, 1996, 02, 29 (2): 38–47.

[3] R Sandhu, V Bhamidipati, Q Munawer. The ARBAC97 model for role-based administration of roles [J]. ACM Transactions on Information and System Security, 1999, 02, 2 (1): 105–135.

[4] R Sandhu, Q Munawer. The ARBAC99 model for administration of roles [A]. In Proceedings of the 15th Annual Computer Security Applications Conference (ACSAC. 99) [C]. Scottsdale, AZ, USA, IEEE Computer Society, 1999, 12. 229–238.

[5] S Oh, R Sandhu, X W Zhang. An effective role administration model using organization structure [J]. ACM Transactions on Information and System Security, 2006, 05, 9 (2): 113–137.

[6] D F Ferraio lo, R Sandhu, S Gavrila, et al. Proposed NIST standard for role-based access control [J]. ACM Transactions on Information and System Security, 2001, 08, 4 (3): 224–274.

[7] J M a, K Adi, M M ejri, et al. Risk analysis in access control systems [A]. In Proceedings of the Eighth Annual International Conference on Privacy, Security and Trust [C]. Ottawa, ON, IEEE Press, 2010, 08. 160–166.

[8] C Y Pang, D Hansen, A Maeder. Managing RBAC States with transitive relations [A]. In Proceedings of the 2nd ACM symposium on Information, computer and communications security (ASIACCS, 07) [C]. Singapore, 2007, 03. 139–148.

[9] R Thomas, R Sandhu. Task-based authorization controls (TBAC): A Family of models for active and enterprise oriented authorization management [A]. In Proceedings of the 11th IFIP WG11. 3 Conference on Database Security [C]. Lake Tahoe, 1997, 08. 166–181.

[10] G Coulouris, J Dollimore, M Roberts. Role and task-based access control in the PerD iS groupware platform [A]. In Proceedings of the 3rd ACM Workshop Role-Based Access Control [C]. Fairfax, VA, U SA, ACM Press, 1998, 10. 115–121.

[11] 邓集波, 洪帆. 基于任务的访问控制模型[J]. 软件学报, 2003, 01, 14 (1): 76–81.
Deng Jibo, Hong Fan. Task-based access control model [J]. Journal of Software, 2003, 01, 14 (1): 76–81 (in Chinese).

[12] O Sejong, P Seog. Task-ro le-based access control model [J]. Information System, 2003, (28): 533–562.

[13] 朱君. 角色协同中群体感知和访问控制技术研究 [D]. 广州: 中山大学计算机软件与理论博士学位论文. 2009.
Zhu Jun. Research on group awareness and access control technology of role co operation [D]. Guangzhou: Computer Science of Sun Yat-sen University. 2009 (in Chinese).

[14] E Bertino, E Ferrari, V Atluri. The specification and enforcement of authorization constraints in workflow management systems [J]. ACM Transaction on Information System Securi ty, 1999, 02, 2 (1): 65–104.

[15] K Knorr. Dynamic access control through Petri net workflows [A]. In Proceedings of the 16th Annual Computer Security Applications Conference (ACSAC' 00) [C]. Washington, DC, USA, IEEE Computer Society, 2000, 12. 159–167.

[16] R Botha, J Eloff. Designing role hierarchies for access control in workflow systems [A]. In Proceedings of the 25th International Computer Software and Applications Conference on Invigorating Software Development (COM PSAC' 01) [C]. Washington, DC, USA, IEEE Computer Society, 2001, 10. 117–122.

[17] Y Q Sun, X X M eng, S J Liu, et al. Flexible workflow incorporated with RBAC [A]. In Proceedings of the 9th International Conference in Computer Supported Cooperative Work in Design (CSCWD.05) [C]. UK, LNCS 3865, 2005. 525-534.

[18] R Thomas. Team-based access control (TMAC): A primitive for applying role-based access controls in collaborative environments [A]. In Proceedings of 2nd ACM Workshop on Role-based Access Control [C]. New York, U S, 1997, 12. 13-19.

[19] F T Alotaiby, J X Chen. A model for Team-based access control (TMAC 2004) [A]. In Proceedings of the International Conference on Information Technology: Coding and Computing (IT CC'04) [C]. IEEE Computer Society, 2004, 04. 450-454.

[20] C N Zhang, C G Yang. An Object-oriented RBAC model fordistributed system [A]. In Proceedings of the Working IEEE/ IFIP Conference on Software Architecture (WICSA'01) [C]. Amsterdam, Netherlands, IEEE Press, 2001, 08. 24-32.

[21] E Freudenthal, T Pesin; L Port, et al. dRBAC: D istributed role-based access control fordynamic coalition environments [A]. In Proceedings of the 22nd International Conference on Distributed Computing Systems (ICDCS'02) [C]. Vienna, Austria, IEEE Computer Society, 2002, 07. 411-420.

[22] S Y Liu, H J Huang. Role-based access control for distributed cooperation environment [A]. In Proceedings of 2009 International Conference on Computational Intelligence and Security [C]. Beijing, China, IEEE Computer Society, 2009, 12. 455-459.

[23] M C M a, S Woodhead. Constraint-enabled distributed RBAC for subscription-based remote network services [A]. In Proceedings of the Sixth IEEE International Conference on Computer and Information Technology (CIT'06) [C]. 2006, 09. 01-06.

[24] W Yao, K M oody, J Bacon. A model of OASIS role-based access control and its support for active security [J]. ACM Transactions on Information and System Security, 2002, 06, 5 (4): 492-540.

[25] B Shafiq, J B D Joshi, E Bertino, et al. Secure interoperation in a multi domain environment employing RBAC policies [J]. IEEE Transactions on Knowledge and Data Engineering, 2005, 11, 17 (11): 1557-1577.

[26] X Wu, P D Qian. Research on policy domain access control model in distributed systems [A]. In Proceedings of Nine International Conference on E-Business and Information System Security [C]. WuHan, China, IEEE Press, 2009, 05. 01-06.

[27] J Park, R Sandhu. Towards usage control models: beyond traditional access control [A]. In Proceedings of the 7th ACM Symposium on Access Control Models and Technologies (SACMAT'02) [C]. Monterey, California, USA, 2002, 06. 57-64.

[28] J Park, R Sandhu. The $UCON_{ABC}$ usage control model [J]. ACM Transactions on Information and System Security, 2004, 02, 7 (1): 128-174.

[29] X W Zhang, J Park, F Parisi, et al. A logical specification for usage control [A]. In Proceedings of the 9th ACM symposium on Access control models and techno logies (SACMAT, 04) [C]. Yorktown Heights, New York, USA, 2004, 06. 01-10.

[30] A Pretschner, J Ruesch, C Schaefer, et al. Formal analyses of usage control policies [A]. In Proceedings of the International Conference on Availability, Reliability and Security [C]. Fukuoka, Japan, IEEE Computer Society, 2009, 03. 98-105.

[31] Z G Z hai, J D Wang, Y G Mao. Study and safety analysis on $UCON_{onA}$ model [A]. In Proceedings of the First International Workshop on Database Technology and Applications [C]. Wuhan, China, IEEE Computer Society, 2009, 04. 103 – 106.

[32] G Russello, N Dulay. xDUCON: Coordinating usage control policies in distributed domains [A]. In Proceedings of the Third International Conference on Network and System Security [C]. Gold Coast, QLD, IEEE Computer Society, 2009, 10. 246 – 253.

[33] G P Zhang, W T Gong, J Z Tian. The research of cross-do-main usage control model in webserv ices [A]. In Proceedings of the Second International Conference on e-Business and Information System Security [C]. Wuhan, China, IEEE Press, 2010, 03. 01 – 05.

[34] L Krautsevich, A Lazouski, F Martinelli, et al. Risk-aware Usage Decision Making in Highly Dynamic Systems [A]. In Proceedings of the Fifth International Conference on Internet Monitoring and Protection [C]. Barcelona, ESP, IEEE Computer Society, 2010, 05. 29 – 34.

[35] 初晓博, 秦宇. 一种基于可信计算的分布式访问控制研究[J]. 计算机学报, 2010, 33 (1): 93 – 102.
Chu Xiaobo, Qin Yu. A distributed usage control system based on trusted computing [J]. Chinese Journal of Computers, 2010, 33 (1): 93 – 102 (in Chinese).

[36] M J Covington, W Long, S Srinivasan. Securing context-aware applications using environment roles. In Pro ceedings of the 6th ACM Symposium on Access Control Models and Technologies. ACM Press, Chantilly, Virginia, USA, 2001, 05. 10 – 20.

[37] 张宏, 贺也平, 石志国. 一个支持空间上下文的访问控制形式模型[J]. 中国科学 E 辑: 信息科学, 2007, 02, 37 (2): 254 – 271.
Zhang Hong, He Yeping, Shi Zhi guo. A formal model for access control with supporting spatial context [J]. Science in China Series F: Information Sciences, 2007, 50 (3): 419 – 439.

[38] C Ardagna, M Cremonini, E Damiani, et al. Supporting location-based conditions in access control policies [A]. In Proceedings of the 2006 ACM Symposium on Information, computer and communications security (ASIACCS' 06) [C]. Taipei, Taiwan, ACM Press, 2006. 212 – 222.

[39] I Ray, L J Yu. Short paper: towards a location-aware role-based access control model [A]. In Proceedings of the First International Conference on Security and Privacy for Emerging Areas in Communications Networks [C]. Athens, Greece, IEEE Computer Society, 2005, 09. 234 – 236.

[40] I Ray, M Kumar, L J Yu. LRBAC: a location-aware role-based access control model [A]. In Proceedings of the Second International Conference on Information Systems Security (ICISS 2006) [C]. Kolkata, India, Springer-Verlag, 2006. 147 – 161.

[41] E Bertino, B Catania, M Damiani, et al. GEO-RBAC: A spatially aware RBAC [A]. In Proceedings of the 10th ACM Symposium on Access Control Models and Technologies [C]. New York, ACM Press, 2005, 07. 29 – 37.

[42] M Damiani, E Bertino, B Catania. GEO-RBAC: a spatially aware RBAC [J]. ACM Transactions on Information and System Security, 2007, 02, 10 (1): 01 – 42.

[43] 张颖君, 冯登国, 陈恺. 面向空间索引树的授权机制[J]. 通信学报, 2010, 09, 31 (9): 64 – 73.
Zhang Yingjun, Feng Dengguo, Chen Kai. Authorization mechanism based on spatial index [J]. Journal on Communications, 2010, 09, 31 (9): 64 – 73.

［44］E Bertino, P Bonatti, E Ferrari. TRBAC: A Temporal Role-Based Access Control Model［J］. ACM Transactions on Information and System Security, 2001, 08, 4（3）: 191－223.

［45］王小明, 赵宗涛. 基于角色的时态对象存取控制模型［J］. 电子学报, 2005, 09, 33（9）: 1634－1638.
Wang Xiaoming, Zhao Zongtao. Role-based access control model of temporal object［J］. Acta Electronica Sinica, 2005, 33（9）: 1634－1638（in Chinese）.

［46］C Z X u, Q X Wang, W M Zhang, et al. Temporal Access Control based on Multiple Subjects［A］. In Proceedings of International Conference on Multimedia Information Networking and Security［C］. HuBei, China, IEEE Computer Society, 2009, 11. 438－441.

［47］J B D Jo shi, E Bertino, U Latif, et al. A generalized temporal role-based access control model［J］. IEEE Transactions on Knowledge and Data Engineering, 2005, 01, 17（1）: 04－23.

［48］H C Chen, S J Wang, J H Wen, et al. Temporal and location-based RBAC model［A］. In Proceedings of the Fifth International Joint Conference on INC, IMS and IDC［C］. Seoul, Korea, IEEE Computer Society, 2009, 08. 2111－2116.

［49］张颖君, 冯登国. 基于尺度的时空RBAC模型［J］. 计算机研究与发展, 2010, 47（7）: 1252－1260.
Zhang Yingjun, Feng Dengguo. A role-based access control model based on space, time and scale［J］. Journal of Computer Research and Development, 2010, 47（7）: 1252－1260（in Chinese）.

［50］S Chakraborty, I Ray. TrustBAC: integrating trust relationships into the RBAC model for access control in open systems［A］. In Proceedings of the 11th ACM Symposium on Access Control Models and Technologies（SACM AT' 2006）［C］. California, USA, 2006, 07. 49－58.

［51］C Z Xu, Y Q Wang, Q Wei, et al. A novel trust model based on temporal historical data for access control［A］. In Proceedings of the International Conference on Computational Intelligence and Security［C］. Beijing, China, IEEE Computer Society, 2009, 12. 446－449.

［52］郎波. 面向分布式系统访问控制的信任度量化模型［J］. 通信学报, 2010, 31（12）: 45－54.
Lang Bo. Access control oriented quantified trust degree representation model for distributed systems［J］. Journal on Communications, 2010, 31（12）: 45－54（in Chinese）.

［53］李晓峰, 冯登国, 陈朝武, 等. 基于属性的访问控制模型［J］. 通信学报, 2008, 04, 29（4）: 90－98.
Li Xiaofeng, Feng Dengguo, Chen Zhaowu, et al. Model for attribute based access control［J］. Journal on Communications, 2008, 04, 29（4）: 90－98（in Chinese）.

［54］王小明, 付红, 张立臣. 基于属性的访问控制研究进展［J］. 电子学报, 2010, 07, 38（7）: 1660－1667.
Wang Xiaoming, Fu Hong, Zhang Lichen. Research progress on attribute-based access control［J］. Acta Electroni ca Sinica, 2010, 07, 38（7）: 1660－1667（in Chinese）.

［55］M Coetzee, J H P Eloff. Towards web service access control［J］. Computers and Security, 2004, 23（7）: 559－570.

［56］V S Mewar, S Aich, S Sural. A ccess control model for web services with attribute disclo sure restriction. In Proceedings of the Second International Conference on Availability, Reliability and Security［C］. Washington, IEEE Computer Society, 2007, 04. 524－531.

［57］B Lang, N Zhao, K Ge, et al. An X ACML policy generating method based on policy view［A］. In

Proceedings of International Conference on Pervasive Computing and Applications [C]. IEEE Press, 2008, 1. 295 – 301.

[58] R Laborde, M Kamel, S Wazan, et al. A secure collaborative web based environment for virtual organizations [J]. International Journal of Web Based Communities, 2009, 05 (2): 273 – 292.

[59] M Pirretti, P Traynor, P M cDaniel, et al. Secure attribute-based systems [A]. In Proceedings of the 13th ACM Coference on Computer and Communication Security [C]. New Y ork, A CM. 2006. 99 – 112.

[60] V Goyal, O Pandey, A Sahai, et al. Attribute-based for encryption for fine-grained access control of encrypted data [A]. In Proceedings of the 13th ACM Conference on Computer and Communications Security [C]. New York, USA, ACM Press, 2006. 89 – 99.

[61] G J Wang, Q Liu, J Wu. Hierarchical attribute-based encryption for fine-grained access control in cloud storageservices [A]. In Proceedings of the 17th ACM conference on Computer and communications security [C]. New York, NY, USA, ACM Press, 2010. 735 – 737.

[62] 洪澄, 张敏, 冯登国. AB-ACCS: 一种云存储密文访问控制方法[J]. 计算机研究与发展, 2010, 47 (z1): 259 – 265.
Hong Cheng, Zhang Min, Feng Dengguo. AB-ACCS: A cryp-tographic access control scheme for cloud storage [J]. Journal of Computer Research and Development, 2010, 47 (z1): 259 – 265 (in Chinese).

[63] F H Li, W Wang, J F Ma, et al. Action-based access control model [J]. Chinese of Journal Electronics, 2008, 07, 17 (3): 396 – 401.

[64] 李凤华, 王巍, 马建峰, 等. 基于行为的访问控制模型及其行为管理[J]. 电子学报, 2008, 10, 36 (10): 1881 – 1890.
Li Fenghua, Wang Wei, Ma Jianfeng, et al. Access control model and Administration of action [J]. Acta Electronica Sinica, 2008, 10, 36 (10): 1881 – 1890 (in Chinese).

[65] 李凤华, 王巍, 马建峰, 等. 协作信息系统的访问控制模型及其应用[J]. 通信学报, 2008, 09, 29 (9): 116 – 123.
Li Fenghua, Wang Wei, Ma Jianfeng, et al. Access control model and its application for collaborative system [J]. Journal on Communications. 2008, 09, 29 (9): 116 – 123 (in Chinese).

[66] F H Li, W Wang, J F Ma, et al. Action-based access control for web services [A]. In Proceedings of Fifth International Conference on Information Assurance and Security [C]. Xi'an, China, IEEE Computer Society, 2009, 08. 637 – 642.

[67] E Lupu, M Sloman. Conflicts in policy-based distributed systems management [J]. IEEE Transactions on Software Engineering Management-Special Issue on Inconsistency Management, 1999, 11, 26 (6): 852 – 869.

[68] N Dulay, E Lupu, M Sloman, et al. A policy deployment model for the ponder language [A]. In Proceedings of the IEEE/ IFIP International Symposium on Integrated Network Management (IM '2201) [C]. Seattle, 2001. 01 – 12.

[69] OASIS. XACML 3. 0 work in progress [S]. 2009, 09.

[70] OASIS. XACML v3. 0 administrative policy version 1. 0 [S]. 2009.

[71] 王雅哲, 冯登国. 一种 XACML 规则冲突及冗余分析方法[J]. 计算机学报, 2009, 32 (3): 516 – 530.

Wang Yazhe, Feng Dengguo. A conflict and redundancy analysis method for XACML rules [J]. Chinese Journal of Computers. 2009, 32 (3): 516 - 530 (in Chinese).

[72] P Bonatti, S D Vimercad, P Samarali. An algebra for composing access control policies [J]. ACM Transactions on Information and System Security, 2002, 05 (1): 01 - 35.

[73] J Lobo, R Bhatia, S Naqvi. A policy description language [A]. In Proceedings of the sixteenth National Conference on Artificial Intelligence (AAAI-99) [C]. Orlando, Florida, 1999, 07. 291 - 298.

[74] 姚键, 茅兵, 谢立. 一种基于有向图模型的安全策略冲突检测方法[J]. 计算机研究与发展, 2005, 42 (7): 1108 - 1114.
Yao Jian, Mao Bing, Xie Li. A DAG-based security policy conflicts detection method [J]. Journal of Computer Research and Development, 2005, 42 (7): 1108 - 1114 (in Chinese).

[75] C Basile, A Lioy. Towards an Algebraic Approach to Solve Policy Conflicts [M]. FCS' 04, 2004.

[76] X D Dai, X Y Chen, Y L Wang, *et al*. An improved state transition- based security policy conflict detection algorithm [A]. In Proceedings of the 2010 International Conference on Computational and Information Sciences (ICCIS2010) [C]. Chengdu, Szechwan, China, 2010, 12. 609 - 612.

[77] 曲延盛, 罗军舟, 李伟, 等. 可信可控网络资源控制的冲突检测机制[J]. 通信学报, 2010, 31 (10): 79 - 87.
Qu Yansheng, Luo Junzhou, Li Wei, *et al*. Resource control conflict detection mechanism in trustworthy and controllable network [J]. Journal on Communications, 2010, 31 (10): 79 - 87.

[78] 汤帜. 新一代结构化版式文档技术 [OL]. http: // www. ccf. org. cn/resources/2567814757318/tang12242010 - 12 - 24 - 03_ 32 - 00. pdf.

细粒度超媒体描述模型及其使用机制[*]

苏铓　史国振　李凤华　申莹　黄琼　王苗苗

1 引言

分布式计算、云计算、移动计算等多种计算模式的出现以及手机、移动设备等手持设备的发展,推动了数字媒体技术的进步,并催生出一种具有自适应性强、表达内容丰富的超媒体文档表现形式。超媒体融合了超文本和多媒体两种概念,具有导航和标注的特征[1],针对超媒体最初的研究主要集中在数据模型方面,先后提出了 Hyperbase、Intermedia、gIBIS、HDM 等模型。文献[2]结合上述模型的特点提出了一种动态、可扩展的超媒体数据模型,为超媒体的表示奠定了基础。随着网络技术的发展,网页媒体通过超链接的方式实现了信息的互联,提高了使用互联网查询信息的便利程度,在因特网上存在着数以亿计的超链接,该技术已经成为超媒体研究的重要组成部分,出现了 PageRank、HITS、CLEVER、Web Archaeology 和文献[3]提出的 STED 算法。超链接分析算法主要用于提高 Web 页面信息搜索效率[4,5]。文献[6]给出了一种简单地将传统检索技术与基于链接文本技术相结合的方法。文献[7]提出了一种语义链接分析模型。目前针对超链接的研究主要集中于超链接分析算法、链接描述模型等方面,在超媒体文档安全和权限描述方面鲜有研究。

现在的超媒体包括了文本、音频、视频、图片、3D 图形等多种多样的形式,对于形式多样的超媒体的权限控制需要一种合理的管理来满足用户的需求。文献[8]提供了一种在开放环境下的陌生实体之间进行授权的有效途径,为实现 Internet 环境下网络资源的虚拟化提供了有力的支持。但是,传统信任管理模型大都不能有效支持高细粒度的委托控制,难以保证权限传播的可控性,不利于系统的安全性。文献[9]提出了基于角色的细粒度委托限制框架,将角色分为对象角色和委托角色,实现细粒度的控制,防止了权限滥用,但多个委托限制规则之间可能会产生冲突。文献[10]是通过 Web 系统增加一个 XML 的权限配置文件,将系统的整体权限结构动态地管理起来,而把具体用户的权限存储在数据库中,通过两者的配合使用提高系统权限维护的灵活性,并降低授权管理的复杂性。

目前,多个关联数字媒体文件通常以独立存储、采用数据库的方式进行文档管理,缺乏灵活性。不能满足具有不同权限等级的用户通常希望在进行学术文献阅读的同时能够通

---

[*] 本文选自《通信学报》,第 34 卷 Z1 期,2013 年 8 月,第 223–229 页

过点击获取相应权限等级的相关参考文献的需求。为了应对上述问题,本文在存储介质的性价比、介质存储空间及其价格不再是问题的情况下,提出了一种支持增量修改的超媒体文档权限管理描述模型及其 XML 描述语法体系,并给出了针对该描述模型的超媒体创建、浏览和修改方法以及针对该描述文件的权限描述文件创建、浏览、修改方法。

2 应用场景分析

本节将针对用户所处时态、环境以及具备角色的不同,给出相应的超媒体访问控制应用场景。用户往往希望在进行超媒体文档使用的同时,能够访问文档中的相关参考资料,以便更加全面地去了解文档内容,理解作者所要表达的信息,并给所拥有的超媒体文档设定访问权限,只有符合条件的用户才能对超媒体文档进行使用。如图 1 中所示,同一个用户 A 针对同一个超媒体文档,由于访问时段的限制,所能使用的资源将会不同,上午 8:00~12:00,用户 A 可以使用该文档的视频、3D 图形以及复合对象;而 12:00~17:00 仅能使用该文档的文本和图片对象。同一用户 B 在公司内部和公司外部针对相同超媒体文档的访问权限不同,在公司外部出差时,用户 B 仅仅可以访问并使用文档的文本对象、图片和音频对象;而在公司内部,则可以使用 3D 图形、视频、复合对象等内容。同样在公司内部,不同的用户 A 和用户 B 由于角色的限制,针对同一超媒体文档的使用权限不同。

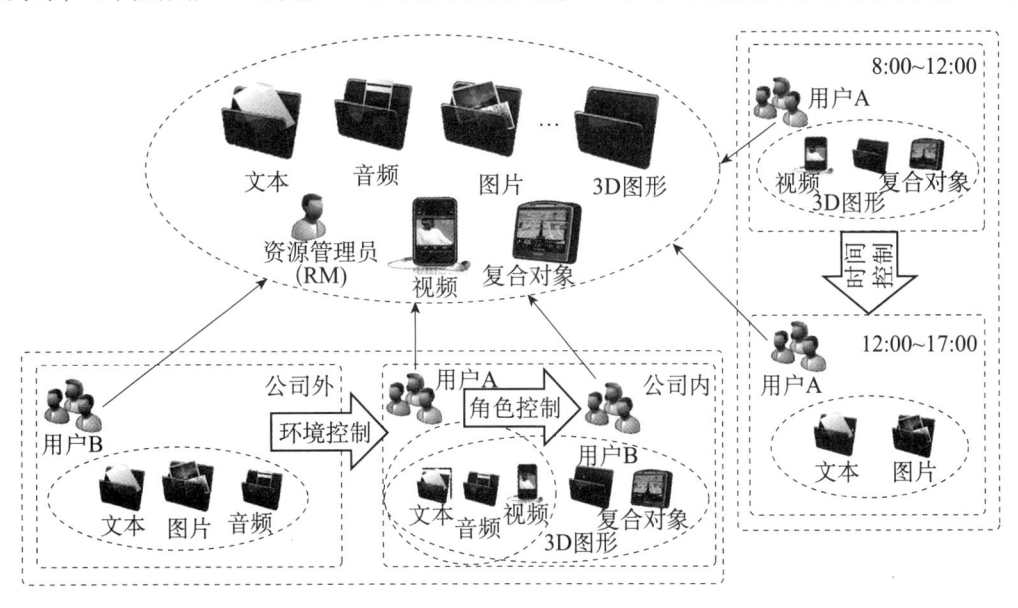

图 1 超媒体文档访问控制场景分析

3 超媒体文档描述模型

3.1 超媒体文档描述模型概述

多维数字媒体文档可以包含版式信息和流式信息,其涵盖资源涉及文字、表单、图像、多媒体、复合对象以及 3D 图形,下面给出超媒体文档权限描述模型,如图 2 所示。

其中超媒体文档对象通过根文档对象 SMr 实现对文档整体对象的管理，SMr 描述了超媒体文档的属性及文档入口；一个超媒体文档中可以包含多个多维数字媒体对象 Mo，每一个多维数字媒体对象中包含文档入口，该对象文档的属性描述、版式和流式信息、资源描述以及相应的物理对象；由于多维数字媒体内容丰富的特点，资源中可以包含文字、表单、3D 对象等，为了满足资源访问控制权限的对象化管理，资源中设置对象权限描述。

该模型对象的 XML 描述语法结构如图 3 所示，生成的 XML 语言描述实例如下：

```
<?xml version="1.0" encoding=UTF-8"?>
<HypermdiaDoc
xmlns:xsi="http://www.w3.org/200
/XMLSchema-instance"
xsi:noNamespaceSchemaLocation="文档描述.xsd">
    <HypermdiaDocEntrance/>
    <HypermdiaDocID/>
    <HypermdiaName/>
    <HypermdiaAuthor/>
    <CreatTime/>
    <ModifyTime/>
    <HypermdiaDocAttrDes/>
    <MDMediaDocADes>
        <BaseInf/>
        <ID/>
        </MDMediaDocADes>
        <MultidimDigMediaDoc>
        <DocEntrance/>
        <DocAttributeDes/>
        <SteamInfo/>
        <FormatInfo/>
        <Resource>
            <type/>
            <security/>
        </Resource>
    </MultidimDigMediaDoc>
    <PhysicalData/>
</HypermdiaDoc>
```

3.2 超媒体文档模型具体实现流程

针对上一节提出的模型及其 XML 描述语法，本节将对模型对应的文档创建、修改、浏览步骤进行设计和说明。

（1）超媒体文档创建

Step1 生成超媒体文档基本信息。

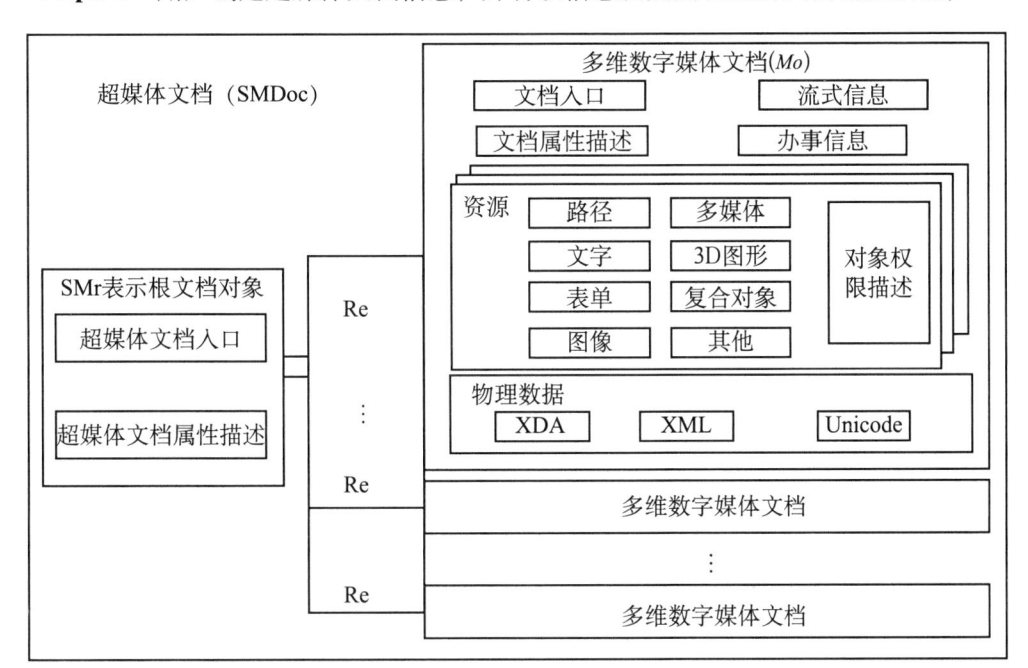

Step1.1 用户创建超媒体文档信息，并将该信息提交到相应的文档创建系统；

图2 一种支持增量修改的超媒体文档

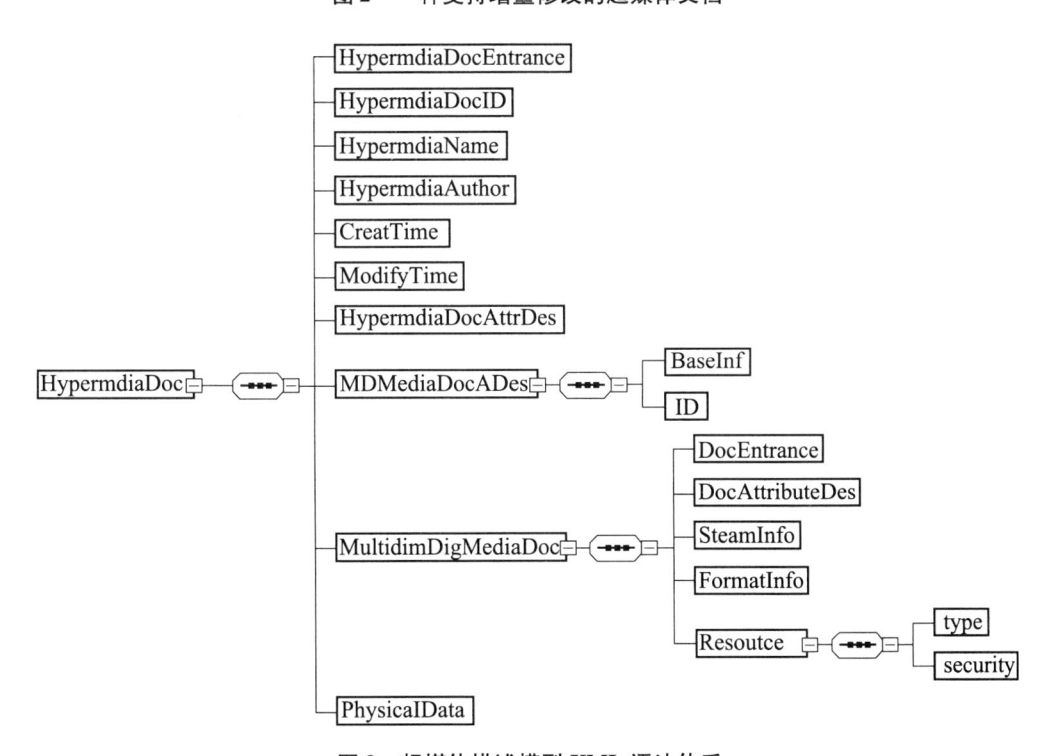

图3 超媒体描述模型 XML 语法体系

Step1.2 系统获取相应的信息，将获取的超媒体文档基本信息填写到 XML 指定标签处，并将修改时间初始化，填写为创建时间。

Step2 关联文档处理。

Step2.1 若用户需要则接收用户填写关联多维数字媒体文档信息，包括多维数字媒体文档的数量、名称、作者等信息；

Step2.2 若不需要则执行 Step5。

Step3 填写关联多维数字媒体文档的属性描述信息。

Step4 填写超媒体文档属性信息。

Step5 生成描述文档，打包封装，完成超媒体文档的创建。

Step6 获取超媒体文档的权限信息，生成权限描述文档，提示用户文档创建成功。

步骤描述如图 4 所示。

（2）超媒体文档的修改步骤

Step1 系统判定用户的身份信息，若为非法用户则返回错误信息。

Step2 用户提交修改申请，文档管理系统进行处理。

Step2.1 系统获取用户信息，包括用户的角色、环境、时态以及名称和唯一标识符；

Step2.2 系统查找超媒体的文档描述信息，包括超媒体文档的属性，即安全属性描述或权限属性描述；

Step2.3 系统根据文档权限属性描述文档，判定用户是否具有提出的修改权限，如具有则执行下一步，否则停止操作，并返回修改失败信息。

Step3 依据用户的要求对超媒体的描述文档进行修改。

Step3.1 修改相应的多维数字媒体文档描述信息；

Step3.2 若涉及多维数字媒体对应资源描述的修改，则进行下一步，否则跳至 Step6。

Step4 依据用户的要求对多维数字媒体对应资源的描述进行相应的修改。

Step5 填写/修改超媒体文档中的修改时间，并返回修改成功信息。

Step6 完成对超媒体文档的修改。步骤描述如图 5 所示。

（3）超媒体文档的浏览步骤

Step1 获取超媒体文档描述信息和用户信息。

Step1.1 获取超媒体文档描述信息，包括文档名称、作者信息、创建的时间等；

Step1.2 获取超媒体文档权限描述信息，包括允许访问的时间信息、地理信息等；

Step1.3 获取用户信息，包括用户角色、环境、时态以及名称和唯一标识符。

Step2 根据获取的超媒体文档权限描述信息，判定用户对该超媒体是否具有提出的查看权限，如具有则执行下一步；否则停止操作，并返回打开失败信息。

Step3 判定用户对关联多维数字媒体文档是否具有访问和使用权限，若有权限，则执行下一步；否则返回没有访问权限信息。

Step4 打开关联多维数字媒体文档，判定用户是否对多维数字媒体对应资源具有访问权限，若有权限，则进行访问，完成对创建的超媒体文档的浏览；否则返回没有访问权

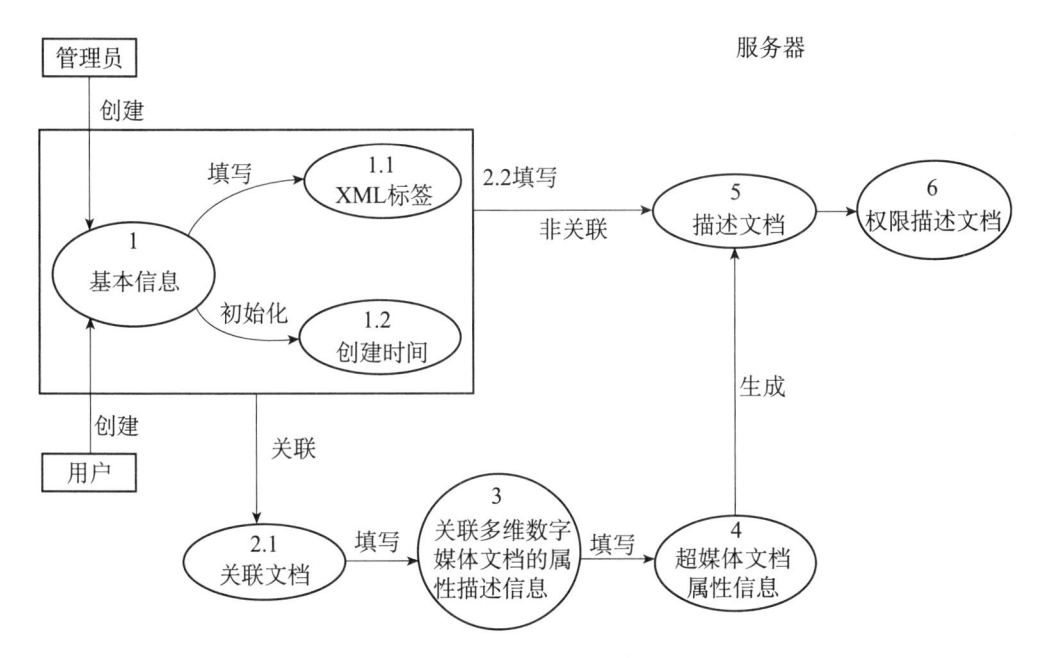

图 4　超媒体文档创建步骤

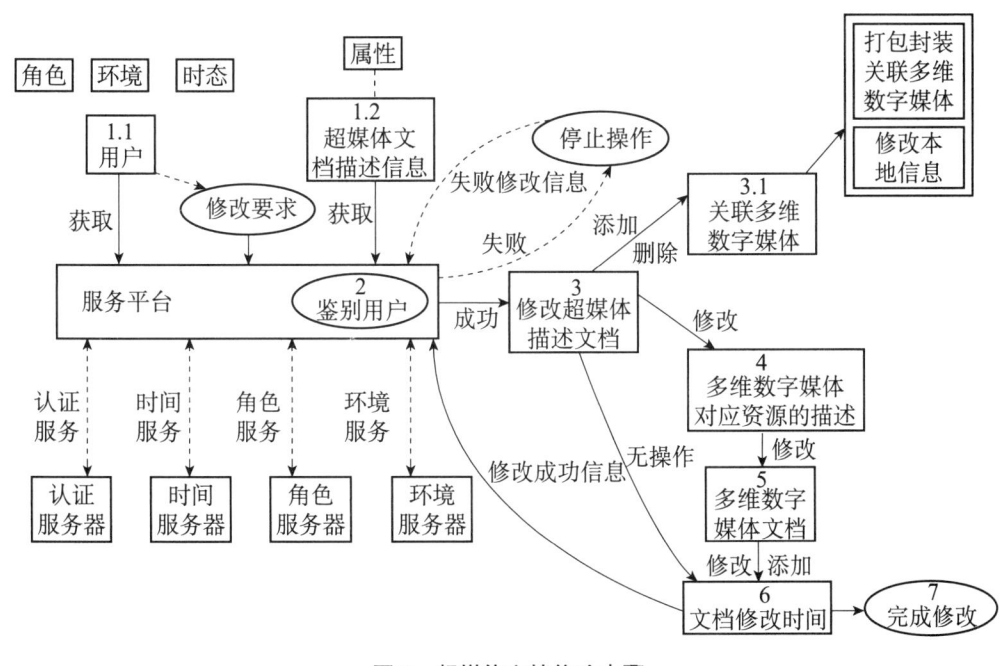

图 5　超媒体文档修改步骤

限信息。

步骤描述如图 6 所示。

上述的方法（1）、（2）、（3）可以实现对本文中提出模型的基本使用，为了能够适应用户可能的自定制需求，XML 描述框架可以依据用户的要求进行扩充。

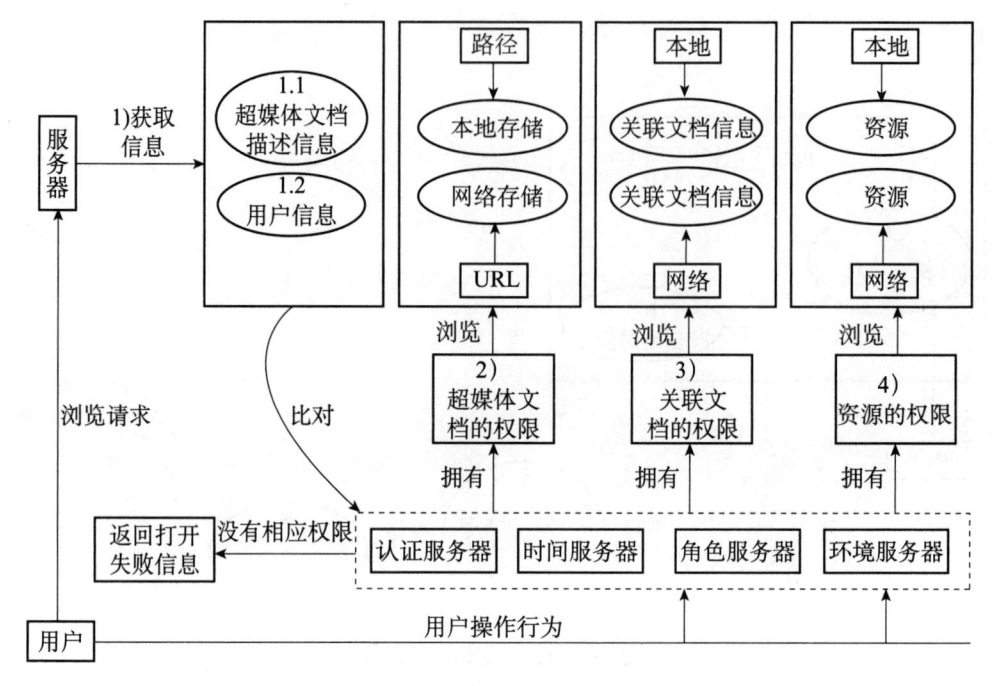

图 6　超媒体文档浏览步骤

4　分析

4.1　安全性

超媒体文档描述模型为超媒体文档及其所包含的资源定义了属性描述标签,该标签可以依据用户意愿进行扩展,包含完整性标记,确保资源在网络传输过程中的完整性和不可篡改性。同时,可以定义对应的加解密算法、工作模式、密钥以及初始化向量。能够保证在文档传输和使用过程中数据信息的机密性。

4.2　对象化访问控制

上述文档描述模型可以依据用户的意愿对超媒体文档及其所包含资源进行任意的划分与描述,通过为不同的划分单元添加相应的文档属性描述实现细粒度的管理与控制。并且,文档属性描述可自定义域属性、时态和环境属性,为用户描述访问时所处的物理环境、软硬件平台、时间状态等信息,并对结构化文档进行对象级的环境、时态约束。文档管理系统通过定义用户与超媒体文档,添加主客体环境、时态标签,实现结构化文档的多要素访问控制,同时,针对不同的安全级别设置不同的访问规则及其操作类型,对文档定义多级安全标记等信息。进一步适用于分布式计算、云计算、泛在计算等复杂网络环境。

5　结束语

超媒体集成多维数字媒体资源与超文本描述于一体,本文在分析了云计算、分布式计算以及移动计算等多种计算环境下多维数字媒体文件表现形式以及多个多维数字媒体文件关联关系的基础上,提出了一个细粒度超媒体文档描述模型,该模型能够对超媒体文档中所包含的数字资源进行对象化的描述,并给出模型对应的 XML 描述语法体系以及相应的创建、修改和浏览的使用方法。从而实现超媒体文档细粒度、对象化的组织管理。

参考文献

[1] 钱培德,吕强,杨季文,等. 一个动态超媒体映射引擎[J]. 软件学报,1999,10 (10): 1114-1120.
QIAN P D, LV Q, YANG J W, et al. A dynamic hypermedia mapping engine [J]. Journal of Software, 1999, 10 (10): 1114-1120.

[2] 马松伟,孙永强. 动态超媒体数据模型[J]. 电子学报,1999,27 (8): 96-98.
MA S W, SUN Y Q. A dynamic hypermedia data model [J]. Acta Electronica Sinica, 1999, 27 (8): 96-98.

[3] 王晓宇,周傲英. 万维网的链接结构分析及其应用综述[J]. 软件学报,2003,14 (10): 1768-1780.
WANG X Y, ZHOU A Y. Linkage analysis for the world wide web and its application: a survey [J]. Journal of Software, 2003, 14 (10): 1768-1780.

[4] YAN L L, WEI Y B, GUI Z J, et al. Research on page rank and hyperlink-induced topic search in web structure mining [A]. Proceedings of the 2011 International Conference on Internet Technology and Applications (iTAP) [C]. Wuhan, China, 2011. 1-4.

[5] HUYNH D T, CAO T H, PHUONG H T, et al. Using hyperlink texts to improve quality of identifying document topics based on wikipedia [A]. Proceedings of International Conference on Knowledge and Systems Engineering (KSE '09) [C]. Hana, Viet Nam, 2009. 249-254.

[6] 张敏,高剑锋,马少平. 基于链接描述文本及其上下文的 Web 信息检索[J]. 计算机研究与发展,2004,41 (1): 221-226.
ZHANG M, GAO J F, MA S P. Anchor text and its context based web information retrieval [J]. Journal of Computer Research and Development, 2004, 41 (1): 221-226.

[7] LIU H S, LIU G, LV Y Q. Semantic hyperlink analysis model [A]. Proceedings of the Fourth International Conference on Semantics, Knowledge and Grid (SKG '08) [C]. Beijing, China, 2008. 416-419.

[8] 翟征德,冯登国,徐震. 细粒度的基于信任度的可控委托授权模型[J]. 软件学报,2007,18 (8): 2002-2015.
ZHAI Z D, FENG D G, XU Z. Fine-grained controllable delegation authorization model based on trustworthiness [J]. Journal of Software, 2007, 18 (8): 2002-2015.

[9] 刘伟,蔡嘉勇,贺也平. 协同环境下基于角色的细粒度委托限制框架. [J]. 通信学报,2008,29 (1): 83-91.
LIU W, CAI J Y, HE Y P. Role-based fine-grained delegation constraint framework in collaborative environments [J]. Journal on Communications, 2008, 29 (1): 83-91.

[10] 薛凯,崔杜武,崔颖安,等. 基于 XML 与数据库技术的权限管理[J]. 计算机工程,2009,35 (20): 148-150.
XUE K, CUI D W, CUI Y A, et al. Permission management based on XML and database technology [J]. Computer Engineering, 2009, 35 (20): 148-150.

基于 AOP 的数据库应用安全控制的设计与实现[*]

董 源 李培军 许舒人

1 引言

随着计算机软件广泛应用于各个行业，软件系统涉及的领域越来越广，规模越来越大，复杂性越来越高。与此同时，软件系统的安全性也成为人们密切关注的问题。从代码实现角度讲，安全模块属于系统的通用模块，系统各个业务均有涉及。作为开发人员，编写这些模块的代码具有很高的冗余性和复杂性[1]。

首先，对于具体业务逻辑点不同但是领域相近的软件系统而言，除了需要实现各自的功能和领域专业模块外，还需要单独实现一套自用的安全模块，如日志管理、权限控制、异常处理和事务管理等。这些模块虽然处于完全不同的软件系统中，但由于领域知识的共通性，其模块功能、应用场景和架构设计在本质上是相似甚至相同的。在这种情况下，不同的开发人员仍然需要针对各自系统开发一套独立的安全模块，大大降低了开发效率。

其次，对于某个单一系统而言，其内部的业务逻辑需要频繁调用安全模块来实现系统安全检测。以最简单的日志管理为例，为了完成系统完整的日志操作记录，开发人员几乎需要在系统撰写的每个方法中均调用日志模块的相关函数。这种实现方式在一定程度上保证了系统较严密的日志管理，但是其实现成本很高，也不利于系统的后期维护。传统的数据库安全访问控制本质上是对用户请求访问的 URL 或数据库 SQL 语句进行拦截，在其中添加用户筛选等过滤条件，这种方式需要开发人员频繁调用安全模块。

在目前的研究和解决方案中，通过 AOP（Aspect Oriented-Programming，面向切面编程）的方式将诸如系统安全模块这样的通用模块作为横向关注点从系统中提取出来，再通过切面配置的方式将其织入到所需的业务逻辑中，即可减少开发人员对通用模块函数调用的依赖[2,3]。然而这种解决方案同样带来了新的问题：开发人员在进行切面配置的时候需要编写配置信息代码，面对庞大而复杂的系统时，系统的开发者就需要编写大量的配置代码，这无形中又增加了开发者的负担。

针对上述问题，本文采用可视化配置的方式，以数据库安全访问控制模块为例，在 AOP 配置的基础上进行改进和优化，旨在设计和完成一套领域可复用的安全模块原型，同时减少开发人员在 AOP 配置过程中的代码编写，将配置信息以持久化的形式存储。在减

---

[*] 本文选自《计算机系统应用》，第 24 卷 第 12 期，2015 年 12 月，第 74–80 页

少配置代码的同时,能够灵活、便捷地对横切模块的切入策略进行变更,方便系统使用者和开发者管理维护安全模块。

2 相关技术介绍

2.1 AOP 介绍

AOP(Aspect Oriented-Programming),即面向切面编程的主要思想是将业务逻辑中共通的部分从中剥离,再通过切入的方式统一编织到不同的方法中。比如日志管理、权限判断等各个方法都需要的内容就可以利用 AOP 的方式实现。这样做可以使业务逻辑方面的代码更加关注自身的逻辑部分,同时松耦合的关系也使得横向关注点模块在需求变更时更易修改。AOP 编程思想如图 1 所示。

有关 AOP 的相关概念如下:

(1)切面(Aspect):一个切面即一个横向关注点模块,如日志模块、权限管理、异常处理等,它包括通知和切入点两部分;

(2)通知(Advice):在特定的联结点执行 AOP 的动作,是 point cut 执行的代码,是"方面"执行的具体逻辑;

(3)切入点(Point Cut):捕获联结点的结构,指定一个通知引发一系列联结点的集合。在 AOP 中,point cut 一般用来捕获相关方法的调用;

(4)联结点(Join Point):在程序执行中明确定义的切入点,正是联结点提供了描述 AOP 程序的构架。一般的联结点可以是方法调用前后、类成员的访问或者异常处理的执行等;

(5)引入(Introduce):添加字段或方法到目标对象,或者引入新的接口来改变其类结构;

(6)目标对象(Target):即横向关注点织入的业务逻辑对象。如果不使用 AOP 进行织入,其逻辑将要考虑通用的功能需求,如日志、事物等;

(7)代理对象(proxy):即 AOP 框架创建的对象,将通知应用到目标对象后被动态创建;

(8)织入(Weaving):将切面应用到目标对象后创建新的代理对象的过程。

AOP 的应用场景十分广泛,可以在权限控制(Authentication)、缓存(Caching)、调试(Debugging)、懒加载(Lazy loading)、持久化(Persistence)、内容传递(Context passing)、异常处理(Error handing)、性能优化(Performance optimization)、事务(Transactions)等情境下使用[4-6]。本文通过 AOP 的机制对日志管理、权限控制等方面进行优化。

下面介绍这些横向关注点的模块。

2.2 横向关注点模块

对于任何一个系统而言,安全性都是需要考虑的因素。与安全性相关的模块为日志管理、权限控制等。作为横向关注点模块,这些模块具有系统通用的特性。从广义的角度上来讲,任何能够为系统通用的模块都可以作为横向关注点,利用面向切面编程的思想实

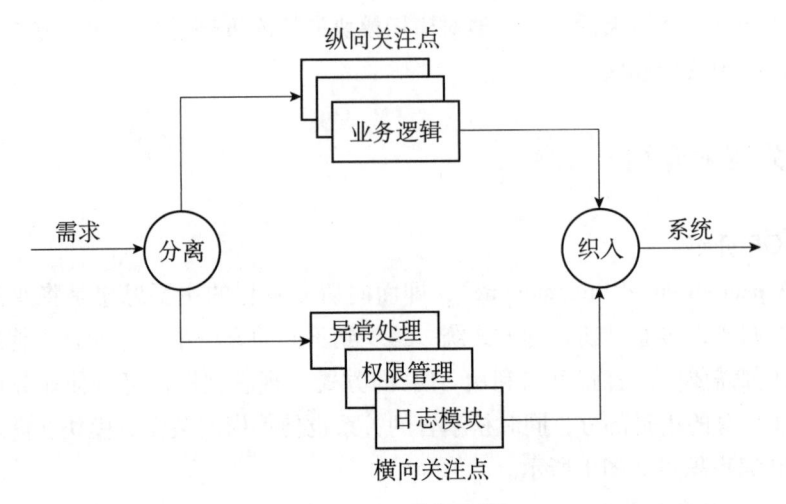

图 1 AOP 编程思想

现。对于功能众多、业务繁杂的系统而言，通过 AOP 的方式对这些模块进行编写显得更为便捷。下面举例介绍这些模块：

日志管理：任何系统的后台都需要记录日志。日志模块是典型的利用横向关注点完成的模块，各个不同的业务逻辑方法中均需要切入日志的记录。

权限管理：针对拥有用户管理的系统，权限管理主要负责用户在使用系统中按照系统赋予用户的权限访问有限的操作、界面和数据。模块操作或数据访问在后台都对应着相应类的方法调用，这需要开发者在系统编程中对每个方法都设定访问权限，并且要求访问权限可以根据需求变更。对大型系统而言，需要单独的切面类模块来配置方法的使用权限。

2.3 利用 xml 方式进行 Spring AOP 配置

本系统基于 Spring AOP 的机制进行横向关注点的注入。Spring AOP 是一个使用标准的 Java 语音编写的框架，它的实现途径不同于其他大部分的面向切面编程框架。Spring AOP 的目标是提供一个和 Spring IOC 紧密结合的 AOP 框架，从而帮助解决企业级应用中出现的一些问题，因此它并不提供完善的 AOP 实现[8]。

在 SSH 框架系统中，Spring 通过两种方式对 AOP 进行配置。基于 Annotation 的"零配置"方式：使用@ Aspect、@ Pointcut 等 Annotation 来标注切入点和增强处理。基于 XML 配置文件的管理方式：使用 Spring 配置文件来定义切入点和增强点。由于 Annotation 的方式需要对多文件进行标签标注，因此 XML 配置文件的方式更适合界面化的实现。

Spring AOP 的 XML 配置方式通过在 Spring 的配置文件中编写配置代码来完成 AOP 的实现。一个完整的 XML 配置方式的配置代码如下：

＜aop：config＞：一段 AOP 程序开始结束符；配置＜aop：config＞元素时，实质是将已有的 Spring Bean 转换成切面 Bean，所以需要先定义一个普通的 Spring Bean。因为切面 Bean 可以当成一个普通的 Spring Bean 来配置，所以我们完全可以为该切面 Bean 配置依赖注入。当切面 Bean 的定义完成后，通过＜aop：config＞元素中 ref 属性来引用该 Bean，就可以将该 Bean 转换成切面 Bean 了；

＜aop：pointcut＞：定义切入点，即在什么位置切入。Pointcut 的作用是明确地为切入的位置进行重命名，帮助切面中的通知便捷地找到切入点。切入点可以为零个至多个；当把＜aop：pointcut../＞元素作为＜aop：config../＞的子元素时，表明该切点可以被多个切面共享；当把＜aop：pointcut../＞元素作为＜aop：aspect../＞的子元素时，表明该切点只能在这个切面内使用；

＜aop：advisor/＞：定义只有一个切入点和通知的切面，在点对点配置时使用；

```
<bean id = "ccBean" class = "aaa.bb.ccBean">
<aop:config>
    <aop:pointcut id = "pc" expression = "execution(* package.class.method(...))"/>
    <aop:advisor/>
    <aop:aspect ref = "ccBean">
        <aop:pointcut/>
        <aop:before method = "before" pointcut - ref = "pc"/>
        <aop:after method = "after" pointcut - ref = ""/>
        <aop:after - returning method = "returning" pointcut - ref = ""/>
        <aop:after - throwing method = "throwing" pointcut - ref = ""/>
        <aop:around method = "around" pointcut - ref = ""/>
    </aop:aspect>
</aop:config>
```

＜aop：aspect＞：定义一个完整的切面，其中包括了切入点 pointcut、切入方式和切入内容 ref；一个切面的切入内容可以同时被多个切入点调用，这也是面向切面编程的核心所在；

＜aop：before＞：前置切入方式，即切入内容在切入点函数调用执行前切入；

＜aop：after＞：后置切入方式，即切入内容在切入点函数调用执行完毕切入；

＜aop：after - returning＞：返回通知切入方式，在调用函数返回 return 值后切入；

＜aop：after - throwing＞：异常处理切入方式，在切入点抛出异常时切入；

＜aop：around＞：环绕切入方式，即在切入方法前后均执行切入代码。

限于篇幅，还有一些诸如优先级等其他使用场景较小的属性，本文在此便不再列出。

2.4 通过 Dom4j 完成配置文件生成

Dom4j 是一个 Java 的 XML API，和 jdom 一样可以用来读写 XML 文件。通过 dom4j 的解析和 XML 转换模块可以快速将数据库中的数据生成到 XML 配置文件中，也可以对已有的配置信息进行修改，从而完成系统的最后一步。

3 系统架构设计

对于一个复杂的软件工程系统而言，通用模块横切入大量的业务逻辑模块需要开发人员手动编写许多相似的配置代码。基于 AOP 的数据库应用安全控制系统旨在通过可视化、界面化的配置方式为开发人员提供 AOP 编程上的帮助。开发人员无须了解面向切面编程的具体实现细节，也无须手动编写 AOP 的配置文件，在可视化的配置界面中进行选择和简单的编写即可完成整个 AOP 的配置工作。同时，对于日志管理、权限控制等通用模块的运用也做到了灵活性、可复用性。

图 2 所示为系统的流程图，分为 AOP 配置和 AOP 执行两阶段。在根据配置文件的信息进行数据安全访问控制之前，需要进行相应的准备工作。

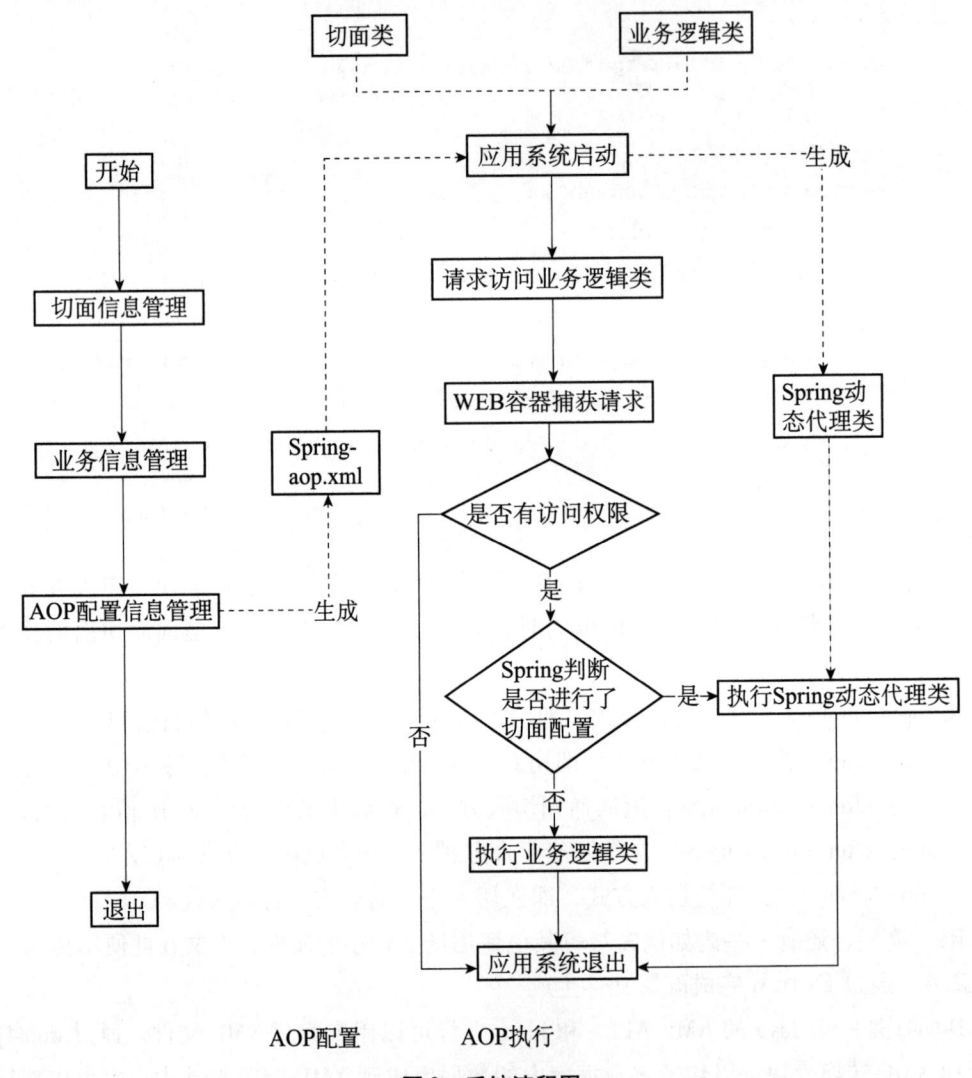

图 2 系统流程图

在 AOP 配置阶段，开发人员可以根据系统需要进行切面信息管理、业务信息管理和配置信息管理。前文提到，切面和业务信息本质上也是类文件，进行切面信息管理和业务信息管理实质上是指定系统中哪些类文件作为横向关注点、哪些作为纵向关注点。在本系统中，以权限管理中的数据安全访问策略部分作为切面类。

AOP 配置信息管理的过程则是将这些关注点切到系统需要的业务逻辑中。AOP 配置信息可随时更改、启用、失效，这是通过传统的代码编写方式所做不到的，而在本系统中通过修改配置文件操作即可自动化完成这一功能。

进行切面信息管理和业务信息管理分别需要系统切面类和业务逻辑类的支持，最终生成切面信息和业务信息到数据库供 AOP 配置信息管理时使用。AOP 配置信息管理最终生成 Spring-aop.xml 文件供应用系统使用。通过以上几项准备，系统的 AOP 配置工作完毕。

在 AOP 执行阶段，应用系统在启动时会根据切面类、业务逻辑类和 Spring-aop.xml 文件生成 Spring 动态代理类。该动态代理类实质上是将切面方法和业务方法组合成一个新的类文件供系统使用。用户在请求访问业务逻辑类时，WEB 容器首先捕获到请求访问，对请求进行访问权限判断，判断用户有权访问后便询问 Spring 访问的函数是否进行了切面配置。如果访问请求设置了切面配置，则执行系统启动时生成的 Spring 动态代理类，否则仍然执行业务逻辑类。

切面类包括数据安全访问策略、日志管理等，和访问权限判断共同构成了数据库安全访问的控制。

根据系统流程图，图 3 所示为系统架构图。本系统主要由 5 个部分组成：

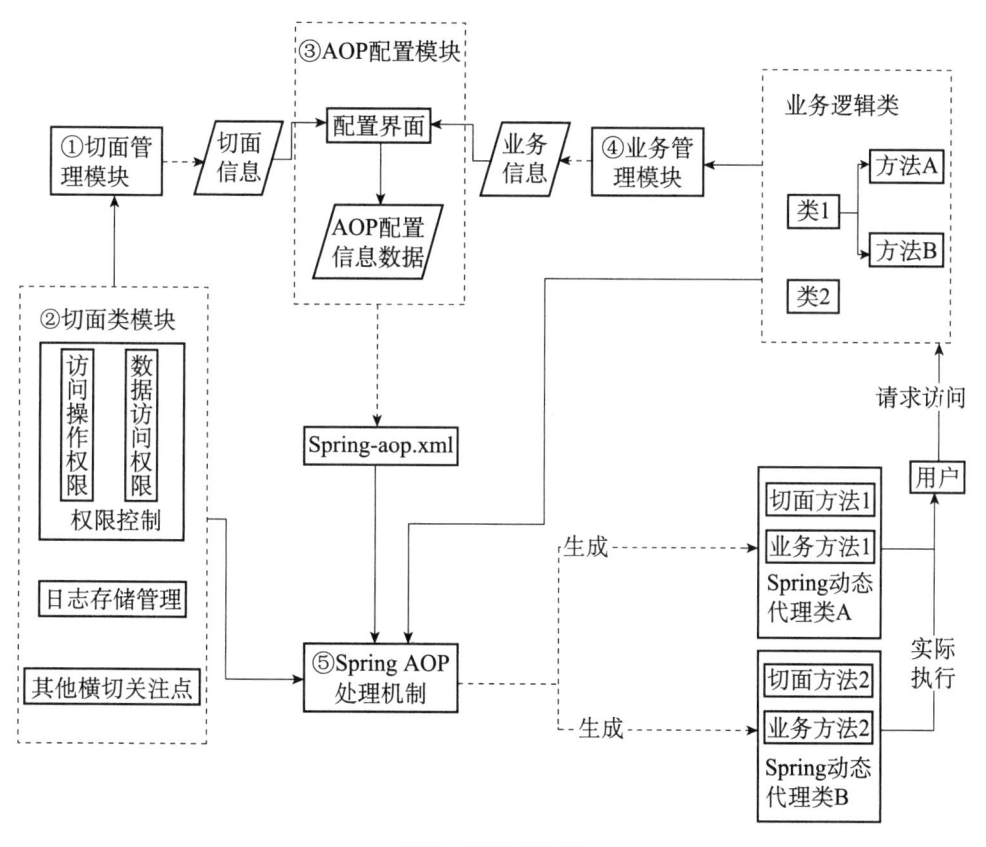

图 3　系统架构图

①切面管理模块：负责切面信息管理，管理系统中的切面类模块，将其文件名、方法参数持久化到数据库，供配置模块配置时使用。

②切面类模块：系统通用模块，通过模块注入的方式应用于系统各个模块。是 AOP 配置部分中切面机制设置的组成部分。在应用系统启动时，切面类根据 Spring-aop.xml 的信息将代码和业务逻辑类代码组合生成动态代理类。本系统以安全访问相关的日志管理、

权限控制为例作为系统实现。

③AOP 配置模块：包括系统表示层的可视化配置、业务逻辑层的自动化生成 XML 配置文件等内容。主要完成 AOP 配置流程的部分。

④业务管理模块：负责业务信息管理，管理各个系统本身的业务逻辑部分，将其文件名、方法参数持久化到数据库，供开发人员配置 AOP 信息。

⑤Spring AOP 处理机制：根据 Spring-aop.xml 文件和切面类模块、业务逻辑类的输入信息处理生成 Spring 动态代理类，供用户在访问业务逻辑类时实际调用执行。

4 系统模块实现

4.1 切面管理模块

切面管理模块主要负责持久化切面类模块的类名、方法名和参数信息，生成切面信息数据。这些数据将供 AOP 配置模块配置时使用。目前为止，系统仅支持权限管理、日志管理等涉及数据库安全访问控制的切面类模块调用。从可扩展性角度上讲，还有许多可以作为切面的性能模块没有被引入到系统中来。这些模块并非适用于每个应用系统，因此切面管理模块会根据不同的应用系统进行管理，持久化需要的切面类模块即可。

4.2 切面类模块

作为系统中的通用模块，我们以数据库的安全访问切面类模块作为样例。其实任何可以从业务逻辑中提取出来的模块都可以作为横向关注点的切面类模块，而不仅仅是传统意义上局限的日志管理、权限控制、事务处理等等。

安全访问控制模块中包含日志管理、权限控制管理、异常处理、性能监控等多项涉及数据库安全的部分。本系统以日志存储管理和权限管理为例实现[7]。

4.2.1 日志存储管理

与一般意义上的日志管理不同，这里说的日志是面向最终用户设计的访问、操作记录日志。因此并不是简简单单记录下系统内部的函数调用和数据传输过程，而要详细地记录下用户登录后进行的一系列操作和动作，这些操作和动作背后实际上就是已经注入了日志管理的业务逻辑模块。

系统的日志管理模块 LogService.java 类中有 addLog 和 deleteLog 两个方法，系统的日志数据表包括日志编号、日志等级、日志类型、操作人、所属单位、IP 地址、操作细节（××单位的××在什么时间做了什么操作）、操作时间。其中除日志编号是数据库自动加载以外，其余项均需要业务逻辑获取或生成。当 addLog 方法执行时，程序会获取当前登录的用户信息，根据日志数据表的设计完成一次记录操作。

4.2.2 权限控制

数据库的安全访问控制重点就在于权限的控制，它包括功能操作级的权限和数据访问行列级的权限。其中功能操作级权限主要指用户是否具有访问某个界面和操作某项数据的权利；数据访问行列级权限则指对于某一项具体的数据，用户是否具有访问的权限，具有哪些数据、哪几项数据的访问权限。

图 4 所示为权限控制模块的数据库设计表。图中包括用户表、角色信息表、权限信息表、数据访问策略表等主表，用户状态表、用户角色关系表、角色权限关系表和权限策略关系表等附属表或关系表。

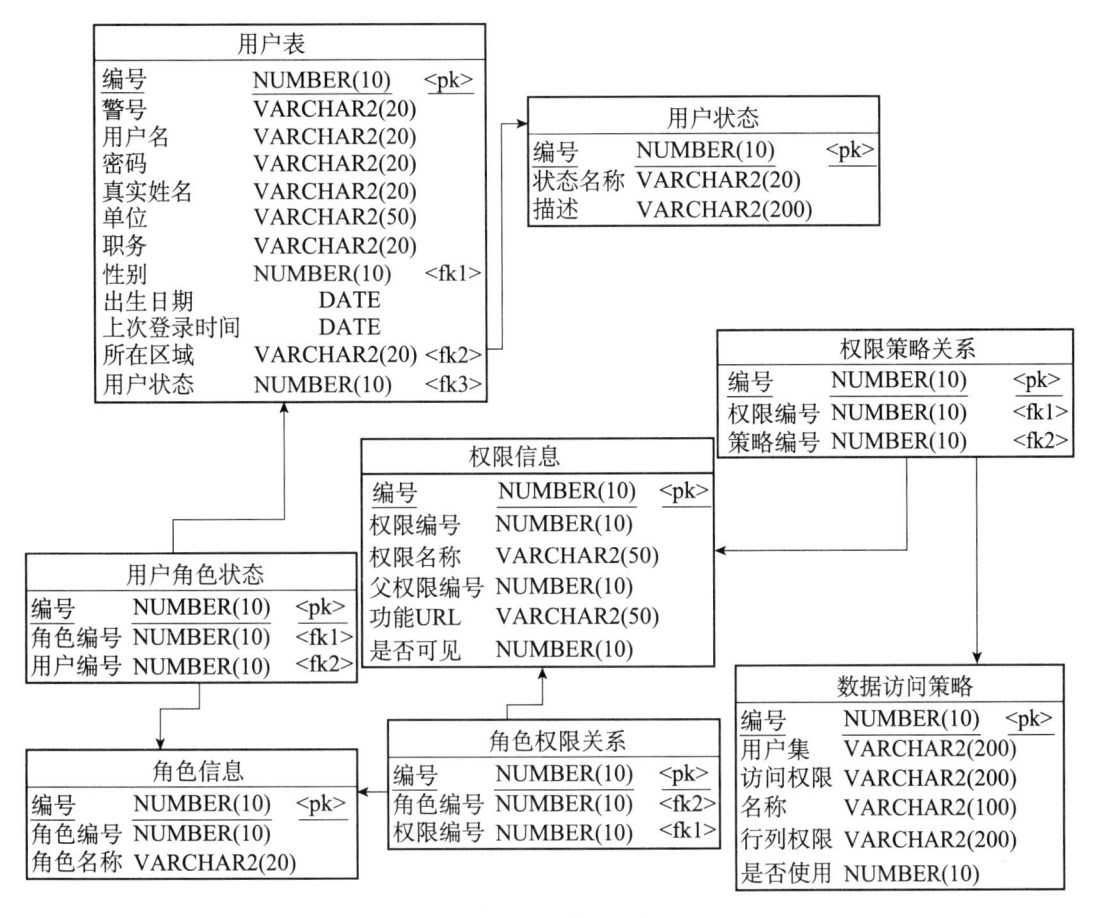

图 4　权限管理模块

用户表用来记录系统注册的用户基本信息。角色信息表记录系统中可能的不同角色，如管理员、高级用户、普通用户等。权限信息表记录访问某个功能模块所需要的最低权限。通过用户状态表、用户角色关系和角色权限关系三个中间表便可构成完整的功能操作级权限判断。通过 AOP 机制注入到业务逻辑组件中后，一旦登录用户访问某个功能界面而调用了组件中的函数，权限控制模块就会根据所访问的 URL 权限信息和用户角色的权限进行判断来决定用户是否成功访问或操作。

对于数据访问行列级权限同样可以通过 AOP 的方式注入业务逻辑当中。数据访问策略表记录了行列级数据访问的权限，和权限信息表一同完成数据访问行列级权限的控制。当登录用户访问数据列表时，系统会根据用户的身份和权限以及预先设定的行列访问权限判断数据列表中哪些数据项可以被访问。

权限控制渗透在系统关键业务模块当中，利用 AOP 的方式配置实现动态的权限配给和收回，而不再需要开发人员每次更改大量的代码来完成。用户、角色和权限之间通过关联表连接后，系统读取登录用户编号就可以根据编号得知该用户的权限和角色，也基于此对用户的访问权限进行判断，从而决定访问成功与否，完成数据库访问安全控制中的用户访问权限控制。

图 5 所示为通过 AOP 切入机制设置数据访问行列级权限的数据库访问示意图。系统管理员对角色权限和数据访问策略进行设定。当用户发起一个数据库数据请求时，根据用户的角色和权限进行判断，在系统的 SQL 请求语句后添加角色和权限信息如"where data.create_user =_ $User{User.getId}"或者"where data.create_user.location = 'XXX'"，筛选出只有自己创建的信息或者同一地区用户创建的信息。数据经过初次筛选后匹配数据访问策略，同样基于 SQL 注入的方式筛选出部分可见字段和数据，最终展现给不同用户不同的数据，如图中普通用户 A 只能看到 X 部分数据，而普通用户 B 只能看到 Y 部分数据，从而完成数据库安全访问的控制。

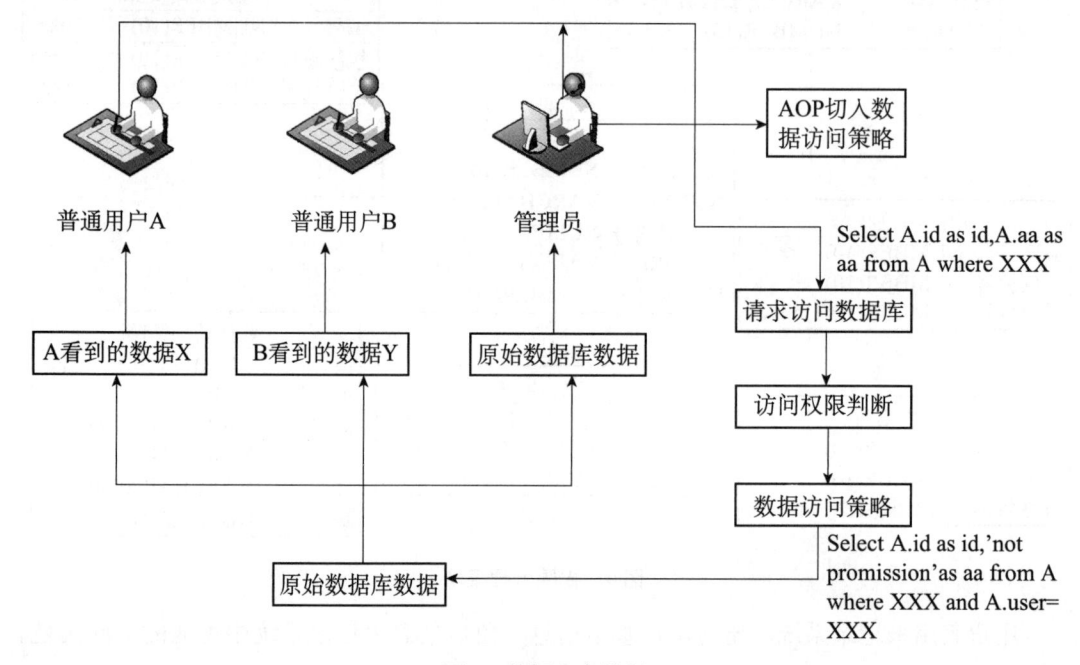

图 5　数据安全控制

4.2.3　其他扩展模块

安全访问控制不仅仅是日志存储管理和权限管理，还包括性能监控、攻击防范等一系列内容。同样，作为横向关注点的切面类模块不仅仅限于安全访问控制。如前文所述，在缓存、调试、懒加载、内容传递、异常处理、事务等情境下均可以作为横向关注点完善切面类模块。在这种思想的引导下，系统的可复用内容也会越来越广泛。

4.3　AOP 配置模块

4.3.1　AOP 的可视化配置

在安全访问控制系统中，通过可视化的界面进行 AOP 配置是系统关键的模块之一。

图 6 所示为 AOP 配置模块的数据库设计图，通过持久化的存储自动生成 XML 配置文件信息，从而替代手动编写的麻烦。图中共包含 5 张数据库表，通知表记录每一项配置的

具体信息,包括切入方式、切入位置和切入内容等主要信息和添加人等辅助信息;ASPECT 切面表则记录下一个具体的切面信息,它和 BEAN 表一同完整记录了切面的信息;POINTCUT 切入点表和 POINTTYPE 切入类型表则反映了在什么业务逻辑模块中切入所需的内容,记录了包括切入的方式和位置等内容。有了这些数据,系统就可以根据数据库中的数据进行动态生成配置文件的过程了。

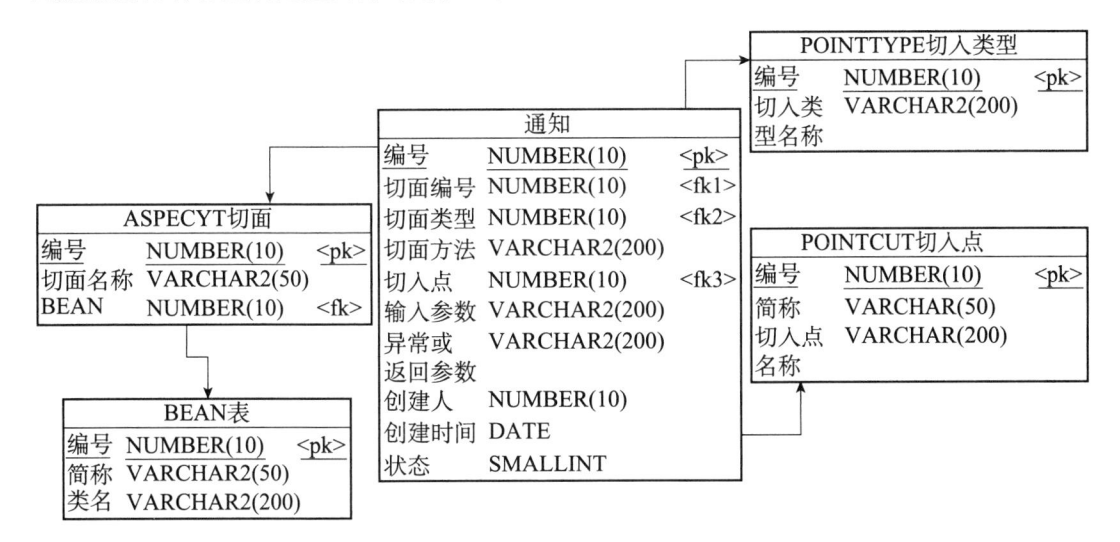

图 6　AOP 配置模块

图 7 所示的 AOP 配置界面示意图显示了开发人员在配置时需要填入的信息,包括选取切入点(pointcut)、联结点(BEAN 表和通知表中的"切面方法")和切入类型(pointType)。在用户填写好这些信息后,后台逻辑会根据参数的有无和切入类型将 pointcut 信息拆分成方法名和参数名,并自动添加上相应的附属信息。

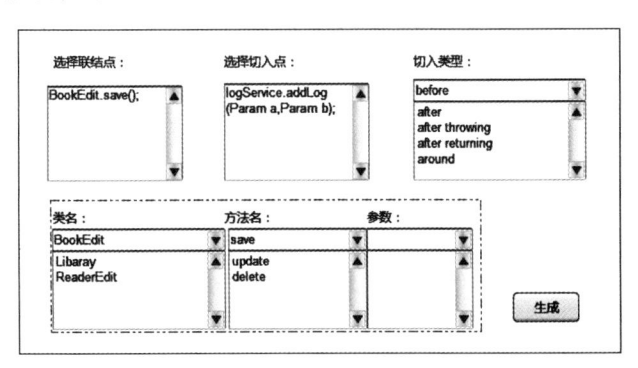

图 7　AOP 配置界面示意图

4.3.2　自动生成 XML 的配置处理部分

在完成安全访问控制的 AOP 配置之后,开发人员或领域专家可以根据配置好的信息自行设定想要执行的部分,对于那些暂时不需要或者已经无效的配置信息可以选择不生成配置信息或者删除。这些灵活的操作不需要开发者重新编写代码,极大降低了系统的维护成本。

4.4 业务管理模块

业务管理模块主要负责持久化业务逻辑类的类名、方法名和参数信息生成应用信息数据。这些数据记录了业务逻辑类中相应的信息，将供 AOP 配置模块配置时使用。配置过程中，将业务信息中业务逻辑类的参数信息和切面信息相结合，从而将业务信息的参数传递给切面。

4.5 Spring AOP 处理模块

Spring AOP 使用动态代理的机制实行横向关注点的切入。在系统运行时，Spring 会根据 Spring-aop.xml 文件读取相应的切面类、业务逻辑类，将其组合成各自的 Spring 动态代理类。当用户访问某个具有切面配置的业务逻辑类时，实际上系统执行的是已经切入了切面代码的代理类，从而完成切面的织入，但这一切对用户而言是不透明的。

5 总结与展望

数据库应用的安全访问关系到整个系统的安全。作为系统通用的功能，安全访问控制模块会被业务逻辑中的各个模块调用，这种客观存在的业务需求使得开发人员必须通过有效的方式解决。无论是传统的函数调用方式还是通过 AOP 的配置方式，都需要开发人员进行大量的代码编写工作。而这种编写很多都是冗余的工作，降低了开发效率。通过可视化的 AOP 配置，将安全访问控制模块灵活、可定制、简便地注入各个模块中。同时，通过可视化的系统，开发人员和领域专家可以共同制定系统的安全访问控制机制，并且随着时间的推移随时改变已有的安全机制，从而使得安全访问控制更加灵活、简洁和多变。

在目前的系统中还存在不足，例如切面类模块的设计还较为简单，其他可以作为横向关注点的模块还没有完善到系统中来，在未来的设计和实现工作中，这将是努力完善的方向。

参考文献

[1] 高海洋, 陈平. AOP 综述. 计算机科学, 2002, 29（10）：133–135.

[2] 张国平, 万仲保, 刘高原. Spring AOP 框架在 J2EE 中的应用. 微计算机信息, 2007, 23（36）：254–256.

[3] 古全友, 王恩波, 胥昌胜. AOP 技术在 J2EE 系统构建中的应用. 计算机技术与发展, 2006, 16（4）：150–152.

[4] Nusayr A, Cook J. Using AOP for detailed runtime monitoring instrumentation. Woda the Sixth International, 2009.

[5] Kim DK, Bohner S. Dynamic reconfiguration for Java applications using AOP. Southeastcon, IEEE. IEEE, 2008：210–215.

[6] 张献, 董威, 齐治昌. 基于 AOP 的运行时验证中的冲突检测. 软件学报, 2011, 22（6）：1224–1235.

[7] 唐建. 农产品供应链管理平台的应用安全设计与实现［学位论文］. 中国科学院大学, 2013.

面向动态框架的数据交互规范研究*

史国振　李凤华　谢绒娜　唐志涛

引言

为了保证密码算法的可用性，针对密码算法的各类测评软件和工具的研究成为国内外研究的热点[1-2]。许多国家先后启动密码算法标准化工作，大量国内外专家致力于密码算法及测评标准的研究与开发[3-8]。文献[9]设计并实现了一种分组密码算法的测试平台，将分组密码各个组成部件包括S盒、轮函数、密钥扩展等设计方法归类总结，同时也给出了一些比较实用的方法；文献[10-12]设计并实现了一种密码算法测试平台，分别从算法、软件和硬件等方面给予说明及实现。但上述密码算法和测试方法在使用上缺乏灵活性。文献[13-14]提出了动态可重组的软件设计框架，为用户提供一种动态、可扩展和可定制的密码算法测试环境，但并没有给出各组件间灵活的数据交换规范，使得在设计过程中软件的灵活性和实用性受到了一定的限制。

本文针对密码算法测评及其动态框架的设计需求，在动态可重构软件框架的基础上研究了可扩展和可定制的各组件之间数据交互规范。

1　动态可重组框架

1.1　动态可重组的组件集成框架

动态可重组系统框架如图1所示。基本框架由集成调度平台、组件管理模块、公共组件以及组件信息数据库和配置文件构成。组件信息数据库记录、管理和维护系统中的组件信息及其运行状态；组件管理模块根据组件信息数据库、配置文件管理系统中的组件；集成调度平台是系统的主控程序，实现当前系统所加载的组件，将其功能以直观的形式显现给用户，根据用户的选择调用组件中的具体功能；公共组件为系统提供输入输出功能。

密码组件和测评组件在系统中统称为私有组件，可以由用户根据个体需要进行订制、添加和删除，形成不同的使用环境。测评组件在系统中体现为测评的具体功能，密码组件在系统中体现为具体的密码算法资源。系统中各个部分的交互关系如图2所示。

---

* 本文选自《计算机工程与设计》，第33卷第6期，2012年6月，第2192-2196页

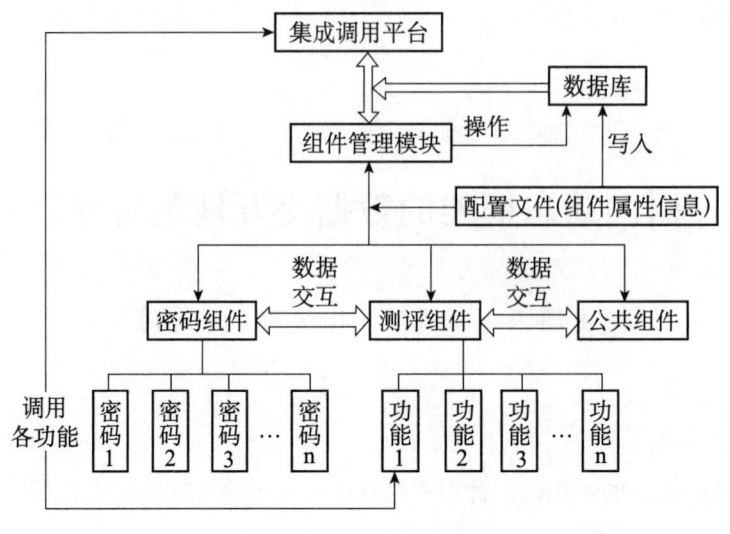

图 1 系统框架

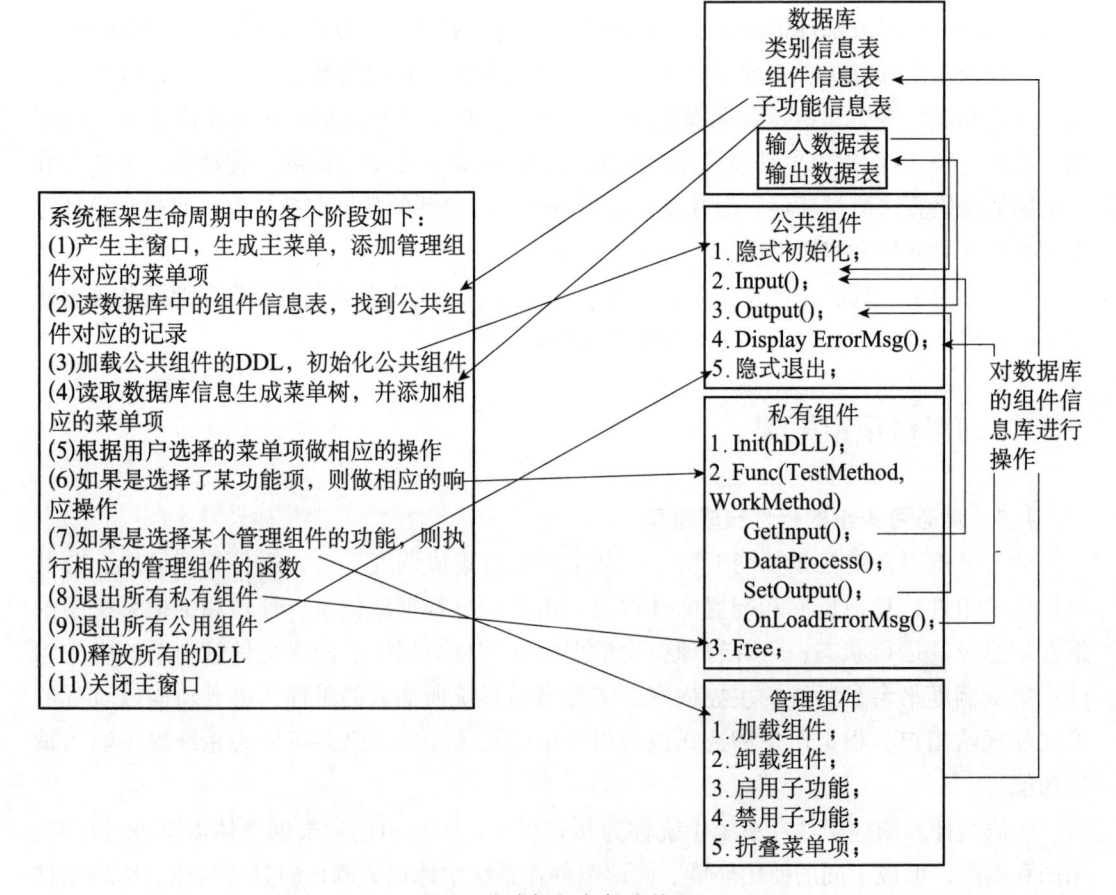

图 2 集成框架各部分关系

1.2 组件间数据交互流程

该动态可重组的软件集成框架由数据库、集成调用平台、组件管理模块和组件组成。

其中，集成调用平台负责界面的显示、对组件功能的调用以及系统的调配；组件模块包含了公共组件、私有组件、管理组件3个子模块，其主要是作为最小的系统加载在最初的集成调用平台上。公共组件主要对系统内部信息进行初始化；私有组件通过与公共组件进行数据交互，对公共组件接收到的外部数据进行处理；管理组件主要是负责对组件的加载、卸载以及子功能和菜单的管理。当组件做加载操作时组件的相关信息被记录到数据库中，集成调用平台则通过读取数据库中的相关表格相关字段获取信息，实现内部的操作。各个部分的交互关系如图3所示。

测评系统中各个组件交互的具体流程如下：

步骤1　运行测评系统，输入测评配置文件。如果用户选择手动配置XML文件则弹出对话框，要求用户输入测评所需的信息和数据，由测评系统生成XML文件；如果用户选择自动配置XML文件则执行步骤2。

步骤2　动态框架解析XML文件获取用户选择的测评方法的信息。

步骤3　动态框架获取一个测评方法，调用测评组件，将该测评方法的信息传给测评组件，进行一个测评方法的测评。

（1）测评组件调用公共库组件获取该测评方法对应的密码算法的信息和数据。

（2）测评组件解析公共库组件传过来的数据，统计测评所需的密码算法组件数目。

（3）测评组件调用密码算法组件进行密码算法测评。

①密码算法组件对数据进行加密/解密操作。

②测评组件利用测评方法对密码算法组件处理过的数据进行测评。

③测评组件调用公共库组件输出测评结果。

（4）判断所有的密码算法组件是否已全部调用，如果没有则返回（3）处执行。

步骤4　判断所有的测评方法是否已完成测评，如果没有则返回步骤3处执行。

步骤5　综合处理测评结果，测评结束。

2　通用可扩展数据交互规范的设计

2.1　数据交互规范的定义

为了为系统各组件之间进行数据传递提供一种统一的数据交互规范，各组件间数据交互采用n层次的数据格式，以 $n = 3$ 为例，数据格式如图3所示。

第一层次为主结构体，该层次主要包括：数据交互的版本号，用于区别数据传递的基本类型；结构体层数，用于解析数据的程序进行数据的结构化分类；算法个数，用于对属于本次测试的不同算法所需要的数据进行分割；具体结构体，填写相应算法的基本信息以及进行相应测试时所需要的所有数据。

第二层次算法结构体，该层次具体描述在某个算法范畴内进行测试所需要的数据信息，主要包括：算法的功能号FunID，用于唯一标识系统中的算法；该类测试中测试类型数目（子结构体数目）：用于解析数据的程序进行数据的结构化分类；子结构体指针，用于标示本项目中数据存放的起始位置；子结构体，用于存放本类算法测试所需要的相关数据。

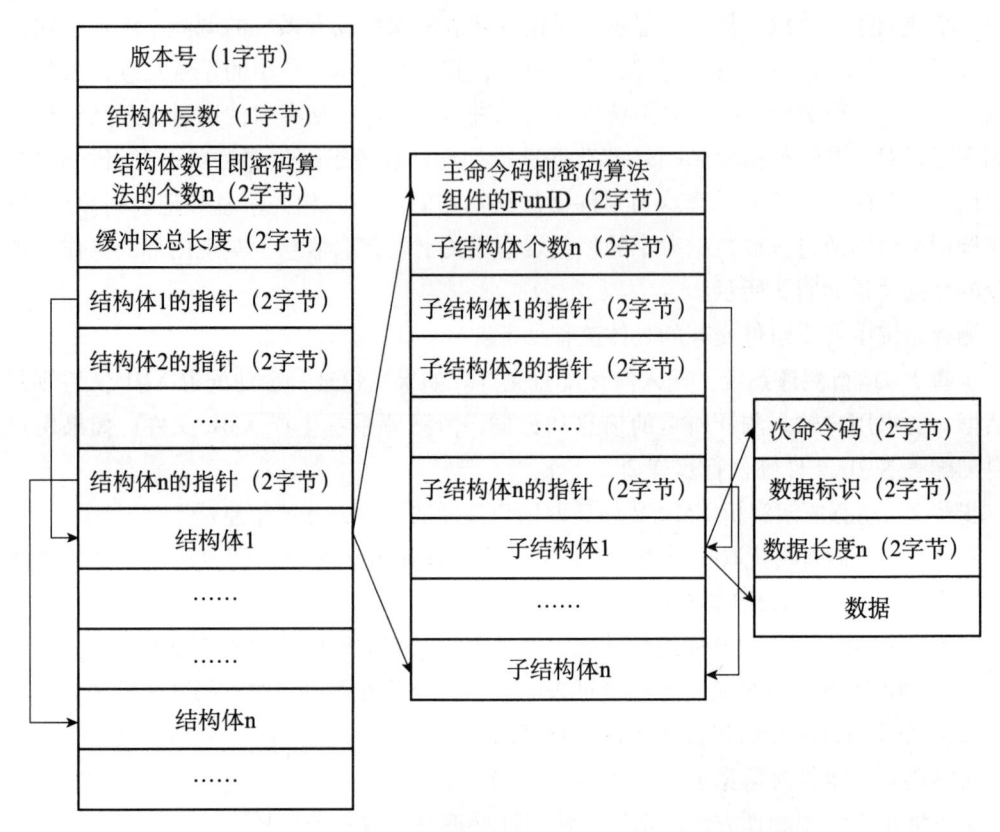

图3 版本号为 1.0 即 FunID 为数字形式时缓冲区中数据结构定义

第三层次测试数据结构体，具体描述算法测试所需要的各种数据。主要包括：子命令字，表示数据类型；数据标示，用于标示数据的输入格式和来源；数据长度，用于表明数据的具体长度。

结构体的具体定义如下，每个结构体只列出了部分成员变量。

（1）主结构体。

```
struct InBufferHdr
{
unsigned char Version;
……
unsigned char LayerNum;
};
```

Version 标识了现在所用数据交互规范的版本，每个数据交互的规范都对应着一个版本号。LayerNum 表示数据交互规范中使用的结构体层数，结构体层数可以根据用户开发的系统的具体需求定义，本系统中根据密码算法测试的具体需求定义了三层结构体的具体数据交互形式，该值固定为3。

（2）算法结构体。

```
struct AlgInfoHdr
```

```
{
unsigned int MainCmdCode;
……
unsigned short int SubStructNum;
};
struct AlgInfoHdr2
{
unsigned int MainCmdStrBytes;
……
unsigned short int SubStructNum;
};
```

为了方便用户对系统的扩展，密码算法 FunID 提供了数字和字符串两种形式，对应的算法结构体就分为了 AlgInfoHdr 和 AlgInfoHdr2。若主结构体中的版本号为 1.0，则表示密码算法的 FunID 使用数字形式表示，调用算法信息结构体 AlgInfoHdr，MainCmdCode 用于表示密码算法对应的 FunID 或者 0；若主结构体的版本号为 2.0，则表示密码算法的 FunID 使用字符串形式表示，调用算法信息结构体 AlgInfoHdr2，MainCmdStrBytes 表示密码算法对应的 FunID 所占的字节数。SubStructNum 用于标识命令参数结构体的数据，包括密码算法组件的 DLL 名、密码算法组件的接口函数名、测试次数、密钥、初始向量和明文数据。

(3) 数据子结构体。

```
struct CmdParaHdr
{
unsigned short int SubCmdCode;
……
  unsigned short int DataLength;
};
```

SubCmdCodl 用于标识测评所需的数据，包括密码算法组件的 DLL 名、密码算法组件的接口函数名、测评类型、测试次数、密钥、初始向量和明文。DataLength 用于表示测评所需数据的数据长度。

数据交互过程中，测评系统根据数据交互规范的版本号调用不同的算法信息结构体，根据定义好的数据结构向测评组件与公共库组件交互的缓冲区和测评组件与密码算法组件交互的缓冲区中填充数据，具体交互格式分为版本 1.0 和版本 2.0。版本号 1.0 其中 FunID 使用第二层算法信息结构体成员变量即可表示；版本号 2.0FunID 需要第二层算法结构体中额外的空间用于存放其对应的字符串形式。

2.2 命令码定义

测评系统通过命令码来获取测评所需的信息从而调用不同的数据处理函数。测评系统组件间数据交互规范是为了方便组件间正确地获取数据、解析数据和传递数据而制定的。测评所需的信息需要在命令码中标识出来。因此测评系统组件间的数据交互的规范需要给主命令码和次命令码的每一位都赋予含义,确保该命令码包含所有测评所需的信息。每个组件获取主命令码和次命令码并对其解析从而调用不同的数据处理函数来处理数据,最终将测评所需的信息和数据传给下一个组件。主命令码和次命令码的定义分别如图 4、图 5 所示。

```
测评组件与哪个组          测评组件对何种数据           15-0bit
件通信(31-24bit)         进行测评(23-16bit)

分类、预留    分型    分类、预留    分型    预留空间    主命令码或主命令码长度
(31-27bit)  (26-24bit) (31-19bit) (18-16bit) (15-12bit)      (11-0bit)
```

测评组件与公共库组件通信   对密码算法进行测评
         ……   ……

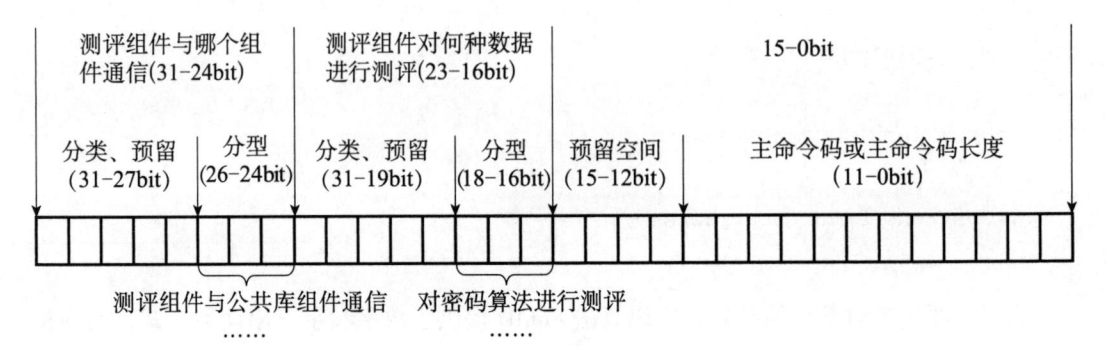

图 4　主命令码

```
                                    00：数据来源于buffer
                                    01：数据来源于文件
              0：单次测评            10：数据来源于随机数组件
              1：多次测评            11：预留备用

         相互通信的组件                测评所需的                       测评所需数据类型
         15-10bit       测评次       数据类型8-6bit      数据来     对应的信息3-0bit
预留                    数类型                          源5-4bit
15-13bit    12-10bit    9bit
```

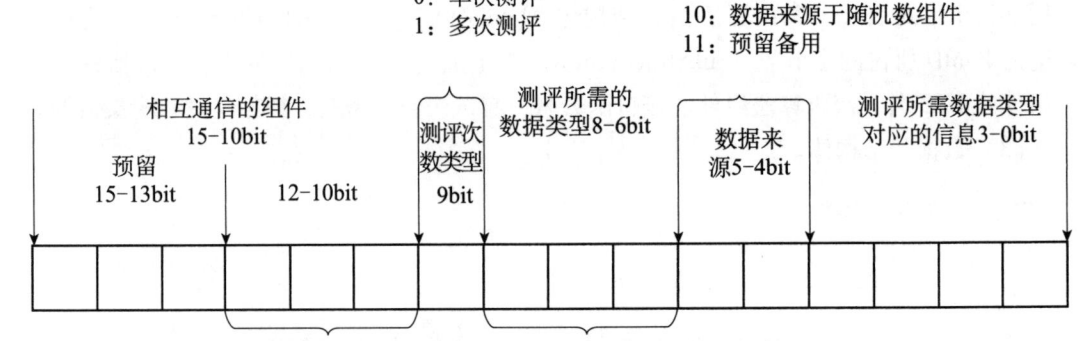

000：公共库组件对测评组件通信　　000：密码算法组件的信息Ke
001：测评组件对密码算法组件通信　001：y
010：密码算法组件对测评组件通信　010：IV
011：测评组件对随机数组件通信　　011：Plain
100：随机数组件对测评组件通信　　100：测评次数
101：测评组件对测评组件自身通信　101-111：预留备用
　　对样本数据进行测评
110-111：预留备用

图 5　次命令码

3　通用可扩展数据交互规范的实现

基于上述通用可扩展数据交互规范,本文设计并实现了动态可重组的自动化测评系统。测评系统各组件都按照统一的数据交互规范获取数据、解析数据和传递数据,从而实现对密码算法或样本数据的测评。下面以密码算法多次测评所需的数据部分相同来描述通用可扩展数据交互规范的实现过程。

公共库组件解析 XML 文件获取测评所需的数据总长度小于缓冲区所申请的内存空间,

因此测评组件解析缓冲区中数据传给密码算法组件。该测试的主要目的是检验测评系统是否严格按照数据交互的规范正确地组织数据，测试结果如图6所示。

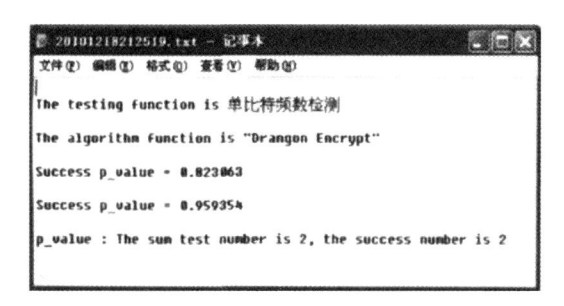

图6 测试结果

4 结束语

本文通过对密码算法测评系统动态可重构软件框架的组件间数据传递规范进行研究，详细分析了各个组件间的相互关系和工作流程，定义了一种可进行动态扩展并能够适应各种密码算法测试的数据交互规范。通过对 AES、Grain128 等 18 种密码算法的单比特频率、矩阵秩检验等国际通用的 16 种算法测试标准[15]进行了相关的测试应用，该规范可以满足所用的相关算法、相关测试项目的测试需求。该数据交互规范统一了组件间数据交互的格式，方便了用户自定义组件的编写，满足了多种密码算法、多种数据、多种测试需求的密码算法测试过程中的数据传递，有利于系统可重构性和动态性的体现。

本文中提出的数据交互规范及动态框架已经在 863 计划"密码算法和安全协议自动化检测工具开发及测评系统"中得到了应用，并获得了相关使用单位的肯定。

参考文献

[1] Stinsond D R. Cryptography: Theory and practice [M]. Boca Raton: Chapman & Ilall/CRC Press, 2005.

[2] Junod P. Statistical cryptanalytis of block ciphers [D]. Switzerland: Federal Polytechnic School of Lausanne, 2004.

[3] WU Wenling, HE Yeping, FENG Dengguo, et al. Brief commentary on the 21st century european data encryption stand and candidate algorithms [J]. Journal of Software, 2001, 12 (1): 49-55 (in Chinese). [吴文玲, 贺也平, 冯登国, 等. 欧洲21世纪数据加密标准候选算法简评[J]. 软件学报, 2001, 12 (11): 49-55.]

[4] LI Fenghua, YAN Junzhi XIE Rongna, et al. Research on the programming language for symmetric cryptographic algotithms [J]. Chinese Journal of Electronics, 2010, 19 (2): 303-306.

[5] FAN Limin, FENG Dengguo, ZHOU Yongbin. Parameter selection of autocorrelation test for block ciphers [J]. Journal on Communicaions, 2009, 30 (7): 86-90 (in Chinese). [范丽敏, 冯登国, 周永彬. 分组密码算法的自相关检测参数选择[J]. 通信学报, 2009, 30 (7): 86-90.]

[6] FAN Llimin, FENG Dengguo, ZHOU Yongbin. A fuzzy-based randomness evaluation model for block cipher

[J]. Journal of Computer Research and Development, 2008, 45 (12): 2095-2101 (in Chinese). [范丽敏, 冯登国, 周永彬. 基于模糊评价的分组密码随机性评估模型[J]. 计算机研究与发展, 2008, 45 (12): 2095-2101.]

[7] MO Xi, ZHAO Fang. Data-model-driven software automation test framework [J]. Computer Engineering, 2009, 35 (21): 78-81 (in Chinese). [莫熹, 赵方. 一种数据模型驱动的软件自动化测试框架[J]. 计算机工程, 2009, 35 (21): 78-81.]

[8] CHEN Hua, FENG Dengguo, FAN Limin. A new statistical test on block cipher [J]. Journal of Computers, 2009, 32 (4): 595-601 (in Chinese). [陈华, 冯登国, 范丽敏. 一种关于分组密码的新的统计检测方法[J]. 计算机学报, 2009, 32 (4): 595-601.]

[9] PENG Wei, ZHOU Liang. Testing platform with block cipher [J]. Journal of Chengdu University of Information Technology, 2005, 20 (5): 530-534 (in Chinese). [彭巍, 周亮. 分组密码算法测试平台设计[J]. 成都信息工程学院学报, 2005, 20 (5): 530-534.]

[10] JIN Lina. The testing platform of cryptographic algorithm-research of the implementation of the algorithm [D]. Xi'an: Xidian University, 2007 (in Chinese). [金丽娜. 密码算法测试平台—算法实现技术研究[D]. 西安: 西安电子科技大学, 2007.]

[11] YANG Ning. The testing platform of cryptographic algorithm-the study of system software design [D]. Xi'an: Xidian University, 2007 (in Chinese). [杨宁. 密码算法测试平台—系统软件设计研究[D]. 西安: 西安电子科技大学, 2007.]

[12] JIA Qun. The testing platform of cryptographic algorithm-the sutdy of hardwar design [D]. Xi'an: Xidian University, 2007 (in Chinese). [贾群. 密码算法测试平台—硬件设计研究[D]. 西安: 西安电子科技大学, 2007.]

[13] LIANG Xiaoyan, LI Fenghua, SHI Guozhen, et al. Dynamic reusable component integration framework [J]. Control and Automation Publication Group, 2009, 25 (27): 189-191 (in Chinese). [梁晓艳, 李凤华, 史国振, 等. 动态可重组的组件集成框架研究[J]. 微计算机信息, 2009, 25 (27): 189-191.]

[14] LI Fenghua, SU Haoxin, SHI Guozhen, et al. Research on the framework integrated by scalable components [C]. Xiamen: Proceedings of the World Congress on Software Engineering IEEE Computer Society, 2009: 442-446.

[15] Rukhin A, Soto J, Nechvatal J, et al. A statistical test suite for random and pseudorandom number generators for crypto-graphic applications [S]. NIST Special Publication, 2001.

基于 iOS 系统阅读的数字版权保护技术初探*

姜波　张国文　李腾高

随着经济和科技的不断进步，数字媒体也得到了飞速发展，而数字版权保护技术就在这种背景下出现，并且在该相关领域成为一个非常重要的研究内容。当前，在人们的日常生活中，移动互联网越来越占据重要地位，同时人们的生活和学习方式也随之发生了很大改变，如阅读方式的改变，其逐渐发展成为数字化阅读。因此数字版权保护技术在当前这种移动互联网背景下就显得十分重要，而在移动系统中，IOS 系统虽然起步较晚，但是在其技术平台上占据了一定地位，因此基于 IOS 系统阅读的数字版权保护技术研究将具有十分重要的现实意义。

1 IOS 系统与数字版权技术概念简介

1.1 IOS 系统

安卓系统和 IOS 系统是我国智能手机操作系统发展至今的两种主要操作系统。其中 IOS 系统是针对移动设备由苹果公司开发出来的，主要用于该公司下的一些产品，如 ipad、iphone 以及 Touch 等设备中。IOS 系统与 Unix 操作系统类似，都是由 Mac OSX 衍生而来。IOS 操作系统能够实现移动设备的语音通信、文本阅读、影音视频以及上网等功能。

1.2 数字版权保护技术

DRM，即数字版权保护技术，它指的是用一定的计算机方法，来保护移动设备中诸如电子书、图片、音频和视频等数字内容的技术。数字版权保护技术的目的就是对数字内容的版权进行有效保护和维护，在技术上实现对数字内容非法复制的控制和阻止，或者使得这种非法复制变得更加困难，只有得到授权的用户才能够实现对数字内容的复制。数字版权保护技术主要涉及很多相关的计算机技术，如电子交易技术、数字标识技术、存储技术以及安全技术和加密技术等。

2 基于 IOS 系统阅读的数字版权保护技术分析

2.1 基于 IOS 系统阅读下数字版权保护技术应解决的问题

第一，由于 IOS 操作系统具有很强的加密功能，因此数字版权保护技术首先就要确保

---

* 本义选自《科学家》，第 3 卷第 11 期，2015 年 11 月，第 20 页、第 23 页

数字内容的安全性。在数字内容的阅读和使用过程中，要确保其安全性，这是数字版权保护的最基本要求。一般是对数字内容的完整性、机密性等进行有效保护。

第二，数字版权保护技术要实现权力描述，即对数字内容授权信息进行描述。IOS系统的庞大功能下，数字版权保护技术必须能够对不同商业模式下的数字内容进行支持，并实现使用权利的描述。

第三，基于IOS系统阅读的数字版权保护技术要实现合理实用和有效的使用控制。不仅要能够支持对数字内容的合理使用，还要对其使用进行有效控制，确保只有具有授权的用户才能够对其保护的数字内容进行使用。

第四，基于IOS系统阅读的数字版权保护技术要实现可信执行和权力转移。当IOS系统处于不安全的环境时，数字版权保护技术要能够保证其程序按照预期方式执行操作，并且要保证执行的程序是安全可靠的。另外，要支持数字内容可以转移到另一台设备上，从而使用户能够达到更好数字内容存储设备的目的，还可以对数字内容进行转卖、赠送和出租等。

2.2 基于IOS系统阅读下数字版权保护技术功能框架设计

2.2.1 版权保护平台设计

（1）内容管理功能设计：数字版权保护技术对IOS系统阅读平台的数字内容进行格式转换，并将其注册成唯一标识符号，然后在IOS系统的秘钥管理中对数字内容进行加密和打包。

（2）安全引擎设计：为IOS系统阅读的加密和解密提供技术支撑，如利用安全引擎，可以实现内容管理模块的内容加密功能。

（3）许可证管理功能设计：实现生产、分发和存储许可证的功能。

（4）域管理功能设计：要能够实现对用户与终端设备唯一标识信息的唯一绑定，并对许可证设备以及数字内容进行安全鉴定。

2.2.2 数字版权保护终端设计

（1）内容解密功能设计：在IOS系统阅读下，数字版权保护技术要能够实现解析数字内容的功能，并对其数字内容实现解密。

（2）许可证管理功能设计：该模块主要是解析许可证并对数字内容的使用进行有效控制。

（3）安全引擎设计：为IOS系统阅读的加密和解密提供技术支撑，如利用安全引擎，可以实现内容管理模块的许可验证和解析。

（4）内容阅读功能设计：在对电子书内容保护的同时，实现对其数字内容的展示。

（5）终端管理功能设计：在IOS系统阅读下，数字版权保护技术能够实现在线状态的平台交互功能，并对其设备的合法性进行判断。

（6）域管理功能设计：在数字版权保护技术中，将一个用户作为一个域，而对客户端的绑定也属于一个域，而设备对该域内的所有合法权限都能够实现共享。这一模块的功能主要是为用户提供与设备进行绑定的服务。

3　结语

综上所述，随着移动通信技术的发展和移动终端设备的便利化，移动智能终端阅读方式就成为当前人们使用最为广泛的一种阅读方式，但是在其使用过程中引发了数字版权问题。数字版权保护技术随着科技的成长的越来越成熟，逐渐发挥不可忽视的作用，具有广阔的发展空间，因此加大对数字版权保护技术的分析和研究将具有十分重要的现实意义。

参考文献

［1］刘哲.基于 IOS 系统的 app 开发—图书阅读助手［J］.山东大学，2014，4（10）.
［2］弋荣静.iOS 平台手机阅读客户端的设计与实现［J］.北京邮电大学，2012，11（25）.
［3］施勇勤，张凤杰，马畅.数字版权保护技术的概念、类型及其在出版领域的应用［J］.科技与出版，2012，03（08）.

基于移动客户端的电子阅读器客户端设计与开发*

蔡利君　楼永植　陈峻峰

科技的发展改变了人们的生活方式，使人们的生活方式日趋方便和快捷。伴随着3G网络的日益发展和智能手机的日益普及，传统的阅读方式：报纸、杂志等已经逐渐向手机客户端转移。因此，利用Android和Windows phone 8平台设计和开发出一款移动客户端的电子阅读器软件有着以下方面的意义：①和传统的报纸、杂志这种实体阅读媒质，电子阅读器资源内容更加多样化，即一个电子阅读器包含各种人群需求、各种类型的资源，便于携带；②和传统方式相比，可以节约纸张资源；③碎片时间也可以阅读。

Android平台是谷歌开发的一种开放性的移动综合平台，是以Linux为核心的一款开放式操作系统。用Android进行移动电子阅读器的开发，可促进系统的创新，降低开发成本，创造出有特色的阅读器。

一个完整的Android程序通常包含以下四个部分：活动对象、广播接收者、服务和内容提供者。一个活动对象代表了用户可见的一个界面，Android运行程序的进行就是在不同的活动之间切换的过程。广播接收器是一个接受广播消息并相应的组件。广播消息可以由系统产生，同时也可以由其他应用程序产生，对于这两种广播，在广播接收器里都可以设置相应的过滤规则来进行接受。服务是具有长生命周期并且没有用户界面的一段代码。

Windows phone 8是微软公司2012年发布的一款手机操作系统，Windows Phone 8采用和Windows 8相同的针对移动平台精简优化NT内核并且内置诺基亚地图，这标志着移动版Windows Phone将提前与Windows系统同步，部分Windows8应用可以更方便的移植到手机上，例如不需要重写代码等（注：与旧版Windows应用不兼容，较难移植，便于移植的是新MicrosoftDesign应用既Windows RT版应用，这是ARM与X86构架的原因，并且可以移植的应用必须是. net编写的应用程序，C与C + +程只需封装成组件）。这意味着系统内核、网络、多媒体、驱动支持等这一切都将在两个平台中共享兼容，开发者仅需很少改动就能将部分Windows 8应用移植到手机上。

1　电子阅读书客户端功能设计和分析

设计的电子阅读书移动客户端包括书库系统、书城系统及阅读系统三大部分。

---

* 本文选自《科学家》，第3卷第11期，2015年11月，第24-25页

（1）书库系统。书库是用户可阅读的图书的集合。用户进入书库不发起联网请求，待有其他联网操作时才发起联网请求。首先读取 SD 卡中目录下的全部文件夹及文件（只读支持格式的文件）；用户通过网上书城下载的图书默认存在"我的下载书籍"文件夹；用户可以自建文件夹，通过"移动""复制"来管理书籍。该系统具有资源管理和资源搜索功能。资源管理功能模块实现用户对电子阅读器上的数字内容进行管理的功能。为用户提供资源管理界面，并针对书籍进行分类管理，提供用户浏览、检索和查找等功能。资源搜索功能模块实现用户对电子阅读器上的数字内容进行搜索的功能。如图 1 所示。

（a）资源管理　　　　　　　　（b）资源搜索

图 1　资源管理和搜索功能模块

（2）书城系统。网上书城主要用于下载、浏览书城书籍。书城的书籍报刊提供了简介入口，可以先查看详细介绍及目录结构，部分书籍还提供了免费试读的入口，可以点击进行试读，对书进行多方面的了解，再进行下载、订阅。图书可以从全部列表中查找也可以按照类别进行查找，并且可以按照"全部、免费、付费"筛选。同时书城还提供了搜索功能，点击搜索框输入关键字可以进行搜索。书城系统包括以下功能模块。书城列表：该功能显示书城上全部图书的列表。图书分为三个标签列表展示，分别是全部图书列表、图书类别列表、作者姓名列表。其中，类别又分为全部、付费、免费三种分类列表。点触书籍进入书城图书简介界面，简介包括：简介、目录、书摘、评价、作者、订阅。点触提供试读的目录，可以在线阅读，可以根据不同的需求进行图书搜索和选择。①图书分类：该功能显示书城上全部图书的分类。②用户注册：该功能实现用户的注册。③用户登录：该功能实现用户的登录，登录后客户端与服务器端自动完成该台设备是否已注册的验证交互，如果未注册，则完成设备注册的过程。④在线搜索：该功能模块实现图书检索的功能。分为分类查找和高级搜索两个方面。分类查找是指在用户没有明确的购书目的的时候，用户可以通过分类查找，选择自己感兴趣的方向，查看图书的相关信息。电子阅读器通过连接无线书城特定接口，获得图书的分类信息，用户可以在电纸书上选择分类进行图书的分类查找。高级搜索是指当用户有明确的购书目的的时候，可以使用电子阅读器中的高级搜索功能。首先将书名、作者、出版社等关键字信息输入电子阅读器中，电子阅读器将信息同某个特定接口发送给无线书城服务器，服务器在将搜索后的结果返回给电子阅读器，用户便可以在电子阅读器中找到自己需要的书籍。

（3）图书订购：该功能实现图书的订购。用户可以通过目录结构进入图书购买界面，也可以通过搜索和各种排行榜，点击相关书项进入购买界面。用户购买图书后，客户端软件可将购买内容的信息返回给用户。用户进入简介界面，客户端向平台发起获取简介界面请求，同时由平台判断该内容是否已经订购，如果已订购则返回用户简介界面中隐去购买入口，直接显示下载及阅读入口。如果未订购，则返回的简介界面中含有购买入口，点击购买后发起订购流程，客户端需解析交互的参数，以弹出对话框的形式将订购结果展现给用户。同时提醒用户进行下载或者直接阅读，如用户选择下载方式，直接进入"我的书架－下载"分类；选择直接阅读，直接返回阅读页。该功能需求还支持分章节购买。用户可以选择先阅读图书的部分内容，当阅读到需要购买下载的章节后，判断有计费点，向平台发起订购请求，平台判断用户是否购买，如果没有则提示用户进行购买。购买成功后，平台根据用户以往该连载内容的阅读方式下发不同的页面消息：如用户采用在线的方式阅读连载内容则返回在线阅读接口，用户直接阅读；如用户采用下载阅读方式阅读则返回下载接口，供用户下载后阅读。①图书简介：该功能显示书城上某本图书的简介，其中包括内容简介、编辑推荐和作者简介。②书籍目录：该功能模块实现查看书籍目录的功能。③书籍下载：该功能模块实现用户进行图书下载的功能。图书下载主要有获取下载地址、下载和断点续传、文件验证三个过程。确认支付后，电子阅读器从无线书城服务器获得经过版权保护的书籍文件的地址，进行下载。下载过程采用 http 协议，可以记录下载的偏移量。当用户发生断网等不可预估的情况中断下载后，重新连接无线书城，可以继续下载。对于下载后的图书文件，电子阅读器会进行文件校验，确认文件的完整性。①在线阅读：该功能模块实现用户进行在线阅读的功能。用户可以通过电子阅读器已注册用户，对未购买书籍的部分开放内容进行在线阅读。在了解书籍大体内容后，用户可以决定是否购买。购买后可以阅读全部内容。电子阅读器在特定的接口获得书籍的开放章节，提供给用户阅读。该方式可以提高用户体验。②账户信息：该功能模块实现用户查看账户信息的功能。

（4）阅读系统。阅读系统用于给用户提供阅读界面，向用户展示所选图书的内容。包括以下几个功能模块。

①内容解密：该功能模块实现对数字资源的内容解密。从许可证文件中解析出加密后的内容密钥，并使用保存在阅读器中的终端或用户的私钥对加密内容密钥进行解密，从而解析出内容密钥。然后，利用内容密钥对密文图书解密，提供格式解析模块进行解析。

②权限控制：该功能模块实现对数字资源的许可证文件进行解析，并使用版权保护控制。阅读器的版权控制模块负责调用公钥密码验证签名功能，验证授权文件的完整性，以保证授权文件没有被篡改。对授权文件中该用户使用该数字内容作品的权限进行检查，实现对用户使用文档的权限控制。

③格式解析：该功能模块实现对数字资源的格式解析。该模块负责解析数字文件，提供给内容呈现模块使用。

④内容呈现：该功能模块实现内容呈现的功能。使用渲染引擎将经过格式解析后的内容呈现在设备上。

⑤内容转移：该功能模块实现支持内容转移功能。

⑥翻页：该功能模块实现阅读过程中的翻页。

2 结论

本文开发了基于 Android 平台和 Windows phone 8 系统的电子阅读器软件系统，可以根据个人爱好建立个人图书馆。相对于传统阅读模式来说，移动客户端的阅读方式在很大程度上改变了人们的生产和生活。

参考文献

［1］张复初. Android 平台移动办公室系统研究［J］. 计算机光盘软件与应用，2011（02）：109.

［2］谢维柱. 基于 Windows Phone 8 的盲文阅读系统设计［J］. 计算机光盘软件与应用，2013（15）.

数字版权保护技术在百科类工具书中的应用探索*

郭蕾蕾

1. 数字版权保护技术的发展

（1）数字版权保护技术的意义

数字版权保护技术是我国信息化建设的重要内容，也是电子书产业可持续发展的关键，增强受版权保护的电子书内容在各系统之间互联互通，进一步保障出版商、各类运营商和用户的利益，才能促使电子书内容出版朝着良性循环的方向发展，取得巨大的社会和经济效益。

（2）常见电子书应用场景和分发模式

用户一般登录到电子书销售终端，浏览电子书产品，对感兴趣的电子书查看介绍，对部分章节内容进行试读、购买或者借阅，最后通过第三方交易平台支付成功后下载电子书，可进行如下几种典型的商业授权模式：①用户通过购买获得授权永久使用，购买即获得永久授权是内容保护系统最基本的商业模式；②用户通过租借获得授权，在一定时间内使用，租借内容具有一定的时间限制，过了时间限制不可使用，需要重新办理租借；③用户通过订阅获得授权，使用订阅期内的电子书内容。通过订阅模式，用户可以同时获得一组内容的授权。典型应用，如期刊的订阅；④用户通过预览/试读功能，对电子书内容有大概了解后才会购买、租借或订阅，通常试读部分为免费内容吸引客户；⑤宜支持用户退货，退货后电子书内容不可使用，为给用户良好的体验，体现一种公平，宜支持分段授权。

（3）数字版权保护技术要求

涉及典型商业模式和应用场景下的电子书内容版权保护，包括电子书版权信息的注册、登记、授权、使用，在公开发布之前，将需要保护的电子书加密打包制作，以防止后续流程中的非授权传播或使用。

1）建立出版单位自主出版的版权保护技术体系。基于数字内容分段控制技术、多硬件环境版权保护技术、内容交易与分发版权保护技术、在线阅览数字版权保护技术等数字版权核心技术，并且通过版权保护可信交易数据管理平台提供的可信交易数据服务，建立出版单位自主出版的技术体系。

---

* 本文选自《现代国企研究》，第 2 期，2016 年 1 月（下），第 198 页、第 200 页

2）研发结构化数据的多层次版权保护技术。对于结构化数据进行多层次的保护，将结构化数据进行加密打包，加密算法基于应用服务器的硬件信息，资源包使用时必须与服务器信息匹配才能使用，防止大批量数据的盗版；系统对于读者的大批量下载行为进行监控，并设置了限制策略，防止非法用户进行大批量的下载；

（3）实现数字内容权利项的持续控制与发放管理。基于数字内容分段控制技术、多硬件环境版权保护支撑技术和内容交易与分发版权保护技术等相关技术，实现对数字内容作品的权利项的持续控制与发放管理。出版单位通过授权模块设置权利项参数形成授权策略后，读者无论在哪种设备使用数字内容作品，无论内部用户还是互联网用户、无论从出版单位自主销售系统还是互联网出版应用系统获得数字内容作品，这些授权策略都持续有效，并且如果授权策略的权利项参数进行了修改，也将在各个应用环节上达到体现，实现对数字内容作品的管控。

2 数字版权保护技术在工具书数字产品的探索应用

目前大多数出版单位缺乏足够的数字版权技术研发能力，出版单位要将本单位的数字内容作品通过自主发行系统运营，或将其委托给发行机构，如没有先进有效的版权保护系统支撑，出版单位和著作权人的权益将无法得到保证。

近年来，以搜索引擎、移动终端、电子阅读器等为主的数字出版技术创新日新月异，数字阅读终端产品不断升级，消费者日益复杂的软硬件环境，对数字出版提出了新的挑战，研究复杂软硬件环境下的版权保护技术和系统，满足消费者各种软硬件环境的阅读需求，成为数字出版产业不得不重视的问题。

（1）出版社的现实需求

单一的服务模式无法满足日益庞大的消费群体的应用需求，越来越多的用户对于服务方式上都提出了新的需求，主要归为如下几类：①对于整书、章节、章节组合、连续出版物等多种内容形态服务上的需求；②对于借阅、购买、章节试读、在线浏览等多种应用上的需求；③对于面向机构的 B2B 服务，面向个人用户的 B2C 服务，面向机构服务，再由机构面向个人用户的 B2B2C 服务等商业模式上的需求；④对于复本数控制，可服务的设备数控制等权利控制方式上的需求；⑤对于复杂软硬件环境方面，如 PC、手持阅读器、iPad 的支持需求；⑥对于包年、包月等服务模式方面的需求。

出版单位一般对数字内容版权保护系统的具体需求，主要体现在开发数字内容加密封装、数字内容使用授权、出版社内部安全使用及数字内容销售四个方面，主要解决出版单位对多种形式的数字内容和作品的灵活的加密和封装；实现对内部用户、渠道服务商及终端用户的授权管理；控制用户对数字内容的访问权限和使用权限；实现数字内容的在线和离线的检索和销售，并在数字版权保护下进行数字内容的安全发送。

（2）探索实践

数字版权保护技术研发工程可以将工程的最新技术和成果应用集成起来，出版单位可以根据业务需求部署相关功能模块。

百科类工具书的数字出版产品主要是百科词条在线阅读和电子书下载阅读，根据产品特点分为三种应用场景：

1）词条在线阅读，以词条检索的阅读形式，向机构用户提供 IP 地址段授权使用，向普通用户提供包年、包月的数据库服务，用户通过输入充值卡号后可以自行购买数据库和时间期限，在购买有效期内可以通过多种检索方式阅读数据库中的条目内容，不在有效期内只能阅读部分内容。百科类词条按学科分类，学科下设学科分支，如果要阅读某些学科或学科分支下的条目内容，可以查阅相关电子书。在线阅读中的数字版权保护技术手段主要是集成技术对大批量下载行为进行监控，防止非法用户进行整包数据下载。

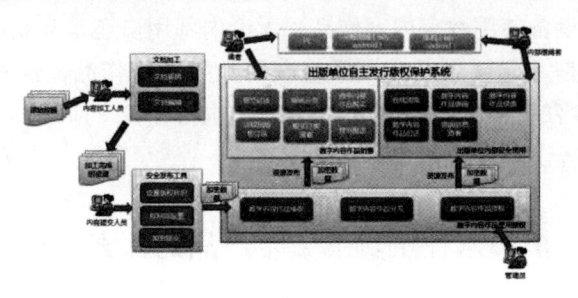

图 2-1 功能业务图

2）百科类工具书，除了检索查阅外，用户也可以购买按学科或学科分支制作的电子书，电子书通过加工工具加工为 DRMCF 格式，电子书采用分段授权模式，通过封装加密的方式进行数字版权保护，用户在销售页面可以试读，按章或整本购买，为了阅读这种授权的电子书需要下载阅读器 aPabi Reader，并在个人中心注册终端设备，注册成功的设备可以下载阅读购买的电子书。为了方便用户使用，每个帐户可以绑定 5 个终端阅读设备（PC、手机、iPad 等），在注册成功的终端设备中都可以下载阅读购买的电子书。

3）内部用户通过内部安全使用模块检索所需的电子书，可以借阅并进行在线阅读。在借阅期限内阅读完后，可以通过客户端阅读器进行归还操作。如果用户在借阅期限内不能阅读完该数字内容作品，也可以通过客户端阅读器进行续借。如果用户在借阅期限结束后，没有归还数字内容作品，系统将自动回收借阅权限。

不同形式的产品可以满足不同用户的个性化知识阅读需求，跟踪和分析用户在线阅读的行为，提供知识的主动推送服务。百科类工具书鼓励用户合理使用，保证读者合理使用的同时，如果有侵权情况发生从网络侵权追踪平台可以查询本出版单位的数字作品的侵权追踪信息，保证出版单位的权益不被侵犯。

3 结语

目前，虽然各出版单位在数字版权保护方面的需求急迫，但大部分出版单位缺乏足够的技术研发能力，没有技术实力去控制数字版权的流通，针对出版单位的自主发行数字版权保护系统可以解决数字出版版权保护的问题，保证数字内容作品在整个生命周期内的合法使用，作为该项目的示范单位在示范运营过程中还需要多做总结和完善，发现新需求提出改进意见，为工具书的数字出版积累经验。

图书在版编目（CIP）数据

数字版权保护技术研发工程论文选辑 / 魏玉山主编．
—北京：中国书籍出版社，2016.10
ISBN 978-7-5068-5845-8

Ⅰ.①数… Ⅱ.①魏… Ⅲ.①电子出版物 – 版权 – 保护 – 文集 Ⅳ.①D913.04-53

中国版本图书馆 CIP 数据核字（2016）第 233373 号

数字版权保护技术研发工程论文选辑

魏玉山　主编

统筹编辑	游　翔
责任编辑	毕　磊
责任印制	孙马飞　马　芝
封面设计	楠竹文化
出版发行	中国书籍出版社
地　　址	北京市丰台区三路居路 97 号（邮编：100073）
电　　话	（010）52257143（总编室）　　（010）52257140（发行部）
电子邮箱	eo@chinabp.com.cn
经　　销	全国新华书店
印　　刷	河北省三河市顺兴印务有限公司
开　　本	787 毫米 ×1092 毫米　1/16
印　　张	17.75
字　　数	519 千字
版　　次	2016 年 12 月第 1 版　2016 年 12 月第 1 次印刷
书　　号	ISBN 978-7-5068-5845-8
定　　价	79.00 元

版权所有　翻印必究